Here Be DRA

STEFAN EKMAN

Here Be Dragons

Exploring Fantasy Maps and Settings

WESLEYAN UNIVERSITY PRESS

Middletown, Connecticut

Wesleyan University Press
Middletown CT 06459
www.wesleyan.edu/wespress
Manufactured in the United States of America
Designed by Richard Hendel
Typeset in Miller and Filosofia by Tseng Information Systems, Inc.

Wesleyan University Press is a member
of the Green Press Initiative.
The paper used in this book meets their
minimum requirement for recycled paper.

Library of Congress Cataloging-in-Publication Data
Ekman, Stefan, 1961–
Here be dragons: exploring fantasy maps and settings / Stefan Ekman.
p. cm.
Includes bibliographical references and index.
ISBN 978-0-8195-7322-3 (cloth: alk. paper) —
ISBN 978-0-8195-7323-0 (pbk.: alk. paper) —
ISBN 978-0-8195-7324-7 (ebook)
1. Fantasy fiction—History and criticism.
2. Landscapes in literature. I. Title.
PN3435.E38 2013
809.3′8766—dc23   2012034770

5 4 3 2 1

Contents

. . . .

Acknowledgments

····························

As a rule, I do not travel alone; and during my explorations of fantasy landscapes, numerous traveling companions have joined me, suggesting better routes, offering invaluable advice, or just generally cheering me on. I have greatly appreciated the company of all of you.

My most heartfelt gratitude goes to Marianne Thormählen, who provided unwavering encouragement during the entire project. My work has benefited enormously from her stimulating advice, attention to detail, and willingness to devote time and energy far above and beyond the call of duty. I could not have hoped for a better cicerone on this trip. I am also immensely grateful for the help and support of Tom Shippey, whose knowledge of Tolkien and numerous other areas of the fantastic has been a tremendous resource.

A number of people have discussed, read, and commented on various stages of this text. Above all, credit should go to the members of the Higher Literary Seminar in the English Studies section at the Centre for Languages and Literature, Lund University, whose willingness to dedicate time and effort to improving this text was always sincerely appreciated. This book owes a great deal to your work. My warmest thanks also go to Lisa Isaksson, Martin Andersson, Petra Andersson, David Sandboge, Susanna Karlsson, Viktoria Holmqvist, Christine Mains, Brian Attebery, Stefan Högberg, Richard McKinney, Mattias Ekman, Farah Mendlesohn, Siv Tapper, and Jenni Tyynelä for reading various drafts and sharing your knowledge (and libraries) with me.

For the quantitative map study in chapter 2, I was in particular need of assistance. If it had not been for the kind support of SF-Bokhandeln, the bookseller that gave me access to its database as well as its stock, that study would have been next to impossible to carry out. Pia Heidrich, Aidan-Paul Canavan, and Lena Ekman: without your help, the chapter would have been much the poorer. I am also indebted to Cai and Bengt Alme, Immi Lundin, Anna Clara Törnqvist, Marie Wallin, and Katarina Bernhardsson, who all made my journey considerably less strenuous and much more pleasant. Furthermore, I would like to express my gratitude to the following foundations for generously funding part of my work: Hjalmar Gullberg och Greta Thotts stipendiefond (Hjalmar Gullberg and Greta Thott Scholarship Fund), Fil dr Uno Otterstedts fond för främjande av vetenskaplig undervisning och forskning (Dr. Uno Otterstedt Fund for the Advancement of Scholarly Education and Research), Knut och Alice Wallenbergs stiftelse (Knut and Alice Wallenberg Foundation), and Hilma Borelius stipendiefond (Hilma Borelius Scholarship Fund).

Finally, I am deeply grateful to my friends and my extended family, who have been invaluable companions on the road of writing. I especially thank my parents for introducing me to fantasyland all those years ago and always accepting and supporting my commitment to the genre. Without you, this journey would never have begun. Most of all, I would like to thank Helena Francke, who has been with me every step of the way toward this book, however rough the going. Were it not for her patience with my constant talk of fantasy, and the generosity with which she gave of her time, expertise, and sound advice, this book would not have turned out the way it did, and my journey would have been a grueling and dreary trek indeed.

Here Be DRAGONS

1 : Introduction

Reading fantasy was always like going on a journey for me. It might have been to a curious place spied through the window, or to an impossibly exotic country far away. Sometimes the landscape was comforting and familiar; at other times, disturbing and alien. Blinding beauty or nauseating ugliness assailed my eyes. In these places, there were adventures and heroes, enigmas and challenges, but what stuck in my mind was often the various locations themselves. Some of them were natural landscapes: grand, open vistas or dense, mysterious forests; others were cities, with dark alleys, labyrinthine sewers, and architectural marvels. Many, admittedly, seemed to echo the European Middle Ages; but all eras and continents, as well as times and places unknown to me, appeared before my inward eye. Somehow, the stories seemed to revolve around these places, weaving in and out of them rather than just using them as backdrops for the action onstage.

This books deals with fantasy settings and the worlds that became so important to me in my reading. Instead of roaming the worlds one at a time, with the plot as my guide, I have explored them more systematically and for their own sakes, to reveal how they are constructed and how they interact with the other elements of the stories. As I delved into the fantasy worlds, I discovered much that surprised me; and my explorations also made me realize how truly intriguing the realms of fantasy are, and how deserving of critical investigation.

THE RELEVANCE OF SETTINGS

It is not uncommon for critics to draw attention to the importance of the natural environment in fantasy.[1] Some even go so far as to suggest that in fantasy, or in some kinds of fantasy, or in some fantasy works, the landscape can function as a character on one level or another.[2] Never-

1

theless, the fantasy landscape's proclaimed importance is not reflected in much of the fantasy criticism that has been produced, and most attention is still being paid to character and plot. John Clute implies the interconnectedness of character, plot, and setting by defining "fantasy geography" (not just the landscape) as a manifestation of the story and a "metaphysical pathos of the emotions and events" therein.[3] In Don D. Elgin's *The Comedy of the Fantastic: Ecological Perspectives on the Fantasy Novel*,[4] the main value of the setting derives from how the characters affect and are affected by it, despite its significance as a world "complete in and of itself."[5]

A number of studies have concerned themselves with the structure of the fantasy setting, discussing it in terms of its main structural components and how they relate to one another. A seminal example is Kenneth J. Zahorski and Robert H. Boyer's "The Secondary Worlds of High Fantasy,"[6] in which the authors propose a rough taxonomy of otherworldly fantasy settings but say little about any natural environments. Some scholars have examined the fantasy environment in connection to the maps that frequently accompany novels in the genre,[7] and multiple studies focus on the landscapes and settings of particular writers and works, most commonly J. R. R. Tolkien and *The Lord of the Rings* (1954–55).[8]

Apart from occasional brief reflections on the landscape's central importance to fantasy, little has been written on the subject. In an article provocatively subtitled "The Irrelevancy of Setting in the Fantastic," Roger C. Schlobin asserts his premise that "[s]etting does not determine the fantastic."[9] I agree with Schlobin's point: the setting should not be made central to a definition of the fantastic. My intention is not to argue in favor of a *topofocal*,[10] or place-focused, *definition* of fantasy, nor to suggest that setting is *more* important than character or plot. I am, however, in favor of topofocal *readings* of fantasy, as a complement to traditional approaches, because setting is *as* important as character and plot. Fantasy offers possibilities to create fictive worlds that are fundamentally different from our own, even in cases when the setting masquerades as a copy of the world we live in. Such differences are common and constitute integral parts of the fantasy stories in which they occur.

A particular kind of difference separating our world from the settings of fantasy provides the focus for this book. A physical environment can be divided in many ways—between sea and land, along tribal, linguistic, or political lines, cut up into any number of types of units on maps—and this is true regardless of whether the environment is actual or imaginary. But most divisions of our world are social constructs, foisted on the land, and the most basic division is that between the landscape and ourselves. In fantasy, the situation can be, and often is, different: the land can be divided into areas where separate sets of rules of causality and laws of nature apply; dividing lines that we are familiar with can be rethought; and the division between people and their environment can be bridged. The setting plays a central role in a fantasy story, and to increase our understanding of the genre, we need to learn more about this role. This book uses a topofocal perspective to examine four basic types of divisions and their function in relation to the world of which they are a part, as well as in terms of the story in which they are used.

My analysis is based on close readings of a variety of divisions in fantasy works written primarily in English, but with occasional references to works in other languages. As my interest has generally concerned the current state of the genre, I have selected works published between the mid-1970s and mid-2000s.[11] The exception is *The Lord of the Rings*: its central position in the genre makes it a useful point of reference, and for that reason I discuss it throughout the book. Each work has been selected primarily for its clear treatment of the feature under investigation, but I have sought to use mainly well-established fantasy writers. Chapter 2 includes a quantitative survey of a random sample of fantasy maps, and the maps brought up for discussion are all part of that sample, with the exception of the Middle-earth maps.

As my main interest lies in how the setting works in relation to the story, my critical affinity leans toward ecocriticism, particularly as defined by Cheryll Glotfelty and Scott Slovic.[12] In the introduction to *The Ecocriticism Reader*,[13] Glotfelty explains that "ecocriticism is the study of the relationship between literature and the physical environment." The questions she proposes that ecocritics and theorists ask include: "How is nature represented in this sonnet?" and "What role does the physical setting play in the plot of this novel?"[14] Together, these two questions largely illustrate my own critical interest in exploring the way in which fantasy landscapes are represented and how those representations interact with the various aspects of the story, not necessarily just the plot.

In "Ecocriticism: Containing Multitudes, Practising Doctrine,"[15] Slovic considers ecocriticism to comprise both "the study of explicitly environmental texts by way of any scholarly approach [and], conversely, the scrutiny of ecological implications and human–nature relationships in any literary text, even texts that seem, at first glance, oblivious of the nonhuman world."[16] In other words, he argues, ecocritics can use any type of scholarly approach if they apply it to a particular kind of text, or any type of text if they approach it in a particular way. Previous scholars have approached literary settings in a wide variety of ways, too many to list them all. Some interesting examples include *Topographies*, in which J. Hillis Miller explores fiction and philosophical texts through the lens of topographical terms and descriptions of landscapes and cityscapes; *Atlas of the European Novel, 1800–1900*, in which Franco Moretti maps various literature-related data and then discusses those maps and their implications; and *A Geography of Victorian Gothic Fiction*, in which Robert Mighall spends a chapter examining how the urban Gothic setting developed from its forbears.[17] I have, as noted, adopted a topofocal approach to fantasy texts, but I do not look for ecological implications within or outside the narratives, nor are my critical tools selected to facilitate the study of such implications. Instead, I complement my topofocal perspective with tools that have developed within fantasy criticism to discuss features peculiar, and relevant, to the genre.

WHAT IS FANTASY?

A great many attempts have been made to define the fantasy genre. In *Critical Terms for Science Fiction and Fantasy* (1986), Gary K. Wolfe included twenty-one definitions of fantasy,[18] and two decades later, Farah Mendlesohn introduced her *Rhetorics of Fantasy* (2008) by stating that "[t]he debate over definition is now long-standing, and a consensus has emerged, accepting as a viable 'fuzzy set,' a range of critical definitions of fantasy." In practice, she suggests, scholars generally choose among the available definitions depending on which area of fantasy and which "ideological filter" they are interested in.[19] I do not wish to add yet another definition of the genre to the large number already proposed, but I have not found a single definition that I fully agree with. Therefore, I will outline the critical opinions about the genre that form the basis of my understanding of what fantasy is.

In this book, the fantasy genre is taken to belong to the mode of writing called the *fantastic*, succinctly defined by Kathryn Hume as "*any departure from consensus reality*."[20] The fantastic in this sense encompasses genres such as fantasy, science fiction, and supernatural horror, as well as any other narratives in which the fictional world and events depart in any significant way from our own. Dainty flower fairies and betentacled monster deities, alternative historical development and unknown utopian societies, magical rings and spaceports are all fantastic elements that signal such departures. In fantasy, the fantastic elements are in some way "impossible,"[21] entailing the presence of events, objects, beings, or phenomena that break the laws of nature of the world as we understand it;[22] in addition, there must be no attempt rationally to persuade the reader of these elements' putative "possibility" (as there is in much science fiction). Magic is magic, not a way of mentally controlling the physical world by tapping into areas of the brain that were not discovered until 2051; dragons simply exist, they are not the result of genetic manipulation of dinosaur DNA; and so on. Not all fantastic elements in fantasy need to be impossible in this respect—many writers have explored the meeting of science fiction and fantasy[23]—but they frequently are; in the discussion that follows, *fantastic* therefore refers to something impossible.

Furthermore, for fantasy to work, writer and reader must agree that there is something impossible—something fantastic—in the story; but for the duration of the story, as part of the story world, they will treat it as if it were possible. The fantastic elements are not allegory, or metaphor, or hallucination, or dream—in the story, the impossible is as "real" and "true" as the possible.[24] Texts in which the author purports to relate a true experience are not fantasy, nor are texts whose content is written to be believed by its readers: fantasy is fiction and does not present itself as anything but fiction.[25] It is, in this regard, written and read in a spirit of "what if?"

In order to be taken seriously, however, the introduction of the fantastic elements must be believable. Tolkien refers to this credibility as "Secondary Belief," which arises when what the author relates "accords with the laws of [the story] world. You [. . .] believe it, while you are, as it were, inside."[26] Fantasy writers are free to make up whatever they like for their worlds, and change the laws by which these worlds work; but once the laws are in place, even the author is bound by them. The story must remain consistent; it must accord with the laws of its world. Rules can be changed and laws broken, but there must be a reasonable explanation for this—rules cannot change for no reason, without comment. The fantasy world must be as stable and predictable as our own, even if it is different. It is, in W. R. Irwin's words, "an arbitrary construct of the mind [. . .] under the control of logic and rhetoric."[27]

Fantasy, in short, is fiction acknowledged by reader and writer to contain "impossible" elements that are accepted as possible in the story and treated in an internally consistent manner. This description is clearly very inclusive, and would result in a large number of works being classified as fantasy. But some of these works would be more typically fantasy than others. Brian Attebery introduces the idea of seeing genres as "fuzzy sets," a "cloud" of works defined by a number of central "prototypes" with which they have some qualities in common (although no qualities are necessarily shared by the entire set). The closer to the center of the cloud, the greater the similarity to the prototypes. The fuzzy edges shade into other genres, explaining why certain works are difficult to place generically, as well as why some works are unarguably fantasy while others only vaguely suggest belonging to the genre.[28] Attebery maintains that Tolkien's *The Lord of the Rings* is one of the prototypes of the fantasy genre, and identifies in it three features that "have become dominant in modern fantasy": a concern with the impossible; a comic structure, which begins with a problem and ends with a resolution; and the process that Tolkien calls "recovery," whereby the familiar is restored to "the vividness with which we first saw [it]."[29]

I would like to add a fourth feature that can be found in all manners of literature but is particularly common and noticeable in fantasy stories: the widespread reliance on material ladled from what Tolkien calls the "Cauldron of Story."[30] He employs this metaphor to show that even though it may be fascinating to examine a tale's source materials, it is of greater interest to consider the story as it is served. Fairy stories, he asserts, are not the result of myths dwindling into epics, which then dwindle into folktales, but are the outcome of various ingredients having boiled together in the Cauldron. Over time, and as new bits are added to the pot, the various flavors combine, until it makes little sense to try to determine how each contributed to the final tale. One example would be Arthur, who, Tolkien explains, simmered in the Cauldron "for a long time, together with many other older figures and devices, of mythology and Faërie, and even some other stray bones of history [. . .] until he emerged as a King of Faërie."[31] Tolkien also notes how the author or teller of a story—the Cook—chooses carefully among the many ingredients in the Cauldron of Story,[32] and even though Tolkien's focus is not explicitly on fantasy literature at this point, I would claim that fantasy writers in particular rely on material from the Cauldron. As a rule, they are also quite frank about using such material, selecting from old myths, legends, and tales in the Cauldron, as well as from more recent material, adding their individual spices to the mix. Typically, many ingredients have been boiled down beyond recognition while others have retained some distinct characteristics. Stories of varying degrees of antiquity are used and reused;[33] magical creatures appear, altered yet recognizable, so that, for instance, dragons can enter a story in shapes either mighty or meek, taking the part of protagonist, antagonist, or both—but, nevertheless, clearly related to the wyrm in *Beowulf* or to St. George's adversary;[34] and, as the following chapters point out, settings are borrowed and adapted from numerous places. Tolkien himself picked medieval tales and characters from the Cauldron and served us Merlin and Arthur as Gandalf and Aragorn. Other writers ladle up bits from Shakespeare or Dante, from Eastern myths or Celtic fairy tales, and from urban legends or medieval romances.[35] Fantasy is a genre where old tales, motifs, and characters are brought to life again, in ways that make them relevant to their contemporary readers.

The texts that provide examples for the following chapters are mostly located close to Tolkien's *The Lord of the Rings* in the fuzzy set of the fantasy genre. They do display some structural differences, however, and Mendlesohn proposes a subdivision of the genre into four (equally fuzzy) categories. She bases her divisions on how the fantastic is introduced into the story, observing how, in (successful) fantasy stories, the manner in which a story is told depends on which category it belongs to.[36] The *portal-quest fantasy* introduces the point-of-view character into a fantasy world, either from a version of our own world (through, for instance, a wardrobe) or from a place in the fantasy world that, like the reader's world, is "small, safe, and *understood*"[37] (such as the noneventful, comprehensible Shire). The story is told from this point of origin, and the reader learns about the alien world along with the main character(s). In *immersive fantasy*, the characters, unlike the reader, are at home in the strange world, and the world is described as if totally familiar; the reader has to puzzle out how it works from the clues that are given. *Intrusive fantasy* is set in a world (often our own) into which the fantastic intrudes, causing chaos and confusion. Neither protagonist nor reader is familiar with the fantastic intrusion, and the story is a process of coming to terms with it. The ghost story is a typical intrusion fantasy. In the final category, *liminal fantasy*, the reader's expectations are used to create worlds where the commonplace comes across as strange and wonderful, and the alien is portrayed with an everyday triteness bordering on the blasé. These fantasies are stories in which stylistic manipulation is central to the experience of the fantastic.[38]

These four categories, although helpful in understanding and discussing some basic structures of fantasy stories, do not provide a set of hard and fast rules to which all works in the genre adhere; nor do they offer a comprehensive description of fantasy literature. They are, in themselves, fuzzy sets, each with its own prototypes, and it is quite possible for a work to slip from one category to another, or to combine categories.[39] Mendlesohn observes how intrusions can occur in immersive fantasies, for example, as in the case of the murderous slake moths in China Miéville's *Perdido Street Station* (2000).[40] So whereas Mendlesohn's categories and Attebery's fuzzy-set perspective offer ways in which the fantasy genre can be understood, neither critic claims to have established the nature of fantasy once and for all. Even so, both viewpoints have proved useful in circumventing problems caused by genre definitions that are either too inclusive or too exclusive, and in avoiding the patchwork of subgenres that have arisen from a profusion of categorizing principles,[41] and they have come to inform my own view of the genre. Furthermore, Attebery's singling out of Tolkien as a genre prototype was one of the reasons for the inclusion of *The Lord of the Rings* as a recurrent example in this book.

Any starting date given for a genre will be largely arbitrary, and critics have made a number of suggestions depending on their respective definitions of what fantasy is. On the whole, the closer a fantasy definition lies to what in this book is referred to as the *fantastic*, the farther back in time the starting point is set, in extreme cases as far back as the Epic of Gilgamesh of some three millennia ago. It is more common, however, to set the emergence of the fantasy genre to sometime in the eighteenth or nineteenth century, often with the insistence that an awareness of some literature as fantastic requires the awareness of other literature as "realistic."[42] Rather than trying to identify the decade, year, or work that constitutes the beginning of the genre, I prefer to regard the emergence of fantasy as a fuzzy process, where various authors and movements contributed to what would eventually become the genre of today.[43]

Regardless of when fantasy may be said to have emerged as a genre, there is a general consensus about the enormous influence that *The Lord of the Rings* has had on today's fantasy literature. Elgin, for instance, claims that the novel "introduced fantasy to the general public,"[44] and according to Wolfe, fantasy did not develop a market identity in America until after the U.S. paperback editions of Tolkien's work appeared in 1965.[45] Much as Attebery sees Tolkien's work as a prototype for the fuzzy set of fantasy, Wolfe refers to Tolkien as the genre's "central ideological lynchpin," suggesting that "the dialectic of the [. . .] genre" defines itself by recapitulating or reacting against his worldview.[46]

Although critics may disagree about *why* Tolkien's magnum opus should be considered pivotal to the development of fantasy literature, they agree that the publication of *The Lord of the Rings* changed the genre dramatically. My own view is that although fantasy works had been written for one or even two centuries previously, depending on how one chooses to define the genre, the publication of Tolkien's novel marked the beginning of seeing fantasy *as a genre*, and its influence has shaped modern fantasy and reader expectations alike. That influence and the fact that most people who pick up this book will be familiar with *The Lord of the Rings* are two further reasons why the novel is discussed throughout the following chapters. Fantasy is an enormous field, with no definitive canon. In selecting my examples, I have tried to draw on widely read authors; but even so, I realize that few of my readers will have read every work discussed here. By including Tolkien's novel, I can be reasonably certain that everyone is acquainted with at least one of the example texts.

Some terms used in the following chapters concern the construction of fantasy worlds on a very basic level. In fact, the most basic of these terms is *world*, by which I mean a universe or space in which all positions are, at least in theory, accessible to a person (fictive or otherwise) by means of (nonmagical) travel: by foot, boat, or spaceship, travelers should be able to make their way from one place to another even if it would take them millennia or more. In "On Fairy-stories," Tolkien introduces the concept *secondary world* to designate the literary creation of a story maker. It is a world that the reader's mind can enter, a world of internal consistency. To Tolkien, any setting for a story constituted a secondary world. The *primary world* was the world of the reader and writer, the "real" world.[47] As Wolfe observes, however, secondary world has come to mean fantasy worlds that are different from our own,[48] and a story is even sometimes said to be set in the primary world. Brian Stableford tries to circumvent this problem by talking about settings as "simulacra of the primary world,"[49] but the term is somewhat unwieldy.

To avoid confusion between a literary setting and the world around us, I will borrow a term from possible-worlds semantics and refer to, on the one hand, the *actual world* (the world inhabited by the reader and the writer[50]) and, on the other, the primary world. The latter is a literary construct whose setting imitates, on a general level if not in every detail, the actual world. The primary world thus contains the main social, geographical, and historical features of the actual world, although its population, and laws of nature, might differ.[51] James Bond, no matter how fantastic his adventures, lives in a primary world, as do Molly Bloom and Jonathan Harker. By contrast, secondary worlds provide homes for Frodo Baggins as well as Aslan the Lion and Taran the Assistant Pigkeeper. It should be noted that though a given work can contain any number of secondary worlds, it can contain only one primary world, and *no* work of fiction is set in the actual world. Also, sometimes a tenuous connection (spatial and/or temporal) is suggested between the fantasy setting and the primary world. The connection could be expressed as a formulaic expression ("Once upon a time" implies such a vague connection, for instance), or it is implied or explained in the text how the story is set in the far future or the distant past. Gene Wolfe's The Book of the New Sun series and Terry Brooks's Shannara books are examples of the former, *The Lord of the Rings* and Robert E. Howard's Conan stories of the latter. Such distant settings, not clearly recognizable as a specific place and time from the actual world, Zahorski and Boyer call "remote secondary worlds,"[52] and although there is no need for the subclassification here, I similarly refer to these worlds as secondary. Furthermore, Zahorski and Boyer suggest a main division of fantasy according to setting; what they call *low fantasy* has a primary-world setting whereas *high fantasy* is set mainly in a secondary world.[53] These terms are also used in this book.

Worlds can be divided into separate *domains*. Lubomír Doležel explains how what he calls "dyadic worlds" are fictional worlds divided into two domains "in which contrary modal conditions reign."[54] Depending on modality, the domains differ in terms of, for instance, contradictory value systems, knowledge, or natural or social laws. Nancy H. Traill uses the concept of dyadic worlds to discuss the fantastic, dividing fantastic worlds into natural and supernatural domains.[55] However, Traill defines *natural* as having "the same natural laws as does the actual world,"[56] which leaves her with a "fantasy mode" consisting of a supernatural domain only. I find that even fantasy worlds—in particular secondary ones—can consist of more than one domain, but that the dividing line between the domains does not necessarily run along what accords with the laws of nature in the actual world. Rather than attempt to come up with a blanket term for domains, relevant names for the worlds in question are employed here, such as the land of the living and the land of the dead, Faerie and mundanity, or Ancelstierre and the Old Kingdom. Geographically divided domains will be the topic for chapter 3, the domains of nature and culture that of chapter 4, and the domains of myth and mundanity make an appearance in chapter 5.

Finally, it should be mentioned that words like *realm*, *land*, and *landscape* are used only in a nonspecific sense. Although *The Encyclopedia of Fantasy* uses *land* with the restricted meaning of "a secondary-world venue whose nature and fate are central to the plot,"[57] I use the word in its general meaning. Similarly, a realm is quite simply an area (often a country) ruled by someone or something, and a landscape is taken quite broadly to mean "the shape of the land."

Each chapter in this book applies its own viewpoint, focusing on different types of divisions on various levels within a setting. The general progress is from large scale to small, beginning with fantasy maps, moving on to divisions between geographical domains, then looking at the interrelation of two domains in an urban setting, and ending with the link between land and people. The four main chapters are written to work independently of one another, however, and can be read in any order. Together, they offer a way in which to understand fantasy literature from a topofocal perspective and demonstrate how readings of fantasy settings can contribute to our understanding of the genre in general, as well as of particular fantasy works.

The map is one of humankind's oldest methods of dividing our physical environment into ours and theirs, safe and perilous, known and unknown, and any number of other categories. The fantasy map, while able to express the categorization of actual maps, also brings up questions about other divisions, such as those between presentation and representation, text and image, and fact and fiction. The fantasy map is a work of fiction, as is the text it accompanies; it is often taken to be a hallmark of fantasy and one of the genre's most distinctive characteristics. Chapter 2 presents what previous research there is into fantasy maps and briefly discusses how to regard maps that are not representations of actual places. A survey of the maps found in a random sample of two hundred fantasy novels is then presented, followed by a reading of two maps from *The Lord of the Rings*. The results of the survey are discussed in terms of what is characteristic of a fantasy map, but the text also pays attention to less frequent features, with special focus on what these features can tell us about the worlds they portray. The readings of the Tolkien maps discuss what assumptions and unspoken values become evident from the (relative) location, presentation, and absence of various map features. These findings are also related to the Tolkien text as a whole.

Chapter 3 deals with divisions that are possible in a fantasy world but do not occur in the actual world. These divisions are discussed in terms of borders, which separate two domains from each other, and boundaries, which circumscribe a domain—I decided to pay special attention to the domains known as *polders*, whose rules are such that the surrounding world would destroy them if the boundary were ever breached. Borders divide life and death in two of Steven Brust's Dragaera novels (*Taltos* 1988, *The Paths of the Dead* 2002); mundanity and Faerie in Neil Gaiman and Charles Vess's *Stardust* (1997–98); and the domains of magic and technology in the Abhorsen series by Garth Nix (1995–2003). The polders examined are Tolkien's Lothlórien, Robert Holdstock's Mythago Wood (1984–2009), and Terry Pratchett's Djelibeybi (in *Pyramids* 1989). Many fantasy plots are constructed around the crossing of such dividing lines; but a particular characteristic of boundaries is that they connect geography with history, and they are components that help construct a world that extends in time as well as in space.

Western civilization has long divided the world into nature and culture, tending to consider the latter superior to the former. Fantasy worlds are not bound by divisions that spring from a Western worldview, however. Chapter 4 examines how the relation between nature and culture is expressed in four fantasy cities: Tolkien's Minas Tirith, Charles de Lint's Newford (novels and short fiction 1988–2006), Miéville's New Crobuzon (mainly *Perdido Street Station* 2000 and *Iron Council* 2004), and Patricia McKillip's Ombria (*Ombria in Shadow* 2002). A city provides the most obvious interface between nature and culture; on a very basic level, the nature outside meets the culture within at the city wall. In most cities, the meeting between the two domains is not that simple, with nature and culture interrelating in a variety of ways. In a fictive city, these interrelations are not restricted to what can be found in the actual world; in such places, nature can relate to culture in ways limited only by the author's imagination. The four cities display quite varied relations between the two domains; but in each case, the manner in which the relation is portrayed can be linked to central concerns in the stories.

The final chapter deals with the question of how the division between people and their environment, which we perceive in the actual world, is bridged in fantasy stories. The focus in chapter 5 is on the way in which ruler and realm are directly linked to each other in much fantasy. After providing an overview of how rulers and realms may be associated, in different ways and to varying degrees, I discuss how the direct link between the sovereign and the fertility of the land, embodied in the Fisher King figure, is put to use in Tim Powers's *Last Call* (1992). Then I turn to Lisa Goldstein's *Tourists* (1989), in which the struggle for control expresses itself as palimpsests in a city's topology, the signs of one ruler overwriting the signs of another. The final section of the chapter examines the landscapes associated with Dark Lords, including a brief historical background to the predominant imagery of these places of evil. Sauron and Mordor (Tolkien), Lord Foul and Foul's Creche (Stephen R. Donaldson: *The Power That Preserves* 1977), and Shai'tan and the Blight (Robert Jordan: *The Eye of the World* 1990) provide the main examples. The section demonstrates how superficial similarities may be misleading when examining the manner in which a land functions, and how a reading of a landscape of evil may promote an understanding of the nature of evil in the work.

2 : Maps

Maps are wonderful tools that can help us find our way and divide up our surroundings: into our land and theirs, into safe places and unsafe, and, ultimately, into the known world and the unknown. Exploring has become tantamount to mapping, turning the empty margins and blank areas of terra incognita into familiar terrain. In a literary genre as concerned with exploring new worlds as fantasy is, it is hardly surprising that the map is a frequent complement to the texts, a companion on the reader's journey through the alien landscape. The inclusion of maps is not restricted to fantasy novels, however, and it has been done for almost as long as there have been printed books. As a result of the Genevan reform, the second half of the sixteenth century saw a widespread use of maps in printed Bibles[1] and already during the late fifteenth century, numerous illustrations charting Dante's Hell had been produced, based on descriptions in the text.[2] Other well-known works of fiction that are furnished with maps include Thomas More's *Utopia* (1516), Jonathan Swift's *Gulliver's Travels* (1726), and Robert Louis Stevenson's *Treasure Island* (1883)—of the last, it has even been said that the map was not just produced to be published together with the novel; the novel was actually written to go with the map.[3]

In modern fantasy, especially high fantasy, maps are considered common enough to be almost obligatory, mainly because of the maps J. R. R. Tolkien included in *The Lord of the Rings* (1954–55).[4] According to Roz Kaveney, the map has come to be used as an authenticating device and a means to facilitate understanding, but she also suggests that Tolkien supplied maps "much in the same spirit that he provided endless glossaries and appendices."[5] What this spirit is, she omits to mention; but it is clear that to Tolkien, the map aids in the construction of an internally consistent world. Furthermore, the maps in *The Lord of the Rings*, just like the many casual references to Arda's historical events and people, serve to provide the secondary world with the width, depth, and height that Tolkien sought in the realm of fairy stories. Whether provided for authentication, understanding, inner consistency, or world expansion, maps are expected to be supplied in high-fantasy novels today.

PREVIOUS EXPLORATIONS OF FANTASY MAPS

Fantasy maps have long fascinated readers. To my mind, the most impressive collection is still J. B. Post's *An Atlas of Fantasy*, first published in 1973 (with a revised second edition in 1979).[6] Post included more than a hundred maps from modern fantasy worlds as well as from a large range of imaginary places. Few scholars have discussed fantasy maps in writing, however. In 1976, Diane Duane wrote a short piece entitled "Cartography for Other Worlds: A Short Look at a Neglected Subject," wherein she acknowledged the value of maps and insisted that fantasy and science-fiction maps should be created by author and mapmaker in collaboration.[7] A year later, Julian May, writing as Lee N. Falconer, examined the history and cartography of the maps of the fictional world of Conan, including details about map projections, in the preface to *A Gazet[t]eer of the Hyborian World of Conan*.[8] The most in-depth description of fantasy maps can be found in Diana Wynne Jones's satirical commentary on the typical worlds of Tolkien's epigones, *The Tough Guide to Fantasyland*, in which she declares that the first thing to do on any tour of Fantasyland is to "[f]ind the map. It will be there. No Tour of Fantasyland is complete without one."[9] The reader is then encouraged to examine the map, and a number of common features of fantasy maps are noted. Apart from Jones's satire, few studies of fantasy maps have been more than cursory, despite the alleged prevalence and uniformity of the phenomenon.

The importance of maps has not passed the scholarly community by completely, however. In 1979, at the beginning of the mass-market fantasy boom that started in the late 1970s, Frank W. Day points out how the increased popularity of science fiction and fantasy, and the use of maps in these genres, "[makes] analysis of the map communication process in such literature more important than ever."[10] His own study focuses on maps as communicative devices, from the perspective of readers and authors. Coming to maps from a somewhat different angle, Clare Ranson ends her 1996 paper "Cartography in Children's Literature" by expressing the hope that she has demonstrated how maps are "an interesting branch of illustration and worthy of more critical attention."[11] Yet despite

Day's and Ranson's exhortations, few critics have devoted any notable scholarly efforts to fictional maps—and in all fairness, the fact that Day's study is an unpublished master's thesis and Ranson's paper was presented at a conference on school librarianship probably did not add to their impact among fantasy scholars. Ranson only incorporates minimal readings of maps, including brief comments on the map in Ursula K. Le Guin's *A Wizard of Earthsea* (1968). Instead, she proposes a taxonomy of maps in children's books, with three categories, comprising maps of real places, real-place maps adjusted to fit the plot, and "imaginary maps."[12] Regrettably, this last category includes both maps of secondary worlds and maps of fictional places in the primary world, and thus Ranson's taxonomy provides little help in advancing a closer investigation of secondary-world maps. R. C. Walker similarly devotes much of his *Mythlore* piece from 1981, "The Cartography of Fantasy," to a general taxonomy of fantasy settings, noting the importance of settings to the genre.[13] The article proceeds to stress the need for maps in fantasy books, proposing that maps be drawn for books that do not have them.[14]

The past three decades have seen a few articles that treat fantasy maps as cartographic objects. Peter Hunt connects maps with landscapes and journeys, bringing up the significance of maps in English fantasy—maps that, he argues, "are both reductive and suggestive." Fantasy maps, according to Hunt, "stabilize the fantasy, while releasing greater imaginative potential."[15] His discussion does not differentiate between maps of primary and secondary worlds; in fact, his focus is on primary-world maps, and he notes that the maps might be said to "symbolize the tension that exists for the writer between the real landscape and the fantasy which inhabits it."[16] That tension is important to Hunt's readings of the fictionalized versions of the English landscape, and the map becomes, to him, a tool for tapping into "landscapes of profound national symbolism."[17] The Middle-earth map is thus discussed in terms of how the secondary world it describes can be matched with the English landscape. The problem is that Hunt glides between map and setting in his discussion, so while many of the landscapes described in *The Lord of the Rings* might fit Hunt's vision of Englishness, the map of Middle-earth itself does not.

Where Hunt focuses on maps in English—primarily low—fantasy, Myles Balfe looks at genre fantasy from an Orientalist perspective. He uses the map from Robert Jordan's Wheel of Time series (1990–2013) to demonstrate how, rather than portraying a completely imaginary landscape, it "continues a Western historical convention of representing the 'Orient' and the 'Orientals' who exist there as both *opposite* and *inferior* to the West, and its Westland heroes."[18] Like Hunt, however, Balfe discusses both setting and its (re)presentation, somewhat undermining any cartographic point he tries to make, and he leaves maps out of his discussions of Feist's *Magician* (1982) and the Dungeons & Dragons setting Al Qadim (1992).

Pierre Jourde dedicates a chapter of his study of imaginary geographies to cartographic representations. After a brief discussion of how map relations can be read (using the allegorical "Carte de Tendre" from Madeleine de Scudéry's *Clélie* [1654–60] and the map of Utopia from More's work as examples), Jourde focuses on the maps from *The Hobbit* (1937) and *The Lord of the Rings*.[19] He sees two basic divisions in Middle-earth's geography. The first is that between east and west, roughly along the central mountain range. The western regions are, according to Jourde, the more civilized, with a great number of "microcosms" and innumerable rivers, a land open to the western sea. The regions to the east are more corrupted by the forces of evil, with vast, undefined areas, open to an unknown continent from which Sauron's troops come.[20] Jourde also sees a second division between northern and southern Middle-earth, observing how the northern communities are more "rudimentary" than their southern counterparts and comparing the elven realms of Mirkwood and Lothlórien, the human lands of Esgaroth, Rohan, and Gondor, and even Sauron's two guises, as the "diffuse necromancer" of Dol Goldur and the "quasi-omniscient potentate" of Barad-Dur.[21] Jourde's map readings offer some valuable insights, although his search for patterns sometimes makes him ignore those map features that do not fit, such as the uncivilized interior of Eriador; his desire to support his argument also leads him to overstate some map features in his outlines.[22]

The most extensive study to date of fantasy maps as cartographic objects is presented by Deirdre F. Baker. She carries out what she refers to as "a casual survey" based on a convenience sample of fantasy maps.[23] Her findings confirm the similarities Jones satirizes in the *Tough Guide*. Regrettably, given that Baker's stated purpose promises much more, her actual reading of the maps turns out to be rather shallow, and she forces the Middle-earth map from *The Lord of the Rings* into an allegory based on "what we know of Tolkien."[24] To suggest that the map illustrates the threat of Nazi Germany by virtue of its physical layout feels like a somewhat outdated interpretation of Tolkien. Also regrettable is that when Baker identifies the Earthsea map as intriguingly different from the other maps she has examined, she turns from the physical map to what she terms "metaphysical" maps. The unique vision of Le Guin's map is coupled with a "mapping" (in the text of the novels) of Earthsea's spiritual world, according to Baker, and she eventually suggests that "the sameness of geographical layout determines a sameness in simplistic moral or metaphysical vision."[25] Unconventional maps and originality in plot and metaphysics go together, she argues, yet while her discussions of a number of fantasy works are not without merit, they do not necessarily substantiate that conclusion.

Ricardo Padrón investigates fantasy maps together with other types of maps of imaginary worlds, offering a wider consideration of cartographic objects that map fictional geographies. He discusses the functions of a wide array of maps, from Dante's Hell to William Faulkner's Yoknapatawpha County, even including examples from the visual arts, such as Adrian Leskiw's road maps of imaginary places. Given such a comprehensive collection of examples, it is not surprising that Padrón includes Tolkien's map of Middle-earth along with user-created maps of the online computer game World of Warcraft (2004–present) and maps of the land of fairy tales by Jaro Hess and Bernard Sleigh. As opposed to the maps of Utopia and Gulliver's travel locations, these various fantasy maps all invite us to revel in imaginative travel.[26] Padrón's analysis, while on the whole interesting, is occasionally so brief as to suggest that he bases his discussion on a personal view of fantasy as escapist fiction, an impression made especially strong when he fails to support his arguments.[27] His conclusion is that the maps he has investigated are not radically different from other maps *as maps*, and that they work because of their similarity with those other maps. It is the imaginary worlds of the maps that trigger our imagination, but that is something any map can do—if we let it.[28]

Among the many recent online essays and blog posts that wax lyrical about fantasy and imaginary maps, I have found one example worth mentioning here. In his nicely argued and beautifully illustrated piece "Here Be Cartographers: Reading the Fantasy Map,"[29] Nicholas Tam sketches out a theory of how to analyze fantasy maps. He proposes a number of angles from which to approach a map, based on ways in which the fantasy map can relate to the story and the fictive world. Tam's discussion ranges from material conditions of mapmaking to worldviews encoded in maps, and his examples make clear why the various angles are worth considering in theoretical investigations of the genre's numerous maps. This is a brief essay rather than a scholarly article, lacking theoretical depth, but it provides a useful starting point for anyone who wants to think critically about fantasy maps.

Over the past four decades, many scholars have argued that fantasy maps deserve more critical attention, but what little scholarship has been published has either offered only a cursory exploration or too narrow a scope to provide any deeper insight into the subject. A greater understanding of the genre's maps requires both a more comprehensive study of a large number of maps and more thorough examinations of particular maps. It is also important to bear in mind that Padrón's point—that maps of imaginary worlds are similar to other maps—implies that fantasy maps can be analyzed in the same way as maps of our world. However, any textbook in cartography will quickly reveal a difference between the two types of maps that is significant enough to call into doubt whether fantasy maps are maps at all, a topic next up for consideration.

WHAT IS A FANTASY MAP?

A map is a symbolized representation of geographical reality, representing selected features or characteristics, resulting from the creative effort of its author's execution of choices, and is designed for use when spatial relationships are of primary relevance.[30]

If this is how a map is to be defined, the maplike illustrations found in a vast number of fantasy works present a problem. Although they undeniably "[result] from the creative effort of [their authors'] execution of choices," an overwhelming majority of them are *not* representations of "geographical reality." Their "features or characteristics" bear little or no relation to anything in the actual world. They are simply not maps, as they violate the deeply ingrained notion that a map must in some way represent the world of the cartographer. Even the most concise definition I have found, that of American cartographers Arthur H. Robinson and Barbara Bartz Petchenik, ultimately falls back on this notion. To them a "map is a graphic representation of the milieu," wherein the word *milieu* "connotes one's surroundings or environment in addition to its meaning of place."[31] Cartographically, a fantasy map seems to be a contradiction in terms.

Actually, Robinson and Petchenik seem to have no problems with maps of imaginary places, as they include them among their examples.[32] Historian Jeremy Black brings up the problem of mapping politics in maps of imaginary worlds, but he never questions their status as maps.[33] In his influential book *The Power of Maps*, map scholar Denis Wood similarly acknowledges the existence of *fictional* and *fantastic* maps.[34] In a later book, Wood discusses maps of imaginary places (mentioning, for instance, the maps of Middle-earth, Dungeons & Dragons, and the Marvel Universe) at some length, concluding that they illustrate how maps need not represent a part of the Earth's surface.[35] Consequently, fantasy maps are treated as maps here, with one important caveat. The difference between the map that graphically represents the milieu and a map of an imaginary place is one of priority: a map *re*-presents what is already there; a fictional map is often primary—to create the map means, largely, to create the world of the map. (This is the case even though maps that are made to fit an existing literary work are by no means uncommon. Padrón includes the many maps of Hell that are based on Dante's *Divina Commedia* as examples of this phenomenon.[36]) Some points, then, on terminology before proceeding: First, the maps in the fantasy novels to be examined are not maps in the sense that they necessarily correspond to anything in the actual world. Drawing inspiration from Wood's terms, I refer to *fictional maps* and *fantasy maps*, where the former category includes any map that does not represent the actual world and the latter is a map of a fantasy world, generally found in a fantasy novel (although the term would fit maps from fantasy role-playing games equally well). Maps of the actual world are consequently *actual maps*. Second, to avoid suggesting that fictional maps in any way correspond to a position in the actual world, I say that they *portray* rather than *represent* something.

The status of the fictional map in relation to the text is in no way clear-cut, and various points of view yield different insights. In *Paratexts: Thresholds of Interpretation*, Gérard Genette uses the term *paratext* to refer to the various "verbal or other productions, such as an author's name, a title, a preface, illustrations" that accompany a text.[37] Whether they belong to the text or not, he explains, these productions surround and extend it. Genette mainly considers textual paratexts, but in his conclusion, he mentions some paratextual elements that he has not examined. Among these are "certain elements of the documentary paratext that are characteristic of didactic works" but that sometimes appear in works of fiction.[38] Genette's examples of such elements include fictional maps, for instance Faulkner's map of Yoknapatawpha County and Umberto Eco's plan of the abbey in *The Name of the Rose* (1980).

It makes sense to regard a fantasy map as something that extends the fantasy text. The maps are generally not part of the narrative, in that they do not refer directly to any object in the text (with a few exceptions, such as Thror's Map in *The Hobbit*, which is also parenthetically referred to by the narrator[39]). Instead, they and the text both refer to the fictional world or to a part of it—that is, to the story's setting. Thus, they become, in Genette's terminology, a *threshold*,[40] a liminal space between the actual world of the reader and the fictional (generally secondary; see Table 2.2) world of the fantasy story. The maps blur the distinction between representation and imagination, suggesting that the places portrayed are in fact representations of existing places. This suggestion would explain why fictional maps are usually considered to be maps, even though they do not share the actual maps' representing of the "milieu."

Alternatively, fantasy maps can be interpreted as *docemes*. A doceme is defined by documentation-studies scholar Niels Windfeld Lund as "any part of a document, anything that can be identified and isolated analytically as part of the documentation process or the resulting document." Moreover, Lund explains that although, for instance, a photograph can be a document in itself, if it is part of a newspaper article, it (as well as the article text) is only a doceme—"[a] doceme can never be something in itself."[41]

Thinking of the fantasy map as a doceme puts a stronger emphasis on the relationship between narrative (text) and map. Rather than offering a threshold between fiction and reader, the map is part of the total fantasy document. Lund's observation that the doceme is part of *the documentation process* or *the resulting document* is also highly relevant. The map is not only one of several parts of the finished document; it can, as in the case of Stevenson's Treasure Island, be a central part of the creation process: according to Orson Scott Card, maps are basic to Card's world creation and provide him with story ideas;[42] Poul Anderson explains how, "[w]hen a story has an imaginary setting, I draw a map as part of the planning";[43] and in a letter, Tolkien relates how he "wisely started with a map, and made the story fit (generally with meticulous care for distances)."[44] Three authors do not, of course, represent a genre, but they all point in the same direction, and Tolkien proceeds to explain why the map's priority is important: "The other way about lands one in confusions and impossibilities, and in any case it is weary work to compose a map from a story." In the same letter, he also apologizes for "the Geography" and acknowledges how difficult it must have been to read *The Lord of the Rings* proofs without maps. In other words, Tolkien felt the map doceme to be necessary both during the documentation process and when reading the resulting document.

In the two discussions on maps that follow, we can see how fantasy maps can be fruitfully interpreted as both paratexts and docemes. The two perspectives are not mutually exclusive but relate the map differently to the text. Constituting thresholds between the actual and fictional worlds, they are also an essential part of the document that is the fantasy book.

A SURVEY OF FANTASY MAPS

To take a quantitative approach to the fantasy map, I carried out a survey of two hundred randomly selected fantasy works and looked at the maps I found in them. This section is devoted to a presentation of the survey results, examining the maps' general features as well as the types of map elements found, and discussing what these findings can tell us about specific settings and the genre as a whole. The small number of works in the sample, and the low proportion of maps among those works, resulted in fairly large margins of error, but the results still indicate some interesting features of fantasy maps. (A more thorough presentation of the survey method and the assumptions on which it is based, along with the statistical method used for calculating margins of error, can be found in appendix A; a list of works in the sample can be found in appendix B.)

The Prevalence of Maps

Here is the most basic question: how common is it for fantasy novels to contain at least one map? Of the two hundred novels in the sample, sixty-seven (34 percent) contained one or more maps. In terms of the entire genre, this means that no more than 40 percent and possibly as few as 27 percent of all fantasy novels actually contain any maps. In other words, maps are not the compulsory ingredients they are widely held to be. The main explanation for this apparent lack of maps has to do with setting. The sampling frame (and thus the sample) comprises the entire genre, high fantasy as well as low, but maps are much more common in fantasy set in a secondary world. In the sample, of the sixty-seven novels that have maps, only six contain maps portraying the primary world

# of Maps	% of Fantasy Novels with Maps, in Sample (n)	% of Fantasy Novels with Maps	% of All Fantasy Novels
1	73.1 (49)	60.9–83.2	18.7–31.1
2	22.4 (15)	13.1–34.2	4.3–12.1
> 2	4.5 (3)	0.9–12.5	0.3–4.3

N = 67

(corresponding to 3 to 18 percent of all novels with maps), and these are all set in historic or prehistoric times. While there are low-fantasy works in contemporary settings that have maps, their numbers are small enough not to crop up in the sample (constituting fewer than 5 percent of all maps and less than 2 percent of the genre). Examples include Alan Garner's *The Weirdstone of Brisingamen* (1960), with a map of the area around Macclesfield in Cheshire; Neil Gaiman's *Neverwhere* (1996), with a map of the London Underground; and Charlie Fletcher's *Stoneheart* (2006), with a map of central London.[45] As I had no data on the general distribution of high fantasy to low in the sample, I was unable to pursue this matter further (see also appendix A).

Related to the question of how prevalent maps are in fantasy novels is the question of how *many* maps a fantasy novel contains. While three quarters of the novels with maps contained only a single map (roughly between 20 and 30 percent of the genre), slightly over one fifth had two maps, and novels with three, four, and six maps also appeared (see Table 2.1). In most cases (fourteen out of eighteen), the additional maps provided one or more large-scale views of one or more areas (in four cases, this included a city map). Of the remaining four cases, two had floor plans for buildings, one had maps of two different continents, and one mapped the area's political and physical features on two separate maps. The main reason for including more than one map, in other words, seems to be to provide a general, small-scale map and a larger-scale map of an important setting: a country, province, or city, for instance. The maps in *The Lord of the Rings* provide an example of this tendency. A large-scale map of the Shire, a small-scale map of the entire western Middle-earth, and a medium-scale map of the area around Gondor and Mordor are included, illustrating how the story's quest-narrative is built around long journeys across the world, but also requires detailed maps for locales where central events are set. (Tolkien's large- and small-scale maps are discussed in detail later in this chapter.)

When examining the features of the fantasy map, I use as my sample the ninety-two maps found in the survey. In five cases, the same map (or similar versions of the same map, when, for instance, different artists have drawn maps for books with the same setting) appears in two or more books. Such maps have been counted as separate instances, however, partly because the efforts of different mapmakers may result in very different renditions of the same location (as can be observed from the maps in the Conan books in the sample[46]), but mainly because they constitute docemes in different documents.

General Map Features:
Subject, Orientation, Surround Elements

Only six of the novels with maps portray a primary-world setting. These six novels contain thirteen of the ninety-two maps, and even though there are fantasy books that have maps of primary-world cities, no such maps can be found in the sample, confirming how rare such maps are (corresponding to less than 4 percent of all fantasy maps). The vast majority of maps portray a secondary world or an area in a secondary world (almost four fifths of the sample, or between 68 and 86 percent of all fantasy maps). Of the remaining maps, about 5 percent (2 to 12 percent) portray an imaginary city, either in a secondary world or set in the primary world (an example of the latter is the city of Ys, a map of which appears in Poul and Karen Anderson's *Dahut* [1988]), and 2 percent (0.3 to 8 percent) are plans of buildings or building complexes.

The portrayal by at least two thirds of all fantasy maps of secondary worlds suggests a need in fantasy novels to provide a visual image of the imaginary setting, but also to provide the setting with some sort of structure. The map can help the reader understand complex spatial relationships that the text alone may fail to convey. Conversely, the absence of a map in a fantasy novel in which movements, positions, and spatial relationships in the imaginary world are central to the story may prove bewildering to the reader.[47]

With maps of secondary worlds clearly dominating, the question arises to what extent these maps of alien worlds also reflect alien forms of mapmaking. In *The Hobbit*, Tolkien includes two maps, one of which

	% of Maps in Sample (n)	% of All Fantasy Maps
Primary World	14.1 (13)	7.7–23.0
Secondary World	78.3 (72)	68.4–86.2
Imaginary City	5.4 (5)	1.8–12.2
Building/s	2.2 (2)	0.3–7.6

N = 92

has THROR'S MAP written in the lower left corner and includes some text in dwarvish runes. It is obviously meant to refer to a map in the story, and the brief preface points out that the map has "East at the top, as usual in dwarf-maps."[48] The other *Hobbit* map, that of the Wilderlands, follows the convention of having north at the top. This convention is comparatively modern, however. According to historian P. D. A. Harvey, almost all world maps before the fifteenth century were either zonal (or climatic) maps or T-O (*orbis terrarium*) maps, circular maps with east at the top where the world is divided into three continents (Asia, Europe, Africa) by a T-shape.[49] In fact, of the extant medieval maps from the eighth through the fifteenth centuries, a clear majority are basic T-O maps.[50]

Despite the dominance of secondary worlds or historical settings in the sample, the maps largely follow the modern convention of placing north at the top. Ann Swinfen remarks on how (northern-hemisphere) fantasy writers maintain primary-world compass directions in their worlds.[51] A majority of all fantasy maps—at least 58 percent—come with a compass rose or similar design indicating which way north is. Other maps signal their orientation in other ways; for example, Southern Ithania is located below Northern Ithania in Trudy Canavan's *Last of the Wilds* (2005). For only nine maps in the sample can orientation not be determined from the map alone. Of the eighty-three maps for which orientation can be determined from the map, nine are not oriented with north at the top, but all are oriented so as to have a direction somewhere between northeast and northwest at the top. In the nine cases for which information about orientation is completely absent from the map, re-

	% of Maps in Sample (n)	*% of All Fantasy Maps*
N	80.4 (74)	70.9–88.0
NE to NW	9.8 (9)	4.6–17.8
No Orientation Given	9.8 (9)	4.6–17.8
Compass Rose	68.5 (63)	58.0–77.8

N = 92

lated maps or the texts in question have been used to work out how they are facing. North is at the top of all these maps except for one, which has north-northeast at the top.

So although Thror's Map demonstrates the existence of fantasy maps that are oriented differently, such maps constitute less than 4 percent of all maps. Only very few fantasy writers or mapmakers avail themselves of the freedom to turn the map whichever way according to the conventions of imaginary societies in secondary worlds, or to create completely new directions. Instead, just as Swinfen suggests, the actual-world convention of orienting the map with north at the top dominates almost completely.

A typical feature of the T-O maps, a feature that, according to John Noble Wilford, goes back to the earliest extant world map (a Babylonian map from the sixth century B.C.),[52] is that the "whole [world] is surrounded by a circumfluent ocean."[53] The surrounding water is where the world ends, where even the *possibility* of knowledge ends. It frames the known world, establishing that what is on the map is all there is. Similar circumfluent oceans can be found on fantasy maps, providing the worlds with what John Clute, in *The Encyclopedia of Fantasy*, calls *water margins*. According to Clute, these margins surround the central land or reality and fade away beyond the edges of any map. He adds that secondary worlds often have maps whose edges are water margins.[54]

Such "ultimately unmappable regions"[55] that completely enclose the known world of a fantasy map within regions of the unknown are not, in fact, particularly common; only a small proportion of the fantasy maps are completely surrounded by water margins (9 to 24 percent; see Table

2.4). On at least three maps out of four, land stretches to the edge of the map, suggesting that the world not only continues but is accessible. The term *water margin* is also slightly misleading; a water margin need not consist of water, but can be a region of any "endless" or "impassable" terrain type. Of the fourteen cases in the sample, two maps have water margins that are not water. In Terry Brooks's *The Tangle Box* (1994), the land of Landover is surrounded by a mountain range beyond which are "Mists and the Fairy World." Brooks's fairy world, it is explained in the first Landover novel, *Magic Kingdom for Sale/Sold!* (1986), is a numinous place that borders on all worlds. It can be traversed but only with the help of magic; it cannot be mapped, it is unknowable.[56] In Martin Gardner's *Visitors from Oz* (1998), one of many late additions to L. Frank Baum's classic Oz books, the land of Oz is surrounded by an "impassable desert" (also described as "shifting sands," "great sandy waste," and "deadly desert").[57] While obviously meant to emphasize the futility of any attempt to leave Oz by nonmagical means, other Oz books (for instance, the third book in the sequence, *Ozma of Oz* [1907]) allow for such journeys and open up a world beyond the land of Oz, which illustrates how water margins can be breached, the unknowable made knowable—and known.

The notion that a water margin must enclose the world completely is not unproblematic. On many maps from the sample, there is some land at the edge of the map, providing the possibility of larger landmasses unaccounted for by the mapped area. An example from the sample is Michelle M. Welch's *Chasing Fire* (2005), where a continent surrounded by water takes up most of the map but where a small part of another landmass (Ikinda) can be found along a section of its southern edge. It is obviously the continent that is the map's focus: it features mountains, rivers, and a lake, as well as political borders and various locations (mostly towns, presumably, but names such as Mt. Alaz, Seven Oaks, and Naniantemple suggest that other types of places may also be included). What can be seen of Ikinda, on the other hand, is completely empty. This might mean that it is featureless, unexplored, or simply irrelevant to the story. On the map, Ikinda is portrayed as unknown but knowable, not quite part of the water margin but almost. Welch's Ikinda is hence truly marginalized—not only pushed to (and beyond) the edge of the map but also empty—whereas the map's central continent has a variety of features. Yet setting out to explore the parts of Ikinda that lie beyond the map edges is certainly possible, and such exploration might reveal a small island or a vast continent. We cannot tell which from the map, yet we know that there is something there.

Even when there is a circumfluent ocean, however, the world can be opened up. Expeditions into the water margin have been undertaken in numerous fantasy works. In, for instance, Stephen R. Donaldson's Second Chronicle of Thomas Covenant series (1980–83), the Mallorean series (1987–91) by David and Leigh Eddings, and Raymond E. Feist's *The King's Buccaneer* (1992), sea voyages off the map turn up new continents. On the other hand, as the Landover and Oz maps have already demonstrated, terrains other than water can create an unmappable, unknowable region at a map's edge. The map in Gail Dayton's *The Barbed Rose* (2006) places the central land of Adara between sea to the east and west, whereas to the north and south there are mountains that give the impression of being impassable. The mountainous northern isthmus is called "The Devil's Neck," a name that emphasizes just how impassable it really is. While this is not a complete margin in a strict sense, the map still makes clear that Adara is where the story takes place, and the reader who ponders what can be found beyond the mountains is left with a vague suspicion that there will only be more mountains. (Mountains as map elements will be discussed further in the text that follows.)

Even if the landmass on the map is fully surrounded by water, this does not necessarily constitute a water margin in Clute's sense. The map of the Isles of Glory (map 2.1) in Glenda Larke's *Gilfeather* (2004) may set its islands in a surrounding ocean, but comments on the map make plain that in the diegesis, there is no unknown world to discover beyond the edges of the map. Instead, the islands themselves have been discovered—and, it is implied, fairly recently at that. Not only does the map tell us that the isles were "[s]urveyed by the 2nd Explor. / Ex. Kells 1782–1784," but it also notes by whom and when the various parts of the archipelago were discovered. Known and unknown are turned around here, the well-known residing off the map. Wherever the political, financial, and cultural centers are to be found in this secondary world, they belong in the regions beyond the map's margin—the Isles of Glory, in the middle of the map, are part of the world's periphery.

The absence of complete water margins, with at least some land reaching all the way to the map's edge, indicates that a map does not portray an entire world. Even when the map gives the impression of portraying the whole world, such as the map of Earthsea in Le Guin's *A Wizard of Earthsea*, an extremely short land border still suggests that there is

THE ISLES OF GLORY

Surveyed by the 2nd Explor.
Ex. Kells 1782-1784.

THE MIDDLING ISLES
Discovered by Sallavuard i. Rutho, 1780.

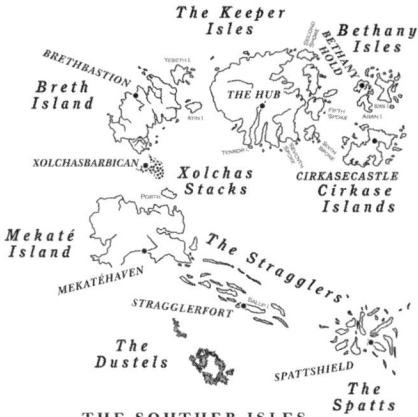

The Keeper
Isles

Bethany
Isles

BRETHBASTION

Breth
Island

THE HUB

XOLCHASBARBICAN

Xolchas
Stacks

CIRKASECASTLE

Cirkase
Islands

Mekaté
Island

The Stragglers

MEKATÉHAVEN

STRAGGLERFORT

The
Dustels

SPATTSHIELD

The
Spatts

THE SOUTHER ISLES
Discovered by Sallavuard i. Rutho, 1781.

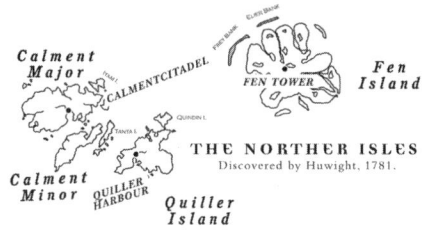

Calment
Major

CALMENTCITADEL

FEN TOWER

Fen
Island

THE NORTHER ISLES
Discovered by Huwight, 1781.

Calment
Minor

QUILLER
HARBOUR

Quiller
Island

SCALE OF NAUTICAL MILES

STATUTE MILES

ISLAND MILES

N

© P Phillips

MAP 2.1. The Isles of Glory from Glenda Larke's *Gilfeather* (2004).
Copyright Perdita Phillips, www.perditaphillips.com.

more to the world than this. It also implies that the region on the map is located somewhere in the larger world.

Of the ninety-two maps in the sample, only one third are clearly set in the northern or southern hemisphere; for the rest, this distinction could not be determined from the maps. Obviously, a secondary world does not have to be set in a hemisphere; Terry Pratchett has demonstrated with his Discworld novels that a world shaped like a disc works as a setting. The change in shape also led to his abandoning the traditional compass points. Instead, the Disc has the main directions "hubward" and "rimward," and the lesser directions "turnwise" and "widdershins."[58] Of the thirty-one maps for which the hemisphere can be determined, twenty-five are set in the northern hemisphere, five in the southern, and one included both hemispheres.

In other words, the northern hemisphere is clearly more common, even when the margin of error is taken into account. One possible explanation is, of course, the preponderance of writers from the northern hemisphere. Despite a growing number of Australian and New Zea-

	% of Maps in Sample (n)	% of All Fantasy Maps
Water Margins	15.2 (14)	8.6–24.2
Map Projection	5.4 (5)	1.8–12.2
Legend	23.9 (22)	15.6–33.9
Scale	16.3 (15)	9.4–25.5

N = 92

land fantasy writers, the vast majority of fantasy writers in English come from the United States and Great Britain. Yet the five maps of a southern hemisphere actually come from three novels by three different writers (Ian Irvine, Sherwood Smith, and Harry Turtledove), with only Irvine hailing from the Antipodes.[59] Another possible interpretation would be that the cultural and political bias toward the northern hemisphere that we find in the actual world rubs off on the creation of secondary worlds and the maps that portray them.

Still, at least half—possibly as many as three quarters—of all fantasy maps lack information about where on the globe they are situated. They may not even be situated on a globe at all. To the extent that they are, or are meant to be, most maps also lack any information about what method has been used to project the spherical surface to a plane (see Table 2.4). This can seem like a minor point in relation to maps of imaginary places; the ideological implications of various map projections may carry political relevance and interest in the actual world,[60] but do such things matter in a fantasy map? An interesting case is provided by the maps created by author and cartographer Russell Kirkpatrick for his fantasy novels, one of which, *The Right Hand of God* (2005), is included in the sample. There are four maps in *The Right Hand of God*: a small-scale map titled "The Sixteen Kingdoms of Faltha"; a medium-scale map of "Westrau, Straux"; an untitled, large-scale map of a mountain pass called The Gap; and a city plan of "Instruere and Environs." Of these, only the Sixteen Kingdoms and Instruere maps contain any information about their map projections. At the bottom of the Instruere map, a note says, "Nestor's Equal-Area Projection © University of Instruere." The Sixteen

	% of Maps in Sample (n)	% of All Fantasy Maps
Northern	27.2 (25)	18.4–37.4
Southern	5.4 (5)	1.8–12.2
Both	1.1 (1)	0.03–5.9
No Data Available	66.3 (61)	55.7–75.8

N = 92

Kingdoms map lacks explicit information about what projection is used, but has a graticule or "web" of latitude and longitude lines that shows the curvature of the surface (see map 2.2). The scale is small enough to let the map reader perceive how the northern parts bend toward the map's vertical axis. This bending causes the squares of the graticule to elongate toward the pole, giving an impression of the mapped area's position between pole and equator. Although no degrees are given, the curves of the longitude lines lead the eye to the projection's central meridian, the one line of longitude that is running parallel to the map's vertical axis. Near the map's center, where the central meridian crosses a latitude line, sits the city of Instruere, its importance emphasized by the map projection.

While the importance of Instruere is made clear by the city's location on, as well as the projection of, the Sixteen Kingdoms map, the note about projection and copyright at the bottom of the Instruere map has a different function. By copyrighting the map to an entity in the secondary world, the map claims itself to be part of the same (fictional) world as that of the city it portrays. The map is no longer an overview of a fictional world; just like Thror's Map, it becomes part of that world, a product of it. This effect is subtly reinforced by the comment about its projection. Nestor's Equal-Area Projection, while cartographically valid, is turned into a product of the secondary world as a result of being attributed to a fictional cartographer.[61] When the map is commandeered by the fictional world, as in this case, it resists a paratextual perspective, stressing instead how it should be considered a doceme, a part that, together with the text, makes up a greater whole. Examining the map is not a question of entering the story; the fictional world has already been entered.

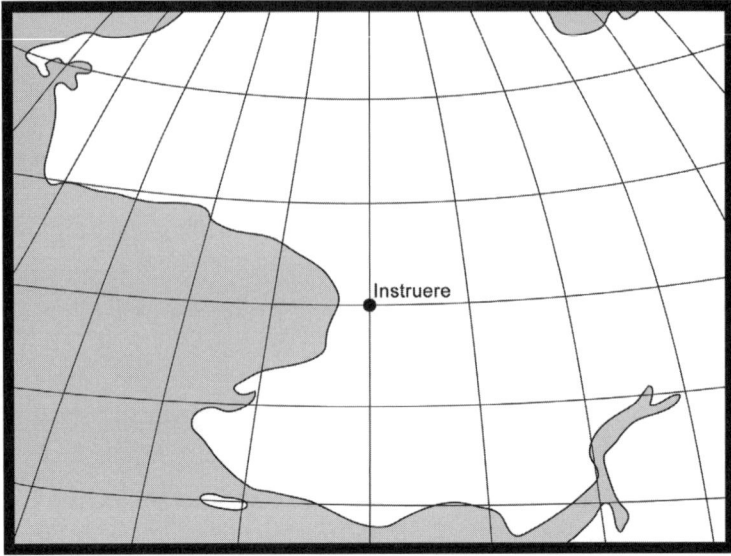

MAP 2.2. Graticule extracted from the map "The Sixteen Kingdoms of
Faltha" in Russell Kirkpatrick's *The Right Hand of God* (2005).
Adapted from the original by the author.

Of all the maps in the sample, only five have any sort of information
about map projection, meaning that of fifty fantasy maps, between one
and six maps say anything about projection (Table 2.4). Apart from Kirkpatrick's Instruere map, only the map of "The World" in Louise Cooper's
Aisling (1994) mentions what projection is used; of the other two maps,
one has a graticule while the second has longitudinal degrees running
along its left side. On Cooper's map, the Winkel Tripel projection has
been used. Unlike Kirkpatrick's Nestor projection, the Winkel Tripel
projection is an actual map projection, used to represent the three-
dimensional actual world in two dimensions; linking it to the map blurs
the map's status as fictional. This emphasizes the map's nature as paratext rather than, as in the Kirkpatrick case, anchoring the map in the fiction as a doceme.

In his oft-cited discussion of the North Carolina highway map, Denis
Wood forcefully denies that legends or keys would be "naturally indis-
pensable to most maps, since they provide the explanations of the various symbols used,"[62] and fantasy maps appear to be no exception. No
more than a third of all fantasy maps have legends or keys of any sort
(see Table 2.4), and of these, none explains all the symbols used. In fact,

HERE BE DRAGONS

only one third of the map legends in the sample (seven legends in total) include any symbols for terrain features. Instead, the legends comment on the map and the fictional world. Wood suggests that "the role of the legend is less to elucidate the 'meaning' of this or that map element than to function as a sign in its own right,"[63] something that is quite obvious from the legends on fantasy maps. These clarify not what separate map symbols mean but what is important about the map; in some cases, they are little more than translation keys that aid in the reader's understanding of where events take place (for instance, the lists on the maps in *Dahut*, which offer translations between contemporary place-names and the names of those places in Roman times). Other legends contain symbols for the travel routes of the protagonists, placing the journey through the world at the center (for example, Orson Scott Card's *Seventh Son* [1987] and Linda Lay Shuler's *Let the Drum Speak* [1996]). Even when the map legend only—or nearly only—contains signs for various terrain features, there is a focus, a comment on the map. Two brief examples:

The legend on Ian Irvine's *Geomancer* (2001) map (map 2.3) lists a number of terrain features, including separate symbols for Conifer Forest, Broadleaf Forest, and Tropical Forest. The legend conveys the impression of a world defined by an abundance of terrain types, a world whose climate ranges from temperate or cold (mountains, hills, coniferous forest) to tropical or warm (reef, desert, tropical forest), with landscapes ranging from dry (desert) to wet (marsh/swamp) and with a variety of landforms (from mountains to grassland). Landscape is what this place is all about, the legend says, adding, almost as an afterthought, that there are also people: a symbol for Main Road (a dotted line) crops up below all the terrain elements, although no road can be found on the maps.

On the map in *The Burning City* (2000), by Larry Niven and Jerry Pournelle, the legend similarly brings terrain features into focus. The first map element (topmost in the left-hand column) is an icon of a coniferous tree that refers to Redwoods. The importance of redwood trees as opposed to other trees is emphasized on at least three levels: their relative position (the Redwood sign precedes the sign for other trees); their being singled out, as opposed to being part of a group (Redwoods versus Other Forest, or all trees that are not redwoods); and the use of an icon rather than a symbol. The legend also stresses the rough terrain: there is a single element for Cultivated Fields and seven that refer to types of wilderness (the legend has no signs for houses or roads, although these

MAP 2.3. Map from Ian Irvine's *Geomancer* (2001).
Copyright Ian Irvine, 2001.

signs appear on the map). No fewer than three of the wilderness signs have to do with elevated land: Hills, Mountains, and High Mountains. According to the legend, this is a wild landscape where people are present but marginalized, a landscape dominated by tall trees and mountains.

A map element that offers a different kind of comment on the map and what it portrays is the scale. As with legends, this is a relatively rare element, which can be found on fifteen of the sample's ninety-two maps (between a tenth and a quarter of all maps; see Table 2.4). In general, a scale allows you to calculate the area covered by the map. With such a low incidence of scales, little can be said about the actual areas that fantasy maps cover. The values are spread fairly evenly, without any noticeable clusters that would suggest typical area sizes. Excluding a city map that covers about 70 square kilometers, the maps that have scales range in size from about 1,100 square kilometers to 27 million square kilometers (approximately the size of Hong Kong and North America, respectively). In other words, they are all significantly smaller than Earth, a fact that, like the prevalence of land borders, hints at a larger, unmapped world beyond the map's edges.

Regardless of map area, the presence of a scale suggests a particular control of the world. It hints at the "meticulous care for distances" that Tolkien mentions in his letter, but even more, it implies that this is a world that *can* be measured. A scale, like information about projection, offers a way to understand positions in map space in terms of positions in "actual geographical" space; the scale on the fictional map announces that there is another space to which the map positions correspond, strengthening the impression that the map not only portrays but represents, that there is a measurable space to which the map refers. This measurability also suggests precision and control, thus either accentuating the author's role as creator and the world's status as fictional or (especially if the map is interpreted as a doceme and refers to a specific or implied map object in the fictional world) requiring a level of scientific knowledge that may be incompatible with the fantasy world as a whole.

Types of Map Elements

Table 2.6 lists the various types of map elements that occur in the sample maps. Significantly more common than any others are topographical elements,[64] especially mountains, coastlines, and rivers (see Table 2.7) as well as various population centers, often without distinctions between villages, towns, and cities. In her *Tough Guide* satirical description of

	% of Maps in Sample (n)[a]	% of All Fantasy Maps
Topographical	92.4 (85)	85.0–96.9
Population Centers[b]	87.0 (80)	78.3–93.1
Other Constructions[c]	67.4 (62)	56.8–76.8
Political[d]	46.7 (43)	36.3–57.4
Demographical/Zoological[e]	10.9 (10)	5.3–19.1
Other[f]	10.9 (10)	5.3–19.1

N = 92

[a] Adds up to more than 100 percent, as each map may contain several types of elements

[b] Cities, towns, villages

[c] Roads, buildings, bridges, and other artificial constructions

[d] Political borders, seats of government, historical sites

[e] Peoples or creatures inhabiting certain areas

[f] Includes a wide range of elements, generally peculiar to particular works

maps, Diana Wynne Jones plays on the perceived prevalence of these elements: "[The map] will show most of a continent (and sometimes part of another) with a large number of bays, offshore islands, an inland sea or so and a sprinkle of towns. There will be scribbly snakes that are probably rivers [. . . .] [The] empty inland parts will be sporadically peppered with little molehills."[65] While inland seas are not as common as Jones implies—large landlocked bodies of water appear on between one and two fantasy maps out of six—she still describes the most common types of map elements (see also Table 2.7). The occurrence of these types of elements in about nine maps out of ten in the sample (corresponding to 85 to 97 percent [topography] and 78–93 percent [towns] of all fantasy maps) is not surprising; on the majority of maps, the landmasses are at least separated from a surrounding sea by coastlines and also include some description of the landforms (two examples of topography). Rivers and mountains seem to be the basic way to define spatial relations; and—especially in portal–quest fantasies—they are both traversed

2.7. THE FIVE MOST COMMON TOPOGRAPHICAL ELEMENTS[a]

	% of Maps in Sample (n)	% of All Fantasy Maps
Rivers	87.0 (80)	78.3–93.1
Bays	84.8 (78)	75.8–91.4
Towns	79.3 (73)	69.6–87.1
Mountains	75.0 (69)	64.9–83.4
Islands	75.0 (69)	64.9–83.4

N = 92

[a] The number of occurrences of an element on each map is not taken into consideration.

frequently and with some difficulty. Because of the hardships involved in crossing (or failing to cross) mountains, these are often used to define the limits of the world; as Jones puts it, there will be "a whole line of mole-hills near the top [of the map] called 'Great Northern Barrier.' Above this will be various warnings of danger."[66] Such mountain ranges (with or without names and warnings) fulfill the same function as a water margin, although they suggest rather more strongly that land exists on the other side. Such ranges can be found, although without any "warnings of danger," on 9 to 24 percent of all fantasy maps. (A number of other maps use a variety of wasteland in a similar fashion, as in the Oz map.)

The group Other Constructions in Table 2.6 (found on two thirds of the maps) is dominated by roads, with only occasional buildings appearing (other than population centers: towers, fortresses, houses). There are rather fewer Ruins, Towers of Sorcery (or other centers of magic), and Dark Citadels (or other edifices of evil) than is implied by the *Tough Guide* (on eleven maps in the sample—somewhere between 6 and 20 percent of all fantasy maps), but Jones is right in pointing to the almost total absence of inns and rest stops. Not even when "camps" are included would this category be found on more than one fantasy map in seven (six maps in the sample).[67] The roads that crawl all over the maps have two main functions. First, as possible travel routes, they tie together the distant points of the map, telling the reader that journeying through this fictional world is possible, even mandatory—the map is a traveling aid, a tool for exploration. This function is particularly prominent in, for instance, Baum's *The Wonderful Wizard of Oz* (1900), in which the yellow brick road is Dorothy's safe way to navigate the fantasy world; and, differently, in D. M. Cornish's Monster-Blood Tattoo/The Foundling's Tale series (2006–2010), in which the protagonist is trained to become a lamplighter, one who lights the lamps along the highways of a dark, monster-infested continent. In both cases, the road is meant to offer safe conduct through a dangerous, fantastic landscape. Second, though, not all fantasy journeys follow the roads; staying away from the road is often more important. The road itself can become a dangerous, unprotected place, open and unsafe. The focus shifts to the wild landscape around the road. The dangers of the road are particularly vivid in *The Lord of the Rings*; it turns into the realm of the enemy, and capture threatens whenever Frodo sets foot on a road. On some maps, the absence or scarcity of roads implies that the world is wild and uncivilized: the few roads that exist are not enough to tame the world, to tie its places together; instead, the world's inhabitants are left exposed and vulnerable to the trackless wilderness.

The political elements mainly consist of political borders between countries or smaller administrative units (for instance, counties), and they are rather uncommon. At most, they appear on two thirds as many maps as do topographical element types. Still, they can be expected to occur on at least somewhat over a third of all fantasy maps. So, while the importance of political units to the fantasy world should not be discounted, it is clear that fantasy maps are more topographical than political.

To fantasy cartographers, it is apparently not particularly important to provide information about what people or creatures live where. In the sample, only 11 percent of the maps contained such information, meaning that as few as one in twenty and as many as one in five of all fantasy maps contain such information in some way. This is a significantly smaller proportion than any of the other map elements, apart from the miscellaneous element types in the Other category. Some of this information might actually be found in the Political category—a certain country could be inhabited by a certain people or type of creature, such as the hobbits in the Shire, or the frequent elven realms, such as Tolkien's Lothlórien and Feist's Elvandar (in *Magician* and other books set in Midkemia). Except for maps in tie-in novels to role-playing game settings (where there are races aplenty, spread over the maps), it is rare to find information such as the "Wood Elves" mark on Tolkien's map of western Middle-earth. The lack of information about what people and creatures live where ("Here Be Elves" or "Here Be Dragons") implies both that the variety of inhabitants found in a fantasy world should be taken as a matter of course and, simultaneously, that the world is, in fact, a terra incognita full of secrets, especially in the cases of portal–quest fantasies, in which the secondary world is explored by protagonist/s and reader together.[68] Rather than being a paratext offering hints to the reader about what to expect once the fictional world is entered, the map in this respect is more of a doceme—a part of the world it describes—for which obvious information is not required, just as we do not often find (actual) general maps that specify "Here Be Germans" in a cursive script over Germany, or have "Here Be Reindeer" printed over northern Scandinavia.

Hill Signs

The signs for mountains offer a useful litmus test in relating the fictional map to maps of actual historical periods. Map projections deal with the transformation of the three-dimensional surface of a sphere to the two-dimensional surface of a plane, but mapmaking also requires another transformation of three- to two-dimensional surfaces. Although it is possible to imagine a world in which the surface is completely flat, most if not all settings tend to have an uneven landscape with hills and mountains as well as plains and valleys. According to geographer Norman J. W. Thrower, "[d]elineation of the continuous three-dimensional form of the land has always been one of the most challenging problems in cartography."[69] The sign for mountains is also among the most ubiquitous topographical elements on fantasy maps—it crops up on three quarters of the maps, which makes it as common as islands but less common than rivers, bays, and towns. (Taking the margin of error into account, it is actually not possible to say which of these five elements is the most prevalent. See Table 2.7.)

The wide variety of signs used for mountains and hills—hill signs—in the sample appears confusing at first. Simple, gray triangles or jagged profiles, pyramids with shadows, even contours and shaded relief can be found. The most common type of hill sign in the sample, appearing on two fifths of the maps (between one third and one half of all fantasy maps), is an oblique (or bird's-eye view) picture of a mountain, shaded to give it an appearance of volume.[70] This kind of hill sign came into use on nonfictional maps during the Renaissance, as copper-engraved, printed maps came to displace hand-painted maps.[71] At the 95 percent confidence level, however, the oblique hill sign is not significantly more common than the sign type it succeeded, the profile view of a mountain, sometimes with hints of shade, a type that can be found on at least 17 percent, and on as many as 36 percent, of all fantasy maps. On medieval maps, the profile view looked "rather like cock's combs" or "serrated bands"[72] or had, at best, basic shading on the sides.[73] The fantasy map equivalents, with or without shading, tend to be simple upside-down V-shapes with no significant difference in prevalence between profiles with and without shading (although the latter is twice as common in the sample).

Around 1680, vertical shading came to be used, an advance that "enabled the cartographers to show [. . .] the length and breadth of a mountain and also to give some approximate idea of the gradients of its slopes."[74] During the eighteenth century, the hatches of the vertical shading sometimes resulted in mountains that looked like "hairy caterpillars"[75] but also led to the development of hachures, "short lines whose thickness indicates steepness of the slope."[76] This type of hill sign is fairly rare on fantasy maps, found in only five instances (or just over 5 percent) in the sample. Given the margin of error, we can expect to find this sign on less than 12 percent of all fantasy maps, possibly on as little as 2 percent. That makes the sign at least 30 percent less common than the profile view and 60 percent less common than the oblique hill signs.

Even less common in the sample, although not significantly so in the fantasy-map population, are the two types of hill signs that are typically used on general survey maps in the actual world today. Contours, which derive from earlier charts of isobaths (lines of equal water depth), appeared on maps as early as 1737 but did not supplant hachures until the second half of the nineteenth century.[77] Expression of landform through shaded relief is related to hachuring and was developed in the 1860s.[78] Only two instances each of these hill signs can be found in the sample, and one book (Kirkpatrick's *The Right Hand of God*) contains one map with shaded relief and one with contours.

Medieval and Renaissance (pre-Enlightenment) hill signs clearly dominate on the maps, however, constituting at least four fifths of all fantasy hill signs. The reason for this is not only that these signs are iconic and self-explanatory but also that they remain highly conventional, part of a cartographic language we acquire along with other cultural knowledge as we grow up.[79] Wood persuasively argues that individuals learn the various types of hill signs in the same sequence that these signs developed historically;[80] the earlier types of hill signs, therefore, appear obvious, self-explanatory. But the relative absence of post-Renaissance hill signs, as well as the general tendencies found in this survey, also agrees with (high) fantasy's general proclivity for pseudomedieval settings.

In "'Fantastic Neomedievalism': The Image of the Middle Ages in Popular Fantasy," Kim Selling discusses why a "significant number of fantasy authors persistently locate their stories in environments where the characters wear medieval dress, fight with swords, and live in hierarchical, vaguely feudal, semi-pastoral societies with low levels of technology."[81] Although Selling uses Umberto Eco's term "fantastic neomedievalism,"[82] Eco as well as Kenneth J. Zahorski and Robert H. Boyer also refer to the "pseudomedieval."[83] Indeed, *pseudo-* rather than *neo-* is the more suitable prefix, as the Middle Ages are evoked rather than recreated. The "vaguely feudal" setting is, in Brian Attebery's words, "essentially a simplified version of the Middle Ages"[84]—simplified in that enough contemporary ideas and sentiments replace their historical counterparts to make the story palatable and comprehensible to a reader of today. The survey indicates that the same goes for the maps.

As the choice of hill signs suggests, the maps pursue a pre-Enlightenment aesthetic. What we generally perceive as late developments, such as map projections and legends,[85] are uncommon. On the other hand, truly medieval conventions are rare. No maps in the sample use the hill signs that were prevalent on actual medieval maps: the serrated bands and cockscombs that represented mountains on many pre-Renaissance maps cannot be deciphered by today's readers. Furthermore, the maps are oriented with north at the top unlike the actual medieval T-O maps, which had east at the top. Rather than appearing medieval, the maps only vaguely suggest the Middle Ages by mixing simplified medieval features with modern conventions.

These modern map conventions are, in fact, only a part of a much larger cluster of social conventions that can be found in fantasy settings, something indicated by the dominance of northern-hemisphere settings. On the whole, the maps indicate a genre-wide conventionality, although some maps, such as the cartographically advanced maps of Kirkpatrick or the landscape-drawing-as-map of Larry and Robert Elmore (as close

	% of Maps in Sample (n)[a]	% of All Fantasy Maps
None	25.0 (23)	16.6–35.1
Profile	26.1 (24)	17.4–36.3
Oblique	40.2 (37)	30.1–51.0
Vertical Shade/ Hachures	5.4 (5)	1.8–12.2
Contours	2.2 (2)	0.3–7.6
Shaded Relief	2.2 (2)	0.3–7.6
Other[b]	2.2 (2)	0.3–7.6

N = 92

[a] Adds up to more than 100 percent, as some maps use more than one type of hill sign.

[b] One map uses white shading to represent mountains; another is a perspectival drawing of the landscape.

as any map in the sample gets to what Ptolemy calls *chōrographica*, a more artistic representation of a small region[86]), try to escape the pattern. Fantasy, especially high fantasy, offers a chance to break with the conventions of the actual world and invent new rules for mapmaking (or return to previous ones), but such inventiveness is actually very rare. Thror's Map in *The Hobbit*, more than any map in the sample, takes advantage of the genre's cartographic possibilities, with its alternative (medieval) orientation and use of an alien alphabet. The vast majority of the maps follow a basic mold established by the two maps in the first edition of *The Fellowship of the Ring*. In the close reading that follows, these two maps are examined to demonstrate what we can learn about a fantasy work and the world it creates by paying attention to its maps.

In Joseph Conrad's *Heart of Darkness*, Marlow reflects on the attraction of maps:

> Now when I was a little chap I had a passion for maps. I would look for hours at South America, or Africa, or Australia, and lose myself in all the glories of exploration. At that time there were many blank spaces on the earth, and when I saw one that looked particularly inviting on a map (but they all look that) I would put my finger on it and say, When I grow up I will go there.[87]

The attraction of Marlow's map apparently lies in its blank spaces, in all the areas left to explore. It is tempting to assume that a fantasy map holds the same attraction—that it opens up an unknown world to explore. Yet, as the ensuing readings of the two Tolkien maps demonstrate, blank spaces on fantasy maps do not necessarily refer to something unknown. On the whole, the fantasy map appears to have a totally opposite function from Marlow's blank spaces. "[T]he very presence of maps at the front of many fantasies implies," according to Farah Mendlesohn, "that the destination and its meaning are known."[88] In other words, the map reflects an effort to make known, not to invitingly offer the unknown. The unknown is largely kept outside the map or along its edges. As was pointed out earlier, at least three quarters of all fantasy maps have land borders beyond which the unknown lurks—or entices. For the greater portion of the mapped fantasy genre, only part of the world is a stage, illuminated and clearly visible.

A "close reading" of a fantasy map means an investigation of what the map makes known and how it makes it known. In such a reading, it must be recalled that although the map is a conspicuous part of how the fictional world is understood, it is never a stand-alone portrayal of that world. Nor should the fantasy map's customary position at the front of the book be taken to mean that the map is to be read without reference to the text. Text and map go together. The map is presumably meant to be consulted during the reading of the text, and it therefore makes sense to read the map in the context of the entire text.

In the reading of the first *Fellowship* map, "A Part of the Shire," the main theoretical underpinnings of literary map readings are presented. The larger, more complex map of the western part of Middle-earth is read according to the same basic theoretical ideas. Some theoretical additions are made when warranted by differences between the two maps. The maps used for the readings come from the Houghton Mifflin Fiftieth Anniversary edition,[89] where they are printed in red and black ink (like the maps in the first edition of *The Lord of the Rings*). In the first (and many a subsequent) hardback edition, volume one, *The Fellowship of the Ring*, contains two maps: the Shire map, a one-page map set just before chapter one in book I; and the general map of western Middle-earth, a foldout map pasted in at the end of the book. The one-volume Fiftieth Anniversary edition has the general map pasted in at the beginning and the larger-scale map of Gondor and Mordor pasted in at the end. For paperback editions, the foldout maps are cut up and printed in black ink only on several pages.[90] Although the readings are based on the maps with black and red print, descriptions are added to make the discussion possible to follow on a map with black print only.

Reading "A Part of the Shire"

Every map, Wood informs his readers, has an author, a subject, and a theme;[91] and while these three characteristics may seem straightforward, they are not as easily identified as one might at first believe. Although a fantasy map does not point to a location in the actual world, it has a subject, a fictional place to which it refers. The map that comes between the prologue and the first chapter in *The Fellowship of the Ring* appears to state its subject clearly: a label in the top right corner announces that it is a map of "A Part of the Shire." Some knowledge of the Shire (gained, for instance, from the preceding prologue) and only the most cursory of glances suggests that this is not completely true, and that "A part of the Shire and some of the land on its eastern border" would be more accurate. Except for the small region of Buckland, carved out between the river and the Old Forest, the land to the east of the Brandywine River is, in fact, *not* part of the Shire (FR, prologue, 5).[92] This small discrepancy might seem irrelevant, but actually emphasizes the insular mentality of the Shire hobbits. Like them, the map does not admit to the presence of anything outside; the Shire is all there is—at least all there is worth mentioning. Any outside world is ignored (this is also the case with the arrows at the map's edges; no mention is made of whether a destination is in or outside the Shire), and everything that appears on the map is subsumed as "A Part of the Shire." Outside or inside is all presented within what further examination will prove to be a discourse of safety and control—regardless of whether it is Woody End, Bindbole Wood,[93] or the Old Forest. By restricting the map's explicit subject, the secondary world is divided into the known, on the map, and the unknown, off it. The label makes the map reassuring, as it implies that everything on the map is described in the prologue and therefore known and safe.

Just like the map's subject, its author appears to be obvious. At closer scrutiny, however, the author's actual identity becomes uncertain, and the reader begins to wonder whether it is part of the fiction or not. These two aspects tie into each other. The Shire map is located between two sections of text (the prologue and the rest of the book), sandwiched, as it were, between two parts of the narrative. Rather than providing a paratextual threshold, it is evidently part of the narrative document. It portrays an area of the world that has already been verbally described in the prologue. There is thus a suggestion that the map is itself part of the fiction or, rather, that the map doceme refers to a fictional Shire map. The author of this fictional map is equally fictional, a cartographer in the secondary world, not an artist in the actual world, even though the prologue casts some doubt over this fictional status by claiming that an extant copy of the Red Book of Westmarch can, in fact, be found in the primary world.

The Shire map is, in other words, not one map but two: a fictional map from the fictional Red Book, designed by a fictional cartographer; and an actual doceme in the actual *The Lord of the Rings*, which refers to the fictional map. This map doceme can be taken to have at least two different authors. The obvious author would be J. R. R. Tolkien, the author of the book as a whole. The map is signed with the initials "C.T.," however, which suggests that someone else has been involved in making the map, if not in creating the secondary world. In a letter, Tolkien relates how he "had to call in the help of my son—the C.T. or C.J.R.T. of the modest initials on the maps"—to help with the maps,[94] and Christopher Tolkien recalls that he is "virtually certain that my father allowed me some latitude of invention in that region of the Shire."[95] Thus, searching for a historical author complicates rather than clarifies matters, as at least two people (to father and son Tolkien could arguably be added, for instance, the editor and the engraver) have contributed to the map's form. Using the concept of an "implied author," an author encoded in the text, simplifies the discussion somewhat[96] and would, for a map, correspond to an "implied cartographer." Along the same lines, the text's narrator would parallel the map's "fictional cartographer." The Shire map still oscillates between fictional and nonfictional authors, however, and since these two authors are difficult—often impossible—to tell apart, I have made no attempt to distinguish between them in the discussion that follows, unless such distinction is relevant to the interpretation of the map.

What we have is thus a map that slips between authors and fudges its subject. At a first glance, the map does not have a particular theme, either. According to Wood, a map's theme is its "focus of attention."[97] No such focus presents itself. In fact, the Shire map is more like a general reference map in that it presents numerous themes that, together, establish the map's general argument.[98] The most prominent (but not the only) themes of the Shire map are topography (including vegetation and water courses), the road system, population centers, and administrative regions. These themes, along with the multitude of names found on the map, are part of an overarching discourse of defining, situating, and familiarizing the Shire—indeed, of instilling secondary belief in the country. Through its themes, the Shire map creates the "small, safe, and *understood* world" that a portal–quest fantasy such as *The Lord of the Rings* requires for its starting point.[99]

The topography of the Shire, as portrayed in the Shire map, is quite ordinary, perfectly safe, and totally understandable. Actually, topography is less important to the map than might be supposed, which is evident from the time and effort it takes to work out the terrain from what appears to be a topographical map. The landscape is one of hill country and river valleys. The west-to-east-running valleys of the Water and the Shirebourn rivers meet the north-to-south-running river Brandywine. That the land at the northeastern part of the map is higher is evident from the hills at Brockenborings and Scary, but also from how the Water tributary runs south. The Water and Brandywine valleys are both fairly densely populated, which suggests arable land (a suggestion that is also confirmed by the text). In the southern valley, separated from the valley of the Water by the Green-Hill Country and the forest at Woody End, the Shirebourn and its tributary (the Thistle Brook) have a similar, but shorter, south-then-east course to the Water. This valley is apparently less farmed, with Willowbottom south of Woody End as the only population center.

It is not this rolling landscape that is most striking, though, especially not on the maps printed in black and red. What stands out most is actually the network of roads (although their impact is somewhat reduced in the black-print-only editions). These roads dominate the map, running over most of it and illustrating how easy it is to travel in the Shire. Every place is accessible by a bright-red road: it is a country with infrastructure. It does not matter where you are on the map, there is always a road you can follow to any other place. To further establish the importance of the road system, more than half of the roads leave the map with a fletched arrow informing the reader that the road leads to other, named and thus known, places rather than into the unknown. Off to Bree to the east and Michel Delving in the west, north to Oatbarton and south to Longbottom—the land on the map exists *somewhere*, anchored by locations outside it. This display of certainty about what exists off the map makes its edges the very opposite to water margins. This land is not afloat in an uncharted sea but instead is clearly a part of something, a message emphasized by the map label: "A Part of the Shire." It is also a place where you travel, and not necessarily to places on the map. The arrows that anchor this part of the land to the world outside also point out directions of travel. In a story that comes with a map that includes so many roads and so many places to travel off the map, journeys are inevitable. In its way, this map is as clear about what will happen in the book as is the title of *The Hobbit, or, There and Back Again.* (And the map's message that the world is mappable and knowable sets readers up for a surprise once the journey takes them outside the Shire.)

All the places that the roads lead to are meticulously named. Names of regions and administrative areas, of rivers and marshes, and in particular of villages of varying sizes are liberally sprinkled over the map. This is not a map of the unknown, it is very much the known, the labeled, the familiar. It is a landscape tamed, not only by the red roads but also by the black names of settlements and topographical features alike, and it is divided into areas even more conspicuously named in red. Through this abundance of names, of labels, the map subjugates the landscape, brings it under control. The names also give "repeated implicit assurances of the existence of the things they label," Tom Shippey argues, assurances that strengthen our secondary belief in the fantasy world.[100] As most of the Shire names are taken from Tolkien's actual-world surroundings, they do not even sound exotic but seem familiar, believable.[101]

The control of the landscape is particularly apparent in the division of the land into four administrative areas: the north, east, west, and south farthings. The farthing names, printed in large red letters, are made even more prominent by facing in different directions around the center of the map: when held with north at the top of the map, "North Farthing" is printed upside down, and "West Farthing" and "East Farthing" are turned ninety degrees clockwise and counterclockwise, respectively. The farthing borders (black, dashed-dotted lines) cross the land without appearing to follow or regard any natural borders, except in the southeast, where the border between the South and East Farthing may run along the river Shirebourn (though this is unclear). Straighter than any river or road, such borders appear on actual maps too. On maps of, for instance, Africa, Australia, or North America, straight administrative borders can be found, borders drawn with a ruler without regard for the landscape the map is meant to represent.[102] The map, not the physical environment, becomes primary. Secondary-world maps are, as was pointed out earlier in this chapter, often primary to the landscape they portray; but the farthing borders also emphasize the priority of the fictional map over the fictional landscape. A colonization of the land is implied; like the many names, the borders present a landscape subordinated to hobbit culture.

Not only space but time is encoded in the map.[103] A map's *tense*, according to Wood, is the direction in time in which it points: whether it refers to its own past, present, or future.[104] The tense is relative to the map; a map from 1858 that refers to the world of 1858 uses the present tense. A map of tomorrow's weather will remain in the future tense when we look at it a week from now. The Shire map, at a first glance, appears to refer neither to its past nor to its future—surely, it uses the present tense? There is nothing on the Shire map that suggests any temporal direction: the map features are the same at the beginning of the story and at its end. To the extent that the Middle-earth maps (and other fantasy maps) have a tense, it is fictional, based on the time when they were created and the direction in which they point in the *fictional time line*. The Shire map, unlike the western Middle-earth map read shortly, lacks any signs of future or past tense, so it must indicate its own present.

Actually, to say that the map uses the present tense is not quite true, as we see when we also take into account the map's *duration*, its "temporal thickness" or the time span it embraces: a few hours, a year, a century . . .[105] The Shire map, by including elements that refer only to that which remains unchanged during the story, spans the time of the entire story. It can be used as the hobbits leave the Shire in the beginning as well as when they return to find Saruman's destruction near the end. Anything transient enough to be changed by story events—for instance, the hobbits' camps or the cut-down trees—has been left out. The time pointed to is thus as much now in the beginning as in the end—the map's tense is not just the present, but a constant present. The time referred to is not a specific now but a now that runs all through the story. This constant present is, to some extent, similar to the present tense employed in discussing a text. The map, like the text, spans all the time in the story and refers to it all simultaneously.

Despite the constant present, however, the map also offers a historical perspective.[106] To have a forest called Old Forest, for instance, automatically suggests that there is history, that some things are old while others are new or young. From the map we can tell that apparently one forest is older than the other two: Bindbole Wood and Woody End may be forests, but they are not old enough to be *old* forests, let alone *Old Forests*. (The Old Forest and its connotations of age are discussed further in relation to the other Tolkien map.) From the text, we learn that the map contains other features that are part of the Shire's history, in that they have not been there always. The prologue refers to some villages as "older," implying that others are younger (FR, prologue, 6; further discussion on this topic follows)—these "older villages" are distinguished on the map by their uppercase script. We are also told that the hobbit area of Buckland—plainly marked as special on the map, something I will return to shortly—is a new addition to the Shire, its development being part of Shire history (FR, I, v, 96–107; vi, 108). Indeed, the very number of hobbit communities that dot the map, and the roads that connect them, carry an implication of the passage of time: the Shire was not built in a day but required time, history, to become that which is shown on this map.

The Shire map does not obey the cartographic conventions of any actual historical period. Instead, through its mixing of conventions and signs from different times, it presents that same pseudomedieval aesthetic that was identified from the survey. Even though there is no compass rose or similar device, the location of the North Farthing shows that the map is clearly oriented with north at the top, and this is not the only map feature that tends to the modern rather than the medieval. As was discussed in connection with the hill signs of the survey, the oblique hills that are used in the Shire map date back to pre-Enlightenment times. They are reminiscent of the "gentle rolling downs" that Edward Lynam says were fashionable with some draftsmen of the late sixteenth century, although, intriguingly, the Shire hills (as well as the hills and mountains on the map of western Middle-earth) are shadowed on the west side rather than the conventional east.[107] Having the farthing names facing different ways suggests, faintly, that this map did not originally belong in a book but was a loose sheet that could be turned in the hands of the user, a convention that Harvey points out among some loose maps of the fifteenth century.[108] The pre-Enlightenment bird's-eye view is not carried through in the hobbit settlements, however, which are represented as black, angular dots, shaped as if the buildings were seen from straight above. The only exception is the Hill, Bilbo's and Frodo's home, which is portrayed with a small, oblique hill sign. This mix of bird's-eye and plan views is particularly noticeable in the case of Tuckborough, where the houses seem almost glued to the hillside. Many other elements, such as script, borders, and labels, similarly follow post-Renaissance conventions.

Deciding what conventions to follow is only one of many choices that face a mapmaker, and the choices affect much more than the map's aesthetic qualities. For a variety of reasons, an actual map does not—cannot—include everything; the work of the cartographer is a process of selection.[109] The same is true for fictional maps. "It is the attempt to cut [the maps] down and omitting all their color (verbal and otherwise) to reduce them to black and white bareness, on a scale so small that hardly any names can appear, that has stumped me," Tolkien complains in a letter to his publisher,[110] and it is reasonable to suspect that only some elements of his fictional world were encoded in the map to begin with. The choices made mirror the map's purpose: by including only those features that remain unchanged during the story, it is possible to make the map refer to a story-long now, as observed before. Choosing one hill sign above another means preferring a certain aesthetic over another; it also means alluding to one historical period rather than another. There are at least three selection processes at work in the construction of a fantasy map: an unconscious process that filters out features that are not even considered for inclusion; a conscious selection of what features to include in the map and what to leave out; and a choice of how included features are to be presented. Interpreting a map involves examining the results of these processes: what are the effects of including some features (and excluding others)? Of portraying some elements like *this* and other elements like *that*? A number of features of the Shire map invite such attention, for instance: the central location of the Three Farthing Stone and the marginal location of a quarry; the distinct red script used for

Buckland; the differences in upper- and lowercase in village names; and how different script is used for the three different forests. Such selections influence what information the map conveys about the secondary world.

Arguably the most privileged location on a map is its center, the spot that, *ceteris paribus*, tends to be the first focus for the viewer's attention.[111] At the center of the Shire map, we find the Three Farthing Stone, the meeting point of the borders of the East, West, and South Farthings, which sits "as near the centre of the Shire as no matter" (RK, VI, ix, 1000). The map, in other words, makes quite clear what the text mentions almost a thousand pages later, near the very end of the story. At the map's center are the geographical and administrative centers of the Shire, and it portrays not only "A Part of the Shire" but also the *central* part of the Shire—the central part of the world, at least as far as the mapmaker is concerned. At this point, it makes sense to distinguish between the implied cartographer and the fictional cartographer: the Shire map has the same implied cartographer as the map of western Middle-earth, but it also has a fictional cartographer. If the Shire map, like the text, is considered to be translated from the (fictional) Red Book of Westmarch (FR, prologue, 1), we can assume a mapmaker from the Shire, an assumption corroborated by the map's center. This center is clearly the hobbit heartland: close by are found the villages of Tuckborough, Bywater, and Hobbiton, the home of the Bagginses. It does not matter that Michel Delving off to the west is *actually* the "chief township"—we see from the map where the center is located, and the fact that one of the villages is called Hobbiton and that there is a separate mark for the Hill just to its north adds to this center's importance. Any reader looking to find where the story begins will have little trouble in hitting the right spot, and what is left off the map is merely periphery.

There is a periphery *on* the map as well, however: a fairly empty landscape with a number of roads leading off to the south and west (and a nameless village on the Michel Delving road), and an eastern fringe of countryside that is not even part of the Shire (although the map does not tell us that). Along the northern edge, there are a handful of communities, all with names that seem somewhat denigrating or belittling: Nobottle, Needlehole, Brockenborings, and Scary.[112] Next to the last of these, we find a quarry, the inclusion of which is quite intriguing. This quarry is the only place of production of any kind on the map, even when fields and mills, coppices and breweries would seem to be more relevant to hobbit culture. Geographer J. B. Harley asserts that "maps—just as much as examples of literature or the spoken word—exert a social influence through their omissions as much as by the features they depict and emphasize,"[113] and the presence of the quarry underscores the absence of the other places of production. Would it not make more sense to include mills, especially as the text presents mills as important means of production and the destruction ("modernization") of them is described as villainy (RK, VI, viii, 990)? Quarries, on the other hand, have negative connotations: Gimli assures Legolas that the dwarves "would tend [the Caverns of Helm's Deep], not quarry them" (TT, III, viii, 535); Saruman's henchmen turn Bagshot Row into a "yawning sand and gravel quarry" (RK, VI, vii, 993); and the ruffians had hidden stolen goods and food in the "old quarries" at Scary (RK, VI, ix, 999). Even though the quarry is "old" (that is, disused), it is a blot on the Shire's peaceful, bucolic nature, a warning on the map that not all is, was, or will be well. The negative connotations of the quarry are added to by its equivocal name. Scary may, as Tolkien points out in his commentary to translators, "contain E[nglish] dialectal *scar* 'rocky cliff'"[114] but more obviously, it means "fearsome." Scary Quarry is clearly a place to be feared, and although it is located at the periphery, away from the road network and thus disconnected from the rest of the Shire, it prophesies the ruin of the hobbit idyll.

The presence of the quarry and the absence of other places of production parallel a greater omission that is brought into focus by the inclusion of its (negative) opposite. As I mentioned before, the Shire map communicates control and safety; it is a map that demonstrates how wilderness has been tamed: only occasional pockets are left, surrounded by blank space. This is not the blank spaces of Conrad's maps, the secretive, alluring unknown. It is the white areas of certainty, of that which is so obvious that it need not be included on the map. The few forests, marshes, and hills are exceptions, just like the quarry; the (positive) norm is left out because it is so obvious. Flat, cultivated land is left blank; it has nothing worth referring to, nothing to get excited about. In particular, nothing that is of any relevance to the story.

Another presence that draws attention to itself as well as to the omissions that it signals is Buckland, or more precisely the red capitals used to mark it. No other "folklands" (for instance, Tookland, where nearly all the Tooks live [FR, prologue, 9]) are mentioned on the map, which indicates that Buckland has a distinct status, that its position is of special interest to the reader (and mapmaker). There are actually several grounds for this distinction. First, in the prologue, Buckland is mentioned as a later addition to Shire territory. It is not, in fact, a farthing, but one of the marches, so it constitutes a separate administrative entity, whereas Tookland is part of the West Farthing. Just as the farthing borders denote hobbit control of the landscape, so does Buckland. When this land was made a part of the Shire, the hobbits had to fight for it against the trees of the Old Forest in a battle against the landscape itself. Second, because it was added comparatively recently, Buckland is not fully regarded as a part of the Shire, and the hobbits who live there are considered "peculiar, half foreigners as it were" by the other hobbits (FR, I, v, 96). Finally, whereas Tookland is only mentioned briefly and "off-stage," Buckland is the goal for the first leg of Frodo's journey. Except for Bridgefields to the north and the Overbourn Marshes to the south, the areas written in red (Green-Hill Country, Woody End, The Marish, Buckland, and the Old Forest) chart the hobbits' journey across the Shire. (The Farthings, although also in red script, are written so differently in size and orientation that they obviously indicate a different category.) Any reader who tracks the journey across the map will have little difficulty even if the actual trail has no marks of its own. Again, the story plays a large part in how the map is shaped, and thus how the world is interpreted. Red draws more attention and conveys greater prominence to elements, and it is made clear to the reader that Buckland is worth paying special attention to.

Employing different types of script for different map elements (color, style, size, and so on) helps indicate various dissimilarities in the referents. On the Shire map, differences in case (using either uppercase only or lowercase with an uppercase initial) are used to signal a relevant difference, although the difference itself is not immediately clear. In terms of the watercourses, the larger ones (rivers) have names written in all capitals whereas the brooks' names are written with only an initial capital. This suggests that the stylistic variations in the script are what Robinson and Petchenik term "mimetic" rather than "arbitrary": in this case, a more prominent style corresponds to a more prominent (or larger) referent.[115] If this correlation is true, uppercase-only villages should be more prominent than the rest. To some extent, the text supports this assumption. Of the five settlements that are all uppercase, three are mentioned in the prologue: the older villages Hobbiton and Tuckborough, and the Shire's chief township, Michel Delving (FR, prologue, 6). The text's juxtaposition of the older villages and the chief township implies that these entities have similar social status, a social status reflected as well as reinforced by the uppercase script. Regarding the status of By-water and Stock, nothing is said; the former is close to Hobbiton and is often referred to in the story, and Stock is mentioned but never visited by Frodo's company. Since social status rather than story relevance appears to be the guiding principle behind the stylistic variation here, it may be assumed that the two villages share the social status of the other three.

The use of upper- and lowercase letters for names, hence, suggests that differences and similarities in script are "mimetically" assigned. A difference in script prominence reflects, in the case of watercourses, a difference in size; in the case of village names, a difference in social status. Consequently, the differences in style, size, and color used to write the forest names should also reflect some difference between the forests. The Old Forest and Woody End have names written in red uppercase but different sizes, with the names placed inside the forest, whereas Bind-bole Wood to the north has its name set outside the forest and written in small, black script with uppercase only for the initials. From the map in general, we find that red script is used for areas and regions (the only exception being the Yale, which, on the map, could also refer to the black dot just beneath it[116]), so Woody End and Old Forest may be considered names for areas or regions rather than for the forests as such. Even so, the difference in script prominence suggests an inexplicable difference in prominence. As both the Old Forest and Bindbole Wood disappear off the map, it cannot be determined whether the question is one of size. Their relative script prominence, from smallest (Bindbole Wood: small, black, lowercase) to largest (Old Forest: large, red, uppercase), corre-sponds to their respective relevance to the story: Bindbole Wood, while appearing on the map, does not play any part; Woody End is the cen-tral setting of most of one chapter; and the Old Forest provides the first encounter with the world outside the Shire and the setting of an entire chapter (named after the forest).

By examining the choices of the mapmaker, it is possible to learn how the map relates to the story it presumably supports, but such an examination also sheds light on some of the social norms and constructions behind the map. In the case of the Shire map, the norms and constructions of the fictional cartographer are braided together with those of the implied cartographer. When it comes to the map of the western Middle-earth, which is more clearly a paratext in that it does not refer to any apparent map in the fictional world, the messages communicated by the map are more clearly those of the implied cartographer (or author). Whereas this map has some traits in common with the Shire map, it offers a worldview different from the controlled safety of the hobbit lands: according to the larger map, Middle-earth is a wilder, older place, and the map is much more explicitly made to serve the story.

Reading "The West of Middle-earth"

The general map of the western parts of Middle-earth was first included on a foldout sheet, printed in black and red, in the first edition of *The Fellowship of the Ring* and *The Two Towers*. In paperback editions, this map was printed in black only and divided into four sections.[117] Although the Shire map and the general map have in common an abundance of names that strengthen the readers' secondary belief (as well as allowing them to identify almost any location mentioned in the novel), the story comes across as much more central to the construction of the general map.

Unlike the Shire map, the general map has a compass rose (with north at the top) and a scale bar. For my edition of the map, one inch equals one hundred miles, which corresponds to 1:6,336,000 and yields a map area of about 6.5 million square kilometers, or about twice the size of India. A quarter of the map is covered by water, which gives a land area approximately half that of Europe or the United States. According to the label, the map is of "The West of Middle-earth at the End of the Third Age," and even though some features are included, much of the eastern and some of the northern side of the map are, in fact, quite empty compared to the western lands. This is a map whose subject is not a nonspecific "west" but a number of regions defined as "The West," a cultural, political, and historical as well as geographical location, something that is confirmed by how its military leaders are repeatedly referred to as "the Captains of the West" (RK, V, x, 867 et passim). These regions (Eriador, Rohan, Gondor, and Rhovanion) are set against the land of Mordor, which is the only land on the eastern third of the maps to be reasonably detailed. The label is signed CJRT, for Christopher Tolkien, but since it is impossible (and in this discussion irrelevant) to decide which features of the map come from which Tolkien, this map is also considered to have an implied cartographer. However, as the general map is more clearly paratextual than the Shire map and exists only on the threshold to the text, I assume it to have no fictional cartographer; this aspect is therefore left out of the subsequent discussion.

Of all the topography portrayed on the map of the western Middle-earth, the mountain ranges attract the most attention. In the middle of the map, extending from the hills beyond Carn Dûm in the northwest to Minas Tirith in the southeast, runs the sinuous mountain range of the Misty Mountains and Ered Nimrais (I use the English rather than Elvish names if they are given on the map). The inverted S-shape of this range neatly indicates where the story's action will take place: in the southeast, it points at the mountains around Mordor; and, together with the Blue Mountains, its northern curve embraces Eriador. The shapes of Mordor's mountain ranges and of the Misty Mountain/Ered Nimrais range give an artificial impression, suggesting that supernatural forces rather than tectonics are behind the very landforms of Middle-earth. This impression is confirmed in *The Silmarillion*, which describes (in *Ainulindalë*) how the semidivine Valar worked to create the landscapes of the world and (in *Quenta Silmarillion*) how the evil Melkor built the Misty Mountains.[118] Given their prominence in terms of location, shape, and quantity, it is hardly surprising that negotiating various mountains is central to the plot, such as the Fellowship's passage through Moria, Aragorn's passage through the Paths of the Dead, and Sam and Frodo's passage through Cirith Ungol. The very goal of the quest is a mountain, Mount Doom, inside which the Ring is destroyed.

Another prominent topographical feature is the enormous forest of Mirkwood. Although the great woodlands are never visited by the protagonists of *The Lord of the Rings*, Mirkwood draws attention to the other forests of the map. Forested areas are far scarcer than would be expected from such a wide stretch of land; apart from Mirkwood, only a few forests are marked on the map, some of them appearing to be quite small. At this scale, however, size becomes tricky to judge. The smallest forest on the map is Chetwood outside Bree, which takes the hobbits and Aragorn more than a full day's walk to get through (FR, I, xi, 178). There ought to be more forests like Chetwood on the map, for instance Woody End and perhaps even Bindbole Wood in the Shire, or the western parts of Middle-earth would be a bare place indeed. This bareness does not agree with the lack of settlements; if there are no people, what keeps the formerly forested areas[119] from turning back into forest? Yet the forests included on the map are not simply those visited in the story, although all forests the hobbits travel through or see outside the Shire are marked, regardless of size. The woodlands along the feet of the Blue Mountains and around the northeast corner of the Sea of Rhûn, which are neither visited nor seen, only add to the impression that most of western Middle-earth is bare, bringing into focus what few forests there are.

Other topographical features reinforce the bareness of the map and consequently bring focus to the few elements that are included. Thus, mostly relevant rivers are found on the map, allowing for easy identification of each river crossed or traveled along. Ultimately, the topography serves the story; that, rather than size, determines what is included and what is left out, with only occasional exceptions, such as the Sea of Rhûn or the Blue Mountain woodlands.

Where the nonverbal map elements serve the story, the verbal ones—the names—serve secondary belief in the world the map portrays.[120] In many cases, features are only marked by the linguistic signs; apart from topographical signs, roads and population centers/strongholds are the only features that have nonverbal signs. In other words, the map is mainly about names. Indeed, when Shippey observes how the characters tend to "talk like maps," he exemplifies this point with characters who tend to list the names and spatial relations of various features.[121] Through the red script, the text is highly visible, and it is emphasized how this is a world where every place is known and named, often even with two names. Names are provided in languages from the secondary world (mostly Elvish) as well as in English, sometimes in both (generally with the English translation within parentheses). With the help of all these names, the reader can navigate the world of the story and follow the characters' journeys; but the names also define the secondary world spatially, by creating a great number of places and spatial relations. Through their multitude and the many translations, these names even allow the reader to puzzle out some of the basic morphemes of the fictional languages, observing, for instance, how mountain ranges are called *Ered* (Ered Luin/Blue Mountains; Ered Lithui/Ash Mountains; Ered Mithrin/Grey Mountains); how *mith-* can mean "gray" (Ered Mithrin/Grey Mountains; Mithlond/Grey Havens); and how Emyn Uial/Hills of Evendim, Nenuial/Lake Evendim, and the [Sea of] Núrnen in Nurn give us *uial* = "evendim," *emyn* = "hills," and *nen* = "lake/water." This is not only a map of a world but a key to its languages.

The fact that places and features on the map often have more than one name also suggests a relation between the languages other than the purely linguistic. Generally, an Elvish name is followed by the English version within parentheses. Typical examples are Ered Luin (Blue Mountains), Gwathló (Greyflood), and Baranduin (Brandywine), with

Weathertop (Amon Sûl) providing an exception. The English names are often a (nearly always literal) translation—*ered* = "mountains," *luin* = "blue"—but sometimes the English name is only notionally similar, so that *gwath-* in Gwathló becomes "gray" rather than "shadow" and Amon Sûl ("windhill") is Weathertop in English. There might be a phonetic similarity only—Brandywine for Baranduin ("brown river")—or no apparent connection to modern English, as when Angren ("of iron") is translated as Isen (Old English for "of iron"). Numerous names are also left untranslated, appearing either in English or (more commonly) in Elvish. Some of the English names are straightforward (e.g., North Downs, Dead Marshes, the Brown Lands); others use more obscure or old-fashioned language or roots (e.g., Trollshaws, Entwash, Rivendell).[122] The Elvish language is made obviously superior to English, partly through its status as the preferred language, partly because although there are a great number of English names, the major names—labeling larger regions and therefore written in larger script—are in Elvish. Middle-earth, we see, contains both the familiar and the alien, although the latter is more prominent.

The variations in script separate the marks on the map into different classes. Small uppercase script indicates names of mountain ranges; regions are written with larger uppercase script, the size of the script increasing with the size of the region (compare, for instance, Eriador and Minhiriath or Mordor and Nurn), although the names of smaller regions (for example, Forlindon, Lebennin, and Lossarnach) are written in uppercase for the initial letter only—as are all other names as well. The script is curved to roughly indicate what region, mountain range, or river it refers to, but the text is straighter when referring to a population center, stronghold, or tower. Outlined capitals are used for the former realm of Arnor and the three kingdoms into which it was divided. The many variations in size, case, and curvature reinforce the impression that this world is fully explored and fully believable. It is not only littered with names; these names appear to be divided into an abundance of categories. Regions are divided and subdivided, rivers have tributaries and marshes, mountain ranges and hills are everywhere: all over the world, the map tells us, there are places whose names are worth knowing.

This profusion of names and categories obscures the fact that there are also places, and kinds of places, apparently not worth knowing about, however. Just as there are actually very few forests on the general map, there are not many places where people live, at least in terms of towns, villages, cities, castles, fortresses, harbors, towers, and so on. These signs of civilization (human or otherwise) are few and far between on the map, giving it an impression not only of bareness but of desolation. Closer examination reveals that the guiding principle for inclusion is, again, the story, not size or social or political relevance. Nor are the respective marks mimetic in relation to a place's relevance to the story. Tharbad (mentioned a few times in passing) is more prominently marked than the Ford at Rivendell (where Frodo faces—and escapes—the Black Riders); Lond Daer (which does not feature in the story) is as prominently marked as the Grey Havens (where the last Elven ship leaves, marking the end of the Third Age). The addition of places other than those of the story affects the reader's perception of the story world, regardless of whether the map is seen as a paratextual element or as a doceme. As the former, the map extends the world of the text; as the latter, the world of the total document is the sum of the world as portrayed on the map and in the text. Both perspectives offer insights into how the many places reinforce secondary belief in the world, implying that Middle-earth is more than the setting of a story.

The west of Middle-earth is not a place that crawls with people, at least if we go by the lack of settlements. This impression is corroborated by the small number of roads, the tiny dotted trails that wind across the land. Compared to the Shire map, where roads are given pride of place, the world outside is clearly not a place to go traveling. It is wilderness, untamed and unsafe (but not unknown). This is stressed even further by the fact that no administrative (political or other) borders are to be found anywhere on the general map. Whatever borders there are coincide with natural borders: the Mountains of Shadow suggest the border to Mordor; the end of the respective forests are the borders of Fangorn and Lothlórien. The Ered Nimrais provides a border between Rohan and Gondor (and the different languages reflected in the names suggest another border between them along the Mering Stream, between Eastfold and Anórien).

Where the Shire map subjects the landscape to its culturally constructed borders, the general map does the opposite. It portrays an internal tension between its natural landscape and cultural control of that landscape. While the profusion of names emphasizes how well known, how defined, the secondary world is, the scarcity of cultural constructions, be they roads, villages, or borders, stresses the world's wilderness and depopulation. This tension runs through Tolkien's text, clearly visible, for instance, in the ambivalent stance between tame and wild nature, where parklike Lothlórien is set against primeval Fangorn, the entwives' horticulture against the ents' forests, even Shire countryside against Old Forest wilderness.[123]

The map does not, however, encode this tension in the schematic structure that Pierre Jourde proposes when he divides western Middle-earth into one region of civilization and goodness (Gondor and Eriador) and one of wilderness and evil (Mordor and Rhovanion).[124] While the conflict between Gondor and Mordor is plain, not least in the text, neither Eriador nor Rhovanion is a region that can easily be interpreted as *either* wild *or* civilized, and even less as good or evil. The former region may contain the Shire, Bree, and Rivendell, but it is also a place of lost realms, both good and evil, where Rangers do battle against evil beings in the wilderness. Rhovanion, on the other hand, contains the evil strongholds of Sauron and Saruman but is also dotted with civilized societies such as Erebor, Dale, Lothlórien, and Rohan. Like the conflict between good and evil, the tension between wild and tame is present all over the map—visible, but never simple. Jeremy Black somewhat misses this point when he claims that the map of western Middle-earth "gives no real sense of the spatial range and potency of wisdom and evil, good and ill, that are important themes in [Tolkien's] narrative."[125] The age-old conflict between the "evil" side of Morgoth and Sauron and the "good" people who oppose them can be traced all over the map: from the notes about Arnor, Angmar, and major battlefields to the very absence of Beleriand west of the Blue Mountains; from Mordor and the empty lands beyond to Dol Guldur and Mirkwood, even to the icebay of Forochel, a remnant of Morgoth's icy reign—the "spatial range" of evil is stamped on the map, a part of Middle-earth's history and development.

Middle-earth's history and the tension between past and present is a theme as clearly visible in the general map as is the secondary world's topography. The very label of the map ensures that the reader comes to this map with a historical awareness: "The West of a Middle-earth at the End of the Third Age." Apart from instilling a sense of finality, it accentuates the fact that Middle-earth has a past (three ages of it, at the very least) as well as a future, a Fourth Age from which it is possible to establish the end of the previous age. Already the map label can thus explain why Ricardo Padrón feels that the suspension of Tolkien's world between a deep past and an impending apocalypse is encoded in the map.[126] Parts of this past are then explicitly marked on the map. In a particular kind of script (outlined capitals), the approximate location of "The Lost Realm of Arnor" is given and, with smaller letters, the regions Arthedain, Cardolan, and Rhudaur are marked. Even if nothing is known about the world, the location of a "Lost Realm" gives the map temporal thickness. Along with the note stating that "Here was of old the Witch-realm of Angmar" in northern Eriador, the references to the old kingdom actually cover the history from the founding of Arnor in the year 3320 of the Second Age, through its division into three realms in the year 861 of the Third Age, the establishing of Angmar (circa 1300), the respective falls of Rhudar, Cardolan, and Arthedain (in 1409, 1636, and 1974), and Gondor's final defeat of Angmar in 1975 (RK, Appx A, 1014–17; Appx B, 1060–61). References to Arnor's history do more than add three millennia to the map's duration, however. Numerous map features are relevant only in connection to the lost realm's long history, such as the old cities of Annúminas and Fornost and the arrow that points off the map to the icebay of Forochel. The map creates temporal depth through the inclusion of references to Cardolan and Rhudaur in much the same way that the text brings temporal resonance to the story events by including the history of Weathertop and the fall of Rhudaur (cf. FR, I, xi, 181; xii, 196). Similarly, the comment that South Gondor is "now a debatable and desert land" adds to the theme of Middle-earth history with its reference to the Gondor civil war (RK, Appx A, 1022–23; Appx B, 1061), and the "now" emphasizes the diachronic nature of the map.

A handful of other marks similarly draw attention to the map's diachronicity, but with less focus on a specific time and more focus on how time passes. These marks invoke the past through the word *old*: Old Forest, Old Ford, and Old Forest Road. In a world where the past is more present than the present, where ancient conflicts and mistakes return to haunt the living, where some of the living actually recall events several millennia in the past, there is, in fact, still a need to refer to a forest, a ford, a road, as *old*. That which is old has the power to withstand the ravages of time, it seems; the Old Forest Road runs straight through the great Mirkwood forest, obviously remarkable enough not to succumb to the forest. The Old Forest is kept back from the Shire by a hedge and a gate. The forest, in particular, appears to be *oldest* rather than *old*. It is associated with Tom Bombadil, who "remembers the first raindrop and the first acorn" (FR, I, vii, 129), but also with Treebeard, "the oldest living thing that still walks beneath the Sun" (TT, III, v, 488); it is a remnant of the primeval woodlands that once covered much of Eriador.[127]

Despite the declaration of the label, the map does not refer merely to its own present but also to its past; its tense is only overtly present. A closer investigation uncovers traces of history, explicit as well as implicit. To Padrón, the many place-names bear witness to the richness of the world's past;[128] but there is more to the map's encoded history than names. Features are included to enable the reader to chart Bilbo's adventures in *The Hobbit*; battlefields and mass graves of old can be found outside Mordor (Dagorlad and the Dead Marshes); and even the rule of, and war against, Morgoth is hinted at. (The icebay of Forochel is the result of the great cold of Morgoth, and the broken Blue Mountains and absent Beleriand are the outcome of the War of Wrath that finally defeated him.) The map's duration thus not only includes the end of the Third Age; it is actually thick enough to go back to the First Age and the battle with Morgoth. This temporal thickness is not immediately apparent to a reader who comes to the map for the first time, but if the map is used as a reference tool during the reading, the encoded history becomes apparent. The land is one that has evolved over the ages, and this evolution is clearly present in the map. Although the story has been a guiding principle for the cartographer, the history of Middle-earth has been just as important. Indeed, the meeting of historical and linguistic setting with story that characterizes the novel is evident already from the general map.

The significance of story as well as history is noticeable from spatial positions. The area where explicit historical features are densest is also where we find the beginning of the story. Unlike the Shire map, where the beginning is located near the center of the map, the story begins near the top left corner of the general map. In Western society, top left is a privileged position: it is where we start our reading on a page, and the Fellowship travels across the map rather the way our gaze scans a newspaper (or web) page, more or less diagonally from top left to bottom right. The landscape, and the characters' journey through it, seems to be set out to make reading the map and finding the characters' route as easy as possible, emphasizing once more how the story is a guiding principle of the map.

A guiding principle it is, but not an unbreakable law: the location

HERE BE DRAGONS

where the story ends is unclear. Certainly, Sam's final return home and announcement that he is back is the obvious ending of the book, in terms of being the last few words of the final chapter; but there are other ways of considering where the story ends. There are at least three main contenders for what constitutes the end of *The Lord of the Rings*, each bringing a particular aspect of the story to a close.[129] The diagonal journey across the map ends with the disposal of the Ring in Orodruin, a moment that marks the end of the hobbits' quest and the victory over Sauron's evil. Spatially, this ending marks the farthest point away from the Shire on the general map, in the same way as the dead and deadly land of Mordor is the total opposite of the fertile and pleasant Shire. The subsequent defeat of Saruman marks another conclusion, with the defeat of an evil that is less cosmic and more human in scale. This ending, as well as Sam's return home in the book's final lines, is set in the Shire. The journey has taken the protagonists full circle; the hero has returned, having traveled, as in *The Hobbit*, there and back again.[130] A third possible ending is the departure of Frodo, Gandalf, and the elves from the Grey Havens, an event that symbolizes the departure of magic from the world, not just the defeat of evil. This ending points to the west, off the map and into the unknown. Each ending thus relates differently to the map and the journey that trails across it, allowing the story as a whole to have a threefold ending of arrival, return, and departure into the unknown.

The Shire and the Grey Havens are located at, or very close to, the place where the story begins. The more far-reaching consequences of the story resolution—the disappearance of magic and the arrival of the Age of Men—are worldwide and have no specific location, but they are alluded to at the center of the map, another privileged position. There, the forests of Fangorn and Lothlórien are found next to each other. These forests offer a much subtler connection to the depths of Middle-earth's history than the verbal signs that refer to Arnor's location of old,[131] but whereas the lost realm of Arnor is restored through the destruction of the Ring and the return of the king, the ancient forest realms come to an end. The end of the Third Age is the end of magic in Middle-earth, and the world changes. The juxtaposition of Lothlórien and Fangorn thus foreshadows Treebeard's meeting with Galadriel and Celeborn near the end of *The Return of the King*. "[T]he world is changing," the old ent says to the elven rulers, "I feel it in the water, I feel it in the earth, and I smell it in the air" (RK, VI, vi, 959). The change he feels is the price for defeating Sauron. "Much fantasy does not have what we could call a 'happy ending,'" Attebery observes in *Strategies of Fantasy*. "Indeed, the fantasist often seems to start with the idea of such a resolution and then to qualify it, finding every hidden cost in the victory."[132] Middle-earth is losing its magic: that is what Treebeard feels, and it is on that loss, on the doom of elves and ents and all things magical, that the map is centered. The "End of the Third Age" proclaimed by the map label is, in fact, the end of magic in Middle-earth.[133]

The middle of the map presents what is at stake, but the periphery warns about the enemy. Ranged around the northern, eastern, and southern borders of the map are names that signal the threats to the people of the West. The Witch-king of Angmar returns as leader of the Ringwraiths, and the peoples of Rhûn, Khand, and Harad—the Southrons and Easterlings—ally themselves to Sauron. Being marginalized also means being primitive. The Forodwaith, or Northmen, became Gondor's allies but were still considered "lesser Men" (lesser, that is, than the Númenorean descendants in Gondor and Arnor), along with the Southrons and Easterlings. The privileged direction in Middle-earth is west: western Middle-earth is superior to other parts; the humans from Númenor (an island once situated in the sea to the west of Middle-earth) are superior to other humans; and to the west of Númenor is the Blessed Realm, where the semidivine Valar reside. Regardless of whether the periphery is teeming with the enemy or offers the only way to sail to an Elysium off the map, it is the unknown margin outside the relevant middle, beyond the reach of the story.

Much of the relevant middle is conspicuously empty, however. While it is littered with names, there are only a few iconic map elements indicating terrain or buildings, roads or rivers. On the Shire map, the blank spaces correspond to a norm that does not need to be mapped. Here, the white emptiness, portrayed on the map by name only, is not a stand-in for fields too obvious to map, nor is it treeless, flat heaths, or desert, tundra, grassy plains, or any other one type of terrain. It is not even simply "wilderness." On the general map, the fields of the Shire are just as blank as the desolate Brown Lands; the grasslands of Rohan are empty white, as is the broken wasteland of the Plateau of Gorgoroth. White is not the unknown or unmapped, nor is it a specific type of landscape: it is landscape that it is irrelevant to map. The only relevant features of this unmapped whiteness are the numerous names by which its areas are known. All those names—in English as well as Elvish, and providing translations between the two—communicate the importance of language in itself. The map shows us a world defined by names and created by language, thus confirming that Middle-earth is a creation centered on language rather than nature—on the creation of new language and the translations involved in understanding it. Given Tolkien's love of languages and philology, it comes as no surprise that one of the principal messages delivered by the map of the western part of Middle-earth is how his fictional world is ultimately a linguistic creation.

• • •

At least since the 1970s, critics have observed the importance of maps to the fantasy genre, although no comprehensive studies have been published before now. Obviously, no study, quantitative or qualitative, can be all-encompassing, and my own contributions to the investigation of fantasy maps in this chapter should be seen as the first tentative mapping of an alien country, not as the definitive exploration of all its blank spaces. As in many studies, time and money came to be unwanted constraints. Maps proved to be more uncommon in the genre as a whole than I originally thought (occurring in at most two fifths of the books rather than in at least half, which a cursory pilot study had led me to believe would be the figure). Their scarcity in the book sample thus led to a smaller map sample that, in turn, resulted in large margins of error. To be certain that the largest margin of error could be at least halved, however, the book sample would need to be considerably larger, requiring almost 360 maps. The advantage of such a large map sample would, of course, be the appearance of more rare features (for instance, oriented any way other than northward; showing a subway system; or portraying modern cities of the primary world); even if a certain phenomenon did not appear in my sample, it might still be found on as many as one fantasy map in twenty-five. (With 360 maps, something not found in the sample would be rare enough only to appear on one map in every hundred in the fantasy-map population.)

My survey made plain that the vast majority of maps mapped settings in secondary worlds. A valid question that remains for a future study would thus be to what extent high-fantasy novels come with maps. Such a study would tell us the proportions of maps in high to low fantasy, but it would require either the books in the sampling frame or (probably more feasibly) those in the sample to be separated into high- and low-fantasy works (something for which there was no time in this survey). Future studies may also want to include more children's and young adult fiction in the sampling frame. My own sampling frame is biased away from fiction for young readers because such fiction was separated from fantasy fiction in the database I used, with the result that the survey largely concerned fantasy for adult readers. Whether there are any major differences between maps in fantasy for adults and in fantasy for children and young adults remains to be investigated, for instance by using another sampling frame.

Certain typical features of fantasy maps were indicated by the survey, features we can expect to find in at least half of all fantasy maps. In brief, a typical fantasy map portrays a secondary world, a compass rose or similar device showing its orientation with north at the top. It is not set in any given hemisphere (not necessarily in a spherical world at all), although there are reasons to believe that clues in the text would indicate north as the direction of colder climates. Apart from topographical map elements such as rivers, bays, islands, and mountains, such a map would also contain towns and other artificial constructions. The hill signs used are typically pre-Enlightenment (either profile or oblique).

Even this brief list reveals the mixture of modern and historical map features. Like much high fantasy, the secondary-world maps follow a pseudomedieval aesthetic according to which dashes of pre-Enlightenment mapping conventions are rather routinely added to a mostly modern creation. Whether this is because of careless research, genre conformity, lack of imagination, or a desire to give the reader the easiest possible access to the map and the world it portrays is hard to say. If the map is meant as an aid for reading (and writing) the story, as a paratext on the threshold between the actual world and the unknown geography of the secondary world, maybe the map should simply challenge the reader's map conventions as little as possible.

Whatever the reason, a mixture of cartographic conventions from various time periods is found in the reading of the two maps from *The Lord of the Rings* as well. The readings also demonstrate that paying close attention to fantasy maps, *as maps*, can reveal information about the maps beyond the elements that were used in their construction. To find that center and periphery are set up against each other on both maps is hardly surprising; to set the familiar in focus, in the center of the map, is a traditional mapmaking strategy. But whereas the Shire map privileges the familiar over the unknown and communicates as its dominant message the control of the land (and the landscape) and the safety this brings, the map of western Middle-earth defines the world it portrays by naming it. The importance of the world's language and history is as central to this map's message as is geography, and both maps contain a link between geography and story. Where the Shire map communicates control and safety, however, the map of western Middle-earth communicates a tension between cultural control and wilderness.

Apart from what the readings of the Tolkien maps tell us about *The Lord of the Rings*, they demonstrate how much any fantasy map can say about the work it belongs to. Each map, it is clear, relates in one way or another to the text. To ignore what the map communicates and only analyze the text means omitting a significant part of the work. Furthermore, as two maps from the same book, portraying parts of the same world, display such significant differences in the messages they communicate, it seems obvious that not only one map but all maps present in a book should be considered. Although the great majority of all fantasy novels that come with maps only include one map, a not insignificant number include two, and at least some come equipped with three or more. Each of these maps is a doceme that adds something to the document as a whole, and each map is a paratext that offers a particular threshold across which the text can be entered.

Whether the map is alone or one of several, typical or idiosyncratic, referring to a fictive map or situated firmly outside the diegesis, we should not dismiss it lightly. Instead, critics as well as readers should let the map do what is—ultimately—its job: to lead us into the fantastic world of the story.

3 : Borders and Boundaries

Just like the actual world, all reasonably complex secondary worlds are divided into areas of various kinds. Divisions may be geographical or administrative in nature, with areas demarcated by, for instance, rivers, mountain ranges, beaches, hedges, ditches, dykes, or simply lines on a map. Crossing from one area into another may be fraught with peril, unexciting, or barely if at all noticeable.

In fantasy settings, whether primary or secondary worlds, other kinds of divisions and types of areas occur as well. Two areas, while side by side geographically, can have quite different rules for how—for instance—time, space, and causality work. A day in one place might be a year on the other side of the wall. In the middle of snowcapped mountains, there might be a valley of eternal summer. The magic power to change one's environment inside the forest might simply be superstitious nonsense outside. This chapter is devoted to an investigation of how demarcations between such dissimilar areas—domains—are constructed, how they reflect the domains on either side, and what their relevance is to the worlds where they occur.

In *The Encyclopedia of Fantasy*, the editors settle for *threshold* as the preferred term for the various dividing lines of fantasy landscapes and stories. The critic behind the "Threshold" article, John Clute, distinguishes between "physical" and "metaphorical" thresholds. The former type of threshold, the type relevant in this context, marks a "gradient between two places or states of being."[1] Although it would be possible to split hairs and wonder if a threshold is not, in fact, a line rather than a gradient, and to observe that in many cases, including the examples that follow, places and states of being are conflated, Clute's is a succinct and to-the-point definition. Clute proceeds to list four functions of the physical thresholds. First, they "normally form the spines of borderlands, demarcating regions which borderlands join together." A borderland, he notes elsewhere, serves as a "marker, resting place or toll-gate between two differing kinds of reality."[2] Presumably, Clute's "normally" is not intended to imply that this is the most common function of a physical threshold in fantasy (I would find that hard to agree with) but that borderlands generally ("normally") have a physical threshold as a defining feature around which they are situated. The function would thus be dual, both separating and joining two regions of different realities.

The second function of the physical threshold is to "announce the presence, or intrusion, of a crosshatch," that is, a place where "two or more worlds may simultaneously inhabit the same territory."[3] This function is clearly connected to the first (thresholds as spines of borderlands), in that borderlands often provide a strip-like crosshatch region.[4] Third, physical thresholds "constitute the perimeter of polders." And finally, "for those of peculiar talents, they may comprise a map of the land."[5] *Land* in this context is taken to mean "a secondary-world venue whose nature and fate are central to the plot: a land is not a protagonist, but has an analogous role."[6] If the third function is the most clear-cut, the fourth is the most puzzling; neither Roz Kaveney's cross-referenced entry on "Maps" nor David Langford's on "Talents" offers much in the way of enlightenment.[7]

The term *threshold* is undeniably versatile when taken as described in the *Encyclopedia*. As a word, however, *threshold* implies not only a dividing line but also the intended crossing of such a line. The *Oxford English Dictionary* gives the figurative meaning of *threshold* as "the line which one crosses in entering,"[8] and Clute's remark that a threshold "may not even be meant to be liminal, or passable"[9] only serves to broaden an already broad blanket term. For all the usefulness of *threshold* as a term, the geographical focus of this discussion requires it to be complemented by two more specific terms: *border* and *boundary*. A border corresponds to the first two functions of the physical threshold. It is a line (or gradient) that separates two places or areas, and it differs from a boundary in that the latter implies a perimeter or circumference. In other words, you can be on either side of a border, but inside or outside a boundary. A polder, for example, is surrounded by its boundary, while two adjacent domains are separated by a border. It should be noted that neither word implies any intended crossing, and thus cannot be fully subsumed under *threshold*.

The fantasy genre offers a great variety of borders, and this section will investigate three examples, representing three different kinds. The first is the border between the land of the living and the land of the dead. Journeys to the land of the dead form a common theme in several mythologies and so-called taproot texts (texts that predate the emergence of generic fantasy but that include the fantastic and are of heightened significance to the genre[10]). The Sumerian goddess Inanna descends into the underworld only to end up captured there. The Japanese god Izanagi enters the dark realm of Yomi to bring back his spouse Izanami. Odysseus and Æneas both venture there for information, and Orpheus attempts to bring back his Eurydice. The Norse gods go down to Hel to bind Fenrir. Examples of how the land of the dead can be reached if one travels to the right place are common in fantasy literature as well. In J. R. R. Tolkien's Middle-earth, elves have to wait out the end of the world in the Halls of Mandos, which are located in the Undying Lands (and thus accessible to those elves who are still alive). Fritz Leiber has his heroes Fafhrd and the Grey Mouser ride to the land of death in "The Price of Pain-Ease" (1970). Raymond E. Feist's protagonists Pug and Tomas journey to the Halls of the Dead (albeit with some magical help, as it is a very long trip) in *A Darkness at Sethanon* (1986). With the Celtic king Urtha, Merlin enters the Ghostland, where the spirits of the dead reside, in Robert Holdstock's *Celtika* (2001). Jasper Fforde writes about how Thursday Next and her colleague Spike drive off the M4 motorway to a service station limbo beyond which the domain of death can be entered (*Something Rotten* 2004). Later, I discuss the Deathgate and the Paths of the Dead in Steven Brust's Dragaera books, mainly *Taltos* (1998) from the Vlad Taltos series and *The Paths of the Dead* (2002) from the Khaavren Romances. Through their very different narrators and the close focus on the actual crossing of borders, these books offer an unusually clear example of the border between the realms of life and death. The Dragaeran realm of the dead is reached easily enough by descending a waterfall, leaving the land of the living at the top. Returning, however, requires special dispensation. The two trips described also illuminate how the border between the realms of life and death can be employed to present very different perspectives on Dragaeran society.

Before I move on to the second border, another term needs to be clarified. Faerie, the mysterious home of any number of magical beings, is a popular location in much fantasy fiction. There is, however, no consensus about what the (often) nonmagical, everyday domain of humans should be called in opposition to Faerie. Many suggestions, such as the *real* world, the *natural* world, the *mortal* world, or the world *of men*, are problematic, since Faerie is often portrayed as a place just as real and natural as its counterpart, where both men and women live as well as die. (These expressions generally include the word *world*; in my own terminology [see chapter 1], Faerie would not be a "world" but a "domain"— that is, a part of a world where the laws of nature and causality differ from the rest of the world.) Tolkien, in *Smith of Wootton Major*, counters Faerie with the World,[11] a distinction that would lack precision in a critical discussion. More precise, and poetic, is Lord Dunsany's "the fields we know," which he uses throughout *The King of Elfland's Daughter*;[12] but such an expression suggests that the critic would look at Faerie from without and at those well-known fields from within. In his introduction to *The King of Elfland's Daughter*, however, Neil Gaiman refers to the *mundane* world,[13] a term that, apart from being somewhat tautological, captures the quality of the earthly as well as the prosaic, connotations that are well suited to opposing the glamour of Faerie. To avoid the tautology, I simply use the term *mundanity* when referring to that which is not Faerie. This noun, while retaining connotations of the world and worldliness, refers to the "quality or fact of being commonplace, trivial, or ordinary" as well as to "that which is commonplace,"[14] and seems an apt designation for the fields we know and inhabit.

The second border I turn to is thus the one between Faerie and mundanity. The exact relationship between the two domains varies widely among those texts that deal with them both: fantasy stories, folktales, and taproot texts. In general, the relations between domains fall into one of three categories: either Faerie is an Otherworld, accessible from mundanity only by magic or certain portals (for example, in John Crowley's *Little, Big* [1981], Susanna Clarke's *Jonathan Strange & Mr. Norrell* [2004], and Tad Williams's *War of the Flowers* [2003]); or Faerie and mundanity intermingle in so-called crosshatches (as in Delia Sherman's *Changeling* [2006], Charles de Lint's Newford books [1998–present], C. J. Cherryh's *Faery in Shadow* [1993]—and, of course, in William Shakespeare's taproot text *A Midsummer Night's Dream* [1600]),[15] where, in many cases, fairies and humans share a common world but the former generally remain invisible to mortals; or Faerie lies next to, or is surrounded by, mundanity. Examples of this third category would include Tolkien's *Smith of Wootton Major* (1967), Poul Anderson's *Three Hearts and Three Lions* (1961), Dunsany's *The King of Elfland's Daughter*, and Hope Mirrlees's *Lud-in-the-Mist* (1926). For the discussion that follows, I have selected the illustrated novel *Stardust* (1997–98), by Gaiman and Charles Vess, for its obvious awareness of the long tradition of Faerie in fantasy. In *Stardust*, Faerie abuts mundanity, if only for a short stretch. The border between them is guarded to keep mundanity from adversely affecting Faerie, a refuge for the imaginary and fantastical, while mundanity itself grows increasingly scientific and skeptical.

The third type of border takes the division between the mundane and the magical even further and divides the world into one domain ruled by science and technology and another domain where magic works. The stories move from one domain to the other and display the differences between them. An early text that separates a place of magic from a world of technology is Theodore Cogswell's "The Wall around the World" from 1953, in which the boundary has been used to allow for the development of magic (although the change takes place in people, not in the environment). The opposition between magic and technology is even more in focus in Garth Nix's Abhorsen series (*Sabriel* [1995], *Lirael* [2001], and *Abhorsen* [2003], and the novella "Nicholas Sayre and the Creature in the Case" [2005]). Nix's border is guarded both by a medieval-looking wall and by guns, concertina wire, and modern troops, portraying a conflict between the two sides. The border defenses' shortcomings are crucial, as the differences between the two sides are central to the plots. Other examples can be found in Roger Zelazny's *Jack of Shadows* (1971) and in the Borderland series of shared-world anthologies and novels (1986–present), created by Terry Windling.

Just as Joseph Campbell's monomythical hero crosses the threshold on his way to adventure, returning in due course, the heroes in the Brust, Gaiman/Vess, and Nix stories cross borders into the unknown. These borders are not what they initially seem, however; they are areas of transition that subvert and undermine the reader's first impressions. They provide the hero with a "there" while never promising that the same hero will come back again.

A Final Injustice: The Dragaeran Paths of the Dead[16]
Hades, Hel, Yomi, Hell—whatever the underworld has been called, journeys there have long been the stuff of myths and stories. In Steven Brust's

Dragaera books, the soul's destination after death is the Halls of Judgment, home of the gods. Two visits to this realm of the dead are described in Brust's books.[17] In *Taltos*, the fourth Vlad Taltos novel, Vlad is sent there together with the Dragonlord Morrolan to bring back an imperial heir. In *The Paths of the Dead*, volume one of the third novel of the Khaavren Romances,[18] the true heir to the imperial throne, Zerika, makes her way to the Halls of Judgment to reclaim the Imperial Orb with which she intends to restore the Empire.

The Dragaeran class system, which permeates both the Vlad Taltos novels and the Khaavren Romances, can also be found in the realm of the dead and is even reflected in the border between the domains of life and death. By examining how each novel's narrator—Vlad Taltos in *Taltos* and Paarfi of Roundwood in *The Paths of the Dead*—treats what is basically the same setting and very similar plots, it is possible to see how the border and the crossing of it can create quite dissimilar views of this class system. The two narrators, from opposite sides of the social spectrum, stress different aspects of how the border is constructed, while agreeing on some fundamental features. The discussion to follow begins with an outline of the Dragaeran social hierarchy and the narrators' respective places in it, followed by an examination of how they present the border and what is required of those who cross it in either direction. Finally, there is a brief consideration of how the portrayal of the border reflects each narrator's social position: Vlad's return journey subverts the social order, whereas Zerika's celebrates it. In either case, death in Dragaera brings no final justice; having a geographically accessible land of death does not change this, but rather emphasizes it.

The narrators of the two novels come from completely different social positions. Dragaeran society is strictly hierarchical, with Easterners as well as members of House Jhereg occupying unprivileged positions. Devoid of citizenship, Easterners are at the very bottom of society. Above them are the commoners of House Teckla, and the sixteen noble Houses are found at the top. The most exalted of all nobles is the Empress (or Emperor). Segregation between Houses is fiercely maintained, and only House Teckla and House Jhereg accept inter-House liaisons and any resulting offspring. While counted among the sixteen noble Houses, Jhereg is in fact more of a criminal syndicate, and its members are therefore despised by the other Houses. Their unpopularity is emphasized by the fact that the animal from which the House has taken its name is a scavenger and generally considered to be vermin. Vlad, both Easterner and Jhereg, embodies the lowest rung on the social ladder, being a part of Dragaeran society and yet an outsider; his (bought) title in House Jhereg grants him citizenship, but it entitles him to very little respect outside his own House. Paarfi, on the other hand, is a nobleman, and very popular at that (*Paths* [xv]–xvii); he writes about the concerns of the noble Houses, the restoration of Dragaeran society, and the establishment of the Empress. While not at the pinnacle of society, he certainly writes from a privileged perspective.

Vlad and Paarfi agree that the most salient features of the border between the domains of the living and the dead can be determined: the actual border is located somewhere between the lip and bottom of a waterfall, hidden by mists. Above it circle giant jhereg, and upstream along the river, animal sculptures indicate where the various Houses launch their dead over the Falls. There is a distinctness about this border, an abruptness evoked by the water cascading down Deathgate Falls, although the actual border is not visible from the top. Here, where the Blood River rushes down a sheer cliff, is the only place where the Paths of the Dead and the domain of death can be entered. Incidentally, the similarity between the Blood River and the Phlegethon is one of several parallels to Dante's *Inferno*[19] that can be found in Vlad's journey into the Paths of the Dead. Others include how Vlad's companion throws down a rope to descend the Falls, just as Virgil does (*Taltos* 105–7; canto xvi), and although Vlad and Morrolan climb down themselves, the serpentine, two-legged jhereg that circle in the air above the Falls echo the monstrous Geryon who carries Virgil and his charge down from the seventh to the eighth circle (canto xvii). Even the encounter with Lord Baritt, believed by Morrolan to be still alive (*Taltos* 131), parallels a similar meeting with the friar Alberigo (canto xxxiii). But where Alberigo's body supposedly remains among the living inhabited by a demon, Baritt explains his presence by the temporal peculiarities in the Paths. (Paarfi discusses the behavior of time in the Paths in detail; see *Paths* 175–76, 358.)

"[T]he foot of the falls," Vlad explains, "isn't in the same world as the lip." He adds that attempts have been made to reach the bottom of the Falls by other routes but that no one has succeeded (*Taltos* 99). The exact point where you pass from one domain into the other is obscured by mists and water spray, which also make it impossible to estimate the height of the waterfall. Vlad relates how people who have returned from the dead (as undead) vary in their assessment of the waterfall's height: "The reports say it is a mere fifty feet, that it is a thousand feet, and any number of distances in between. Your guess is as good as mine, and I mean that" (*Taltos* 99). Vlad's emphatic invocation of the narratee underscores how unknowable the height of the Falls is—if the guess of someone who has never been there is as good as that of Vlad, who has climbed down the cliff, it must be impossible to know. The fact that neither the height nor the exact point of crossing can be determined (and bearing in mind Clute's description of a threshold, discussed earlier) suggests that rather than constituting a distinct demarcation, the waterfall marks a gradual transition from one domain to the other.

The gradual transition may in fact extend into the valley above the waterfall. Depending on who the narrator is, the domain of the dead affects the domain of the living, turning the valley into a crosshatch where both domains inhabit the same space. This crosshatch effect is most evident in Vlad's narrative, as he mentions how two characteristics of the land of death affect the land of the living a fair distance from the Deathgate. Sorcery becomes more difficult to perform as he and Morrolan approach the Deathgate; and the atmosphere of the place is somber—it is too quiet to be in the vicinity of a large waterfall (*Taltos* 96, 100–101). Paarfi, on the other hand, mentions nothing like a crosshatch at all.

The two narrators' differences on this point cannot be reconciled, although it is clear that they owe partly to the narrators' difference in character. Vlad's narrative is informed by his apprehension about going into the domain of the Dragaeran dead, a domain that he has been told he is not allowed to enter. In *Taltos*, the overall atmosphere around the Deathgate Falls thus becomes one of hesitation rather than certainty, as the descriptions tend to emphasize impressions as much as actualities: "it *seemed* like you could wade in it," "[t]his did not *seem* normal," "it *seemed* to me that this was a calculated effect" (100–101; my emphasis). The narrator of the Khaavren Romances employs a different style altogether; both the style and the contents of his story restrict the border to a space between the lip and the foot of the Deathgate Falls, so that the valley does not form part of it. Paarfi attempts to give an account of the events that is as factual as possible (albeit with some poetic license). To him, as a Dragaeran, the Paths of the Dead hold much less mystery than they do to Vlad, and although he professes no personal stake in the affairs he narrates, his is the heroic tale of how the current Empress won her throne and reinstated the Empire. Paarfi's third-person narrative leaves out descriptions of any perceived atmosphere or other crosshatch effects noted by Vlad; the historian's straightforward narration dispels the suspense associated with the Deathgate through meticulous descriptions of the topography, flora, fauna, and population of the surrounding area (*Paths* 314–15). His insistence that there are "mysteries surrounding Deathgate Falls that the historian [i.e., Paarfi] will make no claims to have solved" (*Paths* 319) does not add much in the way of mystery to his hindsight-imbued accounts.

Whether the performance of sorcery is affected by the domain of death is equally impossible to decide from the two narrators' accounts. Where Vlad is clear about this effect, Paarfi mentions no diminution of any sorcerous abilities; one of his protagonists is actually prepared to do magical battle with an opposing sorcerer only a few steps from the water-fall (*Paths* 329). Closer examination makes both cases tenuous, however. Vlad never verifies Morrolan's assertion that sorcery becomes increasingly hard the closer to the Falls one comes (*Taltos* 96, 104). Given that the Dragonlord explains that he discovered this in a fight that he, according to Paarfi's story, was nowhere near, there is cause to doubt him; he might, for some reason, have lied to his companion. As for Paarfi's account, the magical battle he mentions never takes place; sorcery is never employed near the Falls in either case, so Morrolan's claim is not disproved. Consequently, the border might be described as a crosshatch in *Taltos* owing to Vlad's being nervous and misinformed; or it might not be described this way in *The Paths of the Dead* owing to Paarfi's imperfect knowledge.

The two narrators give similar accounts of the way back to the domain of life—that is, of crossing the border in the other direction. In both cases, the return route is indeterminate until the protagonists find themselves back in the land of the living. The actual point of crossing is, again, impossible to determine; it is only clear once the characters have returned that they have in fact completed the crossing itself. Although the way back to life is as much a one-way track as is the way down the Falls, the indeterminate nature of the exit is more pronounced than the entrance. Vlad and Paarfi agree that it is impossible to predict where in the domain of the living people will turn up if they manage to return from the domain of death (*Taltos* 99; *Paths* 315). Yet both Zerika and Vlad leave through a cave. These caves (or this cave; it is never made clear whether they are in fact one and the same) come as surprises to both of them because of their great weariness (*Taltos* 173; *Paths* 387), illustrating how the border cannot be anticipated before it is crossed; it cannot even be identified in retrospect.

Unlike the two examples to follow (from *Stardust* and the Abhorsen series), in *Taltos* and *The Paths of the Dead* entry and exit across the border do not coincide, either spatially or in terms of construction. Both directions have their indistinctness in common: in neither case can the actual point of crossing be identified, which stresses the gradual nature of the border. The entrance to the domain of the dead is always located at the Deathgate Falls, however, whereas the location for the exit varies. Furthermore, the return trips construct a border that does not correspond to any of the functions Clute mentions for a physical threshold: it lacks the distinctiveness of a spine, and there are no borderlands for which it could serve as a spine; nor is there any suggestion of a crosshatch or polder. Instead, it combines a physical aspect (moving, physically, from one area to another) with a metaphorical one (achieving a certain feat, fulfilling some condition, passing some test). Orpheus and Eurydice illustrate this combined border: the border between Hades and the land of the living is a physical location in that they can walk there, but it also entails a test of Orpheus' faith, a test he fails by turning around to look at Eurydice. Brust's protagonists are similarly subjected to a condition: they cannot leave if they fall asleep. The focus when they enter at the Deathgate is on the physical challenge; when they leave, their weariness causes a shift in focus to the metaphorical aspect and to the achievement needed to leave. The border, and the passing of it, cannot be anticipated in their state of weariness; it can only be established once they have passed it. This shift in focus not only constructs the border differently; it suggests that returning to the domain of the living is actually a test, continued life being a gift only bestowed on those who are worthy of it.

From both Paarfi's and Vlad's accounts, it is plain that travelers are tested both when entering and when leaving the domain of death. The main test for entering the domain actually comes once the border has been crossed, in the labyrinthine Paths of the Dead. This test calls attention not only to social segregation but also to injustice in death: both Vlad and Paarfi recount how books are available with instructions that a Dragaeran can memorize before death, as an aid to negotiating the Paths. These instructions are of varying quality, and are passed down in families; reading another family's book is not allowed. Vlad (characteristically for a Jhereg) reacts against this inequality by proposing to steal one of the better books and sell copies. However, he is informed that such a breach of the rules of the domain would not be possible (*Taltos* 115). For the living who wish to enter the domain, another test precedes the Paths, as they must somehow make their way down the waterfall. Although Vlad and Morrolan carefully climb down a rope, Zerika just rides off the cliff edge and survives the fall (although her horse does not; see *Paths* 359–60)—indeed, one character suggests that the Falls will not kill anyone who plunges down them alive (*Paths* 198, 360). Going in is simply a question of boldness—to dare to enter in whatever fashion. Entering the domain of the dead is therefore radically different from leaving it. Anyone can, theoretically, cross the border at the Deathgate Falls and even enter the Paths. Once in the domain of the dead, alive or dead makes little difference, though, since no one is meant to return; people trapped in the domain of death are to all intents and purposes dead, regardless of the state of their physical bodies. The real test is, in other words, the return journey.

Leaving the land of the dead to return to the land of the living is traditionally the tricky part. "*[F]acilis descensus Averno,*" Æneas is told, "*sed revocare gradum superasque evadere ad auras, hoc opus, hic labor est.*"[20] There are always conditions to fulfill for those who want to go to the underworld—and return. Æneas brings a golden bough as a present to Proserpine (Persephone). For Persephone herself, eating a pomegranate seed is enough to give her an annual stretch in Hades. Inanna needs to find someone to take her place in the underworld. In the Dragaeran domain of death, no matter what else, if you fall asleep there, you have to stay. Both Vlad and Zerika are exhausted during their return trip, and their test is simply to stay awake and walk until they eventually find themselves back in the domain of life. Even the awareness of this condition makes them weary: when Vlad is informed that he must not sleep, he "suddenly felt very tired" (*Taltos* 148); similarly, Zerika tells the gods that she needs to return to find somewhere to sleep and then realizes that "she was every bit as weary as she had said" (*Paths* 385). As soon as the characters become aware of the danger of tiredness, the clock starts ticking and the test begins.

Staying awake is not enough, though; only those of the right blood are allowed to return to life. Paarfi makes this into a social issue: Zerika is the heir to the imperial throne and can thus claim the Imperial Orb from the gods, who also want to see the Empire restored. The Orb then facilitates her return. Vlad's account attributes Zerika's return solely to the Orb (and thus her birthright), but although Aliera, next in line for the throne, has the same social reason (imperial succession) to return, the deciding factor is revealed to be blood in a more literal sense: Aliera has inherited the right to leave bestowed on her ancestor—her right to leave is a property of her blood, not her social position; similarly, it is Vlad's non-Dragaeran blood that allows him to return (*Taltos* 156–58). Even the gods' ability to cross the border is connected to their blood (*Taltos* 156), and Morrolan can thus return because he is given a small transfusion of divine blood (172 et passim).

The ability of Loiosh, Vlad's jhereg familiar, to enter and leave the domain of the dead can be argued to be a question of his species. One of the gods informs Vlad that Loiosh "shares [Vlad's] fate" (*Taltos* 156); but whereas the statement gives the impression of being unambiguous, it does not, in fact, say that the fates of Vlad and Loiosh are connected, only that they are shared. Loiosh is allowed to leave, but not necessarily because he is Vlad's familiar. Instead, both narrators refer to giant jhereg that circle over the Deathgate Falls, the only creatures apparently able to cross from one domain to the other as they carry out the necessary task of eating the dead bodies that are sent down the Falls (*Paths* 360). As it happens, apart from the jhereg (and the obscuring mists), nothing can be seen of what lies on the other side of the border, regardless of whether one looks toward the land of the dead or back toward the land of the living. Even though Loiosh never attempts to return up to the lip of the Falls as his giant cousins appear to do, he displays intuitive knowledge about returning to the domain of the living. Vlad recounts how his familiar occupies a very important role during the journey back: "From time to time we'd stop, and Aliera and Morrolan would have a hushed conversation about which way to go. [. . .] When this happened Loiosh would say, 'Tell them that way, boss,' and I'd gesture in the indicated direction" (*Taltos* 172).

This description suggests that any direction conveyed by the exhausted Vlad is telepathically supplied to him by Loiosh. It is reasonable to assume that the jhereg is also the one who ultimately points out the cave that leads them to the realm of the living (*Taltos* 173). Alone of the four, the small reptile is able to navigate his way back from the realm of the dead, sharing at least some of the liminal qualities of his giant relatives at the Deathgate. The fact that a representative of the most despised of the Dragaeran Houses leads two Dragonlords back illustrates how the border crossing can be used to subvert the social order, a topic that deserves further comment.

Paarfi and Vlad clearly express their own social bias in the way they use and comment on the social hierarchy reflected in the construction of the border between the two domains. Death is not a place of social equality. Vlad makes two basic points that display a connection to the social order: Easterners are not allowed to enter this domain of death, only Dragaerans are welcome. This echoes the fact that Easterners can be imperial citizens only if they buy a title in House Jhereg or become serfs in House Teckla (and thus become nominal Dragaerans). Furthermore, Vlad explains how only Dragaerans who are "highly respected by their House" are sent over the Falls (*Taltos* 74; see also 99); high social status is consequently a key to the afterlife. Considering the animal statues along the Blood River, it is also possible to infer that no Tecklas (and possibly no Jheregs) are sent to the Paths of the Dead. Paarfi's account mentions how Zerika's party passes the statue of each noble in the group, but never mentions any Teckla statue or any reaction to such statues by the Teckla lackeys (*Paths* 318–19). Nor are the two lackeys ever included in any discussion about entering the Paths, and they do not discuss it between themselves. While this does not prove that Tecklas are not sent into the Paths, it implies that at the very least, such a journey is of much greater moment to Dragaerans of the noble Houses. A similar argument can be made for House Jhereg—no Jhereg sculpture is mentioned—but on the other hand, no Dragaeran Jhereg passes along the river near the Deathgate Falls in either story.

The animal sculptures, and the Paths themselves, express not only nobility but also the segregation of Dragaeran society. The animal sculptures, and the various places for launching the dead over the Falls, offer a physical manifestation of the social taboo against mixing blood between Houses. This image of segregation is reinforced further by the fact that each House has its own route through the Paths. That House Teckla, and possibly House Jhereg, is not represented along the river—that they are not sent into the domain of death—would accord with the acceptance by both of these Houses of inter-House marriages and children of mixed parentage. Not only a lack of nobility, but also failure to comply with the segregation demanded by society, is emphasized by the border and the Paths of the Dead.

The implicit and explicit discrimination in favor of the upper classes at the Deathgate Falls, while clearly visible in both books, is used in opposing ways by the two narrators. Paarfi's story is one of reestablishing Dragaeran society and maintaining its social order, with an imperial sovereign at the top. The social values of the border match those of Paarfi, and he uses them to reinforce the legitimacy of Zerika's quest. She and her noble friends all in some way acknowledge their respective animal sculptures; and as they approach the Deathgate Falls, Zerika's behavior changes in the direction of the autocratic and self-reliant personality expected of an Empress (see *Paths* 316). Paarfi relates how Zerika deals with the tests both of entering and leaving in a manner appropriate for a strong leader: a constant reliance on her own strength and fortitude, and a focus on how her role as imperial heir and restorer of the Empire (and thus its society) allows her to cross into the domain and return.

In *Taltos*, on the other hand, Vlad uses the superiority of social status and the importance of segregation as a foundation for social criticism. As they enter the Paths, Vlad's account centers on how he is treated with contempt by the Dragaerans for being an Easterner and a Jhereg, and thus neither respected nor allowed into the domain of death; and he counters by refusing to abide by traditions or social rules. Once Aliera's soul has been retrieved, it is made clear how blood rather than social position determines who can leave. That marks the beginning of a subversion of the Dragaeran social hierarchy: in order to return to the domain of the living, the two Dragonlords, one of them the imperial heir, have to rely on an Easterner belonging to House Jhereg (and assisted by a jhereg). Representing the pinnacle of Dragaeran society, the imperial throne itself, as well as a noble House, Aliera and Morrolan need the assistance of Vlad, a criminal from the lowest of the noble Houses, who would not even be a citizen were it not for that House's policy of selling titles; compared to the Dragonlords, he truly belongs on the lowest rung of the social ladder. Furthermore, Morrolan can leave only through the use of witchcraft, a despised form of magic among most Dragaerans, and by mixing blood, a symbolic violation of the taboo against inter-House liaisons. Social mores are turned on their heads and traditional roles reversed. Vlad, doubly unprivileged, saves not only Morrolan and Aliera but, by extension, the Dragaeran Empire—assisted by a despised and reviled animal, a jhereg. At the same time, Vlad himself would not be able to leave without the Dragonlords' help, and the three eventually find themselves friends rather than social opposites. Their return thus celebrates cooperation rather than autocracy and heroic self-reliance.

The narrators thus offer distinct differences in perspective on the Dragaeran afterlife. Vlad focuses on the injustice of an afterlife restricted to the few, and it is his refusal to play by the rules that allows him to return to the domain of life. Paarfi, although he reports Zerika's disapproval of some aspects of the afterlife (*Paths* 365), treats her quest for the Orb as precisely that: a trial for a hero on her way to save the world. Where Vlad's sojourn into the domain of death and back again is an act of social defiance, Zerika's is an act of heroism sprung from social responsibility.

Regardless of whether crossing the border between the domains of life and death is constructed as a means for criticizing or upholding the social order, death in Dragaera is, as was pointed out earlier, not a great leveler. Apart from Dragaerans' ability to live for millennia, Dragaeran sorcery can resurrect recently dead bodies—making someone stay dead therefore requires a special effort from the killer. Even after death, status and wealth are important. Revivification is very expensive, and thus a privilege of the rich. Furthermore, even in those cases in which revivification is too costly (or impossible for some other reason), not everyone is sent to the Paths of the Dead. Only those "deemed important (and rich) enough" are brought to the Deathgate and sent over the Falls to the Paths (*Taltos* 99). In other words, this afterlife is not for everyone—which also implies that either another afterlife exists for everyone else (presumably without a geographical position) or these other souls meet some other fate, for instance reincarnation (see *Paths* 365). The Paths, and the Halls, may be reasonably well known to Dragaerans; but for a large number of the Empire's citizens, they are not the final destination. To them, and certainly to all Easterners, death remains an undiscovered country, one from which no traveler has so far returned. Discrimination is built into the Dragaeran afterlife, but whether the journey into the domain of death and back is used to criticize that discrimination or to uphold the society from which it springs depends on who tells the tale.

Protection from a Hostile World:
Faerie and Wall in Stardust[21]

Stardust tells the story of how Tristran Thorn ventures into Faerie to find a fallen star in order to win the love of the beautiful Victoria Forester. It was originally published as an illustrated story in serialized form in 1997 and 1998, as a result of the collaboration between Neil Gaiman and Charles Vess. Even though it was later published in a text-only edition (in 1998), the illustrations provide an essential paratext that greatly extends the text,[22] and it is thus the illustrated version that is considered here.

The narrator introduces the story of Tristran and Victoria by constructing a bridge between the reader and, ultimately, Faerie. From the village Wall, where the two youngsters live, there is a track, the narrator explains, that if "[f]ollowed far enough [. . .] becomes a real road, paved with asphalt; followed further the road gets larger, is packed at all hours with cars and lorries rushing from city to city. Eventually the road takes you to London, but London is a whole night's drive from Wall" (6 [2]). This almost anxious attempt by the narrator to persuade the reader that Wall is located in the same world as London—that the reader could, in fact, drive from one to the other—could have been written to illustrate Brian Attebery's description of how extension works in reportorial mode to suggest a connection between the fictive place and the reader's location in the actual world:

> Once we know we are in a story in reportorial mode, we can extend the narrator's observations in any direction. If the story mentions London, we can assume Paris. We can fill in Tower Bridge and the dome of St. Paul's, whether or not they are invoked specifically. We can supply Henry VIII and Victoria, Samuel Johnson and Virginia Woolf. Even the least well-read can provide traffic and parks and shops and cinemas to fill in the background of what the narrator actually chooses to notice. Ultimately the world of the story extends in an unbroken path to the reader's own doorstep. Thus the reader does a lot of the hard work of bringing a story to life.[23]

The route from Wall to London is offered as a pattern for further extension. From London, the reader can extend the story world to Cardiff, or Vancouver, or Auckland. And to make certain that the extension is not only geographical, the narrator also supplies a number of historical references, clues that allow anyone with sufficient knowledge or interest to work out when the story takes place.[24] With a narration set in a modern age of cars and lorries and a story set in the early Victorian era, historical extension is thus introduced along with the geographical.

Stardust is not written in the reportorial mode, however, and the part of the world that is extended is biased toward logic and reason. That this is a fantasy story is given away by its title and subtitle (*Being a Romance within the Realms of Faerie*); and as if this hint were not enough, the text quickly mentions curious events that happen on a nine-year basis and odd figures glimpsed on the other side of the wall in Wall. Yet the reader is encouraged to extend the world of Wall, geographically and historically. The extension only brings part of the story's world to life—the lion's share of the "hard work" of bringing to life what I call mundanity is left to the reader. This extension of mundanity is biased in a certain direction by the narrator's encouraging measures: the step-by-step route description and the historical puzzle (with men of science smiling disdainfully at any mention of Faerie) imply an extension of mundanity as a place of reason, of logic and science, but devoid of fairies. The world in *Stardust* thus becomes constructed of two domains: a domain of rational mundanity that extends along the "unbroken path" of the reportorial mode to the reader's doorstep and, separated from it by a stone wall, the domain of Faerie.

In fact, mundanity never manages to extend all the way to Wall, and the extension becomes part of the process that places magic and science in opposition. Whereas the path to London is unbroken, the route description unobtrusively takes the reader off that path. Only if followed "far enough" does the road become a "real road." While the town of Wall and Faerie beyond it are accessible to the reader in a way very different from a formulaic fairy-tale introduction such as "Once upon a time," or the rather more modern "A long time ago in a galaxy far, far away," getting there still requires a leap of imagination. Instead, *Stardust* uses the extension of the reportorial mode to set up a world of two domains, where magic and reason are clearly opposed to each other from the very beginning.

There are several differences between the domains. The starkest distinction between Faerie and mundanity is that in Faerie, magic works. Other differences include disparity in time and season, space and geography. When Tristran enters Faerie, "[h]e felt as if he were walking into summer" (70 [95]), leaving the late October of mundanity behind. The harvest moon that shines down on him suggests a late September that, as he travels deeper into Faerie, becomes more springlike (73 [101]).

Crossing the border thus becomes a movement back through the seasons, but the relation between Faerie time and mundane time is not simply a question of being out of sync. The relationship itself is indeterminable. Some time periods are approximately of the same length in both realms: in Wall, nine months pass from Tristran's conception until the basket with the newborn boy is left at the gate, and the eighteen years that pass as he grows up in Wall correspond to Madame Semele's "nearly twenty years" in Faerie (113 [158]). On the other hand, there is a distinct impression that Tristran's adventure in Faerie takes much less time than the twenty-five or so weeks that pass in mundanity. With this temporal slipperiness, *Stardust* joins a rich tradition of folktales and fantasy texts.[25] Under "Time in Faerie" in *The Encyclopedia of Fantasy*, Langford observes that "[v]isitors to Faerie find that time there is subjective, disengaged from real-world clocks and calendars."[26] He further suggests that there are two types of relations between Faerie time and mundane time. Either a given time interval in Faerie is longer (often much longer) than the corresponding interval in mundanity or it is (much) shorter. Years in Faerie hence equal hours in mundanity or vice versa. The first type, which according to Langford suggests a time polder, is discussed further with regard to polders. The second type is ultimately a way of bringing characters into a more or less distant future. *Stardust*'s Faerie does not fall neatly into either of Langford's categories but has a time flow that denies a simple relation to the time flow of mundanity.

This temporal slipperiness is mirrored in an equally slippery geography and fanciful inhabitants. "Maps of Faerie are unreliable, and may not be depended upon" (61 [84]), the reader is told, and the narrator explains why:

> Faerie is bigger than England, as it is bigger than the world (for, since the dawn of time, each land that has been forced off the map by explorers and the brave going out and proving it wasn't there has taken refuge in Faerie; so it is now, by the time that we come to write of it, a most huge place indeed, containing every manner of landscape and terrain). *Here*, truly, *there be Dragons*. (61 [84])

This unmappable land is, in other words, a land where imagination is real, a land not of proof and evidence but of imagination and belief. The very notion of maps is anathema to its geography. "Here be Dragons" doubly supports the idea that Faerie is a land of the imagined. First, this phrase alludes to the monsters and descriptions of monsters found on some medieval maps, descriptions that "served to fill up embarrassing empty spaces in unknown regions, a custom which went back to Roman times and forward to the sixteenth century."[27] These monsters, which were never found by explorers, are given a refuge in Faerie together with the lands in which they were supposedly residing. But use of the "Here be Dragons" phrase also suggests that not everything is known and that fancy rules Faerie. It is, in fact, a common misconception that the expression can be found on medieval maps. Its only occurrence is on the early sixteenth-century Lenox globe, where the phrase is given in Latin (*Hic sunt dracones*).[28] "Here, truly, there be Dragons" thus brings the monsters of medieval maps into Faerie, but it also becomes a comment on how, even today, people believe in what amounts to fables.

Despite its everyday, solid appearance, the wall from which the town has taken its name does not follow the rules of any common or garden wall. It is "a high grey rock wall" that "is old, built of rough, square lumps of hewn granite, and it comes from the woods and goes back to the woods once more" (7 [3]). This brief description conveys an impression of solidity and antiquity: this is a border that cannot be breached or crossed, and that is how it has always been. The wall is also conspicuously delimited: it appears from the depths of the woods and returns again, surfacing, as it were, briefly at Wall. Rather than being a long border along which the two realms lie side by side, the wall is only a point of contact where they happen to touch. Although it is never mentioned, the impression is that the wall cannot be followed; the circumference of Faerie cannot be traced. This restricted contact is underlined by the bird's-eye view in the illustration on page 209, where the wall is seen coming out of the trees, snaking along the margin of a meadow with Wall on its far side, and disappearing in the forest again. Beyond that, the woods of Faerie and mundanity cannot be told apart, although a flying ship and Stormhold keep on the horizon imply that the viewer is actually looking out from the Faerie side and that everything except the small portion of Wall is part of Faerie.

As in the case of Brust's Deathgate Falls, the border in *Stardust* is not a distinct line between two realms. Some of the land on the far side of the wall also belongs to the border, with a crosshatch stretching from the wall to where Faerie truly begins. Beyond the wall is a meadow; beyond the meadow a small stream; and on the other side of the stream a forest. While the rules of Faerie work all the way up to the wall (the star, Yvaine, can come with Tristran that far without turning into a meteorite), Faerie proper begins in the forest. It is among its trees that inhabitants of Faerie can be glimpsed (7 [3]), and that is where the Market is held. There, October starts changing into summer (70 [95]), and when Tristran sets off in search of the star, it is not until he has crossed the meadow and the stream that he finds himself in Faerie:

> [O]nce in the woods at the top of the hill he was surprised to realize the moon was shining brightly down on him through a gap in the trees: surprised because the moon had set an hour before; and doubly surprised, because the moon that had set had been a slim,

sharp silver crescent, and the moon that shone down on him now was a huge, golden Harvest moon, full, and glowing, and deeply colored. (51 [71–72])

Not until he has passed the meadow and the stream is it mentioned — but then twice — how Tristran walks into Faerie (51 [72–73]). Rather than a single border consisting of the wall, with mundanity on one side and Faerie on the other, there are two borders and a transitional zone between them. The meadow, in other words, is where Faerie and mundanity overlap.

The sentry on duty by the wall draws attention to why the wall is guarded. Leading through the wall to the meadow crosshatch and on to Faerie is a single opening. The gateway is "an opening about six feet in width" guarded on the town side by two townsmen with wooden cudgels (7 [3–4]). That it is the single possible crossing is made plain not only by the many travelers who come to Wall for the Market but also by the comment that "the Market at Wall [. . .] is too close to the world on the other side of the wall" (158 [235]). The diligence with which the border crossing is guarded by the men of Wall raises questions. First of all, against whom do they keep guard—that is, who is prevented from crossing? Is this a self-serving act of protection from some real or imagined danger, or altruistic protection of something or someone? Second, on whose orders (and authority) do they keep guard? These two questions provide a basis for understanding the most central issue about the border in *Stardust*: why do guards monitor the way between mundanity and Faerie so assiduously? The answers to these questions, in no way obvious, reveal interesting facts about the relationship between the two domains.

From the guards' instructions, it can be inferred that passage from mundanity to Faerie must be prevented. The main function of the guard, it is said, "is to prevent the town's children from going through the opening, into the meadow and beyond." Solitary ramblers and visitors to Wall are also discouraged (7 [4]). Travelers who have come for the Market are similarly kept from crossing until the Market opens. There is only one instruction: "It is the task of the guards to prevent *anything or anyone* from coming through *from the village, by any means possible*; and if it was not possible, then they must raise the village" (49 [68]; my emphasis). These instructions can hardly be aimed only at keeping some children from getting into trouble. "[A]nything or anyone" is certainly unequivocal, and would include not only people and animals but also whatever fairy creatures might be returning after a sojourn in mundanity or who might flee from the encroaching power of science and technology. Most frightening in its implication is the order that the guards prevent the crossing "by any means possible." Two grown men armed with long cudgels can easily do serious damage. Whoever issued that instruction is willing to go to any lengths to stop any crossing—from the village side. The seemingly all-inclusive command[29] is modified to include only whatever comes "from the village." It is *entry into Faerie* that is prohibited. When Tristran returns after his adventure, he is forced to debate this point with the guards on duty. He insists that the letter of the instruction is only to stop passage *into* Faerie, whereas the guard, Mr. Brown, claims that the spirit is to stop any crossing of the border. The reason this detail is not part of the guard instruction, Mr. Brown argues, is that no one apart from Tristran has ever tried to cross the border from the Faerie side. Indeed, so certain are the guards of this fact that they stand with their backs to Faerie, and although they are said to stand on either side of the opening (7 [3–4]), they are repeatedly portrayed *in* the opening. Faerie denizens are simply not expected to cross into mundanity and are trusted not to threaten the guards who, apparently, do keep "anything and anyone" out of the Faerie domain.

It is hinted that the watch is organized by Wall's innkeeper, who possibly hails from, and acts as an agent for, Faerie. On the whole, the instructions to the guards suggest that they were issued mainly with Faerie's best interest at heart. It is never made explicit who the master gatekeeper in Wall is; but Mr. Bromios, the innkeeper, appears to carry ultimate responsibility (see 50 [70]; 191 [294–95]), and he is also referred to as an authority on earlier Markets (9 [8]). There are several clues as to the innkeeper's identity, the foremost of which is that his name, Bromios, is one of the names of Dionysus.[30] This tallies with his olive skin, the good wine he serves, his implied longevity, and "items of antique statuary, and clay pots" in his room (192 [297]). The innkeeper's divine identity is further corroborated by the stick entwined with bronze ivy that hangs on his wall (192 [297]; also see ill. pp. 193, 199). This stick closely resembles a thyrsus, a fennel staff topped with ivy, which is one of Dionysus' attributes.[31] The innkeeper in Wall, who apparently controls the entrance to Faerie, is in other words closely associated with the Greco-Roman deity of wine and revelry.

Related to Bromios is the Fellowship of the Castle, a group that acts to protect Faerie and could, conceivably, be behind the watch at the gate.

The connection between the Fellowship and the innkeeper is the hairy little man who calls himself "Charmed." Once in Faerie, Tristran is immediately found by the little man and, at the time, their meeting seems like a coincidence to the boy. The reader, however, can identify Charmed as the man who shared the byre with Tristran's father, Dunstan, almost eighteen years previously, especially by his comment that Dunstan once did him a good turn (94 [131]).

There is more to Charmed than this, though. Even more than Bromios, he seems quietly to watch over Dunstan and Tristran. Even when he is not mentioned in the text, he frequently appears in the illustrations, often at crucial moments.[32] His timely appearance therefore suggests that he was actually waiting for the boy. This explanation is not only possible but probable: in the bloodthirsty serewood, Charmed tells Tristran that he could "castle" but that "there's no one I could castle with'd be any better off here than we are" (76 [107–8]). At the time, the expression "to castle" appears only to mean some mysterious changing of places (as king and castle can change places in chess). Not until Captain Alberic explains to Tristran that the hairy little man is a member of the Fellowship of the Castle does the expression acquire a wider meaning as an early indication of this secret society. Little else is said about the Fellowship, except that Tristran might have joined later and helped break the power of the Unseelie Court (212 [332]). Although the Unseelie Court is never described in *Stardust*, it is traditionally the court of wicked Faerie creatures; fighting it makes the Fellowship come across as being on the side of good (something the reader is likely to have assumed, as only "good" characters are revealed to be members). This also suggests that they work to protect Faerie. The captain tells Tristran that the hairy little man is "not the only member of the fellowship with an interest in your return to Wall" (165 [244–45]). Who else would want Tristran returned to Wall—that is, out of Faerie? Given his probable connection to Faerie, Bromios is the most likely candidate, and indeed, the innkeeper can be seen drinking amicably with Charmed at the Market (199). The Fellowship of the Castle thus comes across as a likely principal behind Bromios and the diligent watch kept at Wall.

Mundanity threatens Faerie, which explains the rigorous guard duty. People from mundanity are kept out of Faerie on Faerie authority. Although dealings with Faerie beings are traditionally perilous for mundane people, and although magic can leak from Faerie to mundanity, it is Faerie that is at risk when mundanity's scientific hegemony threatens to spread across the border. The Market as an arena for regular meetings between Faerie and mundanity emphasizes trade as the driving force behind their interactions. According to folktales and fantasy stories, however, Faerie beings generally have the upper hand when dealing with mundane people, or at least usually attempt to trick them. This sinister side of the Market is further alluded to by the presence of goblin sellers from Christina Rossetti's *Goblin Market* of 1862 (pp. 20–21), where neither purveyors nor goods are beneficial to the consumer. (The goblins' appearance recalls Laurence Housman's illustrations of the 1893 edition of Rossetti's poem. See my note 36, in this chapter.) In this way, the Market reminds the reader of how perilous Faerie can actually be. The opposition between the domains is also evident in the opposition between science and magic, which is brought out from the very beginning of the story. The two scientists, Morse and Draper, and the secular rulers, the queen and the prime minister, would all smile disdainfully at anyone who had mentioned magic or Faerie (8 [5]). Yet, at the border, mundane science meets the magical Faerie. Magic and technology cannot coexist: the former appears to overcome the latter. When the wind blows from Faerie, it carries the smells of Faerie along with the propensity for magic, "and at those times there were strange colors seen in the flames in the fireplaces of the village, and when that wind blew the simplest of devices, from lucifer matches to lantern-slides, would no longer function" (40 [54]). Magic gives the impression of being the stronger force, but this is just an illusion. The scientific knowledge of mundanity is simply too inimical to much of Faerie. When explorers prove the nonexistence of mythical lands, these lands take refuge in Faerie; were the fallen star ever to enter mundanity, she would cease to be a person and become what science has "proven" her to be: a lump of ferrous rock.

In mundanity, magic and wonder are crowded out by science and technology. This dynamic at a time of massive technological breakthrough in the heyday of British industrialization brings into focus the disappearance of magic from mundanity. Such a process of disappearance, or diminishing, Clute refers to as *thinning*.[33] "In low fantasy, crosshatch fantasy, etc., rarely does the world provide venues unthreatened by one or more of a huge range of diminishings or dismissals of the old order," he remarks before listing examples including "the desiccations of the secular and of technology," the draining of magic, and the expulsion of the inhabitants of Faerie.[34] Whereas *Stardust*'s Faerie is reasonably safe behind the wall, mundanity has been suffering from thinning for an unspecified while. As is typical of quest or portal fantasies, according to Farah Mendlesohn, the story "begins with a sense of stability that is revealed to be the stability of a thinned land";[35] but rather than dealing with the thinning, *Stardust* pushes it into the background. Even so, the thinning of mundanity is engaged occasionally: imaginary countries, once they are proved not to exist, are subtracted from mundanity's geography and added to Faerie's. The illustrations of the Market (in particular on pp. 20–21) suggest that legendary and imaginary characters also relocate to Faerie.[36] The Market, which now takes place every nine years, once occurred annually (9 [8]), and Madame Semele claims that fewer visitors come to each Market. Her pessimistic prophesy that it will last "[a]nother forty, fifty, sixty years at the most" (197 [306]) is proved wrong, though. The present-day narrator explains already in the beginning of the story how, even today, the guard at the wall is relaxed every nine years for the Market (7 [4–5]).

Where magic is apparently a property of the air (or at least something that travels with the wind), the thinning of mundanity is a frame of mind. Just as disbelief can destroy the power of a story, it is a force that can threaten the very existence of a magical realm. Thus, only people who would not bring scientific rationality, and thinning, into Faerie are allowed to enter. Unlike the thinning in *The Lord of the Rings*, which is tied to the leaving of the elves, or Tim Powers's *On Stranger Tides* (1988), in which iron drives the magic away, scientific thought (such as the advancements of Draper and Morse) destroys magic in *Stardust*. This is why not only the scientists but also the secular leaders would treat suggestions of magic with disdain—they all subscribe to the rationality brought by science, a rationality inimical to Faerie. In "On Fairy-stories," Tolkien points out how destructive disbelief can be: "The moment disbelief arises, the spell [of the Secondary World] is broken; the magic, or rather art, has failed. You are then out in the Primary World again, looking at the little abortive Secondary World from outside."[37] The spell is broken; magic fails, Faerie (or whatever secondary world the story concerns) collapses. This theme has been treated repeatedly in fantasy fiction. Religious belief is in focus in Terry Pratchett's *Small Gods* (1992), wherein the true belief of the worshippers is required to keep their gods in existence, just as little children's belief in fairies is needed to keep Tinker Bell alive in J. M. Barrie's drama *Peter Pan* (1904). Disbelief brings Hell to an end, cancels death, and threatens the existence of reality in John Wyndham's "Confidence Trick" (1954). The most prominent example in the genre, however, is Michael Ende's *Die unendliche Geschichte* (1979; trans. *The Neverending Story* 1983), in which the entire world of Phantásien (Fantastica) faces destruction unless the diegetic reader shows belief in it.

In *Stardust*, the entire construction of the border focuses on preventing the thinning in mundanity from spreading into Faerie. Imagination and dreams, rather than scientific rationality, are required to be admitted across the border: only "the minstrels, and the lovers, and the mad" (74 [103]) are to be let through. This allusion to *A Midsummer Night's Dream* makes clear why these figures are allowed into Faerie. "The lunatic, the lover, and the poet," Shakespeare writes, "are of imagination all compact,"[38] and such imaginative and irrational people are eminently suited to Faerie. On the whole, however, Faerie must be defended from mundane people and the thinning they could bring. That, more than anything, is why such brutal guard is kept on the border between the two domains.

Apart and Together: Ancelstierre and the Old Kingdom[39]

The opposition between the domains of magic and technology is brought to the fore in Garth Nix's Abhorsen series. The series consists of *Sabriel* and its sequels *Lirael* and *Abhorsen*. (These sequels are technically speaking a two-volume novel, with a single story running through both of them.) The events in the novella "Nicholas Sayre and the Creature in the Case" take place six months after the events in *Abhorsen*. *Sabriel* is a story of the protagonist's coming into her own and defeating a powerful, evil spirit. In *Lirael/Abhorsen*, the destructive force called the Destroyer is trying to escape from its eon-long imprisonment but is thwarted by Sabriel's sister, Lirael, and son, Sam. The novella tells of how Sam's friend seeks to defeat a magical monster woken up by a mad scientist.

For the border between Faerie and mundanity in *Stardust*, the principal question was *why* the border is so well-defended. The same question is resolved almost from the beginning in Nix's books. There, both magical and nonmagical defenses have been put in place to protect the citizens of one domain from the dangers of the other. The Abhorsen series is set in the Old Kingdom, a pseudomedieval, magical realm, and its southern neighbor, Ancelstierre,[40] magicless and roughly corresponding technologically and socially to Western Europe of the 1920s. The border between the countries is thus the border between the domains of magic and technology. These domains are essentially two different

worlds: they have different stars and a different moon, time flows differently (although not completely unpredictably), and seasons and weather
vary (something that becomes distinctly noticeable along the border).
The border between these very dissimilar domains is heavily defended,
but not because of any actual conflict between the two. The defenses are
chiefly meant to stop magical threats from entering Ancelstierre, but
also to prevent Ancelstierrans from venturing into the Old Kingdom.
Among the magical dangers that may enter Ancelstierre from the north
are the Dead—various beings who have been brought back from death or
who have managed to return of their own accord. As Ancelstierre has no
one who, like the Old Kingdom Abhorsen, can send the Dead back into
death, and in general is short on mages to combat any magical threats,
the Wall's protection is necessary. It does not prevent living beings from
crossing, however, and since the land north of the border is a lawless
place (especially in *Sabriel*) where hapless Ancelstierrans would easily
fall prey to necromancers or the Dead, the nonmagical defenses of Ancelstierre are required to prevent entry into the Old Kingdom.

Of the border's two parallel lines of defense, the magical one is closely
linked to the very fabric of magic in the Old Kingdom; but its distinct
appearance belies the fact that the border itself is as gradual as those of
Brust and Gaiman/Vess. To people who cannot see magic, the border
simply looks like a forty-foot-tall, medieval wall in a state of perfect preservation; but it is actually a magical construct. It is created by, and out
of, one of the five Bright Shiners, the semidivine beings that constitute
the Charter, the ordering of the Old Kingdom's magic. In this way, the
Wall is intimately connected not only to the Bright Shiner of the Charter Stones but also to the Charter bloodlines created by the other three
Bright Shiners: the royal bloodline, the bloodline of the Abhorsen, and
the bloodline of the Clayr (see *Sabriel* 285, 299; *Lirael* 559–62; *Abhorsen*
28–29, 167).

This connection ties the physical defense of the border to the ordering of magic, society, knowledge, and death provided by the other parts
of the Charter: Charter magic binds and orders magic; the royal family
brings social stability; the Clayr collect and interpret knowledge from the
past and the future; and the Abhorsen maintains the border between life
and death. In other words, the Wall is not actually a line of defense—it is
part of what maintains order and stability in the Old Kingdom and protects Ancelstierre. Despite being a powerful bulwark of godlike power at
the edge of the magical domain, it does not completely fulfill its purpose,

however. "The only reason that Ancelstierre isn't like the Old Kingdom is the Wall," prince Touchstone explains to Sabriel (*Sabriel* 447–48), although he omits to mention that the Wall is not totally successful in preventing magical influence on the southern realm. Not only does it allow living people through, it fails as a barrier to magical threats: powerful Dead and magical beings can make it to the other side. Furthermore, magic "leaks" across the border (and, as in *Stardust*, it is carried by the wind) into the technological domain; possibly (as is suggested in *Sabriel* [299]) because the Wall itself is a source of magic. As with Deathgate Falls and the Faerie Wall, what appears at first glance to be a sharply defined border turns out to be a crosshatch, where gradual change occurs from one reality to another. Nix's is also by far the largest of the three crosshatches discussed so far: the magic might be barely perceptible to Touchstone in the Ancelstierran capital five hundred miles south of the border (*Abhorsen* 4), but it is strong enough to use without trouble in Sabriel's school, some forty miles from the Wall.

The shortcomings of the Wall are one reason why Ancelstierre needs its own border defense, but this is mainly geared to prevent Ancelstierrans from venturing into the magical domain. Unlike the Wall, its Ancelstierran counterpart, the Perimeter, is a human construction, and while unable to stop magical threats, it explicitly prevents people from Ancelstierre from crossing into the Old Kingdom. The Perimeter, running along the southern side of the Wall, has the appearance of any disputed political border. Its concertina wire, trenches, and concrete strongpoints have a plainly stated purpose: to prevent transgression of the border, in either direction (see *Sabriel* 34; also *Lirael* 203). Because the Perimeter was designed in the southern parts of Ancelstierre, however, where magic is considered to be little more than superstition, it takes little account of the magical nature of incursions from the Old Kingdom:

> [T]he Perimeter was much more successful at keeping people from Ancelstierre out of the Old Kingdom, than it was at preventing things from the Old Kingdom going the other way. Anything powerful enough to cross the Wall usually retained enough magic to assume the shape of a soldier; or to become invisible and simply go where it willed, regardless of barbed wire, bullets, hand grenades and mortar bombs—which often didn't work at all, particularly when the wind was blowing from the North, out of the Old Kingdom. (*Sabriel* 30–31)

The Perimeter is thus no useful complement to the Wall when it comes to hindering creatures from the Old Kingdom: anything that can pass through the magical barrier can pass through the nonmagical one as well. So although its role as barrier to magical intruders is foregrounded (numerous references are made to strange things experienced by the border garrison and to previous incursions from the north), the Perimeter Zone only effectively prevents Ancelstierran people from reaching the Wall. The focus on Ancelstierrans is made evident by signs that proclaim not only that "[u]nauthorized *egress* from the Perimeter Zone is strictly forbidden" but also that "[a]nyone attempting to *cross* the Perimeter Zone will be shot without warning" (*Sabriel* 34; also *Lirael* 203; my emphasis). The signs appear when the Perimeter is approached from the Ancelstierran side, and although they make it perfectly clear that any attempt to *leave* the Perimeter Zone, either into Ancelstierre or into the Old Kingdom, is forbidden, their intended audience obviously comes from the south. Ancelstierre is thus only able to prevent its citizens from straying into danger—they have to rely on the Old Kingdom Wall to keep danger from coming to them.

Along the border, magic is presented as being stronger than technology. As can be seen from the preceding quotation, Ancelstierre's defenses are described as ineffective against the creatures they are meant to keep out. In fact, the border between the domain of magic and the domain of technology is consistently constructed to affirm magic's superiority over technology. This affirmation is not only a question of contrasting the near-divine Wall, a vital component of the magical domain, with the Perimeter, which is ineffectual and ill suited to at least one of its purposes. Technology is only possible in the *absence* of magic; it has no presence of its own. Ancelstierran mages are generally described as incompetent, and the nonmagical country is defamiliarized for the reader. Magic in the Abhorsen books has an almost fluid presence, just as Faerie magic has in *Stardust*. This common characteristic has not only been observed in fiction. Sir James Frazer notes that "that mysterious quality which is supposed to pervade sacred or tabooed persons [. . .] is conceived by the primitive philosopher as a physical substance or fluid."[41] Why proponents of this view are supposed to be "primitive," Frazer does not explain, but the fluidity of magic is certainly a pervasive notion in contemporary fantasy. Both Nix and Gaiman/Vess demonstrate how this fluid magic is actually stronger than supposedly more "advanced" technology. Magic that leaks or blows across the border renders technology in Ancelstierre as well as Wall useless, but technology cannot move across the border in a similar manner. Bringing technological products into the Old Kingdom quickly destroys them: paper decomposes (*Lirael* 339, 380), technical devices break down (e.g., *Lirael* 696; *Abhorsen* 125), and machine-made items are easily destroyed by magic (*Sabriel* 65). Even magic generated from a single, magical creature is sufficient to destroy electrical appliances (e.g., "Nicholas Sayre" 68, 100, 102).

Furthermore, because only small amounts of magic leak across the border, magic users in Ancelstierre are portrayed as less knowledgeable and less proficient than their northern counterparts. Although Sabriel is used to explaining necromantic matters to her magic teacher, she quickly realizes that "a First in magic from an Ancelstierran school [would not] make her a great mage in the Old Kingdom" (*Sabriel* 24, 110). At the border crossing, Colonel Horyse commands "a somewhat motley collection of Ancelstierrans who've managed to gain a Charter mark and some small knowledge of magic" (*Sabriel* 42). Their magic is "crude [. . .] but strongly cast" and their weapons inscribed with "crudely written Charter symbols" (*Sabriel* 39–40). In the battle against the Destroyer's Dead servants, the Charter magic of Major Greene and Lieutenant Tindall is of no use (*Abhorsen* 323–24). Even so, these people are portrayed as wise because of their magical learning, whereas the refusal to admit that magic exists is held up as the main weakness of Ancelstierran society—a weakness that is repeatedly pointed out in connection to the Wall and the Perimeter. In *Lirael/Abhorsen*, for example, the stubborn refusal of Sam's cricket coach and, in particular, of Sam's friend Nick to accept magic as more than superstition has near-disastrous results. Magic is constructed as the norm; technology, so unreliable at the border, is portrayed as an anomaly.

The superiority of magic is paralleled by the familiarization of the magical, and the consequent defamiliarization of the technological, domain. Instead of establishing Ancelstierre as a version of the primary world, as something familiar to the reader, it is the magical domain of the Old Kingdom that is familiarized, and this even though it is substantially different from the largely standardized worlds of Tolkien's epigones. Especially *Sabriel* adheres to a traditional story arc for a portal–quest fantasy, according to which "a character leaves her familiar surroundings and passes through a portal into an unknown place" only to bring restoration to this unknown place.[42] However, it quickly becomes clear that the Old Kingdom is not "unknown" to Sabriel, and since she is the focal character, it just as quickly becomes familiar to the reader. Ancelstierre, on the other hand, loses its familiar features as these are mediated by the focal character's Old Kingdom frame of reference. The defamiliarization is further reinforced by the emphasis on the ridiculous and ineffectual aspects of the technological Perimeter. In *Lirael/Abhorsen*, Nick's constant refusal to accept the magical Old Kingdom reality while it is perfectly understandable to the reader similarly establishes the magical domain as familiar, especially when Nick is contrasted with Sam, who has no problem grasping both realities.

The bias toward magic and the magical domain is undermined, however. While skepticism toward magic is ridiculed in the text, those Ancelstierrans who have accepted magic (like Colonel Horyse, Captain Tindall, and, in the novella, Nick Sayre) are valorized. The Wall fails to keep evil, magical beings from entering the technological domain, almost leading to disaster in both *Sabriel* and *Lirael/Abhorsen*. This circumstance also highlights the fact that the antagonists in all three stories have their roots in the Old Kingdom: a powerful Dead creature, a god-like force set on annihilation, and a magical being, respectively. In particular, the Destroyer demonstrates that unadulterated evil belongs to the domain of magic: its force clearly recalls a nuclear bomb, the most devastating technical device of the actual world, but it is cast in more far-reaching terms, as a powerful entity with hatred for all life. The evil that hails from the domain of magic is defeated in the technological domain, however. The heroic self-sacrifice of Ancelstierran schoolgirls and Perimeter troops in the face of incomprehensible, magical evil in *Sabriel* and *Lirael/Abhorsen*, and, in "Nicholas Sayre," Nick's self-sacrifice and nondefeatist attitude, make the difference between failure and happy ending. For all its supposedly quasi-divine power, the Wall is as ineffectual as the Perimeter when it comes to defeating evil. Instead, it is the valor of Ancelstierrans that allows anything of the day to be saved.

Ultimately, the border between Ancelstierre and the Old Kingdom becomes a focus for courage in the face of the unknown. The unknown is always feared, which is why Ancelstierrans try so hard to defend themselves and still deny that there is anything to defend themselves against. To them, magic can do the impossible. Their attempts either to ignore or to understand this are portrayed as ridiculous, ineffective, or crude at best. The characters from the magical domain, on the other hand, need not fear what is basically only a domain of absence: the Ancelstierran technology is unable to produce anything that cannot be made by magic. At the end of the day, however, magic proves to be just as fallible as technology, and when the Wall's attempts to protect the southern neighbor fail, it is up to the Ancelstierrans to overcome their fear. When they do that, the true heroism of these stories becomes evident: in people entering a battle against the *unknown* threat.

The Threshold with a Thousand Guises

In *The Hero with a Thousand Faces*, Joseph Campbell introduces the concept of the monomyth, the mythological adventure of a hero's journey from the everyday lands into a supernatural region and back.[43] Many fantasy protagonists follow the same trajectory, crossing—like their mythological counterparts—the border between the ordinary and the unknown.[44] To Campbell, the crossing of the *first threshold* occurs when the hero enters the unknown and moves into a realm of adventure. Looking at the examples from Brust, Gaiman/Vess, and Nix from a Campbellian perspective reveals how the borders function in what are essentially hero stories, although these stories do not necessarily follow every step of Campbell's monomyth. He points out that "[t]he two worlds, the divine and the human, can be pictured only as distinct from each other."[45] In the three examples just discussed, that is how the pairs of domains are initially described: distinct from each other and with borders that give a first impression of being clear lines between two domains. In all three cases, this initial impression turns out to be erroneous. The border is fuzzy and vague, an area of transition. Waterfalls and walls appear to be sharply defined; but instead, just as Clute suggests, the threshold is a gradient. It is not possible to stand with a foot on either side, regardless of what we think at first. And even though the fantasy hero can return from the other domain, as Zerika does, the border can also be used to upset, reverse, or complicate the very worldview it seems to advance: the Dragaeran social values apparently upheld by the land of the dead and the Deathgate are subverted by the return of Vlad and his companions; the wall and its guards in Wall defend the imagination of Faerie, not the rational hegemony of mundanity; and magic's seeming superiority is undermined and challenged by the Ancelstierrans' courage.

Courage is vital when confronting the unknown beyond the border. "The hero," Campbell writes, "adventures out of the land we know into darkness; there he accomplishes his adventure [. . .] and his return is described as a coming back out of that yonder zone."[46] "There and back again" is the pattern of the heroes' adventures, not only when they are hobbits. To cross the border, the first threshold, is to enter a magical, unknown, even divine world.[47] No matter if the border is part of everyday life, what lies beyond it is dangerous. "The usual person is more than content, he is even proud, to remain within the indicated bounds, and popular belief gives him every reason to fear so much as the first step into the unexplored," according to Campbell.[48] Venturing into Death, Faerie, or the Old Kingdom is better avoided by everyone but the heroes. In all three cases, however, the heroes cross, not because they are braver but because they have a special inheritance, are bearers of special blood. Vlad, Zerika, Tristran, and Sabriel are all born to the right to cross the border.

Ultimately, as we saw, the challenge lies in returning. Without returning, the journey is for naught; nothing will have been saved. Vlad and Zerika both save the Empire through their return. Only by coming back from Faerie can Tristran learn of his inheritance. Only in Ancelstierre can Kerrigor (the antagonist from *Sabriel*) and the Destroyer be defeated. With the return comes the realization that despite the border, the two domains are parts of one world, not separated from each other. "[T]he two kingdoms are actually one," claims Campbell, for whom this unity is the key to understanding myth and symbol.[49] While it might not be the key to the literary constructions that are fantasy worlds, it is nevertheless a reminder of a central fact about these worlds. Life and death, Faerie and mundanity, magical and technological domains have borders because they belong together, not because they are separate and unconnected.

THE GEOGRAPHY OF HISTORY: POLDERS IN TOLKIEN, HOLDSTOCK, AND PRATCHETT

Not everyone is let in; but those who are will find that regardless of whether they have walked into a mysterious forest, descended into a hidden valley, or entered a curious house, the rules of the world have changed. Fantasy geography is sprinkled liberally with such places, of varying size and (to their respective stories) importance. They might be as small as a single building or as large as a country, and they are often larger on the inside than on the outside. Likening such enclosed domains to the Dutch lowland areas that are protected from the surrounding sea by dykes, Kaveney suggested the term *polder* for them.[50] The term was further developed by Clute in *The Encyclopedia of Fantasy*, in which he defines polders as

> enclaves of toughened reality, demarcated by boundaries [. . .] from the surrounding world. It is central to our definition of the polder that these boundaries are *maintained*; some significant figure within the tale almost certainly comprehends and has acted upon (in the backstory, or during the course of the ongoing plot) the need to maintain them. A polder, in other words, is an *active* microcosm, armed against the potential wrongness of that which surrounds it, an anachronism *consciously* opposed to wrong time.[51]

The assertion that a polder is an anachronism opposed to wrong time deserves further comment. Clute claims that "[s]uccessful polders do not change. Polders change only when they are being devoured from without."[52] In other words, for a polder, the internal and external realities are set up as opposing forces, and as long as the polder is successfully maintained, it does not change. The world outside does, however, and its change widens the temporal gap between the two realities. The polder becomes a maintained anachronism—that is, an anachronism opposed to the time of the surrounding world, actively if not consciously (because it begs the question: whose consciousness?). The external time is, and must be, the *wrong time*, since, in a polder, any time but its own is wrong. Hence, a polder must not only be maintained but also defended from external influence. "Surrounding the polder," Clute continues, "is a world whose effects may—all unconsciously—be inimical."[53]

With reference to *Stardust*, I discussed how a domain on one side of a border might be hostile to the domain on the other side—how mundanity threatens Faerie. Yet the other domain need not be hostile, as in the example from the Brust novels. For polders, danger from without is the rule rather than the exception. Although the surrounding wrongness is, according to Clute, only *potential*, I would like to add that it is also highly probable. Maintenance is required for a reason; without it, the polder boundary would collapse and the polder with it. The threat to the polder's existence is present in one form or another. It might not be part of the plot, but it is always there, as can be seen from the examples that follow.

Three of the genre's multitude of polders have been chosen to illustrate different aspects of how polder boundaries are maintained and crossed. All three are geographical features in one way or another, and they also exemplify how the various realities are protected from their respective surroundings. Tolkien's elven realm of Lothlórien (in *The Lord of the Rings*) is a typical polder. Clearly maintained by Lady Galadriel and her Ring of Power, the elven realm is an anachronism where the long-gone past still remains and where time flows differently from the way it does on the outside. Lothlórien is caught between the devil and the deep blue sea, either falling to the forces of Sauron or fading away once the One Ring is destroyed; its fate is thus inextricably bound to the plot of the novel. Robert Holdstock's Ryhope Wood (in the Mythago Wood cycle [1984–2009]) is also an anachronism, a rather small clump of wildwood that has managed to remain in place since the last Ice Age. As with the elven polder, the past opens up in the forest; but here, time and space are connected: the farther in one ventures, the deeper into the past one ends up. The polder differs from Lothlórien by lacking a clearly identifiable character who maintains it. Instead, it is maintained and defended by the life force of the woodlands. This forest is at the center of the story, not a place to pass through, and characters are attracted to and into it. The plots of the novels have little to do with what danger the surrounding countryside presents, although the obvious threat, the felling of trees, is occasionally alluded to. The final example, Pratchett's Egyptian parody Djelibeybi (in *Pyramids* [1989]), demonstrates how a polder can be maintained by forces less personal than Galadriel and more human than the forest life force. Like the previous examples, Djelibeybi is an anachronism, a place where nothing new happens. Here, the past, and thus the polder, is maintained through a combination of the literal destruction of new time and fierce upholding of traditions. The plot is focused on how influences from the surrounding world are brought into conflict with the traditions and with the high priest who maintains them. These three examples demonstrate some of the various ways in which the core features of a polder, an anachronism whose maintained boundaries separate it from the inimical surrounding world, can be employed.

Damming the Tides of Time: Tolkien's Lothlórien[54]
Although the "Polder" entry in *The Encyclopedia of Fantasy* specifically mentions Tom Bombadil's realm as an example of a polder in *The Lord of the Rings*, J. R. R. Tolkien's most typical polder is the elven realm of Lothlórien, maintained by Galadriel and her Ring of Power. Lothlórien is like a piece of Faerie surrounded by mundanity, the High Elves' last re-

maining kingdom and, as such, an anachronism preserving a piece of the Elder Days (which ended some six millennia before Frodo sets off with the Ring). Lothlórien is presented through its boundaries, whose gradual nature becomes evident as the Company enters the polder. The approach is, as Tom Shippey puts it, "an oddly complex one,"[55] something he demonstrates by examining the Company's crossings of the rivers Nimrodel and Silverlode. These are, however, only two of a number of stages required of the Company as it goes into the polder. The full five stages of the "oddly complex" approach are, I would argue, entering the mallorn forest; wading across the Nimrodel; meeting the guards; crossing the Silverlode; and finally walking blindfolded to Cerin Amroth. Only then does Frodo fully experience how extraordinary a place the elven realm is. Let us examine these stages in greater detail:

The *first* stage, entering the mallorn forest, stresses the danger of the elven realm but also relates it to Faerie. When the Company arrives at Lothlórien's northern border, the trees give a rather uninviting impression. This adds emphasis to the suggestion of an entrance to a magical place where they are all in danger. In the dim light of the stars, tall, gray trees spread their boughs over the road, and the Company hears a rustling of dry leaves in a chilly breeze. There is nothing magical about this part of what Legolas calls "the Golden Wood," only unfamiliar trees, the description of which does not really match Legolas's delight. Gimli's doubt that any elves still live there is perfectly understandable, especially given his previous dismay at finding Moria in the hands of orcs. Despite the enthusiasm of Legolas and Aragorn, Boromir is hesitant, explaining that "of that perilous land we have heard in Gondor, and it is said that few come out who once go in" (FR, II, vi, 329). Although Aragorn rebukes him for thinking evil of Lothlórien, Boromir insists that it is perilous. "Perilous indeed," Aragorn agrees, "fair and perilous," adding that "only evil need fear it, or those who bring some evil with them" (FR, II, vi, 329).

Two details are worth noting in their exchange. First, there is the repeated use of the word *perilous*. Tolkien used the expression *The Perilous Realm* as a synonym for Faerie in "On Fairy-stories,"[56] and the frequent occurrence of the adjective right at the entrance to the elven realm does more than draw attention to the possible dangers to be faced there. It also associates Lothlórien with Faerie, suggesting that the polder is a domain beyond the mundanity of Middle-earth. Second, Aragorn explains to Boromir how the Golden Wood is perilous to "those who bring some evil with them." None of the hobbits has taken part in the discussion at this point, but Frodo is still present, carrying Sauron's Ring around his neck. The Company is, in other words, bringing with it the most evil artifact in the world. On top of the inhospitable description of the forest and Boromir's misgivings, Aragorn actually confirms that Lothlórien is a dangerous place for them. At the first stage, entering the forest thus becomes a question of overcoming fear and willingly walking into danger.

Once in the forest, the *second* stage is the wading across the Nimrodel, which cleanses the Company in preparation for Lothlórien. According to Legolas, "the water is healing to the weary" and "the sound of the falling water may bring us sleep and forgetfulness of grief" (FR, II, vi, 330). This is plainly not just water, a point emphasized by Haldir's vehemence at the thought of orcs wading across: "curse their foul feet in its clean water!" (FR, II, vi, 336). Indeed, when Frodo crosses the Nimrodel, the hobbit feels "that the stain of travel and all weariness was washed from his limbs" (FR, II, vi, 330). *Stain* is an important word here. Shippey observes that this might quite literally mean that "Frodo feels the grime of Moria being washed off, but," he continues, "'stain' is a slightly odd word to use in this context."[57] Instead, Shippey relates it to two later descriptions of Lothlórien, in which *stain* is used to describe a quality of the elven land (cf. FR, II, iv, 341, and TT, III, vi, 503), suggesting that "the 'stain' of normal life is washed off by crossing the Nimrodel."[58] The passage across the stream thus prepares the Company for a land without a "stain" by removing their own "stains." At the time of the crossing, however, the importance of this cleansing is mostly lost on the Company and the reader, because no one tries to stop them. Apart from Legolas's explanation and Frodo's experience, nothing suggests that the passage is in any way special. We only learn this later, through Haldir's explanation: the guards had heard Legolas's voice, and therefore had not prevented the Company from crossing (FR, II, vi, 333). Rather than facing the guards at the Nimrodel, the Company now faces them on the other side.

Haldir and his two fellow guards constitute the *third* stage, and the first sign that this realm is actually defended against inimical surroundings. Not everyone is allowed to enter; in fact, it is only because of Aragorn's previous reputation and because Legolas is also an elf that the Company is admitted. The basic rule is to hinder everyone from entering, because anyone could be a potential enemy. "We live now upon an island amid many perils," Haldir says, justifying his lack of faith in the Company (FR, II, vi, 339); and although he only mentions Sauron's forces, the elf's words imply suspicion of all mortals. Haldir's use of *perils* turns the perspective around. Rather than being a perilous realm, as Boromir and Aragorn agree, it is a place in peril. As in *Stardust*'s Faerie, the elves are very particular about whom they let into their land.

The *fourth* stage takes the Company from the outside world into the polder's distinctive reality. Having been allowed to enter, the Company crosses the Silverlode on a rope-bridge. According to Shippey, "there are continuing hints that the rivers which the Fellowship keeps crossing are leading them further and further out of the world."[59] Certainly, a distinct difference exists between the forests on either side of the river. Once Frodo sets foot on the other side of the Silverlode, "it seemed to him that he had stepped over a bridge of time into a corner of the Elder Days" (FR, II, vi, 340). I will return later to the bridge of time. More relevant for now is to observe that this feeling of Frodo's "deepened as he walked on into the Naith [of Lothlórien]" (FR, II, vi, 340). It is not until the Company has crossed the Silverlode that its members have moved out of the normal world, and they move only gradually away from its influence.

The *final* stage is the walk from the edge of the polder to where its distinct reality comes to full expression. The Company walks along blindfolded from the edge, and although Frodo experiences, more and more strongly, that the group has entered a different place—or rather, a different time—he has not yet fully experienced how much the heartland of Lothlórien differs from the world outside. At some indefinite point during the long walk, however, the Fellowship enters a forest where the power of the elves dominates completely. When Frodo removes his blindfold at Cerin Amroth, the place Aragorn calls "the heart of Elvendom on earth" (FR, II, vi, 343), his experience of the land is radically different from what he felt when they had crossed the river:

> It seemed to him that he had stepped through a high window that looked on a vanished world. A light was upon it for which his language had no name. All that he saw was shapely, but the shapes seemed at once clear-cut, as if they had been first conceived and drawn at the uncovering of his eyes, and ancient as if they had endured for ever. He saw no color but those he knew, gold and white and blue and green, but they were fresh and poignant, as if he had at that moment first perceived them and made for them names new and wonderful. In winter here no heart could mourn for summer or for spring. No blem-

ish or sickness or deformity could be seen in anything that grew upon the earth. On the land of Lórien there was no stain. (FR, II, vi, 341)

This impression is far stronger than when he first entered the forest, or even when he first set foot in the Naith. Although he has the time-bridge experience when he crosses the Silverlode, the breathtaking beauty of Cerin Amroth is clearly absent. Instead of being awed by their surroundings, the members of the Company bicker about whom to blindfold. Once the particular reality of the Golden Wood is revealed at Cerin Amroth, Frodo is lost in wonder. Here, he has finally arrived in the land without a stain that requires those who enter to have been cleansed.

It is at Cerin Amroth that Frodo becomes aware of the force that protects the forest, and the reader understands that the polder is maintained by someone. Haldir first bids that Frodo look toward the capital: "Out of it, it seemed to [Frodo] that the power and light came that held all the land in sway" (FR, II, vi, 342), a power he later learns comes from the elven Ring of Power held by Galadriel. As he looks the other way, across the river, the light goes out; he sees "the world he knew" (an expression that brings to mind Dunsany's "fields we know," again suggesting the association between Lothlórien and Faerie), and, farther off, Mirkwood and the darkness surrounding Dol Goldur. Haldir tells him how the two opposing powers of Galadriel and Sauron "strive now in thought" (FR, II, vi, 342–43). While the borders have so far seemed to be defended by elven guards, a new kind of defense is thus revealed: the power of Galadriel and her Ring that maintains and protects Lothlórien from the hostile world beyond. As foretold by the Lady of Lothlórien, the land fades once the power of the Rings is broken; and when, after Aragorn's death, Arwen returns to the empty land, she "dwelt there alone under the fading trees" (Appx A, I, 1038).

A polder not only defends its inhabitants from attack or invasion, it also defends and maintains a reality that differs from its surroundings. In Lothlórien, two main aspects of reality need protecting: the physical environment and the temporal situation. Physically, the forest of Lothlórien is little more than a park. Treebeard's assertion that the old woodlands that stretched from Fangorn Forest to the Mountains of Lune west of the Shire "were like the woods of Lothlórien, only thicker, stronger, younger" (TT, III, iv, 458) comes across as somewhat peculiar. Fangorn Forest is clearly wildwood, tangled and dark. Looking at the lichen-encrusted trees, Pippin succinctly summarizes his impression of the forest: "Untidy" (TT, III, iv, 450). Lothlórien, on the other hand, appears to consist of nothing but the mallorn trees, with their smooth, silver boles. The ground is level enough for the Company to wander freely without any fear of stubbing toes or falling over (FR, II, vi, 340). The old woodlands are, in fact, nothing like Lothlórien, because rather than being a forest, the Golden Wood is carefully maintained parkland, a monoculture as unnatural as any orchard or tree plantation. In "Taking the Part of Trees: Eco-Conflict in Middle-earth," Verlyn Flieger discusses how Tolkien seems to come down in favor of both wildwood and carefully cultivated nature. Lothlórien, she suggests, is a vision of "nature transcended." It is "a faery forest that is unlikely to be found in a natural state on earth," "an enchanted and enchanting correlative of the Entwives and their ordered, tended gardens."[60] In her book on Tolkien's treatment of time and time travel, *A Question of Time*, Flieger cites a letter from Tolkien in which he describes the elves as "embalmers" who wanted "to live in the mortal historical Middle-earth [and so] stop its growth, keep it as a pleasaunce."[61] Despite its enchantment, or perhaps because of it, Lothlórien is more pleasance (a magically created version of those ancient but well-tended parks found around some old country houses) than nature transcended. It is a perfect example of elven embalming.

Time in Lothlórien is markedly different from time in the world outside. It is quite clearly "an anachronism *consciously* opposed to [the] wrong time"[62] of Middle-earth outside. The gap between outside and polder time recalls the vast history that underlies Middle-earth, and the fact that the power of Galadriel's Ring is required to maintain that gap heralds the end of the elves. To Frodo, crossing the Silverlode is like walking across time into the Elder Days and "a world that was no more." This world is different even from Rivendell, where "there was memory of ancient things; in Lórien the ancient things still lived on in the waking world" (FR, II, vi, 340). A time abyss, "a gap between the present of the tale and some point deep in the past,"[63] opens up in Rivendell when Frodo learns that Elrond not only knows of the Elder Days more than six millennia ago, but can remember them (FR, II, ii, 236–37; cf. Appx B). In Lothlórien, he suddenly finds himself at the bottom of that abyss, in "a corner of the Elder Days," together with elves far older than Elrond. Sam tries to express his impression of the land: "I feel as if I was *inside* a song, if you take my meaning" (FR, II, vi, 342). There is no doubt that he does not mean Pippin's bath song or his own Troll song but rather songs such as Aragorn's about Beren and Lúthien, or Bilbo's about Eärendil, or *The Fall of Gil-galad*, which Sam has learned from Bilbo—songs about events that took place thousands of years earlier. Haldir explains that it is the power of Galadriel that he feels, something that she confirms. Lothlórien's boundary is maintained by the power of her Ring, and as such, it will fail if the One Ring is destroyed. "[T]hen our power is diminished," Galadriel explains to Frodo, "and Lothlórien will fade, and the tides of Time will sweep it away. We must depart into the West, or dwindle to a rustic folk of dell and cave, slowly to forget and to be forgotten" (FR, II, vii, 356). The time of the outside world will rush into the polder if Frodo succeeds in his quest, and not only the beauty of Lothlórien will be ruined. Galadriel's words forebode the loss inherent in triumph: by the defeat of Sauron and destruction of the One Ring, the power of the elves is also forced out of the world. The "sudden joyous 'turn'" that Tolkien calls *eucatastrophe* or "good catastrophe" might bring joy, but it is joy mingled with grief, deliverance mingled with loss.[64]

Time in the polder has not stopped, but it passes differently from time in the world outside.[65] "Elves and Men will live in the world at different speeds, as it were, and their intersecting paths must involve a shift, on some level, from time to timelessness," Flieger observes.[66] Paul H. Kocher draws attention to the relation between passage of time and elven psychology: how, for the deathless elves, time passes both swiftly and slowly.[67] Although the temporal aspect is only called attention to when the Company has left the elves and Sam is puzzled by the new moon (FR, II, ix, 379), a vagueness about the passage of time pervades the entire Lothlórien episode. Flieger discusses in detail how time flows in Lothlórien as compared to the outside world.[68] Having examined Tolkien's musings on time in Lothlórien from *The Treason of Isengard*,[69] she concludes that after an "interior argument," Tolkien appears to have decided that it is "[b]etter to have *no* time difference" between Lothlórien and the outside world. Nevertheless, time in Lothlórien remains vague and imprecise because "Tolkien's theme, if not his plot, needed two kinds of time."[70]

The clearest example of how time in the elven forest flows according to its own rules is provided during the Company's final day there. To summarize their itinerary: they rise and walk with Haldir to the boats, a distance of about ten miles. When "noon [is] at hand," they reach the tongue of land where the Silverlode passes into the river Anduin. They pack the boats and go for a test-drive up the river, run into Celeborn and Galadriel, and have a parting feast. After the feast, Celeborn informs them of the lay of the land along the river and Galadriel imparts her gifts. Then the Company leaves, as a "yellow noon [lies] on the green land" (FR, II, viii, 360–67). Unless the Company and the elves are remarkably efficient with their packing, partying, and presents, something must have happened to time here. It seems almost to have ceased inside Lothlórien, allowing for a greater number of actions than usual to be performed in a briefer (outside) time. The simplest explanation would be to ascribe this temporal anomaly to textual mistakes. According to "The Tale of Years," Frodo and Sam are taken to Galadriel's Mirror on February 14 and the Company departs from Lothlórien on February 16 (RK, Appx B, 1067). Because the hobbits look into the Mirror on what is obviously the Company's last evening in Caras Galadhon (FR, II, viii, 358–60), the critics Wayne G. Hammond and Christina Scull suggest that a mistake has been made and that the correct date for the Mirror of Galadriel in "The Tale of Years" should be February 15.[71]

The question is, would "a writer known for scrupulous attention to the calendar"[72] make not one but two mistakes for two consecutive dates? An alternative interpretation is possible. February 16, the day of departure, is the day with two noons. Does one noon, in fact, belong to the fifteenth and one to the sixteenth? Does the parting feast take them through the night and out on the other side without anyone noticing? Do Lothlórien days and nights, up to the very last, pass faster than on the outside? This would not only explain what seem like inconsistencies, it would also fit Sam's bewildered attempt to recall more than a handful of days of an entire month. The two noons thus suggest both a moment stretched into hours and hours folded into a moment, ultimately indicating how time in Lothlórien, as in *Stardust*'s Faerie, does not simply pass faster or more slowly than in the mortal world but follows completely different rules.

The process of gaining entrance to Lothlórien not only emphasizes the diligence with which this polder is defended, it also displays the gradual nature of the boundary. Gradual, but not that of a crosshatch: despite the stages that the Company passes, it is not until they have crossed the Silverlode that they find themselves in a different reality. The parts of the elven realm that reach beyond the river are clearly part of the land but follow the rules of the outside world. Lothlórien is a Faerie realm that strives to maintain ancient times when the surrounding world moves on, providing a sanctuary for its elven population. That its existence is connected to the One Ring must surely count as the second great tragedy encountered by the reader in the story; but unlike Gandalf's fall into the chasm in Moria, Lothlórien's doom is never negated. Yet this park imparts an eerie vision of time as well as nature: both are constant in the elven realm, ultimately providing sterile beauty and time without change. Tolkien called his elves embalmers, and this polder provides an example of their embalming art.

The Forest of Twisting Paths: Holdstock's Mythago Wood [73]

Ryhope Wood is a patch of wildwood, some six miles in circumference, in rural Herefordshire. Even though a large proportion of Robert Holdstock's Mythago Wood cycle is set in the surrounding countryside, the forest provides a gravitational center for the stories. Within the impenetrable boundaries of this small forest unfold seemingly limitless woodlands where inherited memories from our collective unconscious come to life as so-called mythagos. The novels of the cycle—*Mythago Wood*, *Lavondyss*, *The Hollowing*, *Gate of Ivory*, and *Avilion*—all tell the stories of their protagonists' journeys into, and in, the woods, journeys during which the forest acts upon the characters while allowing them to act in the forest.

Whereas the Lothlórien polder provides stability and constancy, Ryhope Wood, similarly an actively defended anachronism, is a locus of change. Each of the five novels in the series describes a place where space and time are fluid and mutable; and the polder also evolves over the novels into increasingly complex settings for the characters' journeys.

The force that maintains the polder is a nebulous presence in the forest rather than a clearly identifiable entity. The direct action it takes to keep the woodland's secrets bears witness to its power, though. Unable to penetrate the woodland defenses, *Mythago Wood*'s first-person narrator, Steven, seeks to fly over the woodlands to get an overview of their interior. He and the pilot, Harry Keeton, set out to take pictures of the mysterious forest from above, but fail; the plane is tossed by heavy winds, a golden light enshrouds it, and a loud, ghostly wail is heard, forcing them to turn back (*Mythago Wood* 100–101). This powerful display is the only instance when the force that protects the polder takes direct physical action, but it leaves little doubt that there *is* a force that actively maintains the boundaries. George Huxley, Steven's father, believes that the small stand of primordial wildwood

> had survived by *defending* itself against the destructive behavior [. . .] of the human population that was settling around it. Over the millennia, the concentration of time and spirit in the wood had made it into something more than just trees [. . .]. It had become an entity, not conscious, not watching, but somehow sentient and to an astonishing degree timeless. (*Hollowing* 64)

The process suggests a virtuous circle, where successful defense leads to an increased concentration of time and spirit—Huxley uses the word *aura* (e.g., *Mythago Wood* 49)—which in turn results in greater sentience and thus better defenses. This brief description makes clear how central time is in connection with the polder. The process has taken millennia; the concentration of time and spirit has given rise to the sentience; and, somewhat contradictorily, the forest is astonishingly timeless. Over the course of the books, it becomes clear that the contradiction derives from the straightforward progression of time outside the forest polder and the temporal flux inside it.

The sentient woodland force, and the mythagos to which it gives rise, acts on the countryside around it. Its action on the surrounding world is one of the reasons why Mendlesohn considers *Mythago Wood* to be an intrusive fantasy. "[T]he wood's field reaches out into the world," she points out, and the field "allows the wood's inhabitants/manifestations to burst through into modern life."[74] In fact, the forest reaches out— mainly through mythagos, but occasionally through other means—in all five novels. In *Mythago Wood*, a band of oak saplings stretches from the forest to the Oak Lodge, growing far faster than normal, culminating in the sudden appearance of an enormous oak in the study (*Mythago Wood* 88, 141–42). Tallis in *Lavondyss* is insidiously introduced to the forest and taught how to open portals into its depths, so-called hollowings. In *The Hollowing*, Alex's spirit is partially sucked into the wood through one of Tallis's masks, and the boy is subsequently abducted physically by a mythago version of the Green Knight (*Hollowing* 27–29, 296–99). Steven's brother, Christian, is brought into the forest by the schemes of the mythago Kylhuk in *Gate of Ivory*. In *Avilion*, the ancient Amurngoth, or fairies, steal human children and replace them with their own.

The books in the Mythago Wood cycle are, to use Marek Oziewicz's expression, *novels of visitations*, "the kind of visitations the protagonist does not expect, which he dreads and yet becomes increasingly fascinated with while being drawn into wanting them to recur."[75] This power of dread–fascination–attraction is most obvious in the mythago character Guiwenneth, whom Clute refers to as "the seducer seduced."[76] "[T]he notion of the intrusion as seducer," Mendlesohn observes, "is made manifest as the wood in the form of Guiwenneth, who pulls first George Huxley and then his two sons within its embrace."[77]

People are pulled into the forest, through its manifestations or inhabitants, because it needs something from their minds, and they are brought past the boundary defenses. The human subconscious is a source of creative energy used by the mythogenic process to "seed" the forest with mythago inhabitants. In *The Hollowing*, Alex's father, Richard, experiences how "a world [is] forming from his mind in the vampire wood around him" (*Hollowing* 96). Tallis loses energy to the forest, which is "sucking out her soul, her spirit. It was sucking out her dreams. It was draining her" (*Lavondyss* 247). Having been trapped in the forest for years, Huxley's colleague Wynne-Jones is left empty, a native inhabitant of the forest (*Lavondyss* 203), and Steven suggests that he has become a part of the forest in *Avilion* (114). Unlike in the first four novels, it is suggested in *Avilion* that the mythogenic process is not purely passive; the main characters have some slight control. Steven and Guiwenneth's son, Jack, intentionally calls up a mythago of his grandfather (e.g., 161–62); Jack's sister, Yssobel, dreams up parts of Avilion (another name for Lavondyss, the Otherworld at the forest's heart) (e.g., 200–201); and Steven exerts some measure of control in his search for a suitable place to live in the forest (94).

The forest's need for people is why the boundary appears to both pull and push: while the forest does its best to keep outsiders in general away from the heartwood, some are pulled in and helped past the defenses. No character strays into this forest by mistake; all are led by a guide, brought against their will, or consciously force their way in. Steven and Keeton, for instance, very clearly fight their way through the forest defenses; and through their entry, the full extent of those defenses becomes plain:

First, there was disorientation. We found ourselves walking *back* the way we had come. At times it was almost possible to experience the switch in perception. We felt dizzy; the underwood became preter-naturally dark; the sound of the river changed from our left to our right. [. . .] Somehow we passed that first defensive zone. The wood began to haunt us. Trees seemed to move. Branches fell upon us . . . in our mind's eyes only, but not before we had reacted with exhausting shock. The ground seemed to writhe at times, and split open. We smelled fumes, fire, a stench like decay. (*Mythago Wood* 207)

Disorientation is the defense that is most persistently mentioned. Unwelcome visitors are turned away, led out, and never manage to pass the woodland's periphery. On his own and unwanted by the forest, Steven cannot breach this defense and is unable to enter more than two hundred yards into the woods (*Mythago Wood* 92–93). Huxley's diary similarly mentions the difficulty of penetrating into the heartwood. Once humans are drawn in by the forest, however, disorientation also keeps them in, frustrating their attempts to leave. Richard, for instance, is unable to walk even the short distance from the Horse Shrine camp back to Oak Lodge (*Hollowing* 71–72, 74–75). The disorientation can be overcome, however. By keeping to the river, Steven and Keeton manage to maintain their orientation, but they are instead haunted by illusions. On the ground, the forest does not defend itself in such a physically violent manner as when the two attempt to fly over it. Instead, its defenses are related to the first stages of mythogenesis (the creation of mythagos), which are characterized by half-glimpsed images in the corner of the eye, rather than by fully formed (and physical) mythagos.

Humans are kept in the forest, providing material for mythogenesis until they have been emptied of dreams and myths and have been made parts of myths themselves. Because the forest needs people to seed itself with mythagos and also must prevent possible external threats from arising, it maintains its pull, drawing or (physically) dragging back any who manage to escape. Christian leaves at the end of *Gate of Ivory* but cannot give up his search for Guiwenneth, a search that eventually leads to his death in *Mythago Wood* and again in *Avilion*. Steven, Keeton, and Tallis all stay, unable to find their way out. Even in *The Hollowing*, in which the protagonists appear to have a chance of returning, the reader never actually sees them do so, or even start on their way out. Keeton and Tallis's father manages to get out, but he remains spiritually shackled to the forest through Tallis's Moondream mask. Only in *Avilion* does the wood eventually allow Steven and his son to leave, but like his brother before him, Steven keeps returning into the forest, unable to abandon his search for Guiwenneth.

Because of the manifestations of myths, the polder's structure is not only spatial; it is a structure of places connected to the myths: mythago landscapes, buildings, and seasons. W. A. Senior calls this landscape a representation of "the unlimited potential of the mind and creative impulse,"[78] and Tallis is told that the world in the forest "is not nature, it consists of mind" (*Lavondyss* 287). Likewise, the secret behind the polder's impossibly large interior is that it consists not of natural landscape but of the landscapes of myths. This landscape is made up of *mythotopes*,[79] the habitats of myths, places suited to the myths they harbor. Mythotopes are created through mythogenesis along with their heroes (see *Lavondyss* 160), and they are the reason why the woodlands open up endlessly as the characters travel inward.

Looking at the characters' journeys in the novels reveals how the mythotopic structure evolves from novel to novel—the polder is not identical in all five stories. The basic structure is the labyrinth, found in its simplest form in *Mythago Wood*. In his review of *Gate of Ivory*, Clute describes that novel as "an arduous tale which leads its protagonists, arduously, through many labyrinthine meanders, into the arduous heart of fantasy."[80] On one level or another, all the novels can be discussed in terms of labyrinthine structures, although I will focus on the relation between mythotopical structures and character journeys. The path Steven follows through the forest in *Mythago Wood* twists and turns but never really leaves him with any choices.[81] It is a path that conforms to what Umberto Eco calls a linear labyrinth[82] and Penelope Reed Doob describes as a unicursal labyrinth, where "a single unbranched [. . .] circuitous route leads inevitably, if at great length, to the center."[83] The river along which Steven and Keeton travel suggests such a circuitous path, curving and curling through the woodlands (*Mythago Wood* 244, 280); and the only fork that is implied occurs where they leave Christian's trail, guided by a mythago. The inevitability of the unicursal path is echoed in the inevitability of Steven's quest; the further he pursues his brother, and the deeper into the forest he travels, the more he becomes the Kinsman of myth, doomed to eventually kill the equally mythic Outsider that Christian has become, regardless of his own intentions.

In *Lavondyss*, the polder is a forest of forking paths. Tallis's route is not the inevitable, unicursal labyrinth of Steven's journey. Her years of wandering, lost among the protean mythotopes and through unpredictable hollowings, suggest that the forest path is one of innumerable forks and dead ends. It is, in Doob's terminology, a multicursal rather than a unicursal labyrinth,[84] the kind that Eco refers to as a maze. "In a maze," he states, "one can make mistakes. [. . .] Some alternatives end at a point where one is obliged to return backwards, whereas others generate new branches, and only one among them leads to the way out."[85] A mytho-topic maze is more difficult to negotiate than a spatial maze, because it allows for more than spatial choices. The protean nature of the mytho-topes means that backtracking does not return the traveler to an original location, and the forest defenses disorient the travelers. Only slowly are Tallis and her mythago companion drawn inward along the one route that leads not out of the forest but to its center.

The multitude of paths that the forest offers in *The Hollowing*, on land and through hollowings, within and between the numerous layers of woodland Otherworlds, takes the forest beyond the multicursal maze of *Lavondyss*. It resembles the type of labyrinth that Eco calls a net: "The main feature of a net is that every point can be connected with every other point."[86] In the forest in *The Hollowing*, it is implied that every mythotope can be reached from any other mythotope by some route or another. The routes are not necessarily short or obvious, however, and the possibility of losing one's way is ever present. Eco also claims that "the abstract model of a net has neither a center nor an outside,"[87] and whereas Ryhope Wood does have an outside, it is an outside that is im-possibly small compared to the inner vastness. Furthermore, unlike the other three books, *The Hollowing* contains no quest for a Lavondyss at the center of the wood. The heart of the wood and the goal for the quest in this novel is Alex's hiding-place, located somewhere in the forest net, and any one of several routes leads there. As if the net of paths through the forest were not disorienting enough, this structure is further compli-cated by the enigmatic and ubiquitous "rootweb" through which Alex can send his consciousness and see things all over the forest, a web under-lying the net.

In the cycle's fourth book, the complex structure of *The Hollowing* remains, but the journey is one of a small polder within the forest, a polder that creates its own path. When Legion, Kylhuk's host of my-thago heroes, marches through the forest in *Gate of Ivory*, it does not move consecutively through the mythotopes, nor does it move through the net of hollowings and planes. Instead, it breaks the structural com-ponents apart, piecing fractions of time and space together from numerous mythotopes into a new spatiotemporal structure. "Legion moved forward outside what you or I might think of as ordinary space and ordinary time," Christian explains, musing on the effect this might have on mythagos who would see "when Legion flowed for a few seconds through their space and time" (*Gate of Ivory* 139). Legion becomes a mythotope in its own right, with its own structure in relation to the rest of the woodlands, just as the latter have a structure dissimilar to that of the outside world. With a reality of its own, maintained and defended by Kylhuk's warriors and magic users (see, e.g., *Gate of Ivory* 133), Legion is in fact a polder within the larger polder of Ryhope Wood. This small polder moves through its surrounding sylvan polder like a bubble, but a bubble that makes its own paths through the structure that contains it.

Unlike in *Gate of Ivory*, the first three books have labyrinthine structures that emphasize how traveling in the mythago wood is to travel literally into the *selva oscura*, the dark, impenetrable forest where any hope of a straightforward path is lost. Steven, Tallis, and Richard are all at the mercy of their respective labyrinths. In *Gate of Ivory*, Christian is similarly at the mercy of the forest, but not because of its complex structure. Instead, he is brought into the Legion mythotope. So although his tale is arduously labyrinthine, Christian's path takes him and his companions straight to the center along a route that suggests nothing of the circuitous inevitability of *Mythago Wood*. Rather, Kylhuk and Legion become an irresistible force that steadily moves toward its goal. Christian is swept along in their wake—and then sent out again.

In *Avilion*, a change in perspective results in radically different journeys through the mythotopic landscape. Where the first four books all have some aspect of portal–quest narrative to them, in which the reader discovers the forest together with an outsider in the forest, *Avilion* is immersive. The protagonists belong in the wood, leaving the readers to figure out the place without a guide. Jack's visit to Shadoxhurst demonstrates this shift in perspective when, as Paul Kincaid points out in his review of the book, the ordinary is made to seem alien.[88] Thus, the spatial complexity of the mythotopical landscape is treated as commonplace, almost banal, and rather than stressing the arduousness of traveling through the forest, the characters' various paths are emphatically simple: Jack journeys along the Amurngoth trails that cut through the forest mythotopes (e.g., 74 ff.); dreams and supernatural guides lead Yssobel into Avilion; and Guiwenneth joins the Legion as it passes on its march straight through the mythotopic structure.

Rather than emphasizing the arduous journey through the labyrinthine landscape, the text focuses on the liminal regions surrounding Ryhope Wood as a whole as well as those surrounding Avilion at its center. *Avilion* is not a story about traversing a limitless land in search of its heart. It is a story of entering and leaving, of crossing boundaries: of entering but mainly of leaving Ryhope Wood and of leaving but mainly of entering Avilion.

The interior of the polder becomes both anywhere and anywhen, a place where time is as important as space. Its most striking aspects, to the reader as well as to the characters who venture into the woods, resemble the temporal nature of Lothlórien. As one travels inward, mythotopes keep opening up, mythotopes of ever older myths, and at the center is Lavondyss, the First Forest, the first myth and the forest's origin at the last Ice Age. The deeper one ventures, "the deeper the time abysses that open before the traveler: because to travel into the Wood is also to travel back in time."[89] Except, of course, in Ryhope Wood, each mythago opens a time abyss, leaving the human outsider teetering on its edge; to travel inward is to descend into that abyss. In Lothlórien, Frodo suddenly finds himself at the bottom of a time abyss, in a corner of the Elder Days. Steven, Christian, and Tallis find themselves journeying, step by step and myth by myth, to reach the oldest myth of all at the center of the forest. Just as space is distended during this journey inward and backward, so is time. The further one moves toward the heartwood, the faster subjective time passes in comparison to time outside—a trek of weeks might correspond to mere days outside (see, e.g., *Mythago Wood* 53; *Hollowing* 90; *Gate of Ivory* 51). Kincaid sees this as part of a nonlinear, "riverine" concept of time that he argues provides a spine for the Ryhope Wood stories as well as for *The Merlin Codex*, also by Holdstock.[90] Time in the mythotopic forest does more than meander through the story, however; just as space in the forest is protean, so is time, which ultimately suggests that even the time that passes in the woodlands is part of the mythotopes. This idea evolves over the novels, and in both *Lavondyss* and *The Hollowing* the relative passage of time is of central importance. Wynne-Jones's daughter, Morthen, rides off to find a place where she can age faster, and the few hours Tallis spends away from her companions correspond to two days for them (*Lavondyss* 338, 330). In *The Hollowing*, the time differentials work both ways, keeping Alex and James Keeton virtually unchanged in the forest while years pass outside. Richard's brief hesitation before going through a hollowing results in a delay of a day and a half for those on the other side (*Hollowing* 129–30). In *Avilion*, with its polder-internal perspective, the fluctuating time is taken as much for granted as the shifting space. In an ever-changing environment, only Steven, born outside the forest, senses "the steady passage of time" (*Avilion* 98). The passage of time in the polder is specific to each mythotope, as mutable as the spatial aspects of the forest setting, and always unpredictable.

Ryhope Wood is not just a setting—to visit en route elsewhere or to have an adventure in—it is an engine that drives the stories. Holdstock's polder is protean and evolving, an anachronism that constantly redefines its own anachronistic properties. It does not seek to protect a specific old time—it offers access to all old times. Regardless of the intentions of the people who manage to venture into the woods, the woods use the people to create the settings and adventures that they meet. In Ryhope Wood, the mythagos and mythotopes created from the protagonists' minds provide a center for the stories, and the heart of the forest labyrinth is a place that must be reached. The plots are driven by the search for that place, rather than by the actions to be performed there. Places in the forest polder are what they are in myths: the right location for a story to end, not a convenient location for carrying out a particular action.

Time and Time Again: Pratchett's Djelibeybi[91]

Djelibeybi is a small but ancient kingdom in the valley of the river Djel. This parody of ancient Egypt is the central setting of *Pyramids (The Book of Going Forth)*, the seventh of Terry Pratchett's Discworld novels, and is, as Andrew M. Butler puts it in his book on the author, "stuffed full of all the Egyptological details you thought you'd remembered from school."[92] It is a country bound by tradition, where national resources are spent primarily on building pyramids for the dead, religion has a tight grip on both rulers and commoners, and nothing ever seems to change. The novel tells the story of prince Teppic, who returns from his training abroad to accede to the throne only to find himself unable to accept the hidebound traditions and the ubiquitous rituals. Teppic's rebellion eventually results in the deposing of the undying high priest Dios and the modernization of Djelibeybi.

Although most polders include some conscious opposition to the time outside, that opposition rarely takes center stage to the extent that it does in Djelibeybi. Rather than creating an anachronism understandable mainly in terms of history, as in Lothlórien and Ryhope Wood, Pratchett uses the very nature of time to create the opposition between the polder and the surrounding world, making time an exceptionally important part of the setting. That time is of great concern in *Pyramids* becomes clear from the beginning of the novel, when the first description of Djelibeybi is devoted to the flaring pyramids, and the destruction of time caused by these flares drives much of the plot. The pyramids' destructive effect on time is, in the Discworld, a natural phenomenon. "Correctly shaped and oriented, with the proper paracosmic measurements correctly plumbed in" (139), pyramids soak up time during the day and burn it at night in so-called flarelights (plumes of light emitted from the tip of the pyramid, not unlike St. Elmo's fire). Rather than being invisible and abstract, time is given a concrete, visible form, and its destruction has immediate effects for the polder. Instead of living through constantly new time, people in Djelibeybi "use up past time, over and over again" because all new time is turned into flarelights (203). The pyramids act like batteries, turning temporal potential into light and heat just as electric potential is turned into light and heat in an electric discharge. The potential, in both cases, is nullified. Its similarity to electricity (emphasized by the flarelights' resemblance to a coronal discharge) strongly suggests that time is some kind of energy potential.

Time is repeatedly described in terms of energy or power in the novel. To Teppic, the kingdom is a place where "nothing actually changes, even if it doesn't stay the same" (203); without *new* time, there is no way to bring about change. Thus, time has traits in common with physical energy (or power, which is energy over time); and it is often referred to as—or in terms of—power in the novel. Even metaphorically, time and power have similarities; they are both *flows*, of events and energy respectively. Indeed, time is largely visualized through a water metaphor associating it with physical quantities such as energy and electric current as well as power: the time flow can have whirlpools (e.g., 108), and the pyramids are described as "dams in the stream of time" that affect the time flow, just as "a hydraulic ram can be induced to pump water *against the flow*" (139). When time is burned (just as energy can be transformed into different forms) by the pyramids, the time flow ceases, leaving only old time in the kingdom. The handmaiden Ptraci even employs water imagery when she describes the temporal situation in Djelibeybi as "an old pond where no new water comes in," so that "everyone goes round and round in the same old puddle. All the ptime [*sic*] you live has been lived already. It must be like other people's bathwater" (206). The pyramids cause a cessation of the time flow and Djelibeybi is caught in a state in which past and present are conflated, regardless of any attempts to change the kingdom. Having lived through millennia of ever-decreasing change, high priest Dios is, of course, extremely attuned to this temporal conflation, to the point where he even finds the use of the past tense problematic (78)—to him, past and present are the same.

Time is not only a power whose flow can be manipulated, however, it is also one of the four spatiotemporal dimensions. A theoretical discussion on the nature of time is provided by the (inebriated) geometrician Pthagonal, who claims to know why Djelibeybi has disappeared. (This disappearance is discussed later.) He begins by rhetorically asking, "how long did they think they could go on building bigger and bigger pyramids for? I mean, where did they think power comes from?" He then explains how time is "sucked up" and "burned" or "used" up through the flarelights. So far, he indicates that time is a power flow caused by a temporal potential. A few lines further down, though, the geometrician provides an alternative view as he proceeds to tell Teppic that "the power build up" in the Great Pyramid probably moved the dimensions around. "So that length is height and height is breadth and breadth is width and width is [. . .] time. S'nother dimessnon [sic], see? Four of the bastards. Time's one of them" (203). From Pthagonal's explanation, it becomes obvious that time in *Pyramids* is not just one of two seemingly mutually exclusive things; it is a duality: a dimension as well as power. Although Pthagonal's exposition is somewhat muddled, the Great Pyramid is the most obvious illustration of the dimension–power duality of time. The buildup of time-as-power in the pyramid creates a pressure on reality that eventually shifts the four dimensions (the spatial three plus time-as-dimension) by ninety degrees. This dimensional shift is lent further emphasis by the fact that the pyramid builder's son, Ptaclusp IIa, does not shift with the rest of the kingdom and is therefore left completely flat, moving along a spatial dimension rather than through time (173–75). To further intertwine aspects of the duality, the Great Pyramid begins to accumulate time before its construction is finished, because sometime in the future, that is, at another point in the time dimension, it will be finished. Because of its size, the finished pyramid has an effect backward in time-as-dimension, causing premature accumulation of time-as-power (108).

The dual nature of time as both power and dimension is linked to quantum mechanics, a set of scientific principles that is repeatedly invoked in exposition and jokes throughout the novel. Time's paradoxical dual nature echoes a more familiar duality of matter: the seemingly paradoxical, dual nature of subatomic quanta, which exhibit both wave- and particle-like properties. Dios's ability to know how several mutually exclusive things are all true, an ability that "would make even a quantum mechanic give in" (89), alludes to this particle–wave duality: just as Dios knows that the sun is, simultaneously, a celestial orange, a hole into a fiery realm, the eye of a god, and a small ball of fire, quantum mechanics holds that the smallest building blocks of matter are both waves and particles. In fact, quantum mechanics permeates much of the novel. The first use of the word *quantum* (clearly alluding to quantum mechanics) can be found already on the first page (7), foreshadowing the idea of parallel universes (belonging to a particular interpretation of quantum mechanics) that is used to explain the existence of the Discworld universe, the "dimensionette" where Teppic meets the sphinx, and, it is implied, the valley of the Djel itself (219, 233). Most references to quantum mechanics can be found in the discussions of the pyramid builders, especially through their repeated (mis)use of the word *quantum* (e.g., 91, 94, 136, 278), and an explicit reference is even made to the Heisenberg uncertainty principle—a concept central to quantum mechanics (178n).

The plot of *Pyramids* turns on this dual nature of time.[93] Time must be understood as both power *and* dimension for the events that lead to the end of the Djelibeybi polder to be clear. The Great Pyramid that Teppic is tricked into having built stores time-as-power because it exists as a four-dimensional object (one of the dimensions being time-as-dimension). The great potential that this buildup causes results in a shift of the four dimensions, time-as-dimension included. That shift, in turn, causes events that ultimately destroy the pyramids and end Dios's rule. It also brings the polder's boundaries and maintenance into view.

Unlike Lothlórien and Ryhope Wood, the Djelibeybi polder is not introduced to the reader by its boundaries, even though they are implied by more than just the dimensional shift; instead, Dios's attempts to maintain the kingdom as an anachronism define much of the story, as do the protagonist's transgressions of the polder boundaries. A polder requires boundaries that protect it from the hostile reality around it, protection that Djelibeybi initially appears to be without. The clearest sign that the country's boundaries are more than political constructions is the Great Pyramid's shifting of the four dimensions. When this happens,

Djelibeybi is removed from the Discworld universe. The very fabric of the physical reality changes, but only within the boundaries of the polder. As a footnote explains, "Nature abhors dimensional abnormalities, and seals them neatly away so that they don't upset people" (204n). The country is sealed away along its political boundaries, demonstrating that the effect is limited to, but includes all of, Djelibeybi. This removal, or sealing away, of the polder also emphasizes its separate pantheon: once the polder is no longer in contact with the rest of the Discworld, the force of the people's belief is enough to change a number of other natural laws: their gods appear, their mummified ancestors are brought back to life, their ruler is fully responsible for making the sun rise, and so on.

Even before this shift takes place, the Djelibeybi gods as well as the destroyed time indicate that Djelibeybi is separated from the rest of Discworld. "The valley of the Djel had its own private gods," Teppic muses, "gods which had nothing to do with the world outside" (32). In the Discworld, gods exist because people believe in them (179–80) (an idea that Pratchett develops in greater detail in *Small Gods*); but Teppic clearly distinguishes between the Djelibeybi gods and the pantheon of other Discworld gods, just as he sees the world as divided into Djelibeybi and "the world outside." The kingdom is set apart not only politically but also, as suggested before, pantheonically and temporally. The pyramids' burning of time is limited to the polder, providing a basis for its anachronism. Whereas a tradition is connected to its specific society, the lack of new time is a phenomenon that, theoretically, would concern an entire world. The boundaries of the kingdom are also the boundaries for the temporal destruction, however. This localized effect on the time flow becomes particularly evident from the way various characters experience time in the country. Teppic, for instance, reflects on how time might pass everywhere else but not in Djelibeybi (104), and how this makes the air feel "as though it's been boiled in a sock" (203). The lack of time, or at least the absence of change caused by it, is noticeable not only intuitively but as a physical sensation. It is also restricted to the kingdom.

With pantheon, temporal destruction, and dimensional shift all confined to the kingdom, there are obviously boundaries that do the confining, but the plot turns on high priest Dios's attempts to maintain the separate reality of Djelibeybi rather than its boundaries. Recalling Clute's definition of a polder from earlier in this chapter, polder boundaries must be maintained, often by a "significant figure"; it is the defense that protects the polder's separate reality.[94] Whereas Dios is certainly significant, it is not the *boundaries* that he actively maintains; his efforts are aimed directly at protecting the reality in the polder. Instead of preventing the wrong time of the outside world from trickling in, Dios actively opposes change in the kingdom by incessantly manning the bilge pumps, as it were. The death of Teppic's foreign mother is relevant in this context: what little is mentioned about her suggests that she attempted to effect change. For instance, she disliked pyramids, a position that in Djelibeybi is "like disliking breathing" (17). The veiled threat in the simile is carried out: she is eaten by crocodiles when swimming in the river (17). Throwing someone to the crocodiles proves to be the priesthood's favorite way of getting rid of people (this is how Ptraci is meant to be sacrificed [119] and how two blasphemous priests are dispatched [182–83]), so while Teppic's absentminded father supposes that his wife had simply forgotten about the crocodiles, it is far more likely that she was killed by Dios or at least at his command. The late queen is the first crack in Dios's bulwark against change, and he fails to deal with this crack expediently enough; it is because of a promise extracted by the queen before her death that Teppic is actually sent abroad to study, a departure (or "going forth") that sets in motion the chain of events that leads to Dios's undoing.

The failure to maintain the boundaries leads to the end of the polder by allowing Teppic to go forth as well as come back; each transgression constitutes an important turning point in the plot. The novel and its first part both bear the title *The Book of Going Forth* (a title that, as Langford points out, refers to the literal title of the ancient Egyptian guide to the afterlife, "The Book of Coming Forth by Day"[95]), and Teppic's crossing of the polder's boundaries is what makes us aware of those boundaries. Their presence is made obvious by the fact that they are transgressed, rather than by the process of transgression. For both Tolkien's and Holdstock's polders, the entering of the polder is an essential part of how the polder is presented. Djelibeybi, on the other hand, is entered and exited as a matter of course. Teppic crosses the kingdom's border on five occasions in the story (leaving three times, returning twice), and not until Djelibeybi is removed from the Discworld does he encounter any difficulties. Examined in terms of change, Teppic's boundary transgressions—his departures and returns—turn out to be linked to pivotal points in the struggle to reform the kingdom (and thus end the polder).

The first of Teppic's departures gives him the education he needs to oppose Dios's regime of changelessness. When the prince is sent to spend his formative years in Ankh-Morpork, future change is inevitable. As this departure is the main "forth-going" in the first part of the novel, "The Book of Going Forth," the scene becomes further charged with import (obscured but not diminished by the somewhat befuddled focus character of the scene, Teppic's father). At the end of part 1, Teppic returns to Djelibeybi, loaded, as it were, with potential for change and set up as Dios's main opponent. As he wades ashore, illuminated by the flare-lights, he feels ready to rule. He considers the traditional care for the dead and the founding of the country, seven millennia previously (66–67). Unbeknownst to Teppic, this is what his return will ultimately put an end to: the burning of time, the tyranny of tradition, and the ancestor worship, all introduced by Dios when Djelibeybi was founded.

Teppic's second departure comes at the end of book 2, when he and Ptraci escape from Djelibeybi just as the kingdom leaves the Discworld. Teppic seems to have lost the struggle against Dios; the kingdom disappears and becomes a world of its own, with a reality governed by the beliefs that Dios has instilled in the Djelibeybi population over the millennia. The realization of those beliefs, including the appearance of the kingdom's (mutually exclusive and therefore rather irascible) gods and the return of some fourteen hundred mummified ex-rulers, is a greater change than Dios can initially handle, however. Tradition cannot help him deal with Djelibeybi's profoundly different reality: "[Dios] did not know what to do. For him, this was a new experience. This was Change. [. . .] All he could think of, all that was pressing forward in his mind, were the words of the Ritual of the Third Hour" (187). In fact, Dios is at a loss for what to do throughout Teppic's absence (book 3). Not until faced with the prospect of further change, when the old king informs the high priest that the dead intend to destroy the pyramids, does Dios resume control.

Teppic's second return to Djelibeybi, at the end of book 3 and beginning of book 4, is the only time when crossing the boundary is in any way complicated. Since the boundary now separates not only two domains but two worlds, Teppic requires the assistance of his mathematically gifted camel and also has to outwit the sphinx that guards the boundary between the worlds. His goal is to return the country to the world outside by flaring off the stored time in the Great Pyramid, an effort Dios means to stop but never has a chance to deal with. Teppic's success causes not only Djelibeybi's return and the consequent banishment of the gods but also the destruction of the pyramids and restoration of a proper temporal flow, as well as the blasting of Dios back to the time of Djelibeybi's founding.

At the very end of the novel, Teppic goes forth a final time, leaving Ptraci to rule the country. The former handmaiden's escape and short stay in the world outside has changed her enough to suggest that the kingdom is facing a serious modernization scheme. Like that of Teppic, Ptraci's going forth starts a process that allows her to break free from tradition and set about changing the kingdom (see 207). Unlike him, she does not have to work within the polder: she is not opposed by the shrewd Dios but by the "incompetent" Koomi (282), and she has new time to work with—two facts that allow change to actually take place.

It is worth noting how the anachronistic polder is brought to an end by outside education, not only in the main conflict between Dios and Teppic but also in the subplot, which concerns the building of the Great Pyramid. Teppic's going forth to train at the Assassins' Guild in Ankh-Morpork brings skills and ideas almost beyond Dios's control into the country, but only *almost*. In fact, Teppic escapes the high priest's clutches only because of the dimensional shift caused by the Great Pyramid. The "paracosmic" architect behind the pyramid, Ptaclusp IIb, has been sent to the best schools and returned with "an education" (91). The fact that Ptaclusp IIb "worships geometry" and designs aqueducts hints at his having been educated in Ephebe (the Discworld version of ancient Greece), where the people "believe the world is run by geometry" (110; see also 69). Teppic and Ptaclusp IIb are made agents of change by virtue not only of their foreign education but because they have been educated at all—in Teppic's view, an opposition exists between schools and mindless worship (248). In combination, their respective educations eventually result in the destruction of the pyramids and the return of a normal time flow to Djelibeybi.

When time returns to a normal flow after seven millennia, this does not mean the destruction of the polder. As the Great Pyramid explodes, Dios is thrown backward in the time dimension, to find himself, concussed and with memory lapses, at the moment when the valley is brought into existence (at least as a part of the Discworld) by a flock of thirsty camels (284–85). That the high priest is destined to go through another round of Djelibeybi history is obvious: the thought that compels him to pick up his staff of office is that he must "explain about gods and why pyramids were so important" to Djelibeybi's founder-to-be (285). The staff, decorated with snakes that are biting their own tails (284), is a symbol of the never-ending. Dios is destined to create Djelibeybi as a changeless polder, maintain it, and finally see it destroyed over and over again. He more than maintains the polder's anachronistic nature; he becomes the center around which the polder exists. The polder's boundary is not so much spatial as temporal; the polder is a seven-thousand-year-long bubble in time within which Dios is forever trapped. Teppic never destroys the polder, he just ends it, sending Dios back to its beginning. From this perspective, *Pyramids* is very much about transgressing polder boundaries; Teppic's struggle is the process of leaving the temporal polder, of truly going forth.

Turning Geography into History

Unlike its actual-world namesake, the fantasy polder is not so much an area protected from the inimical world around it as the remnant of an era kept safe from the wrong time outside. "They are falling rather behind the world in there," is Treebeard's verdict on the elves of Lothlórien (TT, III, iv, 456), and this assessment is equally true of the other polders. The Elder Days continue on in the diffuse time of the elven realm; ancient myths come to life in Ryhope Woods; and Djelibeybi is kept changelessly stuck in its own past. These are bubbles of long-past days that have been kept in isolation while time has gone by outside.

A polder is not so much a protected area as a protected era. If we revisit Clute's polder definition, we find that the boundaries surround "enclaves of toughened reality" and "*active* microcosm[s]," which certainly implies that polders are spatially defined—enclaves and microcosms tend to be places, after all—but also that they are "anachronism[s] *consciously* opposed to wrong time."[96] Lothlórien, Ryhope Wood, and Djelibeybi have borne out this assertion, that time is an aspect central to polders. In all three cases, a past is protected from the ravages of time in the world. To varying extents, this past is situated sufficiently long ago to cause a time abyss to open for the characters who enter, as well as for the reader. To cross the boundary is to travel in time rather than in space.[97] The experience is one of history rather than of geography.

Polders thus contribute both topology and temporal thickness to fantasy worlds. An anachronism implies that time moves on and the world changes. Polders belie the static impression of many worlds, demonstrating how the present of the story (which is usually but not always that of the protagonists) differs from the past as conserved within their boundaries. Like insects trapped in amber, long-gone eras are preserved in the polders and extend the world backward in time, while letting the reality of the past impinge on the world of the present. Each of the three polders discussed in this chapter reaches back through several millennia, but the pasts they shelter have different functions in their respective stories. In Ryhope Wood lies the past that we all carry within us, the setting neither a landscape nor a timescape but a mythscape, a place of tales that are in some way eternal. In Djelibeybi, the oppressively primitive past is itself an antagonist to escape from, a distorted mirror image of the Edenic wonders of the Elder Days found in Lothlórien. The elven polder stands as a monument to these wonders, maintaining them while simultaneously mourning their disappearance from the world.

Time can thus be spatially encoded in fantasy worlds; with geography comes history. Darko Suvin condemns "heroic fantasy"[98] as suffering from "[g]eographic gigantism." "[O]ne is tempted to say: the less history the more geography," he remarks. But he concedes that some fantasy comes equipped with a "secondary or other history," and he even offers a handful of variations on secondary history.[99] It is thus mainly fantasy's lack of connectedness to the history of the actual world (the author's or reader's "historical web of forces") that Suvin's critical perspective causes him to take issue with. History is inextricably part of the secondary landscape, and not simply because any landscape holds inscribed on it the history of the people who have lived there.[100] Through polders, past eras are given spatial locations, past and present are juxtaposed, and the journey across the land turns into time travel.

· · ·

Borders and boundaries unite rather than divide. A border between two domains would be impossible if those domains were not juxtaposed; a polder boundary would not have a purpose unless the polder were part of the world outside. Both types of thresholds hold the fantasy world together but they also keep it variegated, a patchwork of distinct realities that opens up the geography in a fashion that mere distance cannot do. They expand the world by joining different realities together.

In *Modern Fantasy*, Colin N. Manlove presents a definition of fantasy, a central part of which is that fantasy contains *"supernatural or impossible worlds, beings or objects."*[101] Although the definition is too exclusive to fully suit the purposes of this study, Manlove's explanation of what he means by "supernatural or impossible" has a bearing on the function of thresholds in fantasy worlds. Originally, he explains that it means "of another order of reality from that in which we exist and form our notions of possibility";[102] but he later republished the definition and discussion in a gently revised version with an added afterword, in which he also adds that "no extension of nature can arrive at supernature, just as no extension of possibility can arrive at impossibility."[103] Manlove's remarks are concerned with ways of identifying the edges of the fantastic, but they are also applicable when discussing worlds of fiction.

All fantasy worlds have rules for what is possible and impossible, what is natural and supernatural. These rules may not be—in fact, generally are not—the same as in the actual world, nor are they necessarily shared by several worlds. Once it has been established what these rules are, however, the genre's demand for internal consistency[104] requires them to stay the same. No matter how far you travel in a world, the rules remain unchanged: no extension of nature or the possible will change that. The reality is of a given order, to use Manlove's expression.

The exception—and it is a common exception—occurs when a border or boundary is crossed. On the other side lies another order of reality, a place where the rules *are* different. Extend the journey across a threshold into another domain, and the impossible will become possible; the supernatural of one domain is the natural of another. What is possible or natural is a question of in which domain, not in which world, the story is set. These are the kinds of worlds that Lubomír Doležel calls "dyadic worlds"—and they are often triadic, tetradic, or, occasionally, even more polyadic (such as the place cobbled together by pieces of other worlds in Diana Wynne Jones's *The Merlin Conspiracy* [2003])—where a world's domains have mutually contradictory rules.[105] Each domain holds another order of reality, even if the domain is only the tiniest of polders.

Stories arise from the crossing of thresholds, and in fantasy, they are widely varied. Doležel points out how, in "the divided world with rigid boundaries, the story of the cross-world journey is of perennial fascination."[106] He claims, however, that there are only two variants of this story: that of the observer, who gathers information but cannot physically interact with the other domain (exemplified by Odysseus' visit to Hades); and that of the mission, wherein the human visitor can interact but is bound by some prohibition (Orpheus is the example given). Whereas Vlad Taltos's trip to the domain of the dead clearly belongs to this second category, and Teppic's goings-forth into the outside world could possibly be construed as representative of the first—he only brings back knowledge; his physical interactions are of secondary importance—the four other domains discussed in this chapter illustrate how other stories spring from journeys between domains. In Lothlórien, the Company certainly obtains information; but the items its members bring with them are of even greater importance—in particular, to the hobbits—during the quest but also afterward. Even so, the prohibitions placed on them are quickly lifted. Visiting the elven realm is a small part of the story, but the polder is a key node in the plot, the effects of which affect the characters and the events profoundly for the rest of the novel. In Ryhope Wood as well as in Tristran's Faerie, returning is of subordinate or no importance; the new order of reality is a place of exploration in which the protagonists remain, forging new lives. In the Abhorsen series, there is, ultimately, no privileged direction of transgression; protagonists come from both sides and move in both directions. The fantasy genre, in which the "cross-world journey" is a common trope, thus offers far more than two basic variants of such stories. Instead, the crossing and the differences between the domains provide a deep fount of greatly varied stories.

Other orders of reality are integral parts of fantasy worlds; the possible *can* be extended, geographically at least, into the impossible. Fantasy stories make use of, or even center on, the thresholds between the possible and impossible, turning the domains into some of the genre's most notable settings. There are other domains as well, domains that are not geographical areas but are certainly governed by very different rules from each other. The next chapter investigates one such set of domains: that of nature and culture.

4 : Nature and Culture

One of the most intriguing divisions that fantasy literature enables us to rethink is that between the domains of nature and culture. Many scholars maintain that the principal cause of today's many environmental problems, from ozone depletion to the proliferation of genetically manipulated organisms, is the way in which Western society perceives there to be a difference between nature and culture.[1] While *nature* and *culture* are terms that are both well-known and slippery to define, our cultural relationship with nature is dominated by problems of delimitation as well as of conflicting traditions: Where exactly do we draw the line between nature and culture? Is there even a line to be drawn? Are we not of natural origin and therefore part of nature ourselves? In that case, how can things we do be anything but natural? In the actual world, these questions have become relevant parts of the debate about how to deal with environmental issues; and through the fantasy genre, they may be approached from any number of new directions.

Cities may seem a typically cultural phenomenon, but they are actually among the most interesting, and certainly the most distinct, interfaces between nature and culture. They provide a limit or boundary that is or is not transgressed or permeated, a locus where both sides of the relation can be studied. This is just as true of cities in fantasy fiction. There may well be, as Brian Attebery claims, some "archetypal green world that underlies all fairyland";[2] but generally speaking, the city in fantasy is neither connected to fairyland nor to any archetypal green world. Its magic is of a different kind, less predictable and straightforward. By investigating the relationship between nature and culture, it is possible to understand what function that relationship has in the imaginary cities, but also to see what fantasy cities can tell us about alternative ways of exploring this important and familiar yet complex duality.

Defining "nature" is an undertaking fraught with complications. In *Thinking about Nature*, Andrew Brennan reflects that given the variety of ways in which the term *nature* is used, a case could even be made for dropping it from descriptions.[3] Kate Soper, in *What Is Nature?*, remarks that the term is "at once both very familiar and extremely elusive."[4] A quick glance in the *Oxford English Dictionary* shows us a term that has accumulated a considerable number of only vaguely related meanings. *Nature* can, for instance, mean "[a] malleable state of iron" and "[a] class or size of guns or shot" (both meanings now obsolete). It is a word that can denote anything from bodily functions in need of a handy euphemism (related to, for example, excrement, urine, semen, and menstrual discharge) to the characteristic disposition of a person. It can even mean the entire cosmos.[5]

For the purpose of discussing the relation between nature and culture, the most suitable definition in the *OED* is that of nature as "[t]he phenomena of the physical world collectively; *esp.* plants, animals, and other features and products of the earth itself, as opposed to humans and human creations."[6] The last clause brings to mind Soper's point of departure, namely that "[i]n its commonest and most fundamental sense, the term 'nature' refers to everything which is not human and distinguished from the work of humanity."[7] It is further helpful to consider Brennan's outline of the distinction between broad and narrow (or absolute and relative) notions of "the natural." The basis for his broader notion is that human behavior is natural insofar as we find the same behavior naturally in other animals (particularly higher mammals), and that human management, production, and interference make events and products unnatural.[8] Brennan and Soper are in general agreement with philosopher Keekok Lee, who starts off her list of seven senses of "nature" with what she terms $nature_{nh}$ (non-human). She defines $nature_{nh}$ as opposed to *culture*, which "involves human agency and its products."[9]

"Culture" can have almost as many meanings as the word *nature*. Depending on which discipline we turn to, definitions will vary. It has, for instance, been suggested that "culture" is "a class of phenomena conceptualized by anthropologists in order to deal with questions they are trying to answer."[10] In their 1952 investigation of literature in (mainly) the social sciences, anthropologists Alfred L. Kroeber and Clyde Kluckhohn include nearly three hundred different definitions of the term.[11] In "Classic Conceptions of Culture," Peter Worsley describes the two main ways in which "culture" is used outside of the natural sciences. The first, oldest, and here least relevant way is to use the term more or less synonymously with "the fine arts." The second usage "is the idea of 'culture' as a way of life" which at the broadest level may refer to "almost anything that distinguishes human beings from animals."[12] This is obviously the usage that primarily opposes Lee's nature$_{nh}$ as well as Brennan's and Soper's views of nature and the natural. Daniel G. Bates attempts to define culture in slightly more detail. According to him, culture is the "system of shared beliefs, values, customs, behaviors and material objects that the members of a society use to cope with their world and with one another,"[13] a definition that is useful for my discussion.

The duality *nature—not-nature* (or *culture—not-culture*) has some drawbacks, however. The first, and most obvious, is that if nature is that on which human management, production, and interference—"the work of humanity"—has had no impact whatsoever, then precious little nature is left in the actual world. Through the greenhouse effect and depletion of the ozone layer, humanity has affected the entire biosphere.[14] Humanity's history is one of large-scale changes to its habitats; for millennia, entire landscapes have been artificially changed as the result of human intervention. Historian Lynn White, Jr., points out that the upper valley of the Nile would have been a swampy jungle were it not for some six millennia of irrigation; and both he and Frederick Turner remark on the deforestation and overgrazing that occurred in antiquity, which left the hills of the Mediterranean basin in the state they are in today.[15] As recently as twelve hundred years ago, the first Maori settlers began the process that would soon turn the deep forests of New Zealand into today's rolling hills of tussock grass. The second drawback is that even if there is something left to call nature once we have removed everything on which humans have had any impact (and, in fantasy literature, there might well be), the duality allows for no shades of gray. It is strictly binary. It would seem reasonable to add nuance to this duality. In *De Natura Deorum* (On the Nature of the Gods), Marcus Tullius Cicero writes that "we sow cereals and plant trees; we irrigate our lands to fertilize them. We fortify river-banks, and straighten or divert the courses of rivers. In short, by the work of our hands we strive to create a sort of second nature within the world of nature."[16]

A "second nature" created by human labor would not qualify as natural according to Lee's nature$_{nh}$ or Soper's and Brennan's nature without human impact. Nevertheless, it seems reasonable to consider Cicero's "second nature" not only in terms of culture. A garden, for instance, could be considered to occupy a position between nature and culture.[17] In a garden, apple trees, roses, and lawns grow according to natural principles, and if they were not picked, trimmed, and pruned, they would grow out of control. It is the gardener's control that makes the garden what it is; and without control, the garden, as garden, would sooner or later cease to be. Rather than discussing nature only in terms of human *impact*, we can usefully look at nature in terms of human—or cultural—*control* as well.

Most people would agree that primary rainforest is part of nature but that shopping centers are not, and that a car is not natural but that an ancient oak is. But when it comes to bonsai trees, wheat fields, and pedigree dogs, there is not the same certainty. The difference between the former and latter examples is that the bonsai, wheat field, and dog have been subjected to human control. Their natural behavior has, in varying ways, been checked or changed, turning them into examples of Cicero's "second nature." The rainforest and the ancient oak are (presumably) not culturally controlled but are what I term *wild*, part of a *wilderness*.[18] Once nature comes under our control, we tame it. We force the bonsai, the field, and the dog to develop and behave in ways that fit our culture. Gardens, parks, potted plants, agriculture, and pets are all examples of *tame nature*, nature under culture's control.[19] If that control were to cease, their tameness would give way to another state. The bonsai would grow larger leaves and branches, other plants ("weeds") would mix with the wheat monoculture, and the dog's behavior, if not its appearance, would adapt to a life in the wild—and its offspring a few generations of uncontrolled breeding down the line would certainly no longer be pedigree animals. As culture's control ceases, wildness (re)asserts itself. This shift to a state of wildness and, eventually, wilderness is not restricted to borderline cases such as the ones just mentioned; brownfield land at former industrial sites exemplifies this process, as do the continual battles between gardeners and the invading forces of moss and weeds. If tame nature is not sufficiently controlled, it will not behave according to human wishes. It will go wild. That wildness which manifests itself when nature is no longer controlled is here termed *feral nature*. Over a year, a decade, or a century, wilderness returns, and even though traces of human impact may remain, control is gone; nature is again wild.

The relation between nature and culture varies from society to society.

In the actual world, whether the two are even opposed is open to question. According to Darwin and the theory of evolution, humans are the result of a natural process. To cut a long argument short, if we come from nature, and have developed through a natural process, then why should anything we do be unnatural? Or anything we make?[20] Or is there a sliding scale between nature and culture? Are entities and behaviors more or less natural, more or less cultural? Then there is another notion, namely that humans are in some sense superior to the rest of the (natural) world. In Western society, this notion stems primarily from the Judeo-Christian tradition.[21] Genesis tells us that we "have dominion over the fish of the sea, and over the fowl of the air, and over every living thing that moveth upon the earth."[22] The contemporary, and secular, view of *Homo sapiens* as standing "highest in a natural order of 'lower life forms'" comes to us from the scriptures and from the concept of the *scala naturae* or "ladder of nature," which was originally conceived by Aristotle and later brought into Christian learning.[23] Two impulses thus compete in the Western view of how we and our culture are supposed to relate to nature. From a Darwinian perspective, we are a product of nature, not its masters, while religious tradition positions us above the rest of creation. This contradiction is one of the foremost reasons for our problematic relation between nature and culture.

In fantasy, and particularly in fantasy set in secondary worlds, neither Christian thinking nor Darwinism is a compulsory ingredient. Writers are free to construct their own relations between nature and culture. Tolkien thus uses a Christian foundation when his world, Arda, is explicitly created as the dwelling of the Children of Ilúvatar (elves and humans):

> [T]he Ainur saw that [the creation] contained things which they had not thought. And they saw with amazement the coming of the Children of Ilúvatar, and the habitation that was prepared for them; and they perceived that they themselves in the labor of their music had been busy with the preparation of this dwelling, and yet knew not that it had any purpose beyond its own beauty. For the Children of Ilúvatar were conceived by him alone.[24]

The nature of Middle-earth is thus clearly separated from the cultures of elves and humans. In Aslan's creation of Narnia (C. S. Lewis, *The Magician's Nephew* [1955]), humans are even more external, as they come from outside the world. In both cases, a reading that sees culture as separate from nature is not only possible, it is imposed by how the worlds are created. Other works present other approaches. In David and Leigh Eddings's The Dreamers series (2003–2006) and Terry Pratchett's *Eric* (1990), the world is created by divine labor, but its life develops through evolution. The fantasy genre offers alternative ways of relating to the nature–culture duality, including not regarding it as a duality at all, just as it offers alternative ways of dealing with and relating to any other concepts. When examining the construction of this duality in fantasy literature, my point of departure for each reading was that nature and culture formed separate domains; but as the four following examples demonstrate, that is not necessarily the case.

Returning to Bates's definition of culture, we find that he includes artifacts or "material objects." The most palpable material object, or accumulation of material objects, that "the members of a society use to cope with their world"—that is, to control their surroundings—is the city. The division of labor developed in cities made possible the economies of specialization that led to the urban accumulation of capital (just as agriculture and food preservation allowed for a shift away from hunting and gathering), resulting in a society of specialist professions.[25] In Occidental society, the city has become the locus of cultural interchange and could be considered the pinnacle of culture. The city limit is an obvious meeting point of nature and culture, of outside and inside; but it is also a boundary that, in various ways and in either direction, can be transgressed, permeated, or penetrated. It is a boundary in physical as well as nonphysical terms, and it is a boundary that confines as much as it protects.

Two points need to be made regarding the selection of the four cities discussed here: no assumptions as regards the relation between nature and culture found in them were made when they were chosen; and they were picked for their distinct differences rather than for any similarities they might have shared. It could even be argued that apart from belonging to the same literary genre, all they have in common is that they are imaginary cities. That trait is central to the discussion, however, because a study of the relation between nature and culture in works of fiction is by necessity a study of settings. If a story is set in (a version of) a city from the actual world, such as London or New York, no matter how fictionalized, the relations between nature and culture in the fantasy city could be influenced by circumstances in its actual-world counterpart. As this book aims to examine the relation in fantasy, such an admixture is undesirable. The four cities are thus all imaginary, even in the case of Newford, which is set in a primary world. Apart from that, the four cities have very little in common. Tolkien's Minas Tirith is set in the portal–quest fantasy of *The Lord of the Rings*, in a culture that corresponds somewhat to early medieval Europe. Newford is a city that could well exist somewhere in today's North America. While Charles de Lint's many stories cover a wide range of fantasy, they are mainly of the intrusive type. New Crobuzon appears in immersive-fantasy novels, even though China Miéville's works also contain aspects of both quest and intrusion, and the industrial city is mainly based on Victorian London. Patricia McKillip's Ombria, finally, is a clearly immersive fantasy reminiscent of Renaissance Italy.

The quartet of cities I have selected thus demonstrates some of the many shapes and flavors that fantasy cities come in. In fantasy literature, we find cities scattered in the path of the questing hero, urban oases in the wilderness providing succor before the dangers of the road are braved again. Others are complete settings in themselves, not places to be visited but environments to be explored.[26] Some are beautiful and pleasant; others are dark and oppressive. Some are empty and deserted, others are teeming with life. The vast majority are in some way perilous, threatened or threatening, and, as John Clute observes, "a city in fantasy tends to be a place where the action converges."[27] By looking at the relationship between the city and nature in various texts, we can discuss the relation between nature and culture in those texts and see how the nature–culture division is presented in these places of converging action.

THE RETURN OF THE TREE: BRINGING NATURE BACK INTO MINAS TIRITH[28]

The people of Middle-earth live in a wide variety of dwellings, from the comfortable hobbit holes of Hobbiton to the vast underground halls of Khazad-dûm, from Bree with its friendly inn to Edoras with its gold-roofed Meduseld; but very few of these dwellings are called cities. Certainly, Khazad-dûm was once a light and splendid place, the realm and city of Dwarrowdelf;[29] but when the Fellowship passes through, the place has long been called Moria, the Black Chasm. It is a ruin or ghost town rather than a city, inhabited by orcs and run by a dreaded balrog. Caras Galadhon, the capital of the Galadhrim, is a city of trees and lawns, and while it does not conform to traditional ideas of urbanity, contemplating it offers some interesting insights into an alternative relation between culture and nature. The elven city is therefore briefly examined at the end of this section. Apart from Khazad-dûm and Caras Galadhon, however, most of the communities mentioned in *The Lord of the Rings* are villages or small towns.

The only city proper that the reader encounters in Tolkien's novel is Minas Tirith, the Tower of Vigilance, main city of Gondor after the fall of the original capital, Osgiliath. The city's central importance is stressed by the capital C that has been bestowed upon the word *City* whenever it refers to Minas Tirith in the text. There is what Tolkien calls a "basic opposition" between Minas Tirith and the Dark Tower of Barad-dûr,[30] noticeable from the first time the city is mentioned at the Council of El- rond (FR, II, ii, 238). Minas Tirith is a city that defends itself, most mani- festly from the forces of Mordor but also from the wilderness. Onionlike, the cultural center of the city, the great hall of the rulers of Gondor, is surrounded by ring upon ring of defenses. With each ring closer to the center, wild nature is further removed and the superiority of culture af- firmed; and at the middle, in front of the hall, sits what must have been the ultimate symbol of a culture devoid of nature for Tolkien: an ancient, dead tree. Inside the hall, another symbol of similar meaning appears: a throne under a flowering tree—carved from stone.

Minas Tirith is set in a wilderness that is kept from the city by its outermost defense work and by the tame nature of the Pelennor fields. To the south are the mountains and vales of Lossarnach, and to the north lie Anórien and the Druadan Forest. The text indicates that Lossarnach has been slowly tamed over the years and partly turned into farmland; but it is still a forested country, and Minas Tirith's citizens plainly associate it with wilderness (RK, V, i, 754; viii, 845–46). The Druadan Forest, on the other hand, used to be under Gondor's control but has now gone feral. The wain-road running through it has been forgotten and overgrown, a road known only by the woses who live there (RK, V, v, 814–816). The woses offer a mirror image of the cultural Gondor citizen. Paul H. Kocher points out that Faramir refers to the woses as the lowest class of human civilization—the Wild Men, or the Men of Darkness—in a scale on which the men of Gondor are at the top.[31] If, as it seems to Merry, the woses are indeed related to the Púkel-men statues at Dunharrow that they so much resemble, they have lived unchanged in this part of Middle-earth since the Years of Darkness, more than six millennia earlier (RK V, v, 813–14, 816; iii, 777–78; Appx B 1058). In other words, they have lived in this area longer than the people of both Gondor and Rohan (the "High" and "Middle" Men of Faramir's taxonomy) who are now its masters. The forest is clearly the true element of the woses; clad in grass skirts, they move silently and almost invisibly through it, a part of their natural surroundings. Their willingness to aid the Riders of Rohan despite having been dehumanized and hunted as beasts by the Rohirrim adds the woses' voices to Treebeard's in defense of the wilderness (RK, V, v, 815). From that position, the woses also function as criticism of Gondor's society. The men of Gondor, who style themselves as High, have forgotten their own history (the old wain-road); moreover, they have forgotten to live with nature in their City, which the woses refer to as the "Stone-houses."

Letting the wain-road be forgotten along with the woses of the Druadan Forest is part of shutting the wilderness out, a role more palpably played by the outer defense wall. When Pippin arrives at Minas Tirith, his first encounter is not with the city itself but with Rammas Echor, the twenty-league-long wall that surrounds the Pelennor townlands. This great structure is part of the defense of Minas Tirith, although it actually slows down the enemy forces by less than a day (RK, V, iv, 799–800). What the encircling wall does, however, is surround the urban center with tamed nature. All around the city, apart from right at its back, the land is "rich, with wide tilth and many orchards, and homesteads [. . .] with oast and garner, fold and byre" (RK, V, i, 734). Control over the land is evident from the list of features that tame—or imply the taming of— the natural land, from the growing of crops to animal husbandry. The havoc caused to this farmland by Sauron's armies recalls the ravaging of the gardens of the entwives in an earlier war (see TT, III, iv, 465) and foreshadows the destruction that the hobbits face on their return to the Shire.

Tame nature goes no farther than the Minas Tirith city walls, however. These walls are meant to keep the enemy out; but only nature at its wildest could breach them, and it is implied that even furious wilderness stands no chance of tearing them down. While the city and the Tower of Ecthelion that crowns it are built of white stone, the outward face of the outer defense walls is hard, dark, and smooth. The strength of Minas Tirith's walls is such that it would require "some convulsion that would rend the very earth on which [they] stood" to cast them down (RK, V, iv, 804). The walls' power to withstand enemies from Mordor parallels their ability to withstand natural assault. The black surface recalls a very similar substance that covers Orthanc,[32] and during Treebeard's attack on Isengard, the hard surface even defeats the might of the enraged ents. In her insightful article "Taking the Part of Trees," Verlyn Flieger observes that "[w]hat happens at Orthanc is not merely *like* the work of great tree roots, it *is* the work of great tree roots"[33] — but even when those roots can tear up rock like bread crust, they can do no more than scratch and chip the black surface of Orthanc's walls (TT, III, x, 553; ix, 563). Minas Tirith's walls share this imperviousness to even the wildest nature with the tower of Isengard.

Inside the walls, the city is portrayed as a place of cultural supremacy. To hobbit eyes, it is vast and beautiful but mainly made of stone, giving the impression of being "carved by giants out of the bones of the earth," an image echoed by the leader of the Wild Men, who explains that Gondor's founders "carved hills as hunters carve beast-flesh" (RK, V, i, 734; v, 814). Not only physical "carving" brings the hills under cultural control. In the descriptions of the city, Mindollouin, the mountain on whose side it is built, is anthropomorphized, with metaphors giving it not only body parts like head, knee, face, and heart but also garments such as skirts, helm, and cloak (RK, V, i, 734–36, 743). Rather than encountering the mountain as a feature of the natural landscape, the reader is asked to consider it in terms of the human and artificial. Minas Tirith thus becomes further distanced from the surrounding wilderness even when that wilderness is, in fact, a mountainside to which the city clings like an artificial outcrop of white stone. In this respect, Minas Tirith is markedly different from the capital of Lothlórien. While both cities are strong and beautiful, and while their building material is repeatedly remarked upon by narrator and characters, the elven city is not distanced from the nature surrounding it. It is a city of trees, organic and "weightless," likened to a green cloud (FR, II, vii, 344), whereas the stone city is heavy and artificial.

In Minas Tirith, what little of the natural domain is present only emphasizes its general absence. Given the differences between elven and human cities, Legolas's first observation when he and Gimli enter the city is hardly surprising. "They need more gardens," the elf observes. Through him, we are presented with a city consisting of dead houses and lacking things that, as he explains to Gimli, grow and are glad (RK, V, ix, 854). In the white-paved court at the very heart of Minas Tirith, a fountain plays under the branches of a withered tree. The bright green lawn that surrounds the fountain and sets off the tree's stark deadness is one of only three lawns that the characters come across in this city of stone. The only garden the reader is told of belongs to the Houses of Healing

(RK, V, vii, 837). It is an empty garden, indeed, and far from the verdant profusion of Lothlórien, Ithilien, or even the Shire. During their stay, Faramir and Merry once walk across grass; once they sit under a tree. Nature, then, is evoked by its absence as much as by its presence: when the Ring is destroyed, the reader is told that neither birdcall nor rustle of leaf is heard (RK, VI, v, 940–41), enhancing the impression of sterility and a place in want of things that grow and are glad.

The separation of wild nature and culture is bridged by Aragorn. He comes to Gondor as chieftain for the rangers from the northern wilderness, and one sign of his rightful claim to Gondor's throne is that the herb *athelas* has healing properties in his hands (RK, V, viii, esp. 842, 844). Aragorn thus becomes a symbol of nature rather than culture, especially in opposition to the steward of Gondor, who sits at the center of a stone city, behind a dead tree and in front of a tree of stone. The ranger comes from the wild lands and can heal with an herb that the city's herb masters think has no healing properties (RK, V, viii, 847). Aragorn's use of *athelas* powerfully and positively evokes both wild and tame nature. When he uses it to heal Faramir, Éowyn, and Merry, the herb's fragrance is described in similes that conjure the wonders and beauty of nature; it is, for instance, likened to "the scent of orchards, and of heather in the sunshine full of bees" (RK, V, viii, 851). The intensity of these descriptions, forcefully brought out by the use of the herb to combat the deadly affliction caused by Sauron's servant, links Aragorn to a pristine, natural life-force. The fragrance evokes impressions not just of nature but of nature undefiled, the very antithesis of evil. The vibrant descriptions contrast sharply with the terms employed to describe the fragrance of *athelas* when Aragorn uses it in the wilderness. There, its smell is simply strong and refreshing, not evocative of unsullied nature (FR, II, vi, 327; I, xii, 193). The powerful connection with nature that comes with Aragorn's application of the herb in the culture-dominated Minas Tirith suggests that the ranger's accession to Gondor's throne closes the divide between nature and culture in the White City.

Aragorn's ascent to the throne removes the barrier between the domains and provides the city with more tamed nature. Flowers are brought into the city for the coronation (RK, VI, v, 944); and Legolas makes good on his promise that if Aragorn comes into his own, the elves shall bring "birds that sing and trees that do not die" to the city (RK, V, ix, 854; VI, v, 947). As a final step toward healing the city, the dead tree is uprooted and replaced by its scion. A living tree grows at the center of the city, brought from the wilderness high on the slopes of the mountain, just as Aragorn, a ranger from the wild, assumes his position at the very center of Minas Tirith's culture.

The separation of nature and culture maintained in Minas Tirith is thus brought to an end by the return of the king. The return of nature in the city's culture also signifies the healing of the long-divided people of Númenor. The wilderness that was once the kingdom of Anor, and the rangers who represent it, are brought together with the culture of Gondor, as represented by the city and people of Minas Tirith. The proper order of things, it is implied, not only involves the rightful leader but also a closeness and mixture of nature and culture. This implied order is confirmed by the only other city that is described in any detail in *The Lord of the Rings*, the capital of the Galadhrim. The elven city, similar to Minas Tirith in that it is defended by a wall, is not as markedly cut off from the surrounding nature. The defenses that are mentioned are a moat spanned by a bridge, a circular wall, and, where the wall's ends overlap, tall, strong gates hung with lamps (FR, II, vii, 344). Unlike the defenses of Minas Tirith, which are given great attention, Caras Galadhon's walls are mentioned in passing (and the moat can be inferred only by the presence of the bridge). Instead, this is a city where nature and culture are woven together.

The predominant reason for the nature–culture interweaving of the elven capital is the way in which elven culture is defined by a close relationship to its natural surroundings. Cultural adaptation to the natural environment is one of the main elven traits, not only in *The Lord of the Rings* but also in the other Tolkien works set in Arda. It thus becomes problematic to say whether the mallorn forests of Lothlórien are tame or wild, as well as to identify where the Galadhrim's adaptation to their natural surroundings ends and their control of those surroundings begins. The land's forests are suffused with the power of Galadriel, and the elves have built platforms in the mallorn trees. Whether the capital and the surrounding forests of the Naith of Lórien differ by anything but degree cannot be determined, as the Company is blindfolded for much of its journey from the Silverlode to the capital. The city, however, gives the impression of being a well-tended forest or parkland. In Flieger's words, it is "a city that is its own garden";[34] among the trees, there are paths, stairs, and green lawns, and in the middle of the city, a fountain from which flows a stream. Even the halls of the rulers of Minas Tirith and Caras Galadhon stand in sharp contrast to each other. The lord and lady of Lothlórien sit in a hall in a tall mallorn tree, with their backs to the bole and the crown of the living tree spreading its boughs over their thrones (FR, II, vii, 344–45). In the great hall of Minas Tirith, a crowned helmet of white marble is set over Gondor's throne, with only a carved image of a tree behind it (RK, V, i, 738). Whereas a cultural artifact canopies the center of power in Minas Tirith, nature canopies the elven rulers.

With rightful rulership in Middle-earth follows a blending of culture and nature. Galadriel and Celeborn are certainly the rightful rulers and, in fact, the founders of the realm. In their city, culture and nature flow into each other, blending seamlessly, a condition toward which Minas Tirith appears to move once Aragorn accedes to the throne. The ideal relationship between nature and culture in the cities echoes the ideal relationship between people and the natural world, a relationship expressed in terms of stewardship. Summing up their chapter on stewardship in Middle-earth, Matthew Dickerson and Jonathan Evans observe that "[a]s stewards and tenants, the Children [of Ilúvatar] are given authority over the world, but not to do with what they will. Rather, theirs is an authority accompanied by the responsibility to care for and nourish Ilúvatar's good creation."[35] In *The Lord of the Rings*, the elves of Lothlórien are held up as good stewards of their land, and the brief description of the wonders, beauty, and peace of Caras Galadhon thus anticipates the changes that will occur in Minas Tirith once the rightful king displaces the failed steward. Good cities, the reader is told, must be ruled by the right people in the right way, allowing culture to mix with (tame) nature.

NATURE, MAGIC, AND MISFITS:
WILDERNESS WITHIN NEWFORD[36]

Canadian writer Charles de Lint's city of Newford is, according to the blurb of the collection *Moonlight and Vines* (1999), a "quintessential North American city," seen as Canadian by some and as American by others.[37] It is the setting for more than a dozen novels and several collections of short fiction. The stories are set under the looming shadow of social failures in Western urbanism: child abuse, homelessness, prostitution, and drug abuse. The fantastic elements range from the clearly impossible to the almost possible, from Faerie creatures and dreamworld journeys to vague suspicions and doubt.

The city culture in Newford is challenged in three ways: physically by the wilderness it contains but cannot control; ontologically by the existence of fairies, the Otherworld, and magic; and socially by an alternative culture that comprises those who, voluntarily or involuntarily, lead a life in contravention of social norms: criminals, prostitutes, and the homeless, but also artists, poets, and street musicians. The three sets of domains in Newford intersect and overlap, and de Lint's stories are predominantly about people who find themselves on the border between one or more domains. Newford is a city dominated by culture rather than nature, by mundanity rather than magic, by those who fit into society rather than those who do not; but in the stories, these hegemonic domains are constantly challenged by their subjugated opposites. Rather than merely examining the relation between nature and culture, we can benefit from looking at the three divisions that cut through the city.

The first division is that between nature and culture. Just as with Minas Tirith, a clear distinction exists between wilderness and (cultured) city, with tame nature separating wild nature from culture. When police officer Thomas Morningstar drives up to the Kickaha reserve in *From a Whisper to a Scream* (1992), he observes how the landscape changes around him "from the crowded city streets to blocks of [industrial and commercial estates], the suburbs and finally farmland" and up into the hills, which are "heavy with pine, cedar and hardwoods."[38] The transition happens in stages from the center of cultural control, the crowded streets of central Newford, to the wild nature beyond the city's periphery. The suburbs and farmland recall the tilth, orchards, and homesteads of the Pelennor. Although one need not pass through a wall in order to leave Newford, there is a distinct difference in feeling inside and outside the city. Having left the city behind, Thomas feels reborn; and to the artist Jilly Coppercorn, the most frequently recurring of Newford's many characters, the air outside the city "tastes like it's supercharged with oxygen and everything smells as fresh as a sweet Sunday morning."[39] The dominant picture of Newford is that of a city that keeps the wild at bay, outside and generally quite a distance beyond the city limits.

This external, wild nature is contrasted with the parks, gardens, and other pockets of tame nature that can be found within Newford. These places of controlled nature are few and mostly only implied or mentioned in passing. In this respect, Newford is similar to Minas Tirith. Unlike Tolkien's city, however, Newford encompasses bubbles of wilderness. These bubbles appear all over the city and come in various sizes. The largest is a section of urban blight covering several blocks, but most are as small as a riverbank or a plot of bushes and weeds. Some, like the grounds of the artists' colony Kellygnow in *Forests of the Heart* (2000),[40] are untouched nature, wilderness left uncontrolled but contained by the city culture around it; but most are the result of parts of the city being released, ignored, no longer controlled. Nature is allowed to go feral—the wild percolates into the city.

Wilderness is also found beyond the city in quite a different respect, namely as part of the mostly mythical and always magical worlds accessible only to a few of the city's inhabitants and created by even fewer. The existence of this Otherworld is just one of several indicators of the second division in Newford: the division between the domain of everyday life, very much like our primary world in its mundanity, and a domain of magical places, beings, and events. In *Widdershins* (2006), one of the magical characters explains how Newford is "built on a nexus of time and spirit zones, which means the spiritworld rubs shoulders with this one more than it normally would otherwise[,]" and that this accounts for the great number of unusual events in the city.[41] In the stories, the magical domain actually consists of two settings: the multifarious Otherworld, where time and space behave quite differently from the mundane world, but to which some characters can travel;[42] and the magical part of Newford's reality, sharing time and space with the domain of everyday life. Various human users of magic, who can straddle the border between the domains of magic and mundanity, appear frequently in the Newford stories. The two largest and most prevalent groups of the magical domain's denizens, however, are the native animal people, who can change between human and animal shape, and the various Faerie beings of the Seelie and Unseelie courts, who arrived with the European settlers. Both groups belong to a category of magical beings that have their origin in myth and legend, a category that in Newford also includes, for instance, a few vampires, Bigfoot, a unicorn, and the Devil. Other inhabitants of the magical domain include: spirits that find new abodes (including the powerful entity in *Spirits in the Wires* [2003] that takes up residence in the Wordwood literature website, and the so-called numena that take on physical life through Isabelle Copely's paintings in *Memory and Dream* [1994]); personifications of abstract concepts (for instance, the spirit of the city itself as the eponymous Tallulah and a character's Jungian shadow come to life); and ghosts of dead people that have not yet passed on.

The magical domain and its inhabitants are often perceived as an ontological threat by the citizens of the mundane domain. In "Ghosts of Wind and Shadow" (1990), for instance, fifteen-year-old Lesli's ability to see fairies brings her into conflict with her mother, Anna, who adamantly refuses to acknowledge fairies and magic as part of the real world. Anna's final realization that magic beings are real destroys her worldview and forces her into drug-induced oblivion.[43] Not everyone is as disturbed by the magical domain as Lesli's mother, however. In "The Stone Drum" (1989), Jilly is given evidence that magic and Faerie creatures are real as a punishment. Like Lesli, Jilly is excited by her ability to experience the magical domain, and her wonder at the magical aspects of reality turns the curse into a blessing.[44] The reactions of the majority of Newford's citizens when confronted with the Faerie domain place them somewhere between Lesli's and Jilly's sense of wonder, on the one hand, and Anna's dread, on the other. Most people push the out-of-the-ordinary from their minds and forget what they have experienced.[45] Like the natural domain, the magical domain cannot be controlled and is therefore unseen, invisible. Invisibility is also a key concept when looking at the third way in which Newford is divided.

The final division cuts across the city's social space. While Minas Tirith is defined mainly by its defenses, Newford is defined by its inhabitants, and architecture tends to become a backdrop to human interaction. Although descriptions of the urban environment are allowed comparatively more space in a few stories (in, for instance, *Trader* [1997] and "Tallulah" [1991], the old part of the area called "the Market" is described; and "Pal o' Mine" [1993] includes a description of a number of buildings and their gargoyles[46]), Newford is portrayed predominantly through descriptions of what its inhabitants do, say, and dream, not of the physical structures of houses, streets, and parks that constitute the city's architecture. It is an environment defined by relations, social as well as physical, where the street grid and the complex web of personal connections can be mapped, but where houses are very seldom described. Unlike Minas Tirith, and New Crobuzon and Ombria (as discussed later), this city is almost entirely described as a social and mental space—a collection of people, not a collection of buildings.

In this web of relations, the border between the last two domains stands out sharply. It is a social division, the nineteen-year-old squatter Maisie muses in "But for the Grace Go I" (1991), that is not as simple as dividing the city between the haves and the have-nots. "It's more like some people are citizens of the day and others of the night. Someone like me belongs to the night. Not because I'm bad, but because I'm invisible. People don't know I exist. They don't know and they don't care."[47] The same mechanism is at work when the domiciled members of the city's hegemonic culture relate to the magic domain as when they relate to the "night people": like the magical domain, unwanted people are pushed out of the mind, made to disappear. Thus, invisibility is also frequently used to refer to Newford's homeless and outcasts, just as it is used in other works of urban fantasy as a form of social criticism,[48] linking the metaphorical invisibility of the "night people" to an actual and therefore magical invisibility of the inhabitants of the magical domain. In "The Invisibles" (1997), the narrator sees people no one else sees, and his friend explains a fundamental Newford tenet to him: "Magic's all about perception. Things are the way they are because we've agreed that's the way they are. An act of magic is when we're convinced we're experiencing something that doesn't fit into the conceptual reality we've all agreed on."[49] Be they urban fairies or "night people," such figures are made invisible through the same mechanism of denial.

"Night people" is not synonymous with "homeless," however. "Everybody who spends most of their time on the streets isn't necessarily a bum. Newford's got more than its share of genuinely homeless people," Maisie explains in a later story, but "it's also got a whole subculture, if you will, of street musicians, performance artists, sidewalk vendors and the like."[50] This subculture, or alternative culture, consists of people who do not accept the majority's view of what a proper way of life should be, people who at least to some extent do not subscribe to the consensual reality. It is to this subculture, or to people closely associated with it, that many of the Newford stories' central as well as minor characters, such as Maisie, belong.

Despite the attempts of the mundane society to ignore its opposites, those opposites remain. Together with domains of alternative culture and magic, the penetration of wilderness challenges Newford's city culture from within. One of the numerous epigraphs to the stories illustrates how de Lint weaves together the three domains: "There are seven million homeless children on the streets of Brazil. Are vanishing trees being reborn as unwanted children?"[51] This quotation from the "Poet Laureate of Deep Ecology"[52] links environmental concerns about deforestation to social concerns about street children. In a fantastic context such as de Lint's urban fantasy, the link between social and environmental issues—the transformation of trees into children—also suggests something magical. In "The Forest Is Crying" (1994), a social worker is asked to consider how the spirits of cut-down trees might literally turn into children, and evidence of the world's magical nature eventually persuades him not to dismiss that possibility ("Forest" 68–76). He is made to accept a basic premise of Newford: nothing should be dismissed as impossible simply because it has always been considered as such. If spirits or fairies are living in the trees, it would be equally plausible that the felling of a tree would result in yet another unwanted child on the city streets. Such is the reality of Newford, where the changing world kills spirits with concrete, polluted air, and poisoned water (see, e.g., *Forests* 253). The epigraph thus highlights the links between the three domains that are so central to the Newford stories.

The intersections of the three domains create "bubbles" in the hegemony, free from and thus undermining cultural control. In such bubbles, the links between domains are readily identifiable but are brought out in different ways. Four prominent bubbles of wild nature are considered in the following discussion, of various sizes and relations to the city culture. Stanton Street and All Souls Cemetery are both fairly small, contained areas. The former is a quiet residential street and as such seemingly a part of Newford's social hegemony, the latter a cemetery deserted by that hegemony. Both offer impressions of wilderness and prove to be associated with the magical domain as well as with alternative culture. The two largest bubbles in Newford, for their part, do more than give the impression of wilderness—to a great extent, they are wild: Fitzhenry Park, although linked to city culture along its edges, is wild at heart, a place of wild nature where the magical and alternative cultural domains have the upper hand. The Tombs, finally, is in many ways the park's opposite. The wilderness it contains is feral without any hint of cultural control. It serves as a reminder that the denizens of the subjugated domains are also dangerous, be they magical creatures or social outcasts.

The oak-lined Stanton Street runs through the urban center. On the surface, the avenue looks tame; and certainly, trees lining a street offer little of the imagery that can be expected from wilderness. Some descriptions of the oaks along Stanton Street approach the wild, however. As the street narrows, the hundred-year-old oaks give the impression of a tunnel rather than an avenue. The "two once-tidy rows of manicured shade trees [are] enormous now, and [have] more or less gone feral."[53] When Kerry Madan first arrives in Newford in *Someplace to Be Flying* (1998), the quiet of the street makes her uneasy:

There was something claustrophobic about walking under this long row of enormous oaks. The trees were too big, their dense canopy almost completely blocking the sky. They threw deep shadows against the tall houses and the shrubbery collected against their porches and brick walls, throwing off her sense of time. It no longer felt like the tail end of the day. It was too much like late evening now, a time when anyone could be out and about, watching her, waiting in the shadows for her to step too close. Anyone, or anything. (93)

Noticeable in both quotations is that the oaks are described as "enormous," and to Kerry, they seem "too big"—too big to belong in the middle of a city. Controlling a tree means keeping its size in check, and such control has been relinquished in the case of the Stanton Street oaks. Instead, it seems to Kerry as if the trees control their surroundings. Their shadows obscure the houses, hiding the city's architecture, emphasizing the sensation of wilderness. Kerry feels as if she is walking somewhere dangerous where anyone or *anything* might confront her, and it is not "the usual dangers of a big city" that worry her. Instead, she imagines "other threats, nameless things, creatures with hungry eyes and too many teeth" (93). Her impression is of a place that does not follow the rules of consensual reality, a place of magic. And she is right: Stanton Street is a haunt for a number of inhabitants of the magical domain. Kerry is on her way to the Rookery, where Raven—creator of the world and a being of great mythological importance—lives together with a group of animal people. In *Spirits in the Wires*, numerous Faerie creatures are observed under and among the boughs of the oaks (151). Furthermore, on Stanton Street lies the residence of Cerin and Meran Kelledy,[54] a commonly recurring setting that is a rambling house surrounded by oak trees, "a *regular forest* of them larger and taller than anywhere else in the city, each one of them easily a hundred years old" ("Buffalo Man" 104; my emphasis). Although not every description of the oaks around the Kelledys' house is as explicit, their extraordinary size is stressed, just like the size of the other trees along the street. The implied explanation of the immensity of the trees is that Meran Kelledy is the oak king's daughter. When Meran visits a bookstore, the house fairy there sees her as a "piece of an old mystery" and "an old and powerful spirit walking far from her woods";[55] but to most people, she and her husband are simply a duo playing traditional live music. It is also in a coach house off Stanton Street that the troll-like Rushkin teaches Isabelle the art of the numena paintings that can provide spirits with physical bodies.[56] Similarly to the Kelledys' home, Rushkin's studio is flanked by an oak tree, and the Rookery has an immense elm shading the lawns behind it (*Memory* 32; *Someplace* 86).

Stanton Street, in other words, is a locus where feral nature and the Faerie domain intersect; it is also touched by the alternative culture. While the Kelledys and Rushkin are domiciled, they are not fully part of the "day people." The Kelledys do not have regular employment but make money from their gigs and from teaching music. The deformed artist might be extremely successful, but he is a recluse who shuns society. Still, Stanton Street remains a part of the city, cutting through its center. Other wilderness bubbles are left deserted, pushed to the edge of the city, if not physically then at least socially and mentally, and in Newford, with its social/mental focus, that is highly relevant.

One such deserted bubble is the disused All Souls Cemetery, which provides a central setting for "Held Safe by Moonlight and Vines" (1996) and is also briefly described in *The Blue Girl* (2004). In this novel, a ghost likens it to "something out of a Southern Gothic novel, full of dead and dying trees, old-fashioned mausoleums and crypts, with paths of uneven cobblestones winding narrowly between them."[57] It is a scary place, even to a ghost, a place no longer part of society. Here, the trees formerly under cultural control have not grown to the immense size of the Stanton Street oaks; instead they, along with the mausoleums and crypts, underscore that this is a place of death. Only the rosebush by a particular grave has grown wild again (252). The graveyard is a desolate wilderness, but it still links the magical domain to feral nature. The descriptions in "Held Safe by Moonlight and Vines" match that of *The Blue Girl* (including the dead and dying trees and the rosebush[58]); but in the short story the domains of wild nature, "night people," and the magical intersect even more clearly. It is a place where only drug dealers and junkies come, according to the male narrator, Alex. Everyone else, he claims, "likes the idea of making a place gone wild safe again" (116). By "wild," however, Alex does not simply mean that the nature in the graveyard has gone feral. What scares people, he suggests, is that "a piece of the night" bides there, "thinking about them" (116). Lillie, the female narrator, dismisses any dark, dangerous wildness but suggests a more noticeable intersection with the magical domain. She explains how, when she has spent time in the cemetery, it changes into a different place, a garden, walled but wild, with a "tangle of bushes and briars, trees [she has] got no name for and vines hanging everywhere" (118). This wild place is the dreamed-up sanctuary for an abused child, a young Alex of several years previously (130), and the notions of time travel and a dreamworld combine with de Lint's pervasive theme of child abuse in this bubble of wilderness.

The popular Fitzhenry Park, Newford's equivalent to New York's Central Park and Toronto's High Park, and one of the most frequently used settings in the Newford stories, is also, counterintuitively, a prominent bubble of wilderness. On the surface, the park seems to be a place of tame nature, or possibly even just a cultural construct. Maisie's description of the park almost exclusively defines it in terms of the social (human) interactions that take place there:

> [Fitzhenry Park is] close to the Combat Zone, so you get a fair amount of hookers and even less-reputable types drifting down when they're, let's say, off-shift. But it's also close to the Barrio, so the seedy element is balanced out with mothers walking in pairs and pushing strollers, old women gossiping in tight clusters, old men playing dominoes and checkers on the benches. Plus you get the lunch crowds from the downtown core which faces the west side of the park. ("Waifs" 34)

The impression is of the park as a totally cultural space, an impression common to almost all Newford stories. Like the rest of the city, Fitzhenry Park is a place of social interaction, not of flora. There is a lawn or the odd shrub or tree, insofar as any vegetation is mentioned at all. The major exception to this portrayal occurs in *Trader*, where the park is one of the novel's central settings and the text includes descriptions of more than just a bush or two. When Max Trader, who has woken up in the body of the unpleasant and irresponsible Johnny Devlin, finds himself homeless and penniless, he walks deep into Fitzhenry Park, where there are woods that, like those in the Kellygnow grounds, might be untouched from the days of the first settlers (*Trader* 67). Feeling that he has no other option, Max makes the park his home, only to discover that the wooded tracts are much larger than he has previously believed and that quite a few of the city's homeless are squatting there with him (74–77). Like Max, the various point-of-view characters repeatedly draw attention to the wooded areas of the park, often setting it apart from the surrounding city and associating it with the wilderness outside the city. Max is most explicit about this:

I lie back again, stare at the sky, the stars, feel the warm length of the
dog pressed up against my side. The city seems impossibly far away.
I can't hear it, can't see it except for a hint of its glow refracted in the
boughs of the trees. We could be on a camping trip, up in the mountains behind the city, or out along the lake in cottage country. (85)

Forced into the domain of the homeless and the magical, Max's perception also shifts as regards the natural domain; he now sees wilderness
where he previously saw only controlled nature. The tame nature has
shifted into wilderness in Max's mind, and the park has become a natural
rather than a cultural space. The impression that the city is "impossibly
far away," that Max could be outside the city rather than in its center, is
emphasized, linking the wilderness in Fitzhenry Park with the external
wilderness. A similar dissociation between park and city is experienced
by the strip dancer Nita as she follows a (possibly) suicidal vampire into
the park. "They could have been a thousand miles away, a thousand years
away from this time and place," Nita ponders, echoing Max's sensation
of being "impossibly far away" in a forest predating the first (European)
settlers.[59]

The dominant impression is of Fitzhenry Park as a city location, however, where nature is tame, under culture's control—something that is
not the case with the other subjugated domains. Through numerous
stories, it is made clear that the homeless are not the only "night people"
to be found in Fitzhenry Park. The location is apparently well suited to
criminal activity—from reasonably mild offenses, such as tagging and
unlicensed vending, to teenage gang confrontations and murder. Runaway Lesli is nearly recruited by one pimp and then kidnapped by another ("Ghosts" 204–6). Buskers and fortune tellers work the crowds. In
the controlled natural environment of the park, hegemonic culture has
lost control, not of nature but of the subjugated domain of alternative
culture. Similarly, several stories link the park to the third subjugated
domain, that of magic.

Fitzhenry Park is a center of magic in the midst of city culture. *Widdershins* mentions how fairies need to "replenish" themselves from wild
nature, which they call "the green and the wild" (*Widdershins* 40); and
one of the novel's main plot threads concerns the animosity that has
arisen between the fairies and the animal people who refuse them access
to "the green and the wild" outside the cities. When the two parties are
in need of a common ground for a meeting, the obvious choice is Fitz-

henry Park because, as the Faerie queen's captain explains, it is "in the city, so we have access to it, but there's enough of the wild and the green in its borders for the green-brees [animal people] to feel comfortable" (*Widdershins* 365). The explanation makes the connection between the magical domain and wild nature perfectly clear, and even if it is not as explicit as in *Trader*, it illustrates how the park is not all tame nature. Other stories similarly describe how the magical and natural domains intersect in Fitzhenry Park, mainly through the variety of magical beings that live in or frequent the park. Bodachs, a kind of Celtic Faerie creature, help identify the pimp who has taken Lesli ("Ghosts" 211–12); gemmin, genii loci that safeguard a place's happy memories, have been seen dancing there ("Winter" 161–62); and the park is a haunt for Bones, a recurrent character and an animal person. He and his girlfriend Cassie can be found there telling fortunes; but it is also in the park that Bones imparts knowledge of the magical domain to Max, and it is from the park that he sends Max's friends to the Otherworld (*Trader* 137, 245, 252 et passim).

An intriguing example of how the three subjugated domains overlap in Fitzhenry Park is provided through the part of the park called Silenus Gardens:

Deeper in the park, centered around a series of statues depicting a satyr lipping a syrinx and three dancing dryads, was a small hilltop surrounded by cherry trees in full blossom. The area [. . .] had been funded by a rich Crowsea patron of the arts in honor of the poet Joshua Stanhold. The benches here were marble—the same stone as the statues—and the air was sweet with the heady scent of the blossoms.[60]

From this description, the gardens seem to be a case of tame nature, under the control of culture's hegemony. There is a link between Silenus Gardens and the magical domain, however. In *The Dreaming Place* (1990), Cassie tells a friend how she feels hidden away from the world there, and how no one has ever been mugged or hurt in that part of the park. "There's magic places in the world," she continues, "places where I figure whoever's in charge [. . .] decided that there was only going to be good vibes and this is one of them." She finishes by adding that Newford is lucky to have two such places, the other being an "old house in Lower Crowsea" (*Dreaming Place* 24). The gardens thus combine the notions of magic, nature, and art, not only through their statues, the dedication to a poet, and Cassie's observation that the place is magic, but also through the association to the "old house on Lower Crowsea." It is not clear from the context in *The Dreaming Place*, but the house she refers to is the Kelledy residence, another location where art (in this case, music), magic, and nature meet. It is a place to feel safe and happy.

Where Silenus Gardens is a magic place of good feelings, the largest bubble of wilderness is, at least superficially, quite the opposite. Nowhere in Newford does the intersection of the three subjugated domains become as obvious as in the Tombs, the haunt of runaway children, street people, and drug addicts as well as a wide range of beings from the magical domain. The Tombs is part of a large area originally intended for gentrification, but the investors pulled out, leaving "a mess of empty buildings and rubble-strewn lots."[61] Maisie acknowledges that Fitzhenry Park might give some people a sensation of countryside, but to her it is the Tombs that is "just like a wilderness": it is "like a piece of the city gone feral, the wild reclaiming its own," a reversal of the tamed greenery of the park ("Waifs" 15–16). Although the Tombs is "about as far from the green harbor of Fitzhenry Park as you could get in Newford,"[62] both the blight and the park suggest a connection between culture and wilderness. In the park, wild nature predates city culture, whereas the Tombs was once under cultural control—part of the city—but has now turned into wilderness. There are also connections between the two bubbles in the magic domain. While there are gemmin in the Tombs as well, they are forced to leave because of the area's negative memories ("Winter" 162); but other fairies live there, like the bogans that nearly start a war between fairies and animal people in *Widdershins*, and even though they work in Fitzhenry Park, Bones and Carrie have their squat in the Tombs.

There are also several notional links between this area of feral nature within the city and the wilderness outside Newford. In the winter, the snow is left undisturbed on the ground until it melts in the spring, something common only outside cities ("Winter" 153). The area has derived its name from serving as the dumping ground for old car wrecks ("That Explains" 109), and cars are not the only things people dump there. Packs of feral dogs once thrown from passing cars hunt at the Tombs; the reader is told how unwanted dogs are "returned to nature" in the same way both in the Tombs and in the countryside. Even the descriptions of the Tombs link it to the wilderness outside. Not only is the area frequently referred to as a *wilderness* or *jungle*; unlike the rest of the city, the physical architecture in this part of Newford tends to be more fully described. Streets, dilapidated buildings, squats, even empty lots are described as having a physical presence that is just as important as the people there. The same applies to the wilderness outside the city—its physical locales are described in detail. The Tombs is a bubble of wilderness, of feral nature, within the city's culture.

This scene of urban blight attracts the more sinister inhabitants of the magical domain, such as the monstrous couple who kidnap Harriet in "Pity the Monster" (1991) and the murderous Rushkin and his equally malicious numena in *Memory and Dream*. The dark spirit in *From a Whisper to a Scream* is particularly associated with the Tombs: it is there that the pedophile Teddy Bird is killed, only to return from the grave driven by the need to sexually abuse his daughter. A voodoo priest attempts to exorcise Bird's spirit at a crossroads among the deserted lots, and it is in one of the derelict houses that the final confrontation between the spectral Bird and his daughter takes place. Among the benevolent spirits from the Tombs can be found the ghosts encountered in "Waifs and Strays" (1993) and "Dead Man's Shoes" (1993), and numerous other representatives of the magical domain appear among the "night people" there in a great many of the stories. The resulting portrayal is not one of bleak slum but of true wilderness, with predators as well as prey, a place of great variety that contains good as well as evil and beauty as well as ugliness.

A final example of how nature, magic, and alternative culture intersect is not a bubble of wilderness but a bubble in the social structure. In Newford, art spans the three subjugated domains. A vast majority of the protagonists and recurring characters belong to the city's artists: musicians who subsist on busking and occasional small live performances, painters who work as waitresses to subsidize their art, and more or less well-published poets and writers—true artistic creation, the text repeatedly suggests, has magical properties. Minor bubbles defined primarily by art have already been mentioned (such as the Kelledys' home and Rushkin's studio), and others are prominent in various stories, for instance the Tree of Tales.[63] A bubble of art that clearly presents the connection between art, magic, and wild nature is the artists' colony Kellygnow in *Forests of the Heart*. The rambling old house and the surrounding cottages are inhabited by sculptors, painters, and writers, whereas the properties around the colony belong to representatives of city culture and city control: "stockbrokers and investors, bankers and the CEOs of multinational corporations, celebrities and the nouveau riche" (11). In the forested grounds of the house, there are even huge, towering oaks that "were thought to be part of the original growth forest that had once laid claim to all the land" (12). At Kellygnow, a variety of people and spirits belonging to Newford's magical domain converges: in one of the cottages lives a woman who never ages; the house is protected by a genius loci, a protective spirit, fled from Ireland;[64] a pack of homeless genii loci regularly haunts the grounds; a *curandera*, or magic healer, from Arizona models for the artists and supplies them with amulets; and it is there that the Green Man is eventually conjured forth. Through the bubble of wilderness that is the Kellygnow estate, characters even pass, intentionally and unintentionally, into the Otherworld. The artists' colony becomes a focal point for the domains that challenge the mundane "day people" society.

The Newford stories make clear how the hegemonic culture in Newford contains its own opposites. Bubbles of wilderness abound in the city—areas of nature that culture cannot control, or of which it has relinquished control. An alternative culture of "night people"—the homeless and abused, as well as the artists and musicians—ekes out a living hidden and unseen. Similarly unseen and unwanted, fairies and spirits, ghosts and magicians try to withstand the ravages of a blind culture. Rather than being a city surrounded by wilderness, as is Minas Tirith, Newford turns the image around and presents an internal wilderness of alternative culture, magic, and nature within the city, a wilderness that is both portrayed as a threat to culture and presented as its ultimate hope of survival.

BLURRED BOUNDARIES: CONFLUX IN NEW CROBUZON[65]

Perdido Street Station (2000) is China Miéville's second novel and the first to be set in the world of Bas-Lag. The novel's setting is reminiscent of a mid-nineteenth-century industrial city that is, according to Miéville, "clearly analogous to a chaos-fucked Victorian London" although it also "contains other cities—Cairo in particular."[66] Steam provides the main source of power, but advanced mechanics, chemistry (chymistry), and magic (thaumaturgy) play important parts in the technological makeup of the society. The city, New Crobuzon, is also the setting of the short story "Jack" (2005) and—partly—of Miéville's fourth novel, *Iron Council* (2004), while his second Bas-Lag novel, *The Scar* (2002), is set mainly in the floating city of Armada.

In Miéville's stories, categories mix and dissolve. The publication of

Perdido Street Station sparked a discussion about how it blurred the boundaries between fantasy, science fiction, and horror, and critics have explored other ways in which Miéville's texts have mixed categories.[67] Rich Paul Cooper observes how styles, and thus voices, as well as generic elements blend in the Bas-Lag novels.[68] Christopher Palmer points out how, in Miéville's descriptive language, opposing qualities meet only to interact or overlap, rather than remaining opposites.[69] Joan Gordon investigates the notion of hybridity in *Perdido Street Station*.[70] Whichever categories we turn to, the Bas-Lag stories have found a way to conflate, blur, or mix them up. The texts not only refuse generic description, they reject the very notion of clear-cut categories. As has already been pointed out, a city is a place where nature and culture meet. At the same time, a city is a place of cultural control. The city limits provide a clear demarcation between the wilderness outside and the controlled inside. In New Crobuzon, any meeting between the two domains calls their separation into question.

Waste is a constantly recurring theme in the description of New Crobuzon's environment, becoming a brutal demonstration of the city as a culturally dominated place. When Yagharek, a garuda (eagle-man) exiled from the desert, enters the city in a small boat in the prologue to *Perdido Street Station*, it becomes clear that New Crobuzon is a city radically different from the clean, white sterility of Minas Tirith or the modern, social space of Newford. To the former desert dweller, the dirty, industrial metropolis is "a vast pollutant, a stench, a klaxon sounding" where "[f]at chimneys retch dirt into the sky" (*Perdido* 1).[71] His entry into the city is described in terms that call to mind the descent into a polluted hell, employing imagery of death and disease to describe the urban decay. The garuda travels on a Stygian river, through a foul-smelling warren of rotting buildings and slime-besmirched brick banks. The water "reflects the stars through a stinking rainbow of impurities, effluents and chymical slop, making it sluggish and unsettling" as it carries along the waste of the vast population (*Perdido* 3). Although this view of the city as a hellish place of pollution, sewage, and waste is emphasized especially in the parts narrated by Yagharek (who is the first-person narrator of the prologue and epilogue and of the brief interludes between the novel's eight parts), it informs the portrayal of New Crobuzon primarily throughout *Perdido Street Station* and also to some extent in *Iron Council*.

In New Crobuzon, pollution is the most obvious sign of how culture invades and dominates the natural domain. As the megalopolis is about the size of present-day London,[72] and given that New Crobuzon's technology for cleaning industrial and household waste and sewage is on a par with London's in the heyday of English industrialization, it is hardly surprising that the metropolis suffers from elevated levels of air and water pollution. As we have seen, the portrayals of the city more than acknowledge the pollution; they foreground it, turning it into one of New Crobuzon's most conspicuous features. Frequent descriptions, powerful imagery, even evocative names help place the focus on how culture's waste products dominate the physical environment. The two rivers that meet in the city center are called the Tar and the Canker, clearly indicating how polluted and pathogenic they are. These are rivers filled with floating trash, their riverbeds a sludge mixed with rusting metal (*Perdido* 298). Appropriately, the black waters of the Tar, on which Yagharek enters the city, are said to trickle rather than flow (*Perdido* 19; see also *Perdido* 606).[73] The Canker is somewhat cleaner, but its name, too, is a telltale sign of how the river is changed by the city; when the water is subjected to chymical and thaumaturgical effluence from the Scientific Quarter, the arcane and chymical slop mixes randomly into "bastard elixirs" that can change, enchant, or kill those who encounter them (*Perdido* 24, 607). The Scientific Quarter is also a source of airborne pollutants; but the New Crobuzon air is mainly polluted by the many factories whose smokestacks puncture "the membrane between the land and the air" and disgorge "tons of poisonous smog [. . .] as if out of spite," and by the smoke of millions of household chimneys that turns the air above the rooftops into a stinking haze (*Perdido* 64).

There is never any doubt that the air and water in the city are turned into an unclean, unpleasant, unnatural "second nature." A constant flow of waste resulting from the customs, behaviors, and material objects that the members of New Crobuzon's society use to cope with their world (to return to Bates's definition of culture) maintains the changes even in these fluid elements, turning them into a vivid demonstration of cultural domination. At the same time, the negative connotations of the language used to describe this "second nature," not so much tamed as cowed and bullied into submission, reveal how undesirable this domination is. Pollution is not a necessary, if regrettable, by-product of an industrial, urban lifestyle; it is a disease deliberately passed on, "as if out of spite," to the environment. Even when nature escapes cultural control, it cannot easily recuperate from this disease. The image of disease keeps recurring even when nature reclaims parts that culture has lost or relinquished control of, as in the case of the abandoned, dilapidated docks that have become "massive stinking troughs of malarial slime" (*Perdido* 129). In the city, even nature becomes part, to some extent, of this ambience of filth and disease. Trash is whipped into the air by the wind (*Perdido* 58); slimy, mold-encrusted sewers, ecosystems in themselves, empty the waste of millions of people into the rivers (*Perdido* 419–20, 425); garbage is piled into dumps that have grown to a geological scale. The "second nature" of pollution is not nature changed according to the desires of culture; it becomes its own domain of waste and trash, neither culture nor nature but a disease that affects both, a dirty smear that hides the border between them.

The two domains are even less distinguishable when examined in terms of the shape of the land itself, as the natural and cultural landscapes shift into and imitate each other. The natural landscape, a result of geological, meteorological, and biological factors, is changed by the city into a cultural landscape as "[t]he natural inclines of the land [are] all forgotten by New Crobuzon" (*Iron* 59). This cultural landscape, or cityscape, is sometimes reshaped, in turn, into another sort of landscape, a land in whose shape the cultural and natural merge. The clearest example is that of the "trashscape" (*Perdido* 446). The rubbish dump of the factories and docks along the river Tar has become a "landscape of ruin and refuse and industrial filth [. . .] in a speeded-up parody of geological process" where the "rejected matter settled and shifted and fell into place, affecting some shape, mimicking nature. Knolls, valleys, quarries and pools bubbling with fetid gas" (*Perdido* 314). The natural landscape, the plain on which New Crobuzon is situated, has been transformed and fallen under cultural control, but has then escaped that control in a "parody of geological process" that has reconfigured the land into a trashscape with its own canyons, caverns, and reefs of rubbish (*Perdido* 446–47). Neither nature nor culture is the agent behind this reshaping; it is the refuse itself, culture's *rejected* matter, that forms the trashscape.

The portrayal of the trashscaping process accentuates how the rejected matter becomes something separate from both nature and culture. At first, the matter only settles passively; but for each subsequent verb in the description, there is an increase in both agency and purpose until the matter *affects* a shape and finally *mimics* nature. Rejected by culture and only mimicking nature, trash—like air and water pollution— comes to occupy an indistinct position somewhere between nature and culture, blurring the boundary between them. The land it shapes becomes a haven for feral nature in the form of various tenacious weeds, as well as for *wild culture*; the latter is most clearly represented by the Construct Council, the artificial sentience sprung from discarded difference engines. This renegade culture lies at the center of one of the six plots identified by Farah Mendlesohn in *Perdido Street Station*: "the threat that the city's constructs (robots) have achieved sentience."[74] The trashscape of the dump is thus portrayed as a distorted mirror image of a wilderness, superimposing cultural landforms on natural ones and vice versa.

Layers of trash and ubiquitous pollution are not the only manifestations of the blurred border between nature and culture. The city as a whole is portrayed as a complex topography of urban strata, "a palimpsest of gusting trees and architecture and sound, ancient ruins, darkness, catacombs, building sites, guesthouses, barren land, lights and pubs and sewers" (*Perdido* 673). All the parts of the city flow together, rendering the boundaries between opposites indistinct; light and darkness, ruins and building sites, catacombs and pubs, trees and architecture all meet as aspects of the city. The various layers, possible to arrange spatially, with architecture on top of catacombs on top of sewers, and temporally, with barren land turned into building sites turned into guesthouses and pubs, in fact form their own totality. New Crobuzon is not a neat succession or orderly layering but a chaotic blend, in which other layers are always co-present. The earlier landscape has been scraped off and replaced; the "tons of concrete and tar that [constitute] the city [cover] ancient geography, knolls and barrows and verges, undulations that [are] still visible" (*Perdido* 63).

The natural landscape exists as part of the cultural, in and underneath it, a conflux further emphasized by the employment of natural imagery to portray New Crobuzon's architecture. Not only is the "architectural landscape" referred to as a "townscape" or "roofscape," the cultural and the natural are brought together in the many metaphors and similes with which the text is rife: the city itself is a fen of buildings with concrete forest slums and quagmire ghettos, where the Parliament building is an inselberg of architecture, tower blocks rise like weeds, and the streets run like watercourses between the buildings (*Iron* 71, 442; *Perdido* 96, 145, 129). Occasionally, the imagery moves from the metaphoric to the concrete. The gargantuan proportions of Perdido Street Station itself gives it characteristics generally associated with a natural landscape. There seems to be a cultural triumph in the "chaotic majesty" of Perdido

Street Station as it outdoes even the "magnificent and portentous" foot-hills west of the city, but the massive edifice is geographical rather than architectural. The station building has spread like waves of lava over the surrounding cityscape, a mountain with its own foothills and hillocks, and its roof has a little wilderness floored with scrub and dead, thigh-high grass. Covering the small eponymous street is an architectural sky (*Perdido* 615–21; *Iron* 382, 479–80).

Tame nature, nature controlled by culture but not dominated by its waste products, is rare and disregarded. Another architectural sky arches over the New Crobuzon cactacea (cactus people), who live under the glass and iron girder dome of the Glasshouse, the immense construction that encloses their artificial environment. The constructed desert landscape and gardens, where even sand dunes are carefully sculpted to mimic the ripples made by the never-present wind, is the largest and best-described patch of tame nature to be found in New Crobuzon. Tame nature also oc-curs in a number of minor parks, gardens, and tree-lined avenues, many of them located in the various uptown areas. In the shadow of Perdido Street Station lies BilSantum Plaza with parkland at its center (*Perdido* 615), and the Piazza della Settimana di Polvere is "a trimmed garden of fox-rose and tall stones" in an area where willows "softened each corner" (*Iron* 301). Other parks are occasionally mentioned in passing, equally scantily described, sometimes only as "insignificant parks" or even "small apologetic parks" (*Perdido* 211, 575). All but ignored, these pockets of tame nature give the impression of being exceptions, exotic places visited briefly if at all by the characters.

Even in this place of overwhelming cultural control, the natural do-main finds ways back to the wild. The largest of the parks, and the only one described in some detail, is Sobek Croix, where the scientist Isaac and his companions visit a fair in *Perdido Street Station*. Most of this park is tamed to the point of oppression: the grass and paths are "sticky with spilt sugar and sauce," bushes and tree boughs are decorated with paper bunting, and people of various races crowd the paths (*Perdido* 83). It is a park of flower beds, controlled by culture and surrounded by an iron fence; but there are also acres of untended growth inside (*Per-dido* 83, 17). Unlike the primeval wilderness deep in Newford's Fitzhenry Park, but like all natural wilderness found in New Crobuzon, the un-tended land in Sobek Croix is feral nature, freed from cultural control. A similar lack of control can be seen in the smaller garden that lies at the bottom of the huge concrete rectangle of the Mandragorae Wing. It is "an *unkempt* garden, *overgrown* with darkwood trees and exotic woodland flowers," and it is likened to "moss at the bottom of a well" (*Perdido* 276; my emphasis). The "rude gardens," with their "mutant apple trees and wretched brambles, dubious compost, mud and broken toys" (*Perdido* 675), through which Isaac and the others flee also signal a lack of cultural control. In all three cases, nature is going or has gone feral. Cultural control is slackening, disappearing, enabling the tame to turn wild again. This loss of control can also be identified elsewhere. Feral nature springs up all over the city, intermingling with tame nature as well as with culture. The Griss Twist dump, abode of the Construct Council, is "the size of a small park, though infinitely more feral" (*Perdido* 445; see also 446, 600–601); but incursions of feral nature are generally smaller and more obviously melded with the surrounding city culture. A weed-choked yard and ancient, moldering tables sit outside a pub (*Perdido* 24), and rusted station doors are anchored against the wall by ivy (*Perdido* 130). Empty lots have become "little wildernesses of concrete-splitting bramble and cow-parsley, wildnesses [*sic*] for the insects" (*Iron* 556). The railway arches sprout a "microforest of mould and moss and tenacious climbing plants" that "[swarms] with lizards and insects" (*Perdido* 596). Where there are gaps in the city culture, opened by decay, destruction, or disregard, nature can escape cultural control and turn feral; but rather than establishing a city wilderness, these pockets of feral nature emphasize how they remain part of the cultural surroundings.

The pockets of feral nature suggest a meeting between nature and culture in which the location rather than the boundary is important. There is no transition from one domain to the other, just occasional dots of nature in the cultural surroundings. However, transitions are a central theme in New Crobuzon. In her discussion of the city as hybrid, Gordon cites the crime lord Mr. Motley, whose body incorporates parts from enough creatures to fill a medium-sized zoo: "Transition. The point where one thing becomes another. It is what makes you, the city, the world, what they are. [. . .] The zone where the disparate become part of the whole. The hybrid zone" (*Perdido* 41). Gordon turns her attention to the hybrid dimension of New Crobuzon itself,[75] but a hybrid zone also exists where the city meets the world outside—where its culture meets the surrounding nature. Unlike both Minas Tirith's clear-cut boundary and the gradual but obvious transition between Newford and the surrounding wilderness, New Crobuzon's boundary is porous. Like the allegorical (but biologically inaccurate) frog that will remain in boiling water, rather than jumping out, if the temperature is raised slowly enough, visitors to New Crobuzon do not notice the city as they enter it—until they suddenly find themselves there. To the returning Iron Council, there is a sensation of suddenness in their arrival: "Still empty land, only a few half-kept orchards, a few groves of temperate fruit-trees. There was a moment of transition. They were in the wilds, in unsafe lands, and then with a suddenness and a strange anticlimax they were in domesticated country. They knew they were close" (*Iron* 519). The Councilors cannot see the city limits as they approach; they only realize their position when they have already passed the point of no return, when it is too late for them, as for the unfortunate amphibian, to jump out. Where Thomas Morningstar observes how the landscape changes in stages as he leaves Newford, the Councilors experience only "a moment of transition" between wilderness and tame lands. Yagharek's impression is similar: he observes how New Crobuzon grows around him as he approaches it, but there is still a sense of abruptness when he suddenly finds himself there. "How could we not see this approaching?" the garuda asks himself. "What trick of topography is this, that lets the sprawling monster hide behind corners to leap out at the traveler?" (*Perdido* 2).

Parts of the city limit crumble before, or are permeated by, the surrounding wilderness. An attempt to extend New Crobuzon to the south, into Rudewood forest, fails, and the forest reclaims the train tracks and the railway station (*Perdido* 96, 143). Between the forest and the city proper lies Spatters, a shantytown that is not really part of the metropolis but has simply attached itself to it. While the limit between Spatters and Rudewood is only defined by the random outlines of the shantytown, the city is clearly demarcated from Spatters by a narrow park of grass and trees, and an eight-foot ditch filled with a mixture of polluted water and human waste (*Perdido* 144–46). Similarly to Minas Tirith, New Crobuzon protects itself from the wilderness outside by tame nature, the narrow park and the Pelennor skirting their respective cities. Instead of a protective wall like the Rammas Echor, however, only a trench and its disgusting contents serve as final protection. It is hard to say whether the trench is even part of the shantytown wilderness from which the city and the people of the closest city district try so hard to separate themselves. The wilderness of Spatters is a cultural wilderness, however, which segues into the natural wilderness of Rudewood. The interface between the culture of the city and the natural wilderness outside is not tame nature but wild culture.

The region between the city and the sky above it is another example of how the boundary between New Crobuzon and the world outside is porous. While the sky would generally be assumed to be an aspect of uncontrolled, wild nature, or at least strongly associated with it, the air above the metropolis is controlled (or intended to be controlled) by culture through aeromorphic engines run by meteoromancers (*Perdido* 205; see also *Perdido* 231). Flying insects, lizards, birds, and wyrmen share the urban skies with aerostats, cable-held militia-pods, and trains that traverse the air on their various levels above the rooftops. High-rising buildings thrust upward, and smokestacks and chimneys breach "the membrane between the land and the air" (*Perdido* 64). An alternative, improvised street network stretches from rooftop to rooftop. It is through this interstitial realm that Jack Half-a-Prayer runs on his "Steeplechase" escape from the militia, with skies all fuzzy with airships and wyrmen ("Jack" 207). The air and the skies above New Crobuzon, wild once the city is left far enough behind, are controlled, tamed, and used in the city's vicinity. The city bubbles up into the sky, its boundary as indistinct as those boundaries indicated by the crumbling walls whose "bricks [seem] to effervesce into the air" (*Iron* 91).

The conflux of nature and culture inside the city, and porous boundaries between the city and the wilderness outside, that is found in New Crobuzon can also be detected in *The Scar*. Its central setting, the pirate city Armada, is considerably smaller than New Crobuzon, only about a square mile. It consists of several hundred ships and craft of all kinds and sizes, tied together and facing all directions (*Scar* 79). The wilderness that surrounds the city is the open sea, empty from horizon to horizon and well beyond, and it is through this desolate wilderness that the city constantly travels, tugged (initially) by the "cloud" of tugboats that surrounds it. Like the airborne crafts and vehicles of New Crobuzon, these ships extend Armada's sphere of control beyond the city proper into the wilderness, blurring the boundary between sea and city. The surrounding water flows constantly in between the numerous vessels, through the pores of Armada's boundary. In other words, even as the city moves through the surrounding wilderness, the wilderness flows into and moves through the city and, in doing so, becomes part of Armada, coming under the city's control, if only for a while and to some extent. The multitude of canals between the vessels prevents the water from forming waves even during storms (*Scar* 364) and offers a measure of control over what, outside the city, is wild nature. This control or taming of the wilderness is not enough to make storms safe, however, only less dangerous.

The porous boundary is found above and below Armada as well. In the water under the city, divers, dolphins, seawyrms, and cray (who are part human, part lobster) work with and live in various submerged structures, and "a constant drool of trash" billows from Armada into the sea (*Scar* 75). The air above the city is

> full of craft. Gondolas swayed beneath dirigibles, ferrying passengers across the angling architecture, descending between close-quartered housing and letting down rope ladders, cruising past much larger airships that hauled goods and machinery. [. . .] Masts were mooring posts, sprouting aerostats of various shapes, like plump, mutant fruit. (*Scar* 84; see also *Scar* 235)

The pirate city has no definite limits. On the surface, it dissipates into a cloud of tugboats, letting the ocean in between its component vessels; underneath, Armada citizens of various species and extraction mark the water as a part of the city by living and working there. Even the air is a space claimed by Armadan culture, just as porous and penetrable as the skies above New Crobuzon.

The boundary in Armada is so porous that one wrong step on the slippery bridges that connect the vessels is enough to slip out of Armada into the sea that permeates the city (*Scar* 89); but the half-tame sea is not the only tame nature to occur inside the pirate city. Among the countless naval architectures that make up Armada can be found a remnant of nature, now transformed by cultural usage, in the form of "a barge carved from the ossified body of a whale" (*Scar* 79). Agriculture and animal husbandry are found inside the city, and the large Croom Park is spread across a war-shattered steamer and some smaller ships. For obvious reasons, most manifestations of terrestrial nature give a highly artificial appearance to Armada's decks, hulls, and holds. As in the cactacean Greenhouse, nature has been patiently created. The rusted hull of the steamer has been filled with stolen soil, burying the coke in the coal bunkers and creating an artificial seam of coal in the process (*Scar* 162). But over the centuries, the artificial, controlled nature of the park has become less tame. In Armada, tame nature has been allowed to go feral: "There were cultivated flowerbeds on the Curhouse gunboat, but on the steamer's corpse the woods and meadows of Croom Park were wild" (*Scar* 163). But whereas the sea is an unconditional necessity of the pirate city's existence, wild terrestrial nature could easily be kept in check. Feral nature is accepted, and, should the need arise, possible to bring back under control. The same is generally true for most of the wilderness that intermingles with the city's culture—the tribes of wild animals that roam the city and the greenery that makes the masts look like ancient trees, to name a couple of examples. Just as unlucky citizens can slip into the water and out of the city, however, the wilderness outside can slip in through the porous boundary, for example when predatory fish attack the city's divers from the dark depths (*Scar* 187). Whereas New Crobuzon is a city where culture is as wild as nature, the ever-present wilderness of the surrounding sea is a constant threat in Armada.

The commune of the Iron Council, while much smaller than Armada and New Crobuzon, displays much the same pattern of blurred borders between nature and culture as the larger cities. The rebellious rail workers and prostitutes of the Council cut off the train from the main tracks that stretch back like an umbilical cord to New Crobuzon. No longer tied to the city, "the perpetual train" goes wild and, with it, the Iron Council escapes along constantly reused tracks into the wilderness. When Judah Low returns to the Iron Council after several years back in New Crobuzon studying "the arcane end of golemetry," he finds a utopia, where the train has "gone feral" (*Iron* 338). Its culture is now wild and has flowed together with nature. The old structures of the Council's train are still present, but have been changed and are "crenellated, baroque and topped with dovecots." Some carriages are "thickened with ivy and waxy vines"; two flatbeds are filled with herb gardens and another two with grassy graveyards. One of the new carriages is built with resin-caulked driftwood (*Iron* 338–39). Rather than attempting to bring the wilderness under cultural control, culture is subjugated to nature or at least mixed with it. This conscious bridging of the border between nature and culture is most clearly visible in the ornamentation of the front engine, which is decorated in order to make it zoomorphic:

> Its headlamps were eyes now, predictably, bristling with thick wire lashes, its cowcatcher a jawful of protruding teeth. The huge tusks of wilderness animals were strapped and bolted to them. The front nub of its chimney wore a huge welded nose, the smokestack ajut from it in nonsense anatomy. Sharpened girders gave it horns. (*Iron* 339)

What was patently a cultural artifact has hence been remade into an effigy of a living creature. Still very artificial, it has been given eyes, teeth, nose, and horns, blending nature and culture. In this attempt to mimic nature, the only part of the engine that still betrays a clearly cultural origin is the smokestack, nonsensical in the blended anatomy.

The Iron Council even becomes a part of the landscape through which it moves. The train travels, perpetually, on an ellipse of tracks through miles of gardens, cropland, and fields that, beyond the rails, were "dissipating and merging with wild flora." Tame and wild nature merge around the railway tracks, which describe the path of a wheeled town "neither sedentary nor nomadic" (*Iron* 340–41). Again, there are no clear borders, only a hub where culture and nature have blended together and around which there is a porous boundary where tame and wild nature flow into each other.

In the palimpsestic cityscape of New Crobuzon, among the fettered Armadan ships, and on the perpetual train, culture and nature meet—in different ways, to be sure, but always blurring the boundaries between the domains or even making the concept of separate domains indistinct. Around each of the three cultural centers, there is a fuzzy "hybrid zone" where the centers become part of the world and the world part of them. This indistinctness is also present in other meetings between nature and culture in New Crobuzon. The cultural oppression constituted by the pollution and waste creates a diseased "second nature," a liminal zone situated between the domains, not natural (at least not in the sense of Keekok Lee's nature$_{nh}$) but also rejected by culture. The city landscape is not either natural or cultural but both, architecture and trash turning into landscape, landscape becoming part of city culture; and the cultural domain is dotted by nature, tame and feral, not quite separate from but melding with the cultural domain. The urban sprawl has turned into a cultural wilderness, just as wild as the natural wilderness that surrounds it, and the natural wilderness is brought together with the cultural. In Armada, the wild sea is a nonnegotiable fact of the city's existence. That the tame, terrestrial nature that has been artificially created on the many vessels sometimes becomes wild is accepted and allowed; the small pockets of feral nature pale in comparison to the surrounding wilderness of the sea. The Iron Council, on the other hand, actively moves toward wilderness, turning the cultural artifact of the "perpetual train" into a blend of the natural and the cultural.

Ultimately, the blending of nature and culture constitutes an example of the central concern in Miéville's texts. On every level, blending takes place, from the meeting and mixing of genres to the various hybrid species that populate the world. The blurring of categories lies at the very heart of these stories. When Mr. Motley stresses that the chaotic aggregate that is his body *"is not error or absence or mutancy,"* his words are also a comment on the hybridity, blurring, and palimpsests that make up Miéville's texts—and the world of Bas-Lag. And Motley's emphatic point is as true of his impossible collection of features as of the three cities, where culture and nature flow into each other through porous boundaries: "This is totality" (*Perdido* 115).

Patricia A. McKillip's *Ombria in Shadow* is set in the city-state of Ombria. Technologically and politically, the setting draws on the Italian city-states of the Renaissance, and the novel bases its plot on the political and personal conflicts that follow the ruthless regent Domina Pearl's rise to power. The protagonists must negotiate a complex web of forged and broken loyalties to survive in their struggle against the cruel regent.[77]

The story and its characters move through four clearly demarcated physical zones located between two poles. At the top and center of the city, Domina Pearl and the dark doorway form the duality of the first pole, she representing the city's despair and the doorway its hope. Surrounding them is first the zone of hidden rooms, stairs, and passages of the secret palace, then the zone of the public palace beyond. Outside and beneath the palace lies the zone of the city streets, and under Ombria, furthest toward the periphery, lies the undercity. In this lowest and most peripheral zone, the second pole resides, the sorceress Faey. The crossing from zone to zone is central to the plot structure, something that is reflected in how nature is constructed as a liminal phenomenon in Ombria.

On the surface, Ombria seems to encompass nature–culture relations that are very similar to those already identified in the cities discussed thus far. A closer analysis reveals a different pattern, however. As in Minas Tirith, very little nature is present in McKillip's city; but on the other hand, what nature there is can be found inside the city—whatever wilderness or tame nature exists in the countryside surrounding Ombria is only referred to obliquely. Small patches of both tame and feral nature appear in the city, suggestive of the incursions of feral nature found in

New Crobuzon, and the streets in Ombria certainly share some of the larger city's wildness (for instance, the nightmarish gauntlet that the old prince's mistress, Lydea, is forced to run through the dark streets of Ombria, while accosted by anonymous street people [10–11]). Unlike the situation with regard to New Crobuzon, however, no blurring occurs in Ombria; culture dominates the city without blending with nature. While Ombria shares this clear cultural domination with Newford, McKillip's city sees no challenge from subjugated nature, nor is there any clear connection between nature and any of the city's zones.

Instead, nature appears where one zone is exited and another entered. At the borders between Ombria's four zones, and especially where these borders are crossed, nature tends to turn up, wild or tame or—a common occurrence in the palace—as cultural representation. While this last type of nature is really an aspect of culture, the carvings, paintings, and drawings of flowers in particular are often brought metaphorically to life. On the walls, birds *fly* overhead and roses *open*, while doors *grow* gardens (79); and the painted irises on the black gate's posts *twine* and *bloom* (32; also 288). These cultural representations fit the pattern of nature as a liminal phenomenon, suggesting a desire for the natural in a city where nature is largely if not completely absent. This desire for nature also comes across in Ducon's drawings of what might be found beyond the dark portal. His drawings contain "fantasies of airy palaces, endless woods and frothy seas" and "a city that might have been Ombria, if [. . .] the windows overlooking its twisted streets were filled with flowers" (213). Through his images, Ducon expresses a yearning for a world better than his own yet similar, surrounded by and adorned with nature. At the same time, these drawings reinforce the liminality of nature by associating it with the dark portal and thus with the border between Ombria and its shadow.

Entering the innermost zone often constitutes a search for hope at the risk of finding despair. The prevalence of culturally represented nature is suggested already when Ducon first enters the secret palace with the five-year-old prince Kyel after the death of the boy's father. Although he has used some hidden corridors to get away from Domina Pearl and her guards, it is not until they have passed through "three hinged panels limned with carved roses" (28) that he and Kyel are safe and free to talk. By entering the room behind the panels, they have reached what Ducon hopes is, and Kyel believes to be, a safe space. This feeling of safety and Ducon's love for his younger cousin are further emphasized by the roses carved on the panels. Whereas the roses are only mentioned in passing at this point, the rose has already been introduced as a recurring symbol of safety and love. When Lydea is thrown out of the palace after the old prince's death, her father's tavern, the Rose and Thorn, is her only safe haven, and while, at the beginning, Lydea's hope for her father's love is tainted by despair, mutual if grudging love finally wins out. It is thus from the tavern that she takes her name when reappearing masked as Mistress Rose Thorn; and as Mistress Thorn, Lydea brings comfort to Kyel, who calls her his own secret Rose (215). While love remains strong if not powerful, the safety symbolized by the rose is never uncompromised in Ombria. When Ducon returns to the public palace to find himself at the mercy of Domina Pearl, it is into the old nurse's room he has taken his young cousin. Their passage back leads through a secret door that, rather than being associated with safety, is connected to Domina Pearl's superiority, to a place of despair. Kyel's nurse, Jacinth, has been banished by the Black Pearl, leaving only a scent of violets in her former room (35). In this room, Kyel is taken into custody and Ducon himself is warned not to interfere, first directly and then indirectly through the dead body of a courtier and conspirator, Hilil Gamelyn. It is also here that Kyel leaves the drawings that express the child's own despair. Still, traces of nature linger around this crossing between zones, in the traces of Jacinth's scent as well as in the palm leaf that has been placed over Gamelyn's dead face.

The palm leaf is echoed in the palms in the conservatory, where Ducon leaves the body. Apart from the palm leaf that covers the dead man's face, this is the only place where the border between the secret and public palace is explicitly linked to actual nature. The secret door is hidden behind "a fan of giant fern leaves" (87), and the conservatory contains potted palms as well as representations of nature on its walls. While part of the zone of the public palace, it is a place seldom occupied and thus a suitable meeting place for the older courtiers, including Gamelyn, who are plotting against Domina Pearl. It is a place of transgression, of the border between the two zones, but also of Domina Pearl's power as regent. Here, the courtiers attempt to persuade Ducon to change sides, to make him cross another border. Eventually, they fail in this effort just as they fail to keep their plot from the attention of the regent.

The door through which Faey's protégée Mag sees Ducon disappear in the hallway is a safer door than both the door in Jacinth's room and the one in the conservatory. As on the panels, the rose symbol is employed here: Mag finds that pressing a small rosette in the wall opens a door into the secret palace, allowing her to enter it (125). At this point, she has already fallen in love with Ducon (although she does not understand it herself) and searches for him to prevent his death. Again, the rose symbol is linked to safety and love; but this time Mag fails in her quest. The same door also saves Lydea from the guards, bringing her from certain capture in one zone to an uncertain chase in the maze of another (259). In both cases, the women's attempts are nearly frustrated by Domina Pearl; Mag is locked into the regent's secret library but escapes with the help of Kyel's tutor, and Lydea, rather than accepting capture, leaps through the dark doorway. The rosette that marks the way across the border into the secret palace does not ensure uncompromising safety, but it does not signify any ultimate failure, either.

The most noticeable threshold guardians are found at the palace's west gate. Although some gardens are mentioned, and these might be construed as marking the border between the zones of the palace and the streets of Ombria, these gardens are there in name only. Lydea thinks back on her time as the old prince's mistress, recalling "a view of the gardens and the sea" (193) from high up in the palace. The impression of the gardens as a border phenomenon is reinforced when Ducon uses a passage "beneath the back gardens to the street" (216) to get into the city, which lies between the palace and the sea. In both cases, the gardens remain empty, featureless, and devoid of description; but they confirm that nature is a liminal phenomenon. That pattern becomes more distinct at the palace's west gate, which is the main crossing between the zone of the palace and that of the city streets. There grows "the gaudy patch of sunflowers [. . .] that did nothing all day long but turn their golden-haired, thousand-eyed faces to follow the sun. The Prince of Ombria [. . .] never bothered with what stood outside his iron gates on their graceful, gargantuan stalks and sometimes peered over his wall" (15). Metaphors transform the flowers to animals or even people. The imagery focuses on the sunflowers as spectators of the drama that takes place in the palace and at its gates, seeing that which is hidden to Ombria's citizens. When Lydea is expelled by Domina Pearl after the prince's death, the sunflowers "[hang] their heavy heads like mourners" (8) and seem to watch the proceedings with "[t]heir great, strange faces, all eyes" (9). Even the sunflowers fail to see all the dark dealings that go on, however. When Mag delivers the death spell to Domina Pearl, the flowers droop by the gate, their eyes picked out by birds (24); and once the change has been carried through and a new Ombria has been established, the ersatz witnesses are no longer needed. When Lydea passes through the west gate in what is the novel's final crossing from palace to city streets, only a "crop of blind, withered sunflowers" is left (297). The palace is no longer hidden from the view of the citizenry; there is no more need for watchers at the gate.

The one other entrance into the palace unwatched by the sunflower spectators is still associated with them. Mag has found a way that passes *under* the flowers, and on both occasions when she ventures into the palace it is (explicitly) under the sunflowers she has to go (73, 122). They remain, in the text, the boundary markers that must be passed in the crossing from one zone into the other. To Mag, however, the chamber under the sunflowers is also the only meeting point of Faey's and Domina Pearl's dominions. Neither sorceress can venture into the city streets of Ombria. Although nothing seems to prevent the regent from leaving the palace, she never goes farther than the west gate, whether to expel the unwanted mistress or to receive a charm from Mag. Her information comes from spies, and the only mention of her moving into the city streets (apart from a vague hint that she rides to the old prince's funeral in a carriage) is when the Black Pearl escapes from the forces that come through the portal. She might have vanished, it is suggested, "into the streets of Ombria, where she would find no opening door that would save her, and no bed except her last" (287). Nor are the city streets, or any zone other than her own, accessible to Faey. When she leaves the undercity, and then only to go to Domina Pearl's timeless sanctum in the secret palace, the balance between Ombria and its shadow shifts (278). Like Domina Pearl, she needs an intermediary to act in the no man's (or, rather, woman's) land between them that is Ombria's streets.

Numerous doors between the street zone and the undercity are mentioned in the narrative, most of them merely in passing. The door under the patch of sunflowers has already been discussed, but two other crossings are described in the text in detail. When Lydea searches for Mag, she enters through an old, dilapidated shop from which Faey takes her to an illusory chamber on the bank of the dark river. Not only are its walls "sprigged with painted violets," the chamber is filled with potted plants (108). These plants become emblematic for the room, recurring in the text during Faey and Lydea's discussion there until, eventually, the sorceress disbands the illusion. During their conversation, Faey fans herself with leaves from the plants, nibbles them, and finally lets them wither when the illusion is removed (110–12, 132). Constantly, the reader's attention is drawn back to the plants until they disappear, once Faey has made up her mind to let Lydea enter her house. In this way, the plants become associated with the liminal nature of the "leafy chamber" (131), highlighting Lydea's crossing from the street zone to the zone where Faey resides.

The tutor encounters a different border marker during his crossing with Mag. They meet

> in a small, leaf-choked courtyard surrounded by empty buildings. A century ago they had been an inn and its stables and carriage house. Now, roofs were sunken under the weight of moss and rain; [. . .] Those who needed Faey made their way through drifts of leaves and shadows and fallen roof beams to the cupboard door beneath the stairs. (203)

While probably not the most convenient of doors to Faey's undercity, it certainly suits the tutor's passion for history. The dilapidated buildings show the ravages of time; nature has gone feral, "choking" the courtyard and weighing down the roof. It is a place on the border between the zones, situated in one but only visited by those people who have business in the other.

Across the four zones, a field of power stretches between the two poles. Christine Mains remarks on how a split occurs between positive and negative power in Ombria. Domina Pearl wields power from the top of the palace above the city, just as Faey does from her mansion in the undercity. Mains observes how the two women are a catalyst-figure split in two: even if the regent has preserved the same appearance for generations and Faey changes hers several times a day, they are in many ways similar.[78] Taking Mains's observation further, we can examine how their realms mirror each other. These two locales are "edifices," a type of fantasy setting that dominates its landscape and to which there is always more than meets the eye.[79] In Ombria, one edifice towers above the city, another lurks below, each hiding a labyrinth at its heart. Faey occupies the border between the city's present and its past; the Black Pearl can be found on the border between Ombria's present and its future. This future is split into the despair caused by the cruel regent and the desperate hope offered by the dark doorway at the top of the secret palace. The impenetrable gate cannot be opened through most of the novel, acting as a terminus rather than a border—the only future available remains one of despair. Through the doorway, Lydea springs into "nowhere" with Kyel (266); and when Ducon is cornered there, Domina Pearl offers him the choice between the "quick predictable death here, or the long fall into the unknown or the palace cellar, whichever rises to meet you first" (283–84).

Once Ducon opens the gate to Ombria's shadow, the unknown becomes known; the terminus becomes a border across which Ducon's father arrives with his forces to save the city from the oppression of the Black Pearl. This border is similarly associated with nature. The doorway is "distinguished by painted irises twining up the carved wooden posts. One post was cracked, bent under the shifting weight of the ceiling, the paint long warped away. The other still bloomed irises in delicate greens and purples" (32; see also 212, 288). The differences between the doorposts hint at differences between the two worlds on either side of the gate. The shadow city is not simply a copy of Ombria, it is something other. Through the narrative, we are led to suspect that this other place is, in fact, better, and the similarity between *Ombria* and *umbra* suggests that real and shadow are not absolutes—the cities are shadows of each other. "The shadow world is your hope," Ducon's father tells him. "When you no longer despair, you no longer need us" (286). The cracked and bent post signifies an Ombria troubled by Domina Pearl's misuse of power, while the delicate green and purple irises represent the hope of the shadow city. This tie to nature through representation is further strengthened by other sensations experienced at the black opening. Through the gate, Ducon hears the sound of rain, bird-cry, and wind soughing through tall trees, and sometimes the air on the threshold smells of grass, slow rain, and lavender (212, 32; see also 285). Just as the fragrance of *athelas* is used to evoke nature in Minas Tirith, the smells coming through the gate evoke nature in Ombria. It is not primarily the shadow city that is associated with nature in this way, however, but the doorway itself. The irises decorate the doorposts, and it is *on the threshold* that the fragrance of nature reaches Ducon (32).

Of the four cities examined in this chapter, Ombria is the most self-contained. The setting is concentrated on the city's four zones, with a city limit or surrounding wilderness barely present. Brief mentions are made of farm- and forestland around the city, but the focus is on the land's value as productive units (85, 219). The sea is of some importance to trade, and Domina Pearl's upsetting that trade—through piracy and, later, legislation—constitutes a minor plot element. The border between city and sea is down by the port, with its rotten piers, rough docks, and (implied) prostitution. From beyond the sea, strange plants and animals with magical or poisonous properties come to Ombria, and they are used by both Faey and Domina Pearl (40, 142, 253). Moreover, it is to the distant islands that the tutor is banished when his powerful ally has been destroyed (296). The sea is also invoked as part of the scenery outside the city, but left just as nondescript as the palace gardens. In *Ombria in Shadow*, the sea is not even a backdrop against which action takes place; it is what Clute refers to as *water margins*, the "unmapped and ultimately unmappable regions which surround a central empire" and which "fade indefinitely into the distance."[80] The sea, to all intents and purposes, lies not beyond the city limits; it is the city limit.

When the enemy has been vanquished in *The Lord of the Rings*, the rightful ruler takes the throne in Minas Tirith. Aragorn as King Elessar introduces more nature into his capital, making it a meeting place of nature and culture. Just as in Gondor's capital, nature is wanting in Ombria. When Ducon lets his charcoal imagine what lies on the other side of the dark portal, it draws him endless woods and streets lined with flower-decked windows. Ducon considers these pictures to be wishes or dreams of a "prosperous, perfect world, a city of ceaseless delights" (213), suggesting that Ombria, without forests and flowers, is imperfect. The shadow city, the embodiment of hope, also embodies the hope for something better than the real city, something with more nature. In that respect, however, Ombria is never "transformed into its shadow" in the way Mains suggests.[81] Certainly, the city now has a place for those characters who, in Mains's words, "existed precariously on the margins"; but even when hope is fulfilled, Ombria remains a city dominated by culture. Ducon is more concerned with repairing the piers, making the streets safe, and catching, feeding, and educating the street urchins (293) than in any way bringing nature into the city, the way Aragorn does. Rather than being an interface between nature and culture, Ombria remains a place where nature leads a liminal existence. This is particularly true in the palace, where the thresholds between the zones—shadow/real, hidden/visible, palace/city—are in various ways linked to nature, but it generally holds true throughout the city. It is nature that is controlled, tame, or just a set of cultural representations, and it exists not outside, inside, or with culture but somewhere in between.

• • •

Minas Tirith, Newford, New Crobuzon, Ombria—four fantasy cities with four different relations between nature and culture have been examined in this chapter. The range of differences suggests a great variety of relations between the two domains. Although Minas Tirith and Newford suggest a binary opposition, favoring nature, none of the cities implies that equating one domain with good and the other with evil would be possible. In New Crobuzon and Ombria, no opposition even exists between the domains; in Miéville's city, the domains flow into each other, and neither is promoted in relation to the other. In McKillip's case, nature is not even a domain—the cultural domain is all that matters.

What the four cities all have in common, though, is that with each, the nature–culture relation mirrors some central concern. In *The Lord of the Rings*, the pervasive theme of stewardship and how to relate to the natural environment is reflected in the way in which the rightful king introduces nature to the sterile, cultural environment of the city. The Newford stories show nature linked to two similarly marginalized domains, those of social outsiders and magical beings, and the three domains are brought into focus in the various texts. New Crobuzon and other Bas-Lag cities blur the borders between nature and culture in the same way that Miéville's texts blend and dissolve other categories, mixing humans, animals, plants, and machines, treating science as magic and magic as science, and erasing the borders between fantasy, science fiction, and horror. The plot in *Ombria in Shadow* is centered on the passage between the various zones that structure its urban setting, each crossing in some manner associated with the natural world.

Investigating the relation between nature and culture, as we can see from the four examples in this chapter, offers insights into what lies at the core of a work or world. The obvious question is, why? What is it about this particular relation that appears to be so intimately connected to such basic aspects of works?

As has been observed, one could argue that there is no way to separate nature and culture, that they do not stand in any opposition to each other.[82] However, for ten thousand years, ever since humans first decided that the plants on *this* plot of land were worth protecting and, eventually, worth replacing once they had been harvested—in short, ever since we started farming—we have seen the world in terms of "nature" and "culture."[83] In the beginning, it might have been only in terms of "our garden" versus "the thieving birds" and "the annoying weeds," but over the ages, the idea that we control some things and not others has become deeply ingrained as well as quite complex. Today, it has become part of the way most people see the world, especially in "Western civilization." We may consider there to be a difference, and an opposition, or we may believe this opinion to be a fallacy and the reason behind our environmental problems.[84] In either case, we accept that the nature–culture opposition is a dominant and deep-seated view in our society.[85] As such, it is hardly surprising to find this opposition expressed in works of fiction.

Nor is it surprising that the expression is rooted at the heart of the works' respective worldviews. Miéville's world is one of ubiquitous hybridization, where dichotomies are deconstructed, theses and antitheses synthesized, polarities mixed, and borders blurred. On every level in his world, opposites meet, combine, become something greater than the sum of their parts. Blending nature and culture and turning them into new, impossible, and thus fantastic settings spring from the same underlying thrust that drives the Bas-Lag novels. Miéville offers a thought experiment that, if accepted by his readers, takes them to a world that is radically different from the actual world, as most of us are used to perceiving it. If Tolkien is right that fantasy brings "recovery" and allows us to see things clearly, "freed from the drab blur of triteness or familiarity,"[86] then Miéville's thought experiment allows us to see the world in terms of combinations rather than oppositions.

The Newford stories offer a very different kind of recovery. Rather than ridding the fantasy world of opposites, these stories force the reader to shift focus, to pay attention to the part of the duality that is discriminated against. Like Miéville, de Lint creates a distinct worldview; but it is distinct in *what* we are looking at, not *how* we look at it. His worldview is politically motivated, and the recovery it offers is an awareness of how we, who are part of society and of culture, treat our opposites. These opposites are, in Newford, social outsiders and the natural world. The link between their domains and the domain of magic, fairies, ghosts, animal spirits—in short, of the fantastic—turns fantasy into social critique and social critique into fantasy, and the nature–culture relation thus becomes part of the political core of the stories.

In *The Lord of the Rings*, the narrative constantly returns to the question about the "proper" relation between nature and culture, and the answer is invariably stewardship. The natural world is subordinated to culture, whether hobbit, elven, human, dwarven, or entish; but culture is obliged to care for nature. Nature put to cultural use and kept under cultural control—tame nature—is the ideal; both wilderness and environmental degradation are problems that must be solved, faults that must be rectified. The central battle between good and evil thus becomes a conflict between responsible stewardship and its absence. That this central theme expresses itself in a nature–culture relation that associates the right ruler with natural restoration simply goes along with the more obvious environmental themes, according to which evil means uglifying and destroying the environment (in Isengard, Mordor, or the Shire).[87] Middle-earth may seem to offer a wilderness to explore, but the beauty it recovers for us is the beauty of a park or a garden, an orchard or a field of golden corn.

Where Middle-earth is largely a world of nature, the world of McKillip's *Ombria in Shadow* is one of culture, and its conflicts are played out on this cultural stage. In the power struggle, the characters move between the city's zones, their transitions marked by the use of natural imagery. Where the three other authors offer new ways of perceiving the nature–culture duality of the actual world, McKillip takes it to an extreme where nature as a domain is omitted altogether. Her world is the world of urban culture, a social space where nature performs on the edges. It is a world that may yearn for the natural but does not need it; nature is just a representation — for transition, for hope, even for itself — not absent, only symbolic and, ultimately, ornamental.

Each of the four cities offers a new world to its readers, and as an integral part of each world we find an alternative to the traditional nature–culture opposition of the actual world. Even so, they have one thing in common with the actual world: they maintain a division between people and their environment. This division is not necessarily unbridgeable in fantasy worlds, however, and that is the subject of the following chapter.

5 : Realms and Rulers

The previous chapters discussed divisions that are, in one way or another, mainly peculiar to fantasy—either because they do not exist in the actual world, such as polder boundaries, or because, as in the case of the nature–culture division, they can be constructed differently in a fantasy world. This chapter addresses a division that a contemporary reader would generally take to exist in the actual world but that fantasy frequently bridges: the division between people and their environment. Michael Moorcock points out that "our oneness with nature" is a constant theme in epic fantasy and that "[m]any of the writers emphasize the existence of a deep bond between humans and their world. It is the persistent element in a large proportion of modern work."[1] That "deep bond" may actually be even deeper than Moorcock suggests. While a person can act upon, and be acted upon by, his or her surroundings, the actual world requires some sort of physical intermediary for the action to have any effect. In a fantasy setting, a change in someone's state (physical or otherwise) may result in, or from, a corresponding change in the surroundings. This is the case with various nature spirits, for instance; a dryad would suffer and eventually die from the axe blows that felled her tree far away (in C. S. Lewis's *The Last Battle* [1956]), and a water god's body would be begrimed by all the trash that is dumped into its river (vividly illustrated in Hayao Miyazaki's film *Sen to Chihiro no Kamikakushi* [2001; *Spirited Away*]). There is an implied identity between the spirit and its natural abode, even if they may be physically parted. Other connections do not necessarily imply such identity, even if a direct link is present. A frequent connection between land and people is expressed in the direct links that exist between many fantasy rulers and their realms, and it is this connection that is explored here.

This chapter consists of four parts. It opens with an overview of how rulers may be connected both politically and directly to their realms. Then follow two examples of ruler–realm relationships that provide central themes for their respective novels. The first example is the Fisher King figure, the wounded king who is linked to a land that has somehow been laid waste—a common motif in fantasy fiction and, in many ways, a typical way of presenting the direct link between ruler and realm. The application of wasted lands and wounded kings varies from the obvious to the oblique—as exemplified by Malebron of Elidor in Alan Garner's *Elidor* (1965) and Théoden of Rohan in J. R. R. Tolkien's *The Lord of the Rings* (1954–55).[2] Tim Powers uses this trope as a major plot element in *Last Call* (1992), placing it at the center of a complex of related myths in a primary world where the mythical controls the mundane. The second example demonstrates how the ruler–realm link can be used in a more idiosyncratic manner. In *Tourists* (1989), Lisa Goldstein uses the connection between ruler and realm to inscribe a conflict between two kings, and their supporters, on a country. In her novel, the kings are symbolized by different shapes, and the power struggle is expressed in terms of various kinds of palimpsests, turning the physical landscape into a kind of writing.

The fourth and largest part of the chapter examines the landscape connected to Dark Lords. The "landscapes of evil" do not constitute the most common example of direct links between rulers and realms; but especially in portal–quest fantasy, the Dark Lord and the dismal land that surrounds him[3] offer the most evident connection. After an overview of early instances of evil landscapes that capture the main characteristics of the typical Dark Lords' realms, three such realms are discussed in detail: Sauron's Mordor from *The Lord of the Rings* is set in relation to Stephen R. Donaldson's Lord Foul and Robert Jordan's Shai'tan, and their respective lands, to illustrate how the link between ruler and realm can also provide a useful focus in a comparative reading of presentations of evil in fantasy.

LINKING RULERS TO REALMS: AN OVERVIEW

Whether by finding the rightful heir, identifying a suitable candidate for the empty throne, or curing the ailing king, the restoration of the sovereign is a ubiquitous motif in fantasy literature, particularly that of the portal–quest variety. It may be the object of a quest or simply an unintended result; it may even be a minor side effect of the story's general resolution. Whether central or peripheral to the story, whether a recurring theme or a final twist, restoring the ruler—the *proper* ruler, the ruler who will make everything well—is part of many fantasy stories' happy ending. While little has been written about the proper rulers themselves, scholarship paying attention to the happy ending has often included them as a matter of course, so critical thoughts about the ending provide a natural starting point for the ensuing discussion of fantasy rulers and their realms.

Tolkien considered it near compulsory for "complete fairy-stories" to end happily after a eucatastrophe (an unexpected turn for the better),[4] and the fourth and final part of John Clute's model of "the grammar of discourse of fantasy" is "healing/return."[5] The happy ending is only part of a larger framework that fantasy literature shares with folktales, or *Märchen*, as Brian Attebery points out in *The Fantasy Tradition in American Literature*.[6] He introduces Vladímir Propp's analysis of the folktale as a possible means of understanding the structural organization of fantasy stories.[7] A point Attebery does not make, but that is worth observing in the current context, is that although Propp never discusses his hero in terms of being the rightful ruler, the final event—or "function"—of his morphology is the hero's wedding and award, for instance of a large portion of the kingdom.[8] The restored ruler in a fantasy story does not have to be the hero, but weddings and coronations are certainly common (although, as in Propp's morphology, not mandatory); Clute describes the eucatastrophic ending as being "where marriage may occur, just governance fertilize the barren land, and there is a healing."[9]

The above begs one fairly obvious question: what is so "happy" about an ending in which the proper ruler is restored? Clute's description, in all its brevity, offers an answer. With the proper ruler follows healing: the worst is over and things will get better.[10] The restored sovereign promises an end to tyranny and suffering. Marriage, just governance, healing: we find all three elements in the final volume of *The Lord of the Rings* (with the revealing title *The Return of the King*). Aragorn is the true heir who emerges to claim a throne that has remained empty for centuries; his governance promises to be nothing but just, and he heals the land by removing enmity and banditry, as well as by repairing the environmental damage done by Sauron.[11] Despite having won the throne primarily by virtue of his bloodline, Aragorn proves to be an able and just monarch with great political acumen.

There is something more to the relation between the sovereign and his land than political skill, however, and this something, this mysterious link between ruler and realm, explains why the restoration of the sovereign heals the land. That kingship entails more than politics has been noted by other critics. "Most portal-quest fantasies associate the king with the well-being of the land, and the condition of the land with the morality of the place," Farah Mendlesohn claims in *Rhetorics of Fantasy*;[12] and in *The Tough Guide to Fantasyland*, Diana Wynne Jones offers examples, proposing that

> many Kings have a curious relationship with the patch of land they happen to be entitled to rule. If they are absent too long or failing in their duties, crops will not grow, cattle will die, and there will be general bad luck. Countries where a formerly good King develops a serious personality problem will in sympathy evolve a malign microclimate, entailing drought in winter, snow in summer, and rain during the harvest.[13]

The nature of the "curious relationship" is not restricted to the cases brought up by Mendlesohn and Jones; but no matter what form it takes, it is different from the political rulership of, for instance, Aragorn. The sovereign is in one way or another connected directly to the land and affects it immediately rather than through intermediaries. I have therefore chosen to call this association, this "curious relationship," the ruler's *direct link* to the realm.[14] Fantasy plots can be constructed around variations in direct links and their combinations with the political power (or lack thereof) of the rulers, as can be seen from the examples that follow.

The political aspect of a ruler's rule is different from his or her direct link to the realm, which becomes evident when Aragorn is compared to Arren, from Ursula K. Le Guin's third Earthsea novel, *The Farthest Shore*.[15] At a first glance, the two characters have a great deal in common: they are distant relatives of the previous kings; they ascend the throne after the threat against the world has been removed; and their rule is supposed to heal conflict-torn societies. Both characters are brave and noble enough to carry out various heroic exploits (including a trip through a realm of death), and in both cases, the restoration is not the novel's central quest but an immediate result of it. Despite all their similarities, however, there is at least one major difference: while Aragorn takes the throne by virtue of his royal ancestry, Arren is crowned because he fulfills an ancient prophecy. Arren thus becomes king by historical necessity, by predestination rather than inheritance.

Despite being destined to become king, Arren is predominantly a political leader. Like Aragorn, he heals his land by just governance, primarily introducing social stability rather than fertilizing the barren land. In this way, he is the almost total opposite of the Childlike Empress of Fantastica in Michael Ende's *Die unendliche Geschichte* (1979; transl. *The Neverending Story* [1983]), a story that revolves around the restoration first of the ruler and then of the realm. The Empress is directly connected to her realm to such an extent that discussing ruler and realm as separate concepts is almost meaningless; ruler and realm are metonyms for each other. Her disease and the Nothing that destroys Fantastica are aspects of the same affliction and have the same source; both also have the same cure. When Bastian gives the Childlike Empress a new name, Fantastica is saved along with her. At the same time, she is not a political leader.

> The Childlike Empress — as her title indicates — was looked upon as the ruler over all the innumerable provinces of the [boundless] Fantastican Empire, but in reality she was far more than a ruler; [rather] she was something entirely different. [. . .] She was simply there in a special way. She was the center of all life in Fantastica.[16]

The Empress never exercises any political or military power; her governance is not just or unjust, it is nonexistent. Bastian (and the other people who have attempted to make themselves Emperors of Fantastica) cannot understand this metonymic relation, cannot realize that while the provinces of Fantastica can be conquered, it is impossible to become Emperor. The Childlike Empress and her realm are two sides of the same coin; each is the other, the two always linked. Bastian can rule politically, but the Empress does not rule her realm, she *is* her realm. She is as closely tied to Fantastica as is imaginable. A similar unity between ruler and realm is found — on a smaller scale — in Patricia A. McKillip's Riddle-master series (1976–79), where rulership, or "land-rule," comes with a total awareness of the realm, if only for a moment. When the land-rule is passed on to Prince Morgon of Hed, he briefly sees "every leaf, every seed, every root in Hed"; he even feels himself to *be* every leaf and seed.[17]

Metonymic relations between realm and ruler are uncommon, however; political power is generally combined with some direct link to the realm. For instance, despite the insistence of the murdered king Verence of Lancre that the land and the king are one,[18] the sovereign in Terry Pratchett's *Wyrd Sisters* is quite clearly a political figure. Lancre is explicitly divided into people and "kingdom" (meaning not only the geography but also all its animals and plants, as well as its history),[19] political power first and foremost meaning power over the people. The direct link between realm and ruler only means that the king of Lancre must care for his kingdom; it is, as the witch Granny Weatherwax explains, like a dog, which "doesn't care if its master's good or bad, just so long as it likes the dog."[20] The usurper, Felmet, might not be popular with his subjects owing to his policy of killing people and burning down their cottages; but the kingdom takes offense only when he cuts down its forests out of sheer dislike for them. (*Wyrd Sisters* draws heavily on the life and plays of William Shakespeare, in particular *Macbeth*.) Feeling unloved by its king, the kingdom seeks help from the witches to have him removed. The happy ending is achieved when Felmet is replaced by the Fool, who clearly favors just governance and a healing of the land (even the possibility of a wedding is hinted at). The importance of caring for the kingdom above any political claim to the throne is emphasized when it is revealed to the reader that the Fool has no actual right to the throne, although this is only known to the witches.[21] Political power might be more visible; but throughout the story, the direct link remains a vital plot element and is, ultimately, what being Lancre's ruler is largely about.

In *Wyrd Sisters*, the kingdom is unhappy without a king; in other fantasy stories, the realm's need for a ruler is more pronounced, with countries lacking a sovereign somehow incomplete. One such example is Terry Brooks's Kingdom of Landover, which is first presented in *Magic Kingdom for Sale/Sold!*[22] Devoid of a king, the kingdom experiences social breakdown, environmental degradation, and failing magic. Ben, the buyer of the magic kingdom, realizes how king, land, and magic go together; that the king is more than a figurehead. To become the king that Landover needs, Ben has to do more than buy it and its throne; he has to be recognized as king by his subjects, and in order for them to grant this recognition, Ben must commit himself fully to the kingdom. Like Lancre, Landover needs a king to care for it, but it also needs a king to care for its people. Thus, before the magical healing of the land can commence, the king must use his political skill to heal society. Only by fulfilling his duty to his subjects and showing his commitment to the realm can Ben defeat Landover's enemies, cleanse its environment, bring its magic back, and give new life to its magical royal castle. In Landover, the realm is incomplete without its ruler; political power and the direct link to the land are interwoven.

In Brooks's novel, as in Ende's and Pratchett's, the plot mainly concerns restoring the proper ruler and thus saving the realm. All three novels combine the ruler's direct link to the land with political power, although in various ways—Bastian comes to assume a combination when there is none. My final example demonstrates how the process of separating these two elements of rulership can serve to bring out a story's core theme. Tad Williams's *War of the Flowers* is set in a modernized Faerie whose class society is ruled by a number of powerful Flower families.[23] The novel describes the internal power struggle of these families as well as an uprising of the discontented masses, ending with the transition from a tyrannical oligarchy to a new political order. (Democracy is hinted at but not confirmed.) The world's backstory also tells of an earlier coup, during which a cabal of Flower fairies imprisons Oberon and Titania, the original king and queen of Faerie, and seize power. The coup separates the political power of the rulers from their direct link to the realm. Despite being imprisoned, Oberon and Titania, like Fantastica's Childlike Empress, represent the essence of their realm; and like Ben in Landover, they are needed to bring magic into the land. In Williams's novel, these traits prove to be individual rather than connected to the office of the monarchs. The Flower fairy oligarchs cannot put the dethroned sovereigns to death because such an act would destroy the realm, but they *can* seize political power. When the oligarchy is finally overthrown, the former king and queen are not restored to power, however; instead they disappear, although the protagonist is told that they are in all probability still alive. The original rulers' refusal to make a bid for the throne underscores the separation of power and direct link to the land, showing the latter to be a personal trait rather than a political issue. In Williams's highly politicized version of Faerie, a direct link to the land may be required to channel magic, but it does not guarantee that the ruler will provide just governance. As in any modern democracy, the political power belongs to the people, no matter who happens to constitute the essence of the realm.[24]

The examples just provided suggest some of the many possibilities afforded by a direct link between ruler and realm. The following two sections examine examples of the relationship between ruler and realm, before moving on to Dark Lords and Dark Lands.

RULING THE MYTHICAL LANDSCAPE:
THE FISHER KING IN *LAST CALL*[25]

The first of the books in what Tim Powers refers to as his "Fisher King trilogy,"[26] *Last Call* has a plot that revolves around the mythical King who, unbeknownst to the population in general, rules over the western United States. Powers's name for the three books indicates the centrality of the Fisher King motif, and the author's treatment of it is intimately tied to how he has constructed the world of the novels. *Last Call* is set solely in the primary world, but it is a primary world where, under the surface of the everyday, nonmagical domain of mundanity, there exists a domain of mythical forces. Gary K. Wolfe observes "a genuine mythic sensibility at work in [Powers's] fiction. [. . .] It's an almost totally paranoid universe, where nothing is quite as it seems—in other words, a universe of myth."[27] I would add that the sense of paranoia observed by Wolfe derives from the fact that the mythical is obscured from everyday life; the reasons underlying the mundane events remain mysterious to the protagonists. The mythical causes behind everything that befalls the protagonists only slowly become apparent. The novel's two domains, of mundanity and myth, are thus kept separate yet intimately connected. Mundane events that have their causes in the mythical domain simply lead to incomprehension in those who are unaware of that domain— they understand *what* happens but not *why* (and invented causes and coincidence only take them so far). Rather than insistent explanations, it is leaps of faith in the face of too incredible coincidences that ultimately make the protagonists—Crane, Mavranos, and Diana—accept the mythical domain and the meaning it provides.

In the mythical domain reside "the eternal and terribly potent figures that secretly animated and drove humanity, the figures that the psychologist Carl Jung had called archetypes and that primitive peoples, in fear, had called gods" (26). These mythical forces are represented through symbols in myths, belief systems, rituals, and stories, and are connected to mundanity through such symbols. Each particular force is surrounded by, and defined through, a cluster of symbols shared by and linking those various myths that make up the mosaic of the mythical domain. Each symbol captures a trait or an aspect of the force with which it is associated and can be found in any number of myths and stories: one example would be how the Queen is also the Moon Goddess, both virgin and mother; Pallas Athena and Artemis, Isis and Ishtar, Demeter and the Virgin Mary all symbolize this force, and her traits are captured in the Empress Tarot card (see 273).

Through the symbolism of the mythical forces, the mythical domain interacts with mundanity. An understanding of the symbols imparts meaning to seemingly meaningless events. Wildly blooming rosebushes become an omen of impending demise when they are understood as a powerful symbol of death; by keeping them tamed, their owner symbolically tames death (24). Putting one's tie and sunglasses on one's friend's decapitated head makes it, symbolically, one's own head (199–200). To enter the mythic domain is to understand this domain of symbols, to learn to see the world—to employ Wolfe's expression—as a universe of myth. In *Last Call*, the two domains are not separated by a physical boundary, nor do they exist in parallel. They are separated by knowledge, different in terms of how the world is understood. Symbols provide mundane events with an added layer of causality through the mythical forces they represent, but they also afford means to affect these forces. Rituals are, in Powers's novel, a symbolic manipulation of the forces, but impromptu use of symbols works in a similar manner, such as when the protagonists "psychically camouflage" their car as a bus by adding to it symbols for a great number of personalities (141–42, 169).

Powers draws on a great number of sources for the symbol complexes of the mythical domain and its forces. Four of the most central sources, and most relevant to the mythical King figure on which the plot centers, are Tarot cards, James Frazer's *The Golden Bough* (1890–1915), Jessie L. Weston's *From Ritual to Romance* (1920), and T. S. Eliot's *The Waste Land* (1922). The most explicit collection of symbols related to the forces of the mythic domain are the Tarot cards. In the novel, the Lombardy Zeroth deck is portrayed as having particularly great powers, the symbols employed on the cards tapping the depths of the human collective unconscious. It is a card from the Lombardy Zeroth deck that destroys Crane's eye, and in a poker game played with the deck, he unknowingly sells his body to the incumbent King. The cards are even described as having a life of their own, if only in the mind of the person handling them. By association, however, other Tarot decks and even the modern playing cards derived from them are also powerful symbols in the mythical domain. Buying a hand of cards is thus of great mythical importance. "Fortune-telling by cards [is] *pre*scriptive rather than *de*scriptive," Crane and Mavranos are told. "[A] hand of Poker is a number of qualities," so if "you *pay* money, you've *bought* [. . .] those qualities." (113) By their nature, however, the playing cards represent the most random aspect of the mythic forces, chance rather than fortune or destiny.

Where the cards portray the forces of the mythical domain through their symbolism, other myths and stories offer descriptions of these forces and how to relate to them in their various guises. Apart from a few references to King Arthur, Powers's King character recalls Weston's treatment of the Fisher King figure in the Grail myths and her linking him to nature cults and vegetation gods, such as Tammuz and Adonis. The King character is also associated with the many symbols of the vegetation gods and fertility rites described by Frazer, to the point where any discussion of the King figure in *Last Call* must take these works into account.

The fourth source that Powers has mined for King symbolism, Eliot's *The Waste Land*, resonates powerfully in the novel through numerous quotations, allusions, and explicit references ranging from the obvious (chapter 17 is called "The Sound of Horns and Motors" and contains extensive quotations from "The Fire Sermon") to the oblique (apart from its poker allusion, the novel's title could be taken to allude to the pub closing in "A Game of Chess"). Rather than only using references to the Fisher King figure from Eliot's poem,[28] however, Powers has brought the poem's imagery into the cluster of mythical symbols that surrounds his King, thus facilitating a Fisher King–oriented reading of *The Waste Land* from the perspective of *Last Call*. Many of the Eliot lines quoted in chapter 17, for instance, follow almost immediately after the passage in which the person "fishing in the dull canal" muses "upon the king my brother's wreck / And on the king my father's death before him."[29] In the novel, the quoting is done by the King (associated with the Fisher King figure), which confers Fisher King characteristics on Eliot's fishing royalty regardless of other possible interpretations.[30] Frequently, *Last Call* explicitly demonstrates how to read *The Waste Land*'s symbols in terms of the King. Thus, the "Fire Sermon" line "Old man with wrinkled female breasts" (163; l. 219) becomes an obvious description of the King, who is a man inhabiting the body of an old woman. Less obviously, the end of *The Waste Land* (line 430 translates as "the Aquitanian Prince with his ruined tower") also recalls Powers's King: in the novel, the King's tower is symbolically destroyed, and whereas *Last Call* only tells us that he hails from France, *Earthquake Weather* reveals the King to come from the Bordeaux region in Aquitaine.[31]

With these sources in mind, we can address the question of how the King in *Last Call* is related to his realm through the mythical domain, turning first to Weston's opinion of the Fisher King figure of the Grail texts. Like other characters that have come down to us through medieval romances, the Fisher King lacks a definitive source. Instead, he appears under various names and in various guises in a number of medieval texts. Comparing several of these medieval texts, Weston finds that

> the presentment of this central figure is much confused; generally termed Le Roi Pescheur, he is sometimes described as in middle life, and in full possession of his bodily powers. Sometimes while still comparatively young he is incapacitated by the effects of a wound, and is known also by the title of Roi Mehaigné, or Maimed King. Sometimes he is in extreme old age, and in certain closely connected versions the two ideas are combined, and we have a wounded Fisher King, and an aged father, or grandfather. But [. . .] in no case is the Fisher King a youthful character; that distinction is reserved for his Healer, and successor.[32]

This summary of the Fisher King's characteristics also covers the basic traits of the Kings in *Last Call*. The reader meets a succession of three Kings: the gangster Benjamin Siegel is King during part of the backstory; Georges Leon rules for most of the narrative; and Scott Crane takes the throne in the denouement. All three Kings are associated with fishing, and Leon and Crane are wounded if not incapacitated. Leon most clearly matches Weston's description, even combining apparently contradictory versions: through his ability to take over others' bodies, he is simultaneously in "middle life" and "extreme old age," both father and son—one of the bodies he has taken is that of his son, Richard. Crane is the "youthful" successor, healer of the land if not of his predecessor. In *Last Call*, the land is not healed by healing the King, however, but by having a King of sterility replaced by one of fertility.

All three Kings have traits that associate them with the Fisher King figure, most notably related to fishing and various wounds. For Siegel and Leon, fishing is described as part of their struggle over the Kingship (17, 20); Crane has sustained a number of fishing-related wounds when growing up (69, 93) and is, notably, given a nonhealing wound in his side by a fishing spear, thus adding to the notional link between the Fisher King and Christ already established by the fish symbolism. Apart from their association with fishing, Crane's injuries offer symbolic connections to the (nonhealing) wound that the Fisher King figure, as Roi Mehaigné, has in several versions. In Chrétien de Troyes's *Perceval, ou Le Conte du Graal* (c. 1182), for instance, the Fisher King has a leg wound; the same goes for the later Fisher King figure, King Pelles, in Sir Thomas

Malory's *Le Morte Darthur* (1485)[33] — and Crane suffers throughout the story from a self-inflicted stab wound in the leg. Leon's original body, the ninety-one-year-old "Doctor Leaky," is wounded in a manner similar to the Fisher King Anfortas in Wolfram von Eschenbach's *Parzival* (c. 1210). Anfortas suffers a nonhealing and evil-smelling wound from a spear thrust through his testicles;[34] "Doctor Leaky" has had his genitals shot off, leaving the body sterile and accompanied by a pervasive smell of leaking urine.

The link between the King and his realm in *Last Call* is understandable through his mythical identity with the Fisher King figure and, through this figure, with the gods of resurrection and vegetation.[35] This identity is visible in many symbols found in the various rituals required to remain or become King. Weston observes how "the personality of the King, the nature of the disability under which he is suffering, and the reflex effect exercised upon his folk and his land, correspond [. . .] to the intimate relation at one time held to exist between the ruler and his land."[36] This "reflex effect" may not be relevant to the Fisher King figure in the medieval romances,[37] but it certainly describes the "curious relationship" (to recall Jones's expression) between King and realm in *Last Call*. The well-being of the ruler affects the well-being of the realm; his death, injury, or sterility affects the land adversely.

Pogue, another contender for the Las Vegas throne, focuses on the importance of perfection. His belief that "[t]he man who takes the throne can have no flaws" (199) echoes the old Celtic idea that "a blemished king [is] unsuitable to reign."[38] These flaws need not be of a physical nature (as in the case of Nuadu of the Silver Hand, who relinquished his kingship temporarily after having lost his right arm in battle[39]); kings who were "deficient in character or conduct" would also bring misfortune, and usurpers would bring famine and drought.[40] These "reflex effects" parallel those in *Last Call* but, in his focus on perfection, Pogue errs on one count: the rightful ruler is *made* flawless by becoming king, as Crane eventually discovers (521–22). Powers's novel takes the "reflex effect" further: even the physical features of the King and Queen are imprinted on the landscape, allowing characters to gain insight into the mythical rulership by studying maps where seemingly random roads and terrain features sketch a portrait of the sovereign (see 357, but also 21).

In *Last Call*, the realm not only reflects the King; the King also reflects the realm, as illustrated by the complex of mythical symbols surrounding his stronghold. The Flamingo Hotel, built by Siegel in Las Vegas,

is the defensive focus of the King's realm, and the various myth frag-
ments associated with it are part of the relation between ruler and realm.
Its construction is guided by numerous symbols intended to exploit the
powers of various myths. By strategically opening, closing, and reopen-
ing the Flamingo at Christmas, New Year's, and Easter, Siegel symbolically identifies the hotel with himself as "the modern avatar of Dionysus
and Tammuz and Attis and Osiris and the Fisher King and every other
god and king who died in the winter and was reborn in the spring" (22).
At the base of the hotel, Siegel places an upside-down Tower card, a symbol of "foolishly prideful ambition" which "[r]eversed [. . .] could permit
a King to build an intimidating castle, and keep it" (22). Situated in the
Nevada desert, the Flamingo also becomes a symbol of the Grail castle
in the wasteland, linking the King's stronghold, and thus the King identified with it, to the sterility of the surroundings. This sterility, the nonhealing wound of the maimed king, and the groin injury suggested by
the Emperor card (5) all reflect back on Leon when he usurps the throne,
eventually leading to the gunshot that emasculates him (9–12), and his
sterility is then—again—reflected back on the realm.

With a sterile King on the throne, the realm remains a wasteland.
Crane muses on how the land has changed during Leon's reign: "It was
an Orange County with no orange trees anymore, a region conquered by
developers, who had made it sterile even as they had made it fabulously
valuable" (105). Fertility has given way to sterility, making the land dead
but financially attractive. Death and wealth are linked through Pluto, a
force closely associated with both Leon and Siegel (21). Las Vegas, too, is
kept in dusty, dry sterility because of Leon. "Wild," uncontrolled water is
associated with the Goddess, a force Leon fears (which is why he has its
avatar, Diana's mother, killed). The result is dried-out water tables under
the city, a conflict over water rights, and the use of "tame water" from the
artificial Lake Mead.

A sterile realm is against the nature of things, however. Leon's kingship is not that of a fertility king. Even his henchman, Trumbill, cannot
help thinking that in the past, "Fisher Kings would just *have* children,
not kill their children's minds and steal their bodies—and [. . .] such
a King would reign over a fertile green land and not a sterile desert—
and [. . .] he would share his power with a Queen" (258–59). Trumbill's
sentiments foreshadow the rule of Crane and Diana. As fertility King
and Goddess Queen, they plan not only marriage but also children (the
mythically important incest being neatly sidestepped by their status as

siblings in symbolical terms only—both are adopted). Restoration of both land and King commences, healing Crane's wounds (apart from the one in his side that symbolizes his kingship) as well as giving him a new eye. As the couple drives through the Mojave Desert, the land is no longer described through images of death and emptiness but in terms that indicate healing. The sterile wasteland is no longer dry and dead:

> And the old truck sped on up the highway in the morning sun. And in the desert all around, the Joshua trees were heavy with cream-colored blossoms, and the glowing cholla branches shaded the flowering lupine and sundrops, and in the mountains the desert bighorn sheep leaped agilely down to the fresh streams to drink. (535)

With the new rulers, the desert has become a place of life, verdant and flourishing, recalling Trumbill's "fertile green land." Instead of sterility, fertility; instead of arid wastes, fresh streams. The departure from the wasteland into life promised by this final paragraph also suggests a departure from mundanity into the domain of myth; Crane and Diana drive off into the sun*rise*, leaving their mundane lives behind and taking up their mantles as mythical rulers.

Crane's departure is, in fact, an inversion of King Arthur's departure for Avalon. As if in confirmation of his right to the throne, Crane manages to pull a knife from the cement under the Flamingo Hotel. His last action, after having defeated his father and before departing from Lake Mead, is to throw the knife into the lake where he sees it caught, Excalibur-like, by a hand (417–18, 534). Where Arthur defeats his son but is mortally wounded, Crane wins the throne from his father, his wounds healed. Significantly, he rids himself of the weapon of war before the start of his reign rather than making it his mark, entering a reign of peace, not war. His relationship to the realm promises to differ from Leon's, suggesting that the King figure need not be a Fisher King trapped in a wasteland, but could instead be a healer offering fertility and rebirth.

SHAPING THE REALM: PALIMPSESTS IN *TOURISTS*[41]

Lisa Goldstein's *Tourists* is set in the city of Amaz, which, Wolfe observes, "is vaguely reminiscent of Borges's Tlön, with its odd language, nameless streets, mysterious ruins, and ubiquitous decks of cards which serve as newspapers."[42] In this bizarre place, the American anthropologist Mitchell Parmenter, his wife, Claire, and his teenage daughters, Angie and Casey, find themselves involved in a centuries-old feud between the supporters of two ancient kings. Rather than the interdependency displayed by king and land in the Fisher King legend, as shown clearly in Powers's *Last Call*, Goldstein's novel illustrates how topography can be used to express a conflict between two rulers and their supporters, and how the shape of the land can change in relation to which side is in control. The most prevalent and explicit symbol for the conflict in *Tourists* is the letters of one king written over those of his enemy. Two related concepts are embodied in this overwriting: the palimpsest and the Roman process called *damnatio memoriae*.

According to the *Oxford English Dictionary*, a palimpsest is a "parchment or other writing surface on which the original text has been effaced or partially erased, and then overwritten by another" or, in extended use, "a thing likened to such a writing surface [. . .]; a multilayered record."[43] All kinds of inscriptions, from Egyptian cartouches to engraved brass plates, may constitute palimpsests if they are in some way erased and reinscribed. Sometimes the palimpsest simply represents a case of economic expediency: expensive material (such as parchment or vellum) was washed clean and reused for a more relevant text. Accordingly, the topmost (thus most recent) inscription in a palimpsest is considered in some way more deserving of the writing surface. Ultimately, the reinscription is an expression of power—a case of the winner writing the history book. This expression of power becomes most obvious when the palimpsest is a result not of economic but of political expediency. The written traces of one's enemy are obliterated, whether that enemy is a previous pharaoh with the wrong ideas, the persona non grata of a totalitarian regime, or the holy text of another religion.[44] Palimpsests have been used not only to purge someone from history but also to preserve the memory of the purge. Historian Charles W. Hedrick, Jr., argues that this was the purpose of the Roman repertoire of penalties known, in a modern coinage, as *damnatio memoriae*. "Despite pretensions to the contrary," Hedrick explains, "Roman political attacks on memory were not intended to *destroy* recollection of an individual [. . .] but created gestures that served to *dishonor* the record of the person and so, in an oblique way, to confirm memory."[45]

The most conspicuous palimpsests in *Tourists* are writing on top of writing, expressing a power struggle in which the enemy is supplanted by being overwritten. As with the *damnatio memoriae*, traces of the previous script are left to ensure that the memory of the deposition remains.

Each member of the Parmenter family notices the ubiquitous graffiti that expresses the feud between supporters of the Jewel King and his predecessor, Sozran, although they do not grasp its relevance at first—and Claire, blinkered by alcoholism and culture shock, fails to grasp its palimpsestic nature (15, 42, 49, 78, respectively). The phrase *The King lives* is written twice: first, in the jagged letters of Sozran; then, almost covering them, in the rounded letters of the Jewel King (203). In fact, the graffiti is only a recent expression of a *damnatio memoriae* that goes back twelve centuries to the Jewel King's ascension to the throne. When Mitchell and his Amaz colleague Jara stumble over the Jewel King's old palace in their search for the King's sword, Mitchell finds the remnants of a mosaic along the base of a wall, a mosaic that palimpsestically affirms the Jewel King's superiority over Sozran. The tiles form writing in jagged letters, but "[f]arther on along the wall the letters looked as though they had been pried up, and another mosaic, of newer, more rounded letters, had been put in their place" (89). The Sozranis have employed the same tactic in the mosaic that covers a floor in their house, except that here the jagged writing covers the round one. More observant than her father, Casey makes the connection to the graffiti she has seen, reflecting that it was almost as if "whoever had done the second mosaic had wanted people to know they had desecrated the original" (168).

The *damnatio memoriae* palimpsests are only the most obvious aspects of the feud between the two ancient kings' supporters, however, and once their meaning is made clear to Casey, she realizes that the puzzling Amaz proverb "Jagged and curved things can never marry" (77) is a summary description of how the conflict has affected the city's society as well as its topography:

> The store ahead of her had sharp gables over the windows and a door shaped like a triangle. The store next to that one was rounder, a scallop design on the roof, circular windows and a large arch over the front door. Did the feud extend even to their architecture? [. . .] In twelve hundred years the entire city could have been made over into angles and curves. You'd want to know whom you were dealing with when you went into a store, whether the proprietor was a follower of Sozran or of the Jewel King. (175)

Angles and curves are found everywhere, in cars, driveways, even the shape of the streets. Casey realizes that depending on allegiance, a person would move through the city along curved or jagged streets. Even the map appears vaguely palimpsestic, the very layout of the streets forming a palimpsest with one set of streets superimposed on another.

The influence of the feud on the physical environment of Amaz not only results in bus routes that "snake through every part of the city" (130) and streets that "[loop] like string back and forth and finally [seem] to turn in on [themselves]" (132); the feud also shifts the shape and location of the streets. That the streets move about is suggested already in the directions to the university that Mitchell is given by his Amaz colleague. Although brought up repeatedly, the notion is generally rejected by the rational protagonists. Mitchell and Jara are forced to accept the moving streets for a fact only when they follow a route that spells out the word *sword* on the map. As they have written the word with the Jewel King's rounded script on jagged streets declaring for Sozran, they witness how the city changes shape before their eyes as they walk: "[Mitchell] thought he saw houses jumbled together in front of them, a chimney here, a front door there, a car sticking out of a second-story window. And as they passed the houses re-formed themselves, moved over politely to create new streets" (205).

In this palimpsestic city, moving through the streets is a form of writing. A taxi ride has the car "writing [its] own calligraphy on the streets of the city" (44). Mitchell sees how the streets on the map write *sword* with the jagged letters of Sozran, and Jara changes the word into the Jewel King's script (202–3). The new writing is an expression of power that changes the streets' allegiance, reforges their shape. Writing is necessary to navigate the streets of Amaz. The city's streets are (for the most part) nameless, and there are almost no addresses (14, 21). Mitchell has to rely on written directions to find his way to the university, as well as back home after an excursion through unknown parts of the city. To send a letter, "he'd had to write a whole series of complex instructions on the front of the envelope, instructions that seemed to be directions from the post office to the house" (21). A street map is itself likened to the written manuscript that Mitchell and Jara use as they try to find their way to the Jewel King's legendary sword. The city is truly topo*graphy*—a written place constantly expressed in terms of writing.

Amaz is more than a *written* palimpsest, however; it is a multilayered material record, a palimpsest in an archaeological or architectural sense.[46] The notion of layer upon layer informs the descriptions of the city. History has left palimpsestic traces, with a new layer for each colonial power and foreign occupation (64–65), and other layers are added when parts of the city are erased by fire and earthquake (14). This layering process is so clearly visible that Casey eventually supposes the city as a whole to be like a large version of the *damnatio memoriae* mosaic, repeatedly knocked down and rebuilt over the centuries since the two kings' war (176). Each new layer reflects a new winner in control of the city's physical environment, a new ruler to determine the topography.

The winner determines the present but also the past. The story of the Jewel King competes with the story of Sozran, each version traditionally casting the enemy in an unfavorable light. The dominant story of the Jewel King (the country's national epic) maintains the *damnatio memoriae* policy indicated by the graffiti and mosaic palimpsests, generally refusing Sozran even a name and referring to him simply as "the corrupt king." In palimpsests, however, traces of the suppressed text remain; and in the Jewel King tale, Sozran's name does occur but is mentioned only once (188). Other stories also overlie, superimpose, and leak into each other: the fictive world of the Two Kingdoms, into which Angie has retreated and which she creates through her writing, ends up as a layer over Amaz when she ventures out (41–42, 156–57). Amaz, for its part, leaks into Angie's creation, changing her perceptions and causing her to recreate, in the Two Kingdoms, the old epic of the Jewel King without having read or heard it (165, 236). Even when the Parmenters finally manage to escape from Amaz, the superimposition of stories continues. As Mitchell and the girls tell one another of their adventures, "[t]heir voices overlapped" (235).

Jagged or curved becomes the ultimate question in Goldstein's novel, whether applied to a street, a piece of writing, or a legendary sword. Jagged or curved determines, and is determined by, allegiance, and the ancient feud between the two rulers' supporters shapes and reshapes the city's topography. Amaz thus becomes a place where the outsider is hopelessly lost—sides have to be taken in order to maneuver through the palimpsestic urban landscape and negotiate the stories it tells. It is certainly not a good place for tourists.

WHERE DARK LORDS LIVE: LANDSCAPES OF EVIL IN TOLKIEN, DONALDSON, AND JORDAN

The worst tourist spot that a fantasy world can offer is the territory that surrounds the stronghold, or prison, of the resident Dark Lord. Such a realm reflects the evil of its ruler through highly unpleasant living conditions, being too hot, too cold, or simply too poisonous for normal life to thrive; and like the Dark Lords themselves, their lands share some general characteristics but are on the whole distinctly individual. Although a thorough exploration of the Dark Lord character is beyond the scope of this book,[47] we may note how the genre presents Dark Lords as anything from evil gods and semidivine beings (the three examples in this chapter belong to this end of the scale) to "ordinary" mortals who have turned to evil,[48] and other evil lords are best described as being somewhere between these extremes.[49] Regardless of origin, the lords' association with dark powers invariably turns them into the epitome of evil, frequently reduced to destructive forces with only a single motivating goal[50]—and they all seem to share a predilection for inhospitable dwellings.

I would like to clarify that by using the expressions *landscape of evil* and *evil landscape*, I do not mean that the landscape itself is necessarily evil. That would imply a volition that the land does not generally have; to the contrary, the land is commonly portrayed as a victim of its ruler's evil. (Tolkien provides a clear example of this.) Rather, the land is an expression, through its physical characteristics as well as through its flora and fauna, of the evil that resides there, mainly in terms of a Dark Lord. For this reason, I have refrained from using a (possibly) less ambiguous term such as *cacotopia* or *maletopia* (bad or evil place), as such a term removes the focus from the connection between the moral nature of, in particular, the evil rulers and the landscape of their realm. Furthermore, while the fantasy genre tends to favor a realm ruled by a Dark Lord, an evil landscape may well be constructed as a prison for its denizens (as in the case of Shai'tan). Although there is a fundamental difference between a terrible place created for oneself and one intended for someone else, I have treated these types similarly, focusing primarily on how the evil place is described.

"Such Starved Ignoble Nature": Portrayals of Evil Lands

The idea that certain types of landscapes come with a peculiar, all but built-in, moral character is so widespread in the fantasy genre that when authors avoid it, they do so with an almost palpable self-consciousness. In her section on subversions of the portal–quest fantasy, Mendlesohn cites Barbara Hambly's novel *The Magicians of Night* (1992), observing how Hambly "[severs] the link between landscape and morality. The hills that are splashed with golden sunlight, covered in wild ivy and butter-cups, shelter evil, not elves."[51] Mendlesohn and Hambly both recognize that portal–quest fantasy expects places of evil to be ugly and unpleasant.

The conception of what an evil landscape should look like goes far back among the genre's taproot texts,[52] including any number of dismal hells and realms of the dead. An early example is provided by the "dȳgel lond" (secret, mysterious, or dark land) around Grendel's snake-infested mere in *Beowulf*.[53] With its windswept cliffs, perilous fens, and dark woods full of wolves, it bears more than a passing resemblance to the mountains and the dark, disquieting lake near Moria's western gate (cf. FR, II, iv). Hell (Christian or otherwise), of course, is one of our most typical evil landscapes, Dante Alighieri providing Western literature's most influential depiction of the infernal regions. Dante's *Inferno* notwithstanding, lakes of fire and smoking brimstone tend to appear as the centerpiece of the majority of Christian Hells, but John Milton has some of his fallen angels explore beyond the fiery center and the surrounding cold, where they find other doleful landscapes, places of evil "Where all life dies, death lives, and nature breeds, / Perverse, all monstrous, all prodigious things, / Abominable, inutterable."[54] One of the most vivid descriptions of an evil landscape in English literature occurs in Robert Browning's "Childe Roland to the Dark Tower Came" (1855). Roland explains how he has never seen "Such starved ignoble nature; nothing throve: / For flowers—as well expect a cedar grove!"[55] Plants are scarce no matter how hardy or prolific normally; even grass grows "as scant as hair / In leprosy" (st. 13:1–2). Two stanzas are worth quoting in full, as their echoes appear in the fantasy texts I discuss afterward:

> No! penury, inertness and grimace,
>> In some strange sort, were the land's portion. "See
>> Or shut your eyes," said Nature peevishly,
> "It nothing skills: I cannot help my case:
>> 'T is the Last Judgment's fire must cure this place,
>> Calcine its clods and set my prisoners free." (st. 11)

Places like this, lifeless landscapes of which Nature itself is ashamed and that can (implicitly or explicitly) be redeemed by nothing less than the end of the world, can be found in fantasy's many realms of evil. Browning took the title for his poem from *King Lear* (1623), and according to Tom Shippey, Edgar's snatch of song "Child Rowland to the dark tower came" is also part of the genesis of *The Lord of the Rings*;[56] but it is certainly Browning's grim landscape rather than Shakespeare's line that anticipates Mordor and its Dark Tower. Other early fantasy writers make use of similar landscapes of evil: Sir Kato's Outer Land in Astrid Lindgren's *Mio, min Mio* (1954; transl. *Mio, My Son* 1956) is also a dark, stony, dead realm.[57] Its dreary, dim daylight reminds us of Browning's poem and of the gloom in Dante's *Inferno*, whereas the blackness of its night is more akin to the "darkness visible" in Milton's Hell.[58] The gloom of the evil landscape may, in fact, be a legacy bequeathed by the lands of the dead. The realms of Hades into which Odysseus and Æneas descend are certainly dark, at least on the outskirts; but they also offer groves and quite pleasant fields, making them appear almost cheerful compared to Childe Roland's plain.[59]

It is worth noting that the landscape in Browning's poem changes. While still nightmarish, it does not remain sterile:

> Now blotches rankling, coloured gay and grim,
> > Now patches where some leanness of the soil's
> > Broke into moss or substances like boils;
> Then came some palsied oak, a cleft in him
> > Like a distorted mouth that splits its rim
> > Gaping at death, and dies while it recoils. (st. 26)

This diseased landscape recalls Milton's perverse nature and "inutterable abominations"; rather than offering an image of death, it portrays the process of dying and decay. While less common in fantasy literature, this image still anticipates a number of evil landscapes, places where putrefaction destroys natural beauty.

As Mendlesohn's example from Hambly demonstrates, however, there is also an awareness of this traditional evil landscape among fantasy writers, and attempts have been made to vary the concept. Among the texts most explicitly conscious of the tradition is Glen Cook's *The Black Company*, wherein the Dark Lord is a Dark Lady:

> We sprawled on the flank of a grassy hill. The Tower rose above the horizon due south. That basaltic cube was intimidating even from ten miles away—and implausible in its setting. Emotion demanded a surround of fiery waste, or at best a land perpetually locked in winter. Instead, this country was a vast green pasture, gentle hills with small farms dotting their southern hips. Trees lined the deep, slow brooks snaking between.

Nearer the Tower the land became less pastoral, but never reflected the gloom Rebel propagandists placed around the Lady's stronghold. No brimstone and barren, broken plains. No bizarre, evil creatures strutting over scattered human bones. No dark clouds ever rolling and grumbling in the sky.[60]

Cook's narrator (a mercenary who finds himself fighting on the side of evil) cannot quite believe that this is the Evil Land, partly because Evil, he feels, is neither fertile nor pleasant. Feels, yes; but a reader well acquainted with the fantasy genre would realize that not only emotion but also tradition demands a wasted land of evil, including allusions to wintry Narnia under the White Witch as well as to the volcanic plains around Mount Doom in Mordor. Indeed, the Mordor allusion is reinforced in the second paragraph by references to (the absence of) "brimstone and barren, broken plains" and "dark clouds ever rolling and grumbling in the sky." Even the word *gloom* brings us echoes from Sauron's realm, given that continuous gloom is, as Matthew Dickerson and Jonathan Evans point out, a recurrent image in descriptions of Mordor.[61]

These images of the second paragraph are attributed to a source much more distinct than "emotion": Rebel propaganda. The Rebels are the opposing side; that is, they would be the protagonists of a typical quest fantasy—the forces of Good fighting the Evil Lady. In Cook's novel, they are only good by default, not because they occupy any moral high ground, something that is clear from their willingness to spread lies to vilify their enemy. By invalidating the Rebel propaganda version of the evil land, a version that fits traditional fantasy expectations nicely, Cook also calls into question the goodness of any number of "good guys" throughout especially portal–quest fantasy, suggesting that the black-and-whiteness of the form results from the victors writing the history book.[62]

Nevertheless, the general conception of the evil landscape in fantasy is brought to us through focal characters on the side of Good, and the various realms they describe are everything that the pastoral land of Cook's Lady is not. The three locations explored in the section that follows, from *The Lord of the Rings*, the First Chronicles of Thomas Covenant the Unbeliever, and the Wheel of Time, demonstrate how traditional images of landscapes of evil may be used to reflect the individual characteristics of various Dark Lords and portray evil in different ways. While any number of portal–quest fantasies could provide examples, the two latter Dark

Lords and realms have been chosen for their distinct similarities and differences vis-à-vis Sauron and Mordor. Donaldson offers a quite similar landscape sprung from a different view of evil and its workings; Jordan's fairly Tolkienesque portrayal of evil results in a (superficially) different evil landscape.

Mordor

Sauron is of the lesser order of the Ainur, the angelic beings once involved in the creation of the world who entered it as its stewards. Along with many others, he was swayed by the evil Melkor; and when his master was defeated, Sauron assumed the position of supreme evil being in Middle-earth. The dead lands of Mordor have obvious precursors in Tolkien's earlier work, most plainly in the Desolation of Smaug in *The Hobbit*, a "bleak and barren" land with "neither bush nor tree, and only broken and blackened stumps to speak of ones long vanished."[63] But even before he began writing about Mr. Baggins's adventures, Tolkien had included a burned, desolate plain outside Morgoth's stronghold. In *The Silmarillion* (1977), the plain is called Anfauglith, the Gasping Dust, "full of a choking dust, barren and lifeless";[64] but it is mentioned in a previous synopsis ("Sketch of Mythology") from the late 1920s, as well as in the even earlier *Lay of the Children of Húrin* (early 1920s), under the name Dor-na-Fauglith, the Plain of Thirst.[65] To what extent the landscapes surrounding the antagonists of Tolkien's previous writing actually influenced Mordor is impossible to determine, but Sauron's Dark Land certainly outdoes its precursors in terms of barren gloominess.

It is unclear at what point Sam and Frodo enter Sauron's realm. The Dead Marshes, with their slimy ooze, clammy mists, and spirits of the dead visible in the treacherous pools, are an obvious contender. Gollum, however, claims not to know whether the visages of the dead are Sauron's doing (TT, IV, ii, 614); and as the barrow wights demonstrate in *The Fellowship of the Ring*, old graves, no matter whose, can become the haunt of evil spirits far away from the Dark Land. Randel Helms suggests that the hobbits pass into Sauron's realm once they have traversed the Marshes,[66] but I would argue that they must walk for two more nights, through the Noman-lands and into Dagorlad, the desolation that lies before the Black Gates, before they truly experience the Dark Lord's land.[67] Dagorlad's desolate plain is clearly related to Anfauglith and the Desolation of Smaug, and the description of it is among Tolkien's most chilling:

Here nothing lived, not even the leprous growths that feed on rotten-ness. The gasping pools were choked with ash and crawling muds, sickly white and grey, as if the mountains had vomited the filth of their entrails upon the lands about. High mounds of crushed and powdered rock, great cones of earth fire-blasted and poison-stained, stood like an obscene graveyard in endless rows, slowly revealed in the reluc-tant light. [. . .] [T]he lasting monument to the dark labor of [Mor-dor's] slaves that should endure when all their purposes were made void; a land defiled, diseased beyond all healing—unless the Great Sea should enter in and wash it with oblivion. (TT, IV, ii, 617)

Despite the added details, the dead land before Childe Roland's Dark Tower is clearly recognizable, down to the need for a cleansing cataclysm in order to cure the land—by fire in Browning's case, by flood in Tol-kien's. Sauron's forecourt displays the Dark Lord's complete disregard for any sanctity of life or beauty. The totality of the ecocide brings into sharp focus how the pits and forges of Isengard are indeed "only a little copy, a child's model or a slave's flattery" of the evil that Sauron is capable of inflicting on the land itself (FR, II, ii, 254; TT, III, viii, 542). The first encounter, for the hobbits as well as the reader, with the Dark Lord's realm illustrates the three main ways in which his evil is portrayed as affecting the land: mediated through the actions of others, as a force of decay or destruction, and through emotive language. These ways inter-lace with and amplify one another but are covered separately in the dis-cussion that follows.

John Garth calls the description of Dagorlad an expression of Tol-kien's "anti-industrial animus,"[68] which he also finds in Tolkien's notes for the description of the Marshes. ("Describe the pools as they get nearer to Mordor as like green pools and rivers fouled by modern chemical works."[69]) "Anti-industrial animus," if anything, puts it mildly: Dagor-lad is the most striking image of industrial environmental degradation in *The Lord of the Rings*.[70] That the evil of Mordor lies in environmen-tal destruction and lack of respect for the natural world is obvious from the chapter "The Scouring of the Shire" (RK, VI, viii). When the hobbits return to find the Shire tyrannized and ravaged by Saruman, Sam and Frodo see how Saruman has simply done Sauron's work, although the devastation feels much worse "because it is home, and you remember it before it was all ruined" (RK, VI, viii, 994). Ann Swinfen briefly notes the destruction and exploitation of nature carried out by "Sauron and his imitator Saruman" through machinery and slaves;[71] and that is indeed one of the three ways in which the Dark Lord's evil affects the land. Through minions (including "his imitator Saruman") and other agents, such as the volcano, Mount Doom, and even weather, Sauron affects the world; and in his own realm, these agents can carry out his evil deeds unopposed and unfettered by any regard for the natural environment.

This mediated evil, clearly visible in the poisonous slag heaps and waste pits of Dagorlad, is most conspicuously expressed through the random felling of trees. That misdeed enrages the ents of Fangorn and brings Sam to tears on his return to the Shire, and it is the first sign of Sauron's evil power in the recently conquered Ithilien. Despite the loveliness of the land, Sam and Frodo come across "trees hewn down wantonly and left to die," which reminds them that they are in enemy territory (TT, IV, iv, 637).[72] However, although industrial production and the environmental destruction associated with it might lie wholly within the purview of evil, the Dagorlad waste is not totally gratuitous. Apparently, advanced mining and chemical operations are going on in Mordor, suggested by the slag heaps with their noxious fumes, the poisoned soil, and the multicolored ooze in the pits (TT, IV, ii, 618). From the passage quoted before, the reader can tell that slave labor is used in this industry, and the origin of the slag heaps is hinted at later, when the narrator explains that Mordor's mines and forges are found in the northern parts of the country—conveniently located close to the Black Gates and Dagorlad (RK, VI, ii, 902).

The location is convenient because depositing these dangerous byproducts outside the entrance to Mordor gives Sauron a strategic advantage. The presence of a vast, lifeless area greatly strengthens the defense of the Black Gates, preventing any invading army, such as Aragorn's, from foraging for food, water, or firewood. As Dagorlad was the "battle plain" where Sauron was previously defeated (FR, II, ii, 236–37; see also Appx B, 1059), improving its defensive qualities makes sense.

The Dark Lord does not rely solely on a poisoned and desolate wasteland for his defense, however, nor does he rely only on agents to exert his influence on the land. The second way in which his evil affects the land is more direct: as a destructive force, an invisible energy that works on living things, perverting and ultimately killing them. This falls under what Helms refers to as the fourth internal law of Middle-earth: "[w]ill and states of mind, both evil and good, can have objective reality and physical energy."[73] He illustrates this law with the terror spread by the

Ringwraiths. Sauron's evil similarly affects people, but it also affects the very land. Like an invisible poison or ionizing radiation, it slowly destroys life in his realm without the need for any agents. When the hobbits leave Dagorlad and move south into Ithilien, it becomes clear to the reader how Sauron's evil takes effect over time. A night's walk away from the Black Gates, they find themselves "in a land that had only been for a few years under the dominion of the Dark Lord and was not yet fallen wholly into decay" (TT, IV, iv, 635). While not as verdant as Ithilien (which has been under Sauron's control for an even briefer period of time), it is by no means as horrifying as Dagorlad. It is important to note how being "under the dominion of the Dark Lord" is enough to cause a land to fall into decay, but also that this process occurs over time—his evil corrupts vegetation slowly. This point is corroborated by the glens of the Morgai, on the outer edges of the Dark Land, where "Mordor was a dying land, but it was not yet dead" (RK, VI, ii, 900). What grows there is "harsh, twisted, bitter, struggling for life"—stunted, gray, withered—but apparently not even it has been under the dominion of Sauron long enough to have died.

Not only time but also distance determines the effect of Sauron's evil force. As Sam and Frodo journey through Mordor toward the Dark Tower, they find the land to be completely dead. It is a dark, arid, lifeless place of sharp rocks, dry riverbeds, and broken plains, where what little water they find is as bitter as the air. In their chapter on "The Three Faces of Mordor," Dickerson and Evans point out how Sauron's evil kills even the memory of living nature in Frodo.[74] Other parts of Mordor, farther away from the Dark Tower and the volcano, are comparatively fertile, however. The narrator tells the reader about "the great slave-worked fields away south in this wide realm [. . .] by the dark sad waters of Lake Núrnen," an area that Aragorn later bestows upon Sauron's freed slaves and that apparently cannot be too dreadful (RK, VI, ii, 902; v, 947).[75]

The force of Sauron's evil does not necessarily kill vegetation; it may only stunt or corrupt it. In some cases, the plants themselves are portrayed as turning to evil, like the brambles of Mordor, with their long, piercing thorns and hooked, sharp barbs (RK, VI, ii, 896; 900). While annoying and painful, they are not dangerous, as contrasted with the flowers of the meadows in Morgul Vale. These pale, luminous flowers are "beautiful and yet horrible of shape," with a sickening, corpselike odor (TT, IV, viii, 689). The juxtaposition of *beautiful* and *horrible* signals the perverting effect of evil, just as the juxtaposing of *beautiful* and *terrible* does (twice) when Galadriel warns Frodo of the consequences were she to take the Ring (FR, II, vii, 356). The wrongness of something both beautiful and horrible is made plain by the description of the flowers' shapes as "like the demented forms in an uneasy dream" (TT, IV, viii, 689).

The nightmarish quality of the evil landscape is emphasized even more strongly with the Dagorlad desolation. Frodo and Sam find themselves at the edge of the dead land "like men on the edge of a sleep where nightmare lurks," and some of Aragorn's troops suffer from the same sensation on their arrival; they walk "like men in a hideous dream made true" (TT, IV, ii, 617; RK, V, x, 868). The dream similes illustrate the third way in which a landscape becomes that of evil: through a language that warps the reader's impression of the landscape. Returning to the Dagorlad quotation, we find a number of attributes that intensify the image of the dead landscape, for instance "gasping pools," "sickly white," "reluctant light." Together with another pair of striking similes ("as if the mountains had vomited the filth of their entrails" and "like an obscene graveyard"), they associate the landscape with sickness and death so forcefully that the reader easily accepts that the land is "diseased beyond all healing."

Imagery is used to tie the evil landscape to certain concepts. Nightmares and darkness, disease and death are all typical, but more active characteristics occur as well, which personify the landscape and turn the realm into an extension of its ruler: it is a tormented land of shadows and blind darkness where mountains and cliff faces loom and frown. When Sauron broods, so does the land (iii, 914). In the three chapters in which the hobbits travel through the Dark Land (RK, VI, i–iii), there are numerous examples of anything from dead metaphors to vivid similes: when Sam first gazes out over Mordor, he sees a hard, cruel, and bitter land (i, 879), and toward the end of their trek, the landscape is "rough and hostile," even evil (iii, 917; 914). The Morgai mountain ridge is "grim," with "crags like fangs," air and water are "sad," and roads and pinnacles are "cruel" (i, 879; ii, 900, 902; iii, 914, 921). Mount Doom vomits lava and belches fumes, the entrance in its side gazing toward the Dark Tower, and although it sleeps, it does so "uneasily" (i, 879; ii, 899; iii, 921–22; 918). Despite the personifying imagery, the land remains lifeless; it is a barren landscape, constantly stressing that the Dark Lord's power is never one of life. To enter the wasteland of Dagorlad is to leave "the living lands" (RK, V, x, 868), and the wind that blows into Mordor from the West comes "out of the living world" (RK, VI, ii, 898). Although not a land of the dead, it is a land that has died.

The Spoiled Plains and Ridjeck Thome[76]

Lord Foul is a spiritual being and the enemy of the world's Creator. His attempts to destroy the world in which he is imprisoned stem from his desire to escape it and confront his enemy. In *The Power That Preserves*, the third book in Donaldson's first trilogy about Thomas Covenant the Unbeliever, the final confrontation between Covenant and the Dark Lord takes place in Foul's Creche. Before Covenant makes his way there, Foul's realm is described to him and his Giant friend, Foamfollower: "There the Landrider [River] becomes the Ruinwash, and flows polluted toward the Sea. It is a murky and repelling water, unfit for use by any but its own un-fit denizens" (390). The land is then described in more detail:

> [T]he Spoiled Plains form a wide deadland around the promontory of Ridjeck Thome, where Foul's Creche juts into the Sea. Within that deadland lies Kurash Qwellinir, the Shattered Hills. Some say that these Hills were formed by the breaking of a mountain—others, that they were shaped from the slag and refuse of [Foul's] war caverns, furnaces, breeding dens. However they were made, they are a maze to bewilder the approach of any foe. And within them lies Gorak Krem-bal—Hotash Slay. From Sea-cliff to Sea-cliff about the promontory, it defends [Foul's] seat with lava, so that none may pass that way to gain the one gateless maw of the Creche. (390)

Despite the dispassionate voice, which belongs to Covenant's friend Bannor, and a description that is basically a list of features, we can see how Foul's realm parallels that of Sauron: pollution, deadlands, hills of slag and refuse as a line of defense, even volcanic activity on the doorstep to the stronghold. The apparent similarity is so great that it is tempting to translate directly between the two evil realms: Kurash Qwellinir = Dagorlad, Gorak Krembal = Orodruin, Ridjeck Thome = Gorgoroth, and so on. Apart from highlighting the authors' respective preferences in cre-ating names, however, such one-to-one translations would only stress superficial features while drawing attention away from the radical dif-ferences.

W. A. Senior argues that the "similarities between Frodo and Cove-nant can be traced easily to the paradigm of the fantasy hero [. . .] their parallels are functions of form and plot, not of character and motive."

He proceeds to outline these parallels, including the dangerous quest to confront evil each protagonist embarks upon; both Mordor and Foul's Creche are even situated in the southeast.[77] Although Senior carries out a detailed and highly fascinating examination of parallels and differences between Donaldson and Tolkien, including the role of the ring at the center of each work, he says very little about the evil lands as such.[78] The discussion that follows explores the relationship between character and motives of the respective Dark Lords and how they affect the characteristics of their lands.

When the hobbits arrive in Mordor, the dead land horrifies them. The Middle-earth they have traveled through has not necessarily offered constant vistas of natural beauty, but the utter lifelessness they encounter here is beyond anything they could have imagined. Covenant and Foamfollower, on the other hand, have journeyed through a Land in which Foul has delayed spring by several months. They, and the reader, are also aware that Foul has already once contrived to kill every living thing in the Land. The dead landscape of the Spoiled Plains comes not as a shock but as an expectation fulfilled. This difference in how the evil land is perceived both originates in and is indicative of the distinctive character and motive of the Dark Lord who rules it. Understanding how Foul differs from Sauron helps us understand how his realm differs from Mordor, despite the obvious similarities.

Senior subjects the two Dark Lords to a thorough comparison, observing a number of central distinctions: Sauron as a representation of evil is abstract, universal, and generic, evil as a symbolic force that wants to bind all in darkness. Lord Foul, for his part, is concrete, particular, and specific, wishing to twist and corrupt. He is the ills of leprosy inflicted on the Land.[79] Whereas Sauron may wish to bind all in darkness, he only demands tribute and dominion (RK, V, x, 872). Lord Foul's goals and nature, on the other hand, are spelled out plainly from the very beginning: Foul explains how he was behind the Ritual of Desecration that reduced all life in the Land to dust a millennium ago, lists his various sobriquets (which capture aspects of his character), and warns Covenant that he will eradicate hope from the Earth. His final words are: "Think on that, and be dismayed!"[80]

Dismay and hopelessness: invoking despair is one of Foul's main motives, as may also be inferred from the Giants' name for him, Soulcrusher. Much of Foul's realm appears incomprehensible unless this aspect of him is taken into account. The journey of Covenant and Foamfollower through the Spoiled Plains is a series of exercises in despair, often through the dashing of hope or the marring of relief. (Christine Barkley refers to this as Foul's "psychological torture" and describes its use against Covenant.[81]) Torrential rain and absence of food sources leave them hungry, wet, and cold. Any escape from a threat lands them in a comparatively more difficult situation. Such oscillations between relief and dismay are particularly intense in the eerie "orchard," where every perceived advantage quickly proves to have an even greater disadvantage (400–404). The land thus causes the protagonists to swing between hope and despair, between relief and despondency, and each disappointment erodes their hope further.

The erosion of hope is also the purpose of the last points of defense. The maze of the Shattered Hills (which, contrary to Bannor's description, are not slag and refuse but forms carved from black, igneous rock) is constructed to take people in the opposite of their desired direction. Only by moving *away* from the fiery glow of the lava at Hotash Slay at each junction do the Giant and his friend reach the river of molten rock (424). Next, the lava river understandably ruins any hope Covenant has of crossing, since he has forgotten about the Giant's ability to endure fire (425). Finally, even once Foamfollower has managed to get Covenant across, during the final stretch along the promontory to the entrance into Foul's Creche, and down to the Dark Lord's thronehall, the protagonists oscillate between hope and despair; and the closer they get to their ultimate goal, the more plain it is that these oscillations spring from Foul himself—that his realm's purpose is his own: the eradication of hope.

Foul's second purpose, evident from his nickname "Corruption" as well as from the delight he takes in explaining his involvement in the Ritual of Desecration, is the destruction of life. Senior points out that "[o]ne obvious lesson of the Chronicles addresses the spoliation of our land in stark contrast to the maintenance of the Land by its peoples. There people worship the environment which, in our world, is often no more than a natural resource to be exploited."[82] To this should be added the point that the contrast is not simply between Covenant's primary (and our actual) world and the Land but also between the people of the Land and their archenemy. Yet Lord Foul does not display Tolkien's "anti-industrial animus"; Donaldson's Dark Lord may be a polluter, but his evil power aims for wholesale corruption through any means available. According to Senior, Foul's desire is "to twist and deprave," but also to call attention to how twisted and depraved he has caused things to become;[83] and although Senior does not mention it, the turning of the clean Landrider River into the polluted, murky, repellent Ruinwash certainly exemplifies this desire.

The ruined landscapes of Tolkien and Donaldson thus appear similar, but they result from different attitudes to the natural environment. Sauron's destruction is secondary to his other goals of defense and (military) production; the desolation of Dagorlad is the result of mines and forges—of industry—operated without regard for the environment, just as the darkness is necessary for his troops of nocturnal orcs and trolls to fight during the day. Orcs may enjoy the occasional, arbitrary felling of trees, but it is not their master's main purpose. Conversely, Foul cares very much about nature: twisting and destroying it is a primary objective for him. The "scattering of tough trees and brush had eked out a bare existence until Lord Foul's preternatural winter had blasted them," so that now they stand gray, brittle, and dead (395). The "bare existence" no doubt left the trees just as twisted and bitter as the scrubby trees of the glens of the Morgai in Mordor and all the more pleasing for Foul.

As environmental destruction per se is Foul's motive, there is no need to elaborate on how the land is destroyed. The Landrider is suddenly polluted, likewise the soil. Bannor suggests that there are reasons behind the pollution ("the slag and refuse of [Foul's] war caverns, furnaces, breeding dens"), but no evidence corroborates this claim. As in Sauron's case, Foul's evil is itself a poisonous force or energy—if anything, it is more tangible than Sauron's. On Ridjeck Thome, the force of evil is so powerful that Covenant "felt muffled ill beating up through the rock" (432). It is there, near the very heart of Lord Foul's realm, that the land suffers the worst damage, not (as in Mordor) on the doorstep, because the destruction springs first and foremost from Foul's desire to destroy life. The dead landscape is easily recognizable from Tolkien, and from Browning before that—"a cracked, bare lowland of dead soil and rock, a place which had lain wrecked and riven for so long that it had forgotten even the possibility of life" (431). But here, nothing hints that poisonous waste or volcanic activity lies behind this destruction. Whether the force of Foul's ill is as clearly delimited as Sauron's evil, which stays within the land he controls, or whether, in Foul's case, evil diminishes with distance from its source (like, for instance, electromagnetic radiation) is unclear. There is a fringe of "un-Spoiled flatlands" through which Covenant and Foamfollower pass (395), but whether the Spoiling is gradual is not mentioned. In any case, the landscape of Ridjeck Thome is the type of landscape that Lord Foul desires. Around his stronghold, he has created this landscape—not through his minions, but through the force of his evil alone.

The connection between the Dark Lord and his realm is thus central to understanding Lord Foul's land. By understanding the differences in character and motive between Foul and Sauron, we can see how there can be radical differences between two superficially similar landscapes that evil has turned into places of disease and death. The next example, however, from Robert Jordan's Wheel of Time, entails a turn to an evil landscape that combines life and death, fecundity and disease.

The Blight[84]

The realms of evil discussed thus far are characterized by being dead or dying. Like the grim plain traversed by Childe Roland, they represent a sterile land where the exceedingly sparse vegetation is diseased, corrupted, moribund. The lands affected by the evil of the Dark Lord Shai'tan, or the Dark One, in Robert Jordan's *The Eye of the World* also produce diseased and corrupted vegetation. Rather than dying, however, these plants are deadly, subjected to Shai'tan's carcinogenic evil. Even so, Shai'tan—the protagonists erroneously refer to him as Ba'alzamon during the first three novels in the series, before realizing their error— echoes both Sauron and Lord Foul: he is the opponent of the Creator, bound at the beginning of time; the embodiment of chaos; and the destroyer of reason.

As in *The Lord of the Rings* and *The Power That Preserves*, the goal of the protagonists' quest lies within the realm of the Dark Lord, and Rand al'Thor and his companions venture into the area under Shai'tan's influence called the Blight. Unlike Sauron and Lord Foul, however, the Dark Lord in *The Eye of the World* is imprisoned and only has limited power over the physical world (see 726). The effect Shai'tan's evil has on the landscape even far away from his prison is clearly noticeable, however:

> As the mountains drew closer, so did the true Blight. Where a leaf had been spotted black and mottled yellow before, now foliage fell wetly while [Rand] watched, breaking apart from the weight of its own corruption. The trees themselves were tortured, crippled things, twisted branches clawing at the sky as if begging mercy from some power that refused to hear. Ooze slid like pus from bark cracked and split. (734)

This disease-ridden place is far from the sterility and death of Mordor and Foul's Creche, as well as from the dead landscape Childe Roland first encounters, but it recalls the second stanza quoted from Browning's poem. The tortured trees also echo Dante's Wood of Suicides, where tormented souls have been transformed into twisted trees and bushes.[85] The Blight is a cancer in Rand's world, a slowly growing zone of diseased vegetation. Unchecked growth, the mark of cancer, applies to more than the *area* of the Blight. The very plants grow impossibly. Along with the humidity and heat of the Blight, this fecundity suggests a tropical jungle, a place where vegetation hides dangers of all sizes. The traveler dares not touch anything without careful scrutiny, as deadly surprises may hide behind a branch or leaf. In the Blight, it is equally wise not to touch the leaves (as Rand is cautioned) for the very same reason.

The further into the Blight the companions journey, the less attractive the idea of touching anything becomes. Like any cancer, the growth is not healthy. In the earlier quotation, the black spots and mottled yellow, along with the unnatural heat and humidity, suggest fungal attacks, decomposition that sets in even as the leaves are growing. The deeper Rand and his companions venture into the Blight, the more pronounced the decay becomes, until leafing and rotting occur simultaneously. The disease does not kill the vegetation, however. As in Milton's Hell, this is a place where nature breeds perverse, monstrous things:

> [Rand] could not say what kind [of tree] it was, or had been, so gnarled and tormented was its shape. As he watched, the tree suddenly whipped back and forth again, then bent down, flailing at the ground. Something screamed, shrill and piercing. The tree sprang back straight; its limbs entwined around a dark mass that writhed and spat and screamed. (734–35)

The cancer of evil corrupts the trees into new forms of life, life that is unnatural, abominable, transgressing boundaries between species, even between the animal and vegetable kingdoms. Trees that are completely overcome by the Blight's cancer are no longer just trees; they bear no relation to any kind of tree in the world outside. They have taken on traits of the animal kingdom, such as moving and catching prey, and when Rand lops off a branch, he "almost thought he heard them scream" (736), again recalling the Wood of Suicides and how a bush cries out in pain when having a twig broken off.[86] Nor are trees alone in transgressing the boundaries of taxonomy. "Flowers can kill in the Blight, and leaves maim," Rand is warned, and he is told of "a little thing called a Stick" that looks like its name and will bite anyone who touches it, with disastrous results (724). Whether the Stick is an animal or a plant is never specified; the "little thing" is another transgression, a hybrid impossible outside the Blight.

The boundary between plants and animals is violated in the Blight, as are the boundaries between species. Rand cannot identify which kinds of trees he sees. When he and his companions are attacked by a host of monstrous creatures, the first of these is described thus: "Stiff hair like long bristles covered it, and it had too many legs, joining a body as big as a bear at odd angles. Some of them at least, those coming out of its back, had to be useless for walking, but the finger-long claws at their ends tore the earth in its death agony" (736). The description is one of a mutation beyond any divine creation or natural selection. Body parts from various animals appear to have been thrown together randomly, resulting in the "too many" legs that are strangely joined to the body, with some appearing to have no purpose. The being described is an abomination, clearly diseased, yet alive and ferocious. The arbitrariness of the attacking creatures' shape is emphasized by the fact that no two are alike (737) and none has shapes recognizable to Rand (or the reader).

The focus on cancer and transgressions distinguishes Shai'tan's evil from that of Sauron and Lord Foul, but to fully understand the nature of this evil, some similarities should be considered. Where Tolkien's and Donaldson's Dark Lords destroy the natural environment, leaving a dead, sterile landscape, Jordan's Dark One causes nature to turn into another kind of nightmare. The Blight is nature gone bad, a corruption not only of its plants and animals, but of the very laws that govern the ecosystem. Two important parallels can be drawn between his emanation of evil and those of Foul and Sauron, though. First, as in the case of Sauron, land that has fallen under the control of Shai'tan's troops is also swallowed by the Blight, as in the case of the kingdom of Malkier (711). Yet the degree of corruption of the land, which in Sauron's case mainly appears to depend on how long a land has been under the Dark Lord's control, is related to the distance from the Blight's edge, more along the lines of Foul's evil. To enter the Blight is gradually to enter the corruption wrought by Shai'tan's evil. Rand wonders when the party will move into the Blight, not realizing that the slight change in temperature and the wrongness that this change makes him feel are the first signs (721). This association of the Dark Lord's evil with radiation effects (in that the evil decreases relative to the distance from its source, dying away gradually), as well as with military control of an area, proves relevant somewhat later in this discussion.

The second parallel between the evil force of mainly Foul and Shai'tan, but to some extent also Sauron, is the lifeless lands surrounding Shai'tan's prison. In a dream, Rand sees this place to which "spring had never come [. . .] and never would come. Nothing grew in the cold soil that crunched under his boots, not so much as a bit of lichen. [. . .] [D]ust coated the stone as if never a drop of rain had touched it" (119). This land obviously shares some characteristics with both Mordor and Ridjeck Thome: it is dry, dusty, and dead. Appropriately called the Blasted Lands, it calls to mind a radioactive desert close to a massive radioactive source, as well as the long cold of nuclear winter. In fact, that appears to be the (symbolic) nature of the Dark Lord's evil in Jordan's book: where Sauron represents the ills of industrialization and Lord Foul represents the ills of leprosy, Shai'tan represents the ills of nuclear war and radioactivity.

Quite apart from its association with military control, Shai'tan's evil in *The Eye of the World* shares numerous traits with ionizing radiation. As noted before, it decreases with distance, a tendency that also explains the sterility of the Blasted Lands: Close to its source, nuclear radiation kills and sterilizes. As its effect decreases farther away, it does not kill directly but changes the cellular structures, thus causing cancer and mutations, as well as damage to the immune system—and fungal infections are among the first to take advantage of a compromised immune system. In other words, Shai'tan's evil—as a force—affects the Blight in a manner similar to nuclear radiation: it turns living things into diseased, cancer-ridden wrecks, eventually causing plants and animals to mutate into new, corrupted forms of life. This interpretation is indicated already in the book's prologue, when Lews Therin takes his life with magic tainted by evil: the air turns to fire and the light "would have seared and blinded any eye that glimpsed it, even for an instant." Stone is vaporized, the ground convulses, molten rock is cast into the air, and "[f]rom north and south, from east and west, the wind howled in" (xiv). The image closely resembles the blinding light, shock wave, and mushroom cloud that we have learned to associate with a nuclear explosion.[87]

Examining the relation between the Dark Lord and his realm, we find that the cancer and mutations, the sterile Blasted Lands and the military control not only explain how ruler and realm affect each other. By understanding the nature of evil through the character of the evil land, a central theme of the novel emerges, with evil representing the ills of nuclear war and the misuse of nuclear power.

Evil Landscapes: The Personal Touch

Although the landscape of evil has developed into a fairly traditional trope only occasionally challenged by writers of portal–quest (and some immersive) fantasy, the similarities among the many accounts are largely superficial. As the three evil realms presented in this chapter illustrate, these characteristics include a land where little lives, especially plant life, or where existing life is in some way corrupted, diseased, and dying—traits shared with the genre's taproot texts, in particular Robert Browning's "Childe Roland" poem. Other similarities may be found: the occurrence of temperature extremes, which we recognize from Hell in *The Divine Comedy* and *Paradise Lost* and which is a motif alluded to in Cook's ironic reversal of the evil realm: Sauron has a volcano at the center of his realm but is able to create a snowstorm in the Misty Mountains;[88] Lord Foul protects his stronghold with a river of lava, but the stronghold itself is icy cold, and he afflicts the Land with a preternatural winter; Shai'tan has also prolonged the natural winter, and his realm is unnaturally hot in the Blight, but the Blasted Lands near his prison lacks hope for spring, just like the desolate plains outside Mordor.

Looking beyond such parallels, the relationship between the evil rulers and their realms offers valuable suggestions as to central themes in the stories, not least because the Dark Lords are the principal antagonists—the main obstacles of the heroes' quests. No evil is merely generic, even in fantasy; and the nature of evil is mirrored in the nature of the evil landscape—morality puts its stamp on the land. To Tolkien, industrialization is evil, while Donaldson creates evil by projecting the despair and destruction of leprosy on the Land, and Jordan demonstrates the radioactive evil of nuclear devices. Each theme goes far beyond the dark realms to permeate the entire story.[89]

The three readings here have also presented three alternative ways of exploring Dark Lords and Dark Lands. Each approach uses a somewhat different starting point in discussing the subject: three aspects of Sauron's evil in Tolkien, the nature of Shai'tan's evil influence in Jordan, and the character and motive of Lord Foul in Donaldson. Regardless of point of departure, however, they all demonstrate a connection between ruler and realm and show that exploring that connection yields interesting critical insights.

• • •

The land and the king are one, we are told by Terry Pratchett's king Verence, an assertion that quickly loses some of its edge when Nanny Ogg wonders, "One what?"[90] The witch's question raises a valid point. A direct link between ruler and realm is a common element in fantasy literature, but the various works display little consensus as to the nature of that link. Perhaps the direct link is merely a stylistic device? If, as Mendlesohn suggests, the king is associated "with the well-being of the land, and the condition of the land with the morality of the place,"[91] does this imply that the morality of the *king* is reflected in the condition of the land? Ought we only to consider the realm as a metonym for its ruler and the land's condition as an emblematic correlative of the sovereign's morals or health?

From the cases discussed in chapter 5, we can see how variation rather than conformity best describes how sovereigns are linked to their countries. The direct link can be central to the plot and of great importance to the protagonists, or it can flash by, all but ignored by the story. Being one with the land may mean that ruler and realm are all but identical, or it could mean that a country without a leader is simply prone to political anarchy. Even when the sovereign acts as a conduit for power, that power can involve a combination of politics, magic, and fertility—or it can keep them separate. An explanation for the direct link may be offered, or the link may be left totally inexplicable. The influence may run from ruler to realm or from realm to ruler, and may even work in both directions at once.

These differences are not binary, they exist on a scale; nor is this an exhaustive list. In other words, each direct link that we find between a fantasy king or queen and his or her country is in all probability unique. What these links have in common is merely that they tell the reader something about the rulers by describing the realm that surrounds them. Is that, perhaps, *all* these direct links do? Peter Barry remarks that it is "a common literary-critical ploy" to read the *external* as *internal*;[92] and a critic could, presumably, read the state of the realm—good or bad—as just a metaphor for the state of the ruler. If the pouring rain outside is a metaphor for the grief of the man in the car, and the sunny day and lush greenery is a metaphor for the happiness of the young couple on the picnic blanket, why not read the sterile land as a metaphor for the sterility of a castrated king?

The problem with such an approach is that it is reductive as well as denying fantasy's characteristic ability to create, within its fictive worlds, new rules for how things work. Treating the realm as a metonym for its ruler also implies that the realm is, somehow, less important than the ruler. The land is reduced to a mere setting, a backdrop that at best provides clues for the protagonists (and the reader) and sets an appropriate mood for the story, at worst only allowing us to see the flaws of a sovereign writ large. Implicit in such a reading is the assumption that characters are more important than setting and people more important than place, as if the characters (and people in general) were somehow more "relevant" than settings (and places). As I pointed out in the introduction to this book, I am wary of these attitudes in general; and when it comes to fantasy, whose environments are often radically different from the actual world, there is a distinct risk of misunderstanding a story if its setting is read simply as a metaphor for some internal aspects of the character in charge. In their fantasy worlds, authors are free to set up any rules they like; failing to take such rules into account ignores one of the genre's most fundamental features.

Despite their many differences, the various "curious relationships" examined in this chapter also demonstrate the problem with a metaphoric/metonymic reading of the direct link between ruler and realm. Even in cases in which the state of the land suggests a metaphor, as in Jordan's *The Eye of the World*, it is not necessarily a metaphor for the ruler's mental or moral condition. The effects produced by Shai'tan's evil force suggest that it is possible to read this force, or indeed evil itself, as a metaphor for nuclear radiation—but this tells us nothing about the Dark One himself. Similarly, the palimpsest and the related *damnatio memoriae* that dominate the changing topography of Goldstein's Amaz offer a metaphor for the kings' conflict, but the shapes associated with each king tells us little about either kings or supporters. The rounded shapes associated with the Jewel King are not an external representation of his well-rounded ideas, for instance.

Even when it is possible to read the external landscape in terms of the ruler's internal traits, such a reading is reductive rather than expansive. Sauron's and Foul's realms are superficially alike, to the point where a list of correspondences could be drawn up. These similarities in realms are *only* superficial, however, and adhere to a long tradition of what evil landscapes ought to look like. The structure of those landscapes derives from two rather different characters, however. Were we to assume that outward resemblance implied internal similarity in the Dark Lords, we would fail to understand not only Sauron and Foul but also the nature of evil in Tolkien's and Donaldson's works. Given how central evil and the battle against it are to the respective plots, we would also risk misunderstanding the plots themselves. Although the ruler–realm relationship is marginalized in some works, it is of central importance in others. If the nature of the direct link is of immediate concern for the protagonists, whether they aspire to the throne themselves (e.g., in Brooks's *Magic Kingdom for Sale/Sold!*) or are in some way involved with a sovereign and a land suffering from the same affliction (e.g., in Ende's *The Neverending Story*), an attempt to read the realm as the ruler writ large would make the story well-nigh incomprehensible.

The case is especially pronounced with *The Neverending Story*, in which the direct link allows the realm to affect the ruler: the illness of the Childlike Empress is a direct result of Fantastica being devoured by the Nothing. If anything, the Empress is a version of Fantastica writ *small*, her illness a metaphor for the land's destruction. Yet, for all their metonymic relationship, Fantastica and the Empress—as well as any other ruler and realm in the genre—are also two separate entities; and a special and curious relationship exists between them. When discussing rulers and realms in a fantasy work, we must also understand the nature of the link—direct or indirect—that connects them. It is not enough to realize that ruler and realm are one—the question we need to ask ourselves is: "One what?"

6 : Some Final Thoughts

I consider myself a seasoned traveler in the realm of fairy story. I have long since lost count of all the places I have visited in the myriad fantasy stories I have read over the years. Often, a setting feels more well-known than wonderful, like a vacation resort one has visited several times before. Equally often, however, I blink (my mind's eye, at least) at the fresh wonders that glitter between the pages: windswept tussock grass in lurid colors, a forest of strange beasts and weird trees, a city of miracles . . . Whether familiar or alien, the setting combines with characters and plot to create the fantasy story. There is widespread agreement that settings are central to fantasy works—indeed, that a fantasy setting has much in common with the characters who live in, travel through, or otherwise experience it. Nevertheless, few critics have examined the genre from a perspective where those settings are in focus. It was this discrepancy between proclaimed significance and lack of scholarship that gave rise to my original question: what can we learn about particular works as well as the genre in general by examining fantasy settings? That question sparked this exploration into the representations of fantasy landscapes and the ways in which those landscapes interact with their respective stories.

I have proposed the term *topofocal* to describe an approach to texts that focuses on the setting. This is not to say that characters and plot are of less importance, but it does mean that it is the setting—in any of its many aspects—that provides a critical way into the work. Each of the four main chapters offers a different topofocal perspective, examining one particular aspect of fantasy settings. Chapter 2 presents two studies—one quantitative and the other qualitative—of what is arguably the most visible manifestation of fantasy settings: the fictive map. In about three to four fantasy novels out of ten, the setting is presented by both text and map(s). These maps typically share an aesthetic that is relatively free from modern map elements, such as scale and legend; but they nevertheless mostly adhere to modern map conventions. At least two thirds of fantasy maps portray secondary-world settings, but elements or conventions invented as part of such worlds are rare. Overall, the maps convey an impression of adherence to genre conventionality. This apparent conventionality is deceptive, however, as all maps are the result of a mapmaker's choices about what to include and exclude. If we bear in mind that every map has an author, a subject, and a theme, for instance, a close investigation of an individual map may reveal much about the world of the work. Rather than showing us only where the protagonists are and how they got there, a fantasy map can offer insights about the attitudes embedded in it. These are attitudes to particular map referents, to the culture and land of the map, and to the very world portrayed.

The discussion in chapter 3 springs from a conspicuous difference between fantasy geography and the geography of the actual world. The same reality prevails all over the actual world (with the exception, perhaps, of extreme cases such as black holes and elementary particles), and on the other side of any border or boundary we cross, the same laws of nature and causality still apply. A fantasy world, by contrast, can be divided into different realities. It is possible to find that magic works on the other side of the border, or to walk from the land of the living to the land of the dead. Such borders may appear to be sharp demarcations, but they are often indistinct, gradual transitions from one reality to another. Regardless of what domain lies on the other side, the hero's courage is put to the test when crossing the border into the alien and unknown—but it is generally the return that marks the real trial, of one kind or another. Fantasy landscapes are also dotted with enclosed areas—polders—protected from the outside world by a boundary. Inside these boundaries, climate, the nature of magic, even the passage of time itself may be different from the surroundings. Polders are anachronisms, bubbles of the past that are part of the world's topology as well as its history.

A key element of many fantasy definitions, and one I take as a defining feature of the genre, is the presence of something impossible that is accepted—and treated—as possible by writer and reader. The different realities that the borders and boundaries keep apart are actually territories of different possibilities. What is impossible in one place is possible on the other side of the border. A fundamental function for both boundaries and borders is, in fact, not to separate but to unite; to join opposing realities. To cross from one side to the other is to rethink the world and to see the impossible as possible.

Rethinking the world is the issue underlying chapter 4. Fantasy is a genre that, in principle, allows us to rethink, reimagine, and reconsider anything. One of the central relationships that a setting can present is that between nature and culture. The guiding question for this chapter was how the nature–culture relation is portrayed in fantasy cities. In the four close readings, we encountered highly dissimilar relations between the two domains, relations possible to arrange according to a variety of principles. Looking, for instance, at how nature is or is not incorporated in the cultural domain, we find that in Minas Tirith, nature as a part of culture signals just governance. Newford uses the opposition between the natural and cultural domains as an expression of society's flaws. In New Crobuzon, the two domains dissolve into each other as part of a general inclination against categories and toward hybridity and the grotesque. Ombria turns the natural into a liminal phenomenon that marks out the borders between the city's cultural domains. A range such as this does not in itself reveal much about the role of the nature–culture relation in the genre, even if it is quite revealing in the respective settings. In each city, however, the relation between the domains displays a connection to a key theme or concern in the stories. This kind of topofocal reading can thus indicate an area of a work that deserves further investigation.

Chapter 5, finally, engages more immediately with the connection between setting and characters. Whereas chapter 3 considers geographical divisions found in fantasy but not in the actual world, this chapter explores how fantasy bridges divisions that are taken for granted in the actual world. Fantasy rulers may be linked more directly to their realms than we commonly consider actual-world rulers to be. The sympathy between ruler and realm is greater, and the two act as each other's complement. A sterile king governs a barren realm, a languishing empress reigns over a fading land, and an evil lord rules a blighted and hostile country. The genre offers great variety in type and magnitude of sympathy, although the Dark Lord with his (or, occasionally, her) evil land has become a stock character in much fantasy of the portal–quest variety. Even so, each dark realm deserves careful attention, as the similarities between them are mostly superficial. Furthermore, it is a mistake to read the landscape as only a metaphor for its ruler. The direct link between ruler and realm is a fantastic element; to ignore it, or to regard it as other than "real" within the frame of the story, is to deny the impossible made possible that lies at the very core of the fantasy genre. Whatever other reading of that special connection one makes, the direct link must first and foremost be accepted for what it is. Indeed, the nature of the link—its magnitude and type—may itself be central to the construction of the plot.

My topofocal approaches center on four types of divisions of the fantasy setting, and each approach provides a partial answer to my original question. As I had expected, placing the setting in focus afforded a glimpse of what the fictional worlds contain and how they are assembled or expanded along geographical, historical, and fantastical dimensions. More surprisingly, the topofocal readings revealed much about fundamental aspects of the works, such as their underlying attitudes and central concerns. These readings turned out to be useful in clarifying the roles and nature of certain characters, and they helped demonstrate how plot, character, and setting are interwoven. The reading of any fantasy work, it became evident, would benefit from an exploration of its many environments—and clearly an understanding of some areas of the genre will profit from a focus on settings.

I say "some areas," because even though I strove for the widest possible range in my selection of examples, I did choose works that belong near the center of the genre's fuzzy set—as far as I can tell, they are unmistakably works of fantasy. I also picked texts that would provide the clearest possible examples of the features under discussion. It could thus be argued that other texts, texts that are less typically fantasy, may display other characteristics. A similar case can be made regarding liminal fantasy, the least represented of Farah Mendlesohn's fantasy categories among my examples. These are valid objections; but they do not invalidate my findings, they merely underscore the need for further topofocal explorations of the genre.

One possible area for future exploration is suggested by the Cauldron of Story. In the introduction, I explained how I consider the (mostly unabashed) incorporation of material from the Cauldron to be a fourth dominant feature of modern fantasy (apart from the three features already identified by Brian Attebery). Places as well as characters and plots simmer in the pot, and they are often ladled out and added to fantasy stories. One perspicuous example in this book is the inclusion of an entire complex of related myths surrounding the Fisher King figure in Powers's novel. Another, less obvious, example is how the landscapes of evil tend to share a number of recognizable building blocks. Places such as Faerie and the land of the dead, as well as the polder element itself, have bubbled in the Cauldron for a long time. Other settings have been added more recently: the urban blight, the "Oriental" city, the sewer systems. The most frequently used ingredients, in particular, certainly deserve more critical attention, not to find out where they come from but to see what flavors they contribute to the dish.

This book has provided only a small part of the answer to what we can learn by examining the settings of fantasy. The four approaches introduced here do not constitute the sole way of reading the genre from a topofocal point of view. Fantasy worlds differ from the actual world in innumerable ways: fantastic elements can be introduced as part of the landscape; strange environments can be inhabited or traversed; any number of categories can be rethought. Topography, hydrology, and ecology can exist under different rules. Employing a topofocal perspective does not necessarily mean using one of the approaches outlined and exemplified in the four chapters recapitulated just now. It only means finding an interesting aspect of the fantasy setting and placing it in focus.

By discussing the same work—*The Lord of the Rings*—in terms of maps and boundaries, as well as of the relations between nature–culture and ruler–realm, I demonstrate how analysis of a single text can benefit from all four approaches. My topofocal reading of Tolkien's work is by no means exhaustive, but even this limited exploration of the settings of Middle-earth can clearly provide new insights about a book that has been very thoroughly analyzed over the years. As for the other texts I have used as examples, I have barely scratched their surfaces. I could instead have looked at the relation between the king and his realm in Nix's books; the map in Miéville's *Perdido Street Station*; the border between de Lint's Newford and its Otherworld; the nature–culture relation in Brust's Dragaera books . . . not to mention the construction and function of forests, rivers, mountain terrain, and other landscape types whose stories run through these works. Those topics, and many others, await future scholarship. This book outlines some paths into the vast and varied interior of Fantasyland; but a great deal remains for subsequent applications of topofocal criticism: other worlds to investigate, new landscapes to visit, more fantasy settings to explore.

Appendix A: Method for the Map Survey[1]

To obtain unbiased results with a known margin of error from a quantitative study, a sample should be randomly selected from the entire population, with every unit in the population having the same chance of being drawn. Hence, to sample the fantasy genre, one would compile a list of all the works of fantasy ever written and randomly pick as many works as are necessary to obtain the desired margin of error. This is simple in theory but impossible in practice. Even if a straightforward definition existed that would determine unequivocally whether a given text belonged to the genre or not, it would be impractical to check everything ever published in English (or even everything published in English after 1858 or 1954, or any other arbitrary start date for the genre) against that definition. If one accepts Brian Attebery's suggestion that fantasy is a fuzzy set, where genre affiliation depends on similarity to a number of core works,[2] listing the works of a genre becomes impossible even in theory, as works belong to the genre *to some degree*.

A question that needs to be resolved when sampling a genre is what actually comprises the population. To address this question with some precision, I have borrowed terminology from the International Federation of Library Associations and Institutions. According to its *Functional Requirements for Bibliographic Records*, a *work* is "a distinct intellectual or artistic creation," an abstract entity that is realized through one or more *expressions*. A *manifestation* is "the physical embodiment of an *expression*" and can exist in a number of *items*.[3] For example, as J. R. R. Tolkien made constant revisions of the various impressions and editions of *The Lord of the Rings*, this work exists in a number of expressions. Each such expression is physically embodied in manifestations such as, for instance, the 2002 HarperCollins hardcover edition or the Houghton Mifflin 2004 Fiftieth Anniversary edition, each of which exists in a number of copies (items). Using these terms, we may ask whether a genre is a group of authors who write in the same vein or a collection of works that fulfill a certain set of criteria, or perhaps the totality of all expressions, manifestations, or even items that embody these works. If it is the authors, each author should appear only once in the sampling frame, and the probability for selecting Hope Mirrlees should be the same as for Terry Pratchett. That a writer who has published a single novel of genre interest would have the same impact on the genre as someone who has been writing steadily for decades seems dubious. Also, since we are investigating maps, it is reasonable to see the genre as a collection of fantasy works; the presence of maps *can* vary between expressions, but as a rule, if a work includes a map, a map is found in all of its expressions (although there are exceptions). I therefore decided to consider the population (the genre) to comprise all fantasy *works*, and to give each work in the sampling frame an equal chance of being selected for the sample.

Since listing every work in a genre is impossible, sampling the genre directly is likewise impossible. A popular method for a literary survey is to use an easily available sample. (Deirdre F. Baker, for instance, describes her sampling thus: "I did a casual survey of the maps in some of the many fantasies I have on my own bookshelves."[4]) Such a *convenience sample*, however, is almost certainly biased in one or more ways (in Baker's case, both by what books she has in her bookcase and by which of these she picked for her survey); there is no way of estimating the representativeness of the sample.[5] The survey in chapter 2 draws its sample from a sampling frame, whose possible biases are detailed shortly. The largest database of fantasy books available to me was the inventory list of SF-Bokhandeln (Sweden's main science-fiction and fantasy retailer), which contained titles currently or previously in stock, or ordered, at the time when the list was copied to me.[6] I filtered the list for fantasy novels in English (according to the retailer's classification, it should be noted) and edited it: each title (work) was retained only once (separate editions, for instance hardback and paperback, resulted in multiple listings for some titles in the original list). Works considered not to be fantasy according to the criteria detailed in chapter 1 were removed: Charlotte Guest's *Mabinogion* (1838–49), Walter Scott's *Ivanhoe* (1819), Thomas Malory's *Le Morte Darthur* (1485), and Penguin Classics of various "taproot texts" that predate the emergence of generic fantasy but that include the fantastic and are of heightened significance to the genre.[7] The following categories, while of genre interest, were also removed, as they were deemed to follow rules different from those for original works of fiction for including maps and would thus bias the sample: graphic novels (e.g., Neil Gaiman's Sandman sequence [1989–96]), obvious parodies (e.g., the Barry Trotter books [2001–2004] and *Bored of the Ring* [1969]), non- or semi-fiction spin-offs (e.g., Pratchett et al., *The Science of Discworld* [1999]), and tie-in novels (novels based on worlds originally created in other media, e.g. role-playing and computer games).

Although the list offered a reasonable sampling frame of English-language fantasy currently or recently in print, I improved its correspondence to the population through supplementation in two ways. First, obvious gaps in a number of book series were filled in (e.g., if the first and third titles in a series were listed, the second title was added to the sampling frame). Second, as they could be considered central to the genre, any fantasy novels short-listed for the Hugo and World Fantasy Awards from 2000 to 2007 were added. If a short-listed work was part of a series, all the books in that series were added. For instance, for Gene Wolfe's *Soldier of Sidon* (2006; World Fantasy Award winner in 2007), the previous novels of the series, *Soldier of the Mist* (1986) and *Soldier of Arete* (1989), were also included. (In fact, most of the ninety-seven short-listed works and their pre- or sequels were already on the list, and only twenty-one additions were made.) After edits and additions, the final sampling frame contained 4,292 titles. From the sampling frame, 200 titles were then randomly selected (by computer-generated random numbers) and collected (listed in appendix B).

Obtaining the exact editions in the sampling frame quickly proved too impractical—and expensive—so the sampling has been of the most readily available editions. As I take the genre to be a totality of *works* rather than *expressions*, this should not invalidate the sample. In some cases, I have been unable to get hold of copies of the books myself and have thus had to rely on others to scan or photograph the maps for me. Partially for this reason, I lack data on the distribution between high and low fantasy in the sample.

To determine the margin of error (at a confidence level of 95 percent), I used a method developed by G. H. Jowett. This method gives reliable calculations of potential errors and has the advantage of providing statistically correct margins of error regardless of sample size.[8] The margin of error gives the upper and lower limits between which it is 95 percent certain that the actual value for the total population lies.

$$pU = \frac{(x+1)F_{1-a/2}\left(2(x+1), 2(n-x)\right)}{n-x+(x+1)F_{1-a/2}\left(2(x+1), 2(n-x)\right)}$$

$$pL = \frac{x}{x+(n-x+1)F_{1-a/2}\left(2(n-x+1), 2x\right)}$$

pU upper limit for margin of error
pL lower limit for margin of error
n sample size
x number of units with the quality investigated
a confidence coefficient

Appendix B: Map Sample

Map(s)	Author	Title (Series #)	Year	Series (if any)
	Abé, Shana	*The Last Mermaid*	2004	
✓	Alexander, Alma	*#1: The Hidden Queen*	2005	The Changer of Days Duology
	Amory, Jay	*#2: Pirates of the Relentless Desert*	2007	The Clouded World
	Anderson, Poul	*War of the Gods*	1997	
✓	Anderson, Poul, and Karen Anderson	*#3: Dahut*	1987	The King of Ys
	Anthony, Piers	*#16: Demons Don't Dream*	1992	The Magic of Xanth
	Asprin, Robert Lynn	*#6: Little Myth Marker*	1985	Myth Adventures
✓	Auel, Jean M.	*#4: The Plains of Passage*	1990	Earth's Children
	Bailey, Robin W.	*#2: Talisman*	2004	Dragonkin
✓	Barclay, James	*#2: Shadowheart*	2003	Legends of the Raven
	Barrett Jr., Neal	*#2: The Treachery of Kings*	2001	Finn, the Master Lizard Maker
✓	Barron, T. A.	*#2: The Seven Songs of Merlin*	1997	The Lost Years of Merlin
	Baudino, Gael	*#4: Strands of Sunlight*	1994	The Strands
	Berliner, Janet, and George Guthridge	*#1: Child of the Light*	1991	The Madagascar Manifesto
	Bishop, Anne	*#2: Belladonna*	2007	Ephemera
	Blaylock, James P.	*All the Bells on Earth*	1995	
	Boyer, Elisabeth H.	*#5: The Troll's Grindstone*	1986	Wizard's War
	Bradley, Marion Zimmer	*#1: The Mists of Avalon*	1983	Avalon
	Bradley, Marion Zimmer	*#3: Witch Hill*	1990	Colin McLaren/ Claire Moffat
	Brennan, Noel-Anne	*Daughter of the Desert*	2006	
✓	Brooks, Terry	*#4: The Tangle Box*	1994	Magic Kingdom of Landover
	Brown, Mary	*#4: Dragonne's Eg*	1999	Pigs Don't Fly
	Brust, Steven	*To Reign in Hell*	1984	
	Brust, Steven	*#1: The Phoenix Guards*	1991	Khaavren Romances
	Butcher, Jim	*#6: Blood Rites*	2004	The Dresden Files
✓	Canavan, Trudi	*#2: Last of the Wilds*	2006	Age of the Five
✓	Card, Orson Scott	*#1: Seventh Son*	1987	The Alvin Maker Saga
	Carroll, Jonathan	*Black Cocktail*	1990	

Map(s)	Author	Title (Series #)	Year	Series (if any)
✓	Chamberlin, Ann	*#2: The Merlin of the Oakwood*	2001	Joan of Arc Tapestries
	Chapman, Janet	*#4: Tempting the Highlander*	2004	Pine Creek High-lander
	Cherryh, C. J., and Janet Morris	*#2: The Gates of Hell*	1986	Heroes in Hell
✓	Christian, Deborah	*#1: The Truthsayer's Apprentice*	1999	Loregiver
	Ciencin, Scott	*Wolves of Autumn*	1992	Wolves of Autumn
✓	Clayton, Jo	*#2: Drum Calls*	1997	The Drums of Chaos
	Clayton, Jo	*#2: Wildfire*	1992	Wild Magic
✓	Cobley, Michael	*#3: Shadowmasque*	2005	Shadowkings Trilogy
✓	Cole, Allan, and Chris Bunch	*#3: Kingdoms of the Night*	1995	Anteros/Far King-doms
✓	Coleman, Loren L.	*#3: Songs of Victory*	2005	Legends of Kern
	Constantine, Storm	*#3: Way of Light*	2001	The Magravandias Chronicles
	Cook, Glen	*#3: Water Sleeps*	1999	Glittering Stones
✓	Cooper, Louise	*#8: Aisling*	1993	Indigo
	Crawford, Dan	*#1: Rouse a Sleeping Cat*	1993	Cat and Mouse
	Cutter, Leah R.	*The Caves of Buda*	2004	
	Daniells, Cory	*#1: Broken Vows*	1999	The Last T'En
✓	Dayton, Gail	*#2: The Barbed Rose*	2006	The One Rose
✓	De Camp, L. Sprague, Lin Carter, and Björn Nyberg	*Conan the Swordsman*	1978	
	De Camp, L. Sprague	*#2: The Clocks of Iraz*	1971	The Reluctant King
	De Camp, L. Sprague	*#3: The Unbeheaded King*	1983	The Reluctant King
✓	Deitz, Tom	*#2: Springwar*	2000	A Tale of Eron
	Delacroix, Claire	*#1: The Rogue*	2002	Rogues of Ravens-muir
	Delacroix, Claire	*#2: The Scoundrel*	2003	Rogues of Ravens-muir
	Demarest, Jaki	*The Cardinal's Heir*	2004	
	Dickson, Gordon R.	*#5: The Dragon, the Earl, and the Troll*	1994	The Dragon and the George
	Drake, David	*Vettius and His Friends*	1989	
	Drew, Wayland	*Willow*	1988	
	Duane, Diane	*#1: The Book of Night with Moon*	1997	Feline Wizards

Map(s)	Author	Title (Series #)	Year	Series (if any)
	Durgin, Doranna	#2: Changespell	1997	Dun Lady's Jess
✓	Eddings, David, and Leigh Eddings	#2: The Treasured One	2004	The Dreamers
	Eisenstein, Phyllis	#1: Sorcerer's Son	1979	Book of Elementals
✓	Elmore, Larry, and Robert Elmore	Runes of Autumn	1996	
✓	Emerson, Ru	#2: The Two in Hiding	1991	Night Threads
	Erskine, Barbara	On the Edge of Darkness	1998	
	Estes, Rose, and E. J. Cherhavy	#1: Mountains & Madness	1993	Iron Dragons
✓	Foster, Alan Dean	#2: The Hour of the Gate	1983	Spellsinger
✓	Foxe, Jocelin	#2: Child of Fire	1999	The Wild Hunt
	Freeman, Pamela	#1: Blood Ties	2007	The Castings Trilogy
	Friesner, Esther M.	Child of the Eagle: A Myth of Rome	1996	
	Friesner, Esther M.	#3: Unicorn U.	1992	Gnome
	Friesner, Esther M.	#1: New York by Knight	1986	New York
	Frost, P. R.	#1: Hounding the Moon	2006	Tess Noncoiré
	Gardner, Craig Shaw	#1: Slaves of the Volcano God	1989	The Cineverse Cycle
✓	Gardner, Martin	Visitors from Oz: The Wild Adventures of Dorothy, the Scarecrow, and the Tin Woodman	1998	
✓	Garland, Mark A.	Sword of the Prophets	1997	
	Gemmell, David	#1: Legend	1984	The Drenai Saga
	Gentle, Mary	#1: Ash: A Secret History	2000	The Book of Ash
	Goldstein, Lisa	Strange Devices of the Sun and Moon	1993	
✓	Goodkind, Terry	#5: Soul of the Fire	1999	Sword of Truth
✓	Goodkind, Terry	#6: Faith of the Fallen	2000	Sword of Truth
	Green, Simon R.	#2: Blood and Honour	1992	Blue Moon Rising
	Green, Simon R.	#1: No Haven for the Guilty	1990	Hawk & Fisher
	Green, Simon R.	#8: The Unnatural Inquirer	2008	Nightside
✓	Greeno, Gayle	#1: Sunderlies Seeking	1998	Ghatten's Gambit
	Greeno, Gayle	#3: Exiles' Return	1995	The Ghatti's Tale
	Greenwood, Ed	#1: The Silent House	2004	Chronicles of Aglirta
✓	Hambly, Barbara	#1: The Ladies of Mandrigyn	1984	Sun-Wolf
	Havens, Candace	#2: Charmed & Ready	2006	Bronwyn the Witch
✓	Hearn, Lian	#2: Grass for His Pillow	2003	Tales of the Otori
	Hearn, Lian	#4: The Harsh Cry of the Heron	2006	Tales of the Otori
✓	Herniman, Marcus	#1: The Siege of Arrandin	1999	Arrandin Trilogy
	Hetley, James A.	#1: Dragon's Eye	2005	Dragon's Eye

Map(s)	Author	Title (Series #)	Year	Series (if any)
	Hill, Sandra	*#3: The Very Virile Viking*	2003	Viking Series II
	Holdstock, Robert	*#4: Gate of Ivory, Gate of Horn*	1997	Mythago Wood
	Holt, Tom	*Grailblazers*	1994	
	Howard, Linda	*Son of the Morning*	1997	
✓	Howard, Robert E.	*#7: Conan the Warrior*	1967	Conan Universe
✓	Irvine, Ian	*#1: Geomancer*	2001	Well of Echoes
	Jackson, Lisa	*Enchantress*	2003	
✓	Jacques, Brian	*#8: Outcast of Redwall*	1995	Redwall
	Jefferies, Mike	*#4: The Knights of Cawdor*	1995	Loremasters of Elundium
✓	Jones, Diana Wynne	*#2: Drowned Ammet*	1977	Dalemark
✓	Jones, Diana Wynne	*#4: The Crown of Dalemark*	1993	Dalemark
	Jones, Linda Winstead	*#3: The Star Witch*	2006	Fyne Witches
	Kay, Guy Gavriel	*The Last Light of the Sun*	2004	
	Kearney, Paul	*#3: The Iron Wars*	1998	Monarchies of God
	Kelleher, Anne	*Love's Labyrinth*	2000	
✓	Keyes, J. Gregory	*#3: The Blood Knight*	2006	The Kingdoms of Thorn and Bone
✓	Kirkpatrick, Russell	*#3: The Right Hand of God*	2005	Fire of Heaven
	Klasky, Mindy L.	*#4: The Glasswrights' Test*	2003	Glasswrights' Guild
	Knaak, Richard A.	*#1: The Shrouded Realm*	1991	Origins of Dragon-realm
	Kurland, Lynn	*#3: Dreams of Stardust*	2005	
✓	Kurtz, Katherine	*#3: Camber the Heretic*	1981	Legends of Saint Camber
	Lackey, Mercedes	*#1: The Lark and the Wren*	1992	Bardic Voices
✓	Lackey, Mercedes	*#2: Arrow's Flight*	1987	Heralds of Valdemar
✓	Lackey, Mercedes	*#3: Arrow's Fall*	1988	Heralds of Valdemar
	Lackey, Mercedes	*Brightly Burning*	2000	Heralds of Valdemar Prequels
✓	Larke, Glenda	*#2: Gilfeather*	2004	Isles of Glory
✓	Lee, Rachel	*#1: Shadows of Myth*	2005	Ilduin
	Lee, Tanith	*Reigning Cats and Dogs*	1995	
	Leiber, Fritz	*#7: The Knight and Knave of Swords*	1988	Fafhrd and the Gray Mouser
✓	Lewis, C. S.	*#7: The Last Battle*	1956	The Chronicles of Narnia
	Lickiss, Rebecca	*Eccentric Circles*	2001	
✓	Lindskold, Jane	*#5: Wolf Hunting*	2006	The Firekeeper Saga
✓	Lisle, Holly	*#1: Talyn: A Novel of Korre*	2005	Korre
	Litton, Josie	*#3: Castles in the Mist*	2002	Akoran

Map(s)	Author	Title (Series #)	Year	Series (if any)
	Liu, Marjorie M.	*#7: The Last Twilight*	2008	Dirk & Steele
✓	Mackey, Mary	*#2: The Horses at the Gate*	1996	Earthsong
	MacLeod, Ian R.	*The Light Ages*	2003	
	MacMillan, Scott, and Katherine Kurtz	*#1: Knights of the Blood*	1993	Knights of the Blood/ Vampyr-SS
	MacMillan, Scott, and Katherine Kurtz	*#2: At Sword's Point*	1994	Knights of the Blood/ Vampyr-SS
	Madden, Mickee	*Love Everlastin'*	1998	
	Malan, Violette	*The Mirror Prince*	2006	
	Marco, John	*#3: The Sword of Angels*	2005	Eyes of God
	Marillier, Juliet	*Wildwood Dancing*	2006	Wildwood
	Martin, Gail	*#1: The Summoner*	2007	Chronicles of the Necromancer
✓	McCarty, Dennis	*#5: The Birth of the Blade*	1993	Thlassa Mey
✓	McGarry, Terry	*#2: The Binder's Road*	2003	Eiden Myr
	McKerrigan, Sarah	*Captive Heart*	2006	
	Medeiros, Teresa	*Lady of Conquest*	1989	
	Meier, Shirley	*#5: Shadow's Daughter*	1991	Fifth Millennium
✓	Modesitt, L. E.	*#4: Alector's Choice*	2005	Corean Chronicles
	Modesitt, L. E.	*#1: The Magic of Recluce*	1991	The Saga of Recluce
	Monette, Sarah	*#3: The Mirador*	2007	Mélusine
	Moorcock, Michael	*#5: The Bane of the Black Sword*	1977	The Elric Saga
	Moore, C. L.	*Jirel of Joiry*	1969	
	Moore, John	*Slay and Rescue*	1993	
	Morgan, Alexis	*#3: In Darkness Reborn*	2007	Paladins of Darkness
	Murphy, Shirley Rousseau	*#4: Cat in the Dark*	1999	Joe Gray
	Myers, Edward	*#2: Fire and Ice*	1992	Mountain Made of Light
✓	Myers, John Myers	*#1: Silverlock*	1949	Silverlock
	Nicholls, Stan	*#2: Quicksilver Zenith*	2004	Quicksilver/The Dreamtime
	Nichols, Adam	*#2: Songster*	1999	The Whiteblade Saga
✓	Niven, Larry, and Jerry Pournelle	*#1: The Burning City*	2000	Golden Road
	Norton, Andre, and Lyn McConchie	*Silver May Tarnish*	2005	
	Nye, Jody Lynn	*#1: Waking in Dreamland*	1998	Dreamland
	O'Kerry, Janeen	*Daughter of Gold*	2004	
✓	Paxson, Diana L.	*#1: Lady of Light*	1982	Westria

Map(s)	Author	Title (Series #)	Year	Series (if any)
	Paxson, Diana L.	*#5: The Sea Star*	1988	Westria
✓	Paxson, Diana L.	*#6: The Wind Crystal*	1990	Westria
✓	Paxson, Diana L.	*#8: The Golden Hills of Westria*	2006	Westria
	Powers, Tim	*Declare*	2000	
	Powers, Tim	*#3: Earthquake Weather*	1997	Fault Lines
	Putney, Mary Jo	*#4: A Distant Magic*	2007	The Guardian
	Rabe, Jean	*#3: The Finest Challenge*	2006	Finest
	Rafferty, Carin	*#3: Touch of Lightning*	1995	Sanctuary
	Rice, Patricia	*#1: Mystic Guardian*	2007	Mystic Isles
✓	Rohan, Michael Scott	*#1: The Anvil of Ice*	1986	The Winter of the World
	Rohan, Michael Scott, and Alan Scott	*The Ice King*	1983	
	Rowe, Stephanie	*#1: Date Me, Baby, One More Time*	2006	Goblet of Eternal Youth
	Rydill, Jessica	*The Glass Mountain*	2002	
	Saunders, Charles R.	*#1: Imaro*	1981	Imaro
✓	Savage, Felicity	*#2: Delta City*	1995	Garden of Salt
	Scott, Melissa, and Lisa A. Barnett	*#1: Point of Hopes*	1995	
	Sherman, Josepha	*#1: The Shattered Oath*	1995	Prince of the Sidhe
✓	Shuler, Linda Lay	*Let the Drum Speak*	1996	
	Smith, Clark Ashton	*Monster of the Prophecy*	1983	
✓	Smith, Sherwood	*#2: The Fox*	2007	Inda
	Smith-Ready, Jeri	*#1: Eyes of Crow*	2006	Aspect of Crow
	Snyder, Midori	*The Flight of Michael McBride*	1994	
	St. John, Tina	*#1: Heart of the Hunter*	2004	The Dragon Chalice
	Stasheff, Christopher	*#1: A Wizard in Mind*	1995	Rogue Wizard
	Stasheff, Christopher	*#1: The Shaman*	1995	The Star Stone
	Stemple, Adam	*Singer of Souls*	2005	
	Turner, Delia Marshall	*#2: Of Swords and Spells*	1999	
✓	Turtledove, Harry	*Conan of Venarium*	2003	
✓	Turtledove, Harry	*#6: Out of the Darkness*	2004	Darkness
	Vaughan, Elizabeth	*#3: Warlord*	2007	Chronicles of the Warlands
	Walton, Evangeline	*#1: Prince of Annwn*	1974	The Mabinogion
	Watt-Evans, Lawrence	*#3: Dragon Venom*	2003	The Obsidian Chronicles
✓	Welch, Michelle M.	*#3: Chasing Fire*	2005	Five Countries

Map(s)	Author	Title (Series #)	Year	Series (if any)
	What, Leslie	*Olympic Games*	2004	
	White, T. H.	*#5: The Book of Merlyn*	1977	Once and Future King
✓	Whitlach, Terryl, and David Michael Wieger	*The Katurran Odyssey*	2004	
	Wilkins, Kim	*#1: The Autumn Castle*	2003	Europa Suite
✓	Williams, Michael	*#1: A Sorcerer's Apprentice*	1990	From Thief to King
✓	Williamson, Philip G.	*#3: From Enchantery*	1993	The Firstworld Chronicles
	Witcover, Paul	*Tumbling After*	2005	
	Wylie, Jayel	*Wicked Charms*	2003	
	Wylie, Jonathan	*Across the Flame*	1996	
✓	Young, Roy V.	*#1:Captains Outrageous: Or for Doom the Bell Tolls*	1994	Days of Yor
	Zelazny, Roger	*#4: The Hand of Oberon*	1976	Chronicles of Amber

Note: These works were all tagged as novels although some of them are short story collections. The collections have been kept in the sample because some of them (for instance, the Conan books) actually come equipped with maps. Although the incidence of maps in collections may vary from that in novels, a work's status as a collection does not appear to decide whether or not it contains a map, and simply being a collection was thus not deemed to be sufficient grounds for exclusion. The Internet Speculative Fiction Database (www.isfdb.org) has been used to supplement information that was missing from the SF-Bokhandeln database.

Notes

....

1. INTRODUCTION

1. See, for instance, Michael Moorcock, *Wizardry and Wild Romance* (London: Victor Gollancz, 1987), ch. 2; Colin N. Manlove, "The Elusiveness of Fantasy," *The Shape of the Fantastic: Selected Essays from the Seventh International Conference on the Fantastic in the Arts*, ed. Olena H. Saciuk (New York: Greenwood Press, 1990), 63; Robert J. Branham, "Principles of Imaginary Milieu: Argument and Idea in Fantasy Fiction," *Extrapolation* 21, no. 4 (1980): 328.

2. According to Schlobin, fantastic settings "take on powers and attributes that are normally assigned to characters"; see his "The *Locus Amoenus* and the Fantasy Quest," *Kansas Quarterly* 16, no. 3 (1984): 29; quoted in Roger C. Schlobin, "'Rituals' Footprints Ankle-Deep in Stone': The Irrelevancy of Setting in the Fantastic," *Journal of the Fantastic in the Arts* 11, no. 2 (2000): 156. Mathews explains how fantasy geography and setting "function almost as characters and symbols," and Clute describes how a "land" "is not a protagonist but has an analogous role"; see Richard Mathews, *Fantasy: The Liberation of Imagination* (New York: Routledge, 2002), 39, and John Clute, "Land," *The Encyclopedia of Fantasy*, eds. John Clute and John Grant (New York: St. Martin's Griffin, 1999). Both Mendlesohn and Rosebury observe how Tolkien's landscape is "a participant in the adventure," even the novel's "hero"; see Farah Mendlesohn, *Rhetorics of Fantasy* (Middletown, CT: Wesleyan University Press, 2008), 35, and Brian Rosebury, *Tolkien: A Cultural Phenomenon* (Basingstoke, UK: Palgrave Macmillan, 2003), 34. Mendlesohn makes similar points about C. S. Lewis's Narnia (a "character in and of itself"), and in Bram Stoker's *Dracula* "the landscape becomes a character [. . .] with moods and emotions of its own" (Mendlesohn, *Rhetorics*, 34, 129).

3. John Clute, "Notes on the Geography of Bad Art in Fantasy," *Pardon This Intrusion: Fantastika in the World Storm* (Harold Wood, UK: Beccon Publications, 2011), 111–12.

4. Don D. Elgin, *The Comedy of the Fantastic: Ecological Perspectives on the Fantasy Novel* (Westport: Greenwood Press, 1985).

5. Ibid., 180.

6. Kenneth J. Zahorski and Robert H. Boyer, "The Secondary Worlds of High Fantasy," *The Aesthetics of Fantasy Literature and Art*, ed. Roger C. Schlobin (Notre Dame, IN: University of Notre Dame Press, 1982).

7. Many of these studies are presented in more detail in chapter 2.

8. The most thorough of such Tolkien studies is Matthew Dickerson and Jonathan Evans, *Ents, Elves, and Eriador* (Lexington: University Press of Kentucky, 2006). For a truly excellent reading of a natural environment, see Verlyn Flieger, "Taking the Part of Trees: Eco-Conflict in Middle-earth," *J. R. R. Tolkien and His Literary*

Resonances: Views of Middle-earth, eds. George Clark and Daniel Timmons (Westport, CT: Greenwood Press, 2000).

9. Schlobin, "'Rituals' Footprints'," 154.

10. "With the setting in focus," compare *matrifocal*, "based or centred on the mother"; see "matrifocal, adj.," *OED Online*, December 2011 (Oxford University Press). Schlobin uses Bachelard's term *topoanalysis* for a focus on setting (Schlobin, "'Rituals' Footprints'," 155, citing Gaston Bachelard's *The Poetics of Space*, trans. Maria Jolas [1958; Boston: Beacon Press, 1994], 8). Bachelard's term is closely tied to psychoanalysis, however, and thus implies an almost exclusive focus on the relation between place and personal subject.

11. It should perhaps also be mentioned that however interesting a diachronic examination may be, such an examination is—regrettably—beyond the scope of this book.

12. For a wide range of opinions on how to define or describe ecocriticism, see the position papers on the topic at the website of the Association for the Study of Literature and the Environment (ASLE): Michael P. Branch and Sean O'Grady, eds., *Defining Ecocritical Theory and Practice*, ASLE, 1994, http://www.asle.org/site/resources/ecocritical-library/intro/defining/.

13. Cheryll Glotfelty and Harold Fromm, eds., *The Ecocriticism Reader: Landmarks in Literary Ecology* (Athens: University of Georgia Press, 1996).

14. Cheryll Glotfelty, "Introduction: Literary Studies in an Age of Environmental Crisis," *The Ecocriticism Reader*, xviii–xix.

15. Scott Slovic, "Ecocriticism: Containing Multitudes, Practising Doctrine," *The Green Studies Reader: From Romanticism to Ecocriticism*, ed. Laurence Coupe (London: Routledge, 2000).

16. Ibid., 160.

17. J. Hillis Miller, *Topographies* (Stanford, CA: Stanford University Press, 1995); Franco Moretti, *Atlas of the European Novel, 1800–1900* (London: Verso, 1998); Robert Mighall, *A Geography of Victorian Gothic Fiction: Mapping History's Nightmares* (Oxford: Oxford University Press, 1999).

18. Gary K. Wolfe, *Critical Terms for Science Fiction and Fantasy: A Glossary and Guide to Scholarship* (New York: Greenwood Press, 1986), 38–40.

19. Mendlesohn, *Rhetorics*, xiii. Not all critics agree that the debate over definitions is laid to rest, however; see, for instance, A.-P. Canavan, "Calling a Sword a Sword," *The New York Review of Science Fiction* (May 2012): 1; and Marek Oziewicz, *One Earth, One People: The Mythopoeic Fantasy Series of Ursula K. Le Guin, Lloyd Alexander, Madeleine L'Engle and Orson Scott Card* (Jefferson, NC: McFarland, 2008), ch. 1.

20. Kathryn Hume, *Fantasy and Mimesis: Responses to Reality in Western Literature* (New York: Methuen, 1984), 21. Note that Hume uses the word *fantasy* for what is here called *the fantastic*. Other critics who use the fantastic in a similar sense include W. R. Irwin, *The Game of the Impossible: A Rhetoric of Fantasy* (Urbana: University of Illinois Press, 1976), 8, and Brian Attebery, *Strategies of Fantasy* (Bloomington: Indiana University Press, 1992), 3 ff., esp. 11–12; and it is this broad definition that is referred to as "a general term for all forms of human expres-

sion that are not realistic" by Gary Westfahl, "Fantastic," *The Encyclopedia of Fantasy*. Rabkin's definition, although related to the one just given, is stricter: to him, "the fantastic" is a "diametric reversal of the ground rules of a narrative world"; see Eric S. Rabkin, *The Fantastic in Literature* (Princeton, NJ: Princeton University Press, 1976), 28–29. Also note that Todorov sees the fantastic completely differently, defining it as a hesitation about whether occurrences have a natural or supernatural explanation; see Tzvetan Todorov, *The Fantastic: A Structural Approach to a Literary Genre* (Ithaca, NY: Cornell University Press, 1975), 33. Todorov's term, while of interest when discussing a certain body of work, has no bearing on the discussions in this book.

21. Wolfe refers to this as perhaps "the most frequently cited defining characteristic of fantasy" and notes that the term is problematic in its imprecision (Wolfe, *Critical Terms*, 57; see also 38). For examples of scholars who have used *impossible* in their definitions, see Irwin, *Game*, 9; Attebery, *Strategies*, 14; Brian Attebery, *The Fantasy Tradition in American Literature: From Irving to Le Guin* (Bloomington: Indiana University Press, 1980), 2; Colin N. Manlove, *Modern Fantasy: Five Studies* (Cambridge: Cambridge University Press, 1975), 10, and John Clute, "Fantasy," in *The Encyclopedia of Fantasy*, 338.

22. Shippey, while accepting "known to be impossible" as a rule of thumb for identifying fantasy and its precursors, problematizes the concept, noting that views on what is impossible change over time and from person to person. He concedes, however, that regardless of cultural context, "the unseen or the non-material always remains in a separate category from the everyday"; see Tom Shippey, introduction to *The Oxford Book of Fantasy Stories*, ed. Tom Shippey (Oxford: Oxford University Press, 1994), x.

23. Even a hybrid such as *science fantasy* may exist, although it could be argued that adding something impossible to science fiction would turn it into fantasy. See Ursula K. Le Guin, "Changing Kingdoms: A Talk for the Fourteenth International Conference on the Fantastic in the Arts, March 17–21, 1993," *Trajectories of the Fantastic: Selected Essays from the Fourteenth International Conference on the Fantastic in the Arts*, ed. Michael A. Morrison (Westport, CT: Greenwood Press, 1997) for a discussion of this topic.

24. Irwin describes how "writer and reader knowingly enter upon a conspiracy of intellectual subversiveness" to "make nonfact appear as fact" (Irwin, *Game*, 9). Whether dream stories can be thought of as fantasy generally depends on whether the dream is taken seriously or whether it is used, as Tolkien suggests, as a device to discount the fantastic: J. R. R. Tolkien, "On Fairy-stories," *The Tolkien Reader* (1947; orig. lecture 1938; New York: Ballantine, 1966), 13–14.

25. Obviously, individual readers could happen to believe fiction to be true; if they believe a fantasy work to be true, however, they do so despite the way it is presented, not because of it.

26. Tolkien, "On Fairy-stories," 37. He emphasizes that he is discussing the instilling of belief, not "willing suspension of disbelief," which he believes to be something more passive; cf. Samuel Taylor Coleridge, *Biographia Literaria*, vol. 7:2 (1815; London: Routledge & Kegan Paul, 1983), 397–98 [ch. 14].

27. Irwin, *Game*, 9. Tolkien also stresses the rationality of the fantasy world, going as far as to say that "[t]he keener and the clearer the reason, the better fantasy it will make" (Tolkien, "On Fairy-stories," 54); and Elgin mentions how the reality of a "parallel world" is "drawn from its own internal consistency" (Elgin, *Comedy*, 180).

28. Attebery, *Strategies*, 12–14. He draws on cognitive linguists Lakoff and Johnson's use of fuzzy sets and prototypes to discuss categorization; see George Lakoff and Mark Johnson, *Metaphors We Live By* (Chicago: University of Chicago Press, 1980), 122–24. It is worth noting that in order to make Lakoff and Johnson's categories work as literary genres, Attebery adapts them by combining the fuzzy-sets idea with prototypes, by adding a spatial dimension to the fuzzy-set metaphor, and by suggesting that genres can have (a number of) individual works as prototypes. For an overview of Lakoff's view of categories, see George Lakoff, *Women, Fire, and Dangerous Things: What Categories Reveal about the Mind* (Chicago: University of Chicago Press, 1987), esp. ch. 2.

29. Attebery, *Strategies*, 14–16; cf. Tolkien, "On Fairy-stories," 57.

30. Tolkien, "On Fairy-stories," 26 ff., 19–20, 23.

31. Ibid., 28–29.

32. Ibid., 30.

33. For example: Marion Zimmer Bradley's *The Firebrand* (1986) portrays the Trojan War from Cassandra's point of view; Neil Gaiman offers the Queen's perspective of Snow White in "Snow, Glass, Apples" (1995); in Robert Holdstock's *Celtica* (2001), a young Merlin joins Jason and the Argo for the Celtic tribes' invasion of the Balkans; in *Caliban's Hour* (1994), by Tad Williams, Shakespeare's *The Tempest* is revisited; and Lisa Goldstein has Doctor John Dee help Rabbi Judah Loew fashion a golem in *The Alchemist's Door* (2002).

34. Examples of these respective dragon varieties can be found in, for instance, Erik Granström's *Svavelvinter* (Brimstone Winter; 2004), Patrick Rothfuss's *The Name of the Wind* (2007), Gordon R. Dickson's *The Dragon and the George* (1976), Michael Swanwick's *The Iron Dragon's Daughter* (1993), and the Dragonlance Chronicles (1984–85), by Margaret Weis and Tracy Hickman.

35. Many writers appear to have misunderstood the Cauldron of Story and have tried to use someone else's—frequently Tolkien's—recipe, only adding the literary equivalent of a sprig of parsley, generally with scant success.

36. The categories are thoroughly presented and discussed in Mendlesohn, *Rhetorics*.

37. Ibid., 2.

38. Ibid., 182; see also earlier discussions of liminal fantasy in Farah Mendlesohn, "Toward a Taxonomy of Fantasy," *Journal of the Fantastic in the Arts* 13, no. 2 (2002); Farah Mendlesohn, "*Conjunctions 39* and Liminal Fantasy," *Journal of the Fantastic in the Arts* 15, no. 3 (2005). The outline here only hints at the complexities of liminal fantasy, given that this category has no bearing on the discussions in this book, but interested readers are encouraged to refer to Mendlesohn's book for a more exhaustive description.

39. Mendlesohn, *Rhetorics*, xv–xvii; for a discussion of texts that exist simultaneously in several categories, see ch. 5 of Mendlesohn's work.

40. Mendlesohn, *Rhetorics*, 114. It could even be argued that the episodes narrated by Yagharek, the stranger who has journeyed to the city on a mission of his own, are brief instances of a portal–quest voice.

41. John Clute and John Grant, eds., *The Encyclopedia of Fantasy* (New York: St. Martin's Griffin, 1999), contains some forty types of fantasy, labeled according to, e.g., setting, plot structure, origin of source material, handling of source material, portrayal of magic, type of protagonist, age of (intended) reader, and story themes.

42. See, e.g., John Clute, "Taproot Texts," in *The Encyclopedia of Fantasy*, 921; Attebery, *Fantasy Tradition*, 5–9; Wolfe, *Critical Terms*, xviii; John-Henri Holmberg, *Fantasy: Fantasylitteraturens historia, motiv och författare* [The history, motifs, and authors of fantasy literature] ([Viken, Sweden]: Replik, 1995), 14; and Mathews, *Fantasy*, 2–3. Although he does not call attention to this fact, the earliest "modern fantasy" work Manlove discusses is George MacDonald's *Phantastes: A Faerie Romance for Men and Women* (1858); see Manlove, *Modern Fantasy*.

43. In-depth discussions of some of the genre's historical development can be found in Edward James and Farah Mendlesohn, eds., *The Cambridge Companion to Fantasy Literature* (Cambridge: Cambridge University Press, 2012), and detailed accounts of the evolution of fantasy literature can be found in, e.g., Farah Mendlesohn and Edward James, *A Short History of Fantasy* (London: Middlesex University Press, 2009), and Attebery, *Fantasy Tradition*. For briefer overviews, see, e.g., Shippey, introduction to *Fantasy Stories*, and Mathews, *Fantasy*, 5–20.

44. Elgin, *Comedy*, 31.

45. Gary K. Wolfe, "Evaporating Genres," *Evaporating Genres: Essays on Fantastic Literature* (Middletown, CT: Wesleyan University Press, 2011), 24, 30. He acknowledges the existence of previous fantasy literature, though, in pulp magazines such as *Weird Tales* (1923–54 and later revivals) and *Unknown* (1939–43), digests such as *The Magazine of Fantasy and Science Fiction* (1949–current), and the books of individual writers.

46. Wolfe, "Evaporating," 24.

47. Tolkien, "On Fairy-stories," 37 et passim.

48. Wolfe, *Critical Terms*, 115.

49. Brian Stableford, "The Discovery of Secondary Worlds: Notes on the Aesthetics & Methodology of Heterocosmic Creativity," *The New York Review of Science Fiction* (August 2004): 6.

50. As employed by philosophers such as David Lewis, "Truth in Fiction," *Philosophy of Literature: Contemporary and Classic Readings: An Anthology*, eds. Eileen John and Dominic McIver Lopes (1978; Oxford: Blackwell, 2004); and in applications to literature, see, e.g., Lubomír Doležel, *Heterocosmica: Fiction and Possible Worlds* (Baltimore: Johns Hopkins University Press, 1998), 2 ff.; Nancy H. Traill, *Possible Worlds of the Fantastic: The Rise of the Paranormal in Fiction* (Toronto: University of Toronto Press, 1996), 8–9.

51. For a more in-depth discussion of how the actual world relates to its fictional counterpart(s), see Marie-Laure Ryan, *Possible Worlds, Artificial Intelligence, and Narrative Theory* (Bloomington: Indiana University Press, 1991), esp. ch. 2.

52. Zahorski and Boyer, "Secondary Worlds," 58–63.

53. Ibid., "Secondary Worlds," 56. The authors make clear that *high* and *low* are not to be taken as evaluative terms. Alternative terms, e.g. *indigenous fantasy* (Attebery, *Strategies*, 129), have been suggested but are not as frequently employed.

54. Doležel, *Heterocosmica*, 128.

55. Traill, *Possible Worlds*, ch. 1.

56. Ibid., 8, citing Raymond Bradley and Norman Swartz, *Possible Worlds: An Introduction to Logic and Its Philosophy* (Oxford: Blackwell, 1979), 6.

57. Clute, "Land."

2. MAPS

1. Elizabeth M. Ingram, "Maps as Readers' Aids: Maps and Plans in Geneva Bibles," *Imago Mundi* 45 (1993): 44.

2. Ricardo Padrón, "Mapping Imaginary Worlds," *Maps: Finding Our Place in the World*, eds. James R. Akerman and Robert W. Karrow, Jr. (Chicago: University of Chicago Press, 2007), 261–62.

3. See, e.g., Padrón, "Mapping," 265–66.

4. In a piece from 1981, Walker claims that the interest in fantasy maps engendered by the Middle-earth maps has meant that "a map has become almost *de rigeur* [sic] in new and reprinted fantasy" (R. C. Walker, "The Cartography of Fantasy," *Mythlore* 7, no. 4 [1981]: 37). A quarter of a century later, Padrón expresses the same opinion: the influence of Tolkien and C. S. Lewis has made maps "standard fixtures of the genre" (Padrón, "Mapping," 272). Kaveney concurs that "[i]n imitation [of Tolkien], almost all modern genre fantasies come equipped with a map, to the extent that maps are only much noticed when absent" (Roz Kaveney, "Maps," in *The Encyclopedia of Fantasy*, 624.)

5. Kaveney, "Maps," 624.

6. J. B. Post, *An Atlas of Fantasy* (1973; New York: Ballantine, 1979).

7. Diane Duane, "Cartography for Other Worlds: A Short Look at a Neglected Subject," *SFWA Bulletin* 11, no. 5 (1976).

8. Lee N. Falconer, *A Gazet[t]eer of the Hyborian World of Conan, Including Also the World of Kull, and an Ethnogeographical Dictionary of Principal Peoples of the Era, with Reference to the Starmont Map of the Hyborian World* (West Linn, OR: Starmont House, 1977), vii–xiii.

9. Diana Wynne Jones, *The Tough Guide to Fantasyland* (New York: Firebird-Penguin, 2006), [x].

10. Frank W. Day, "The Role and Purpose of the Map in Science Fiction and Fantasy Literature" (M.A. thesis, Bowling Green State University, 1979), 3.

11. Clare Ranson, "Cartography in Children's Literature," *Sustaining the Vision: Selected Papers from the Annual Conference of the International Association of School Librarianship* (Worcester, UK: International Association of School Librarianship, 1996), 166.

12. Ranson, "Cartography," 165.

13. Walker, "Cartography," 37.

14. Such as the additional maps that have been created for *The Lord of the Rings*; see Karen Wynn Fonstad, "Writing 'TO' the Map," *Tolkien Studies* 3 (2006).

15. Peter Hunt, "Landscapes and Journeys, Metaphors and Maps: The Distinctive Feature of English Fantasy," *Children's Literature Association Quarterly* 12, no. 1 (1987): 11.

16. Ibid., 11.

17. Ibid., 13.

18. Myles Balfe, "Incredible Geographies? Orientalism and Genre Fantasy," *Social and Cultural Geography* 5, no. 1 (2004): 82–83.

19. Pierre Jourde, *Géographies imaginaires de quelques inventeurs de mondes au XXe siècle: Gracq, Borges, Michaux, Tolkien* [Imaginary geographies by some twentieth century inventors of worlds: Gracq, Borges, Michaux, Tolkien] (Paris: José Corti, 1991), 113–32.

20. Ibid., 126–27.

21. Ibid., 131.

22. See, e.g., Jourde, *Géographies imaginaires*, 125, in which the gulf of Lhûn's shape is simplified to look more like a ship—which better fits the author's argument. Jourde also makes too much of the linguistic similarity between Lhûn/Lune and "la lune" (128–29).

23. Deirdre F. Baker, "What We Found on Our Journey through Fantasy Land," *Children's Literature in Education* 37 (2006): 239.

24. Ibid., 240.

25. Ibid., 242.

26. Padrón, "Mapping," 276, 279.

27. See, for instance, Padrón, "Mapping," 272–74. Calling Sauron an evil wizard and referring to the "folksy names" of the Shire (275) also detract from the force of his argument by suggesting that he is either not completely familiar with the text or prone to oversimplification.

28. Padrón, "Mapping," 286.

29. Nicholas Tam, "Here Be Cartographers: Reading the Fantasy Map," *Nick's Café Canadien* (blog), April 18, 2011, http://www.nicholastam.ca/2011/04/18/here-be-cartographers-reading-the-fantasy-map/.

30. International Cartographic Association, "ICA Mission," last modified March 18, 2012, http://icaci.org/mission.

31. Arthur H. Robinson and Barbara Bartz Petchenik, *The Nature of Maps: Essays toward Understanding Maps and Mapping* (Chicago: University of Chicago Press, 1976), 16.

32. Ibid., 15.

33. Jeremy Black, *Maps and Politics* (Chicago: University of Chicago Press, 1997), 100 ff.

34. Denis Wood, *The Power of Maps* (London: Routledge, 1993), 199n43, 126.

35. Denis Wood, *Rethinking the Power of Maps* (New York: Guilford Press, 2010), 36–38.

36. Padrón, "Mapping," 260–65.

37. Gérard Genette, *Paratexts: Thresholds of Interpretation*, trans. Jane E. Lewin (Cambridge: Cambridge University Press, 1997), 1.

38. Ibid., 404–5.

39. J. R. R. Tolkien, *The Hobbit, or, There and Back Again* (1937; Boston: Houghton Mifflin, 1997), 19. Thror's Map is discussed further later in the text.

40. Genette, *Paratexts*, 2.

41. Niels Windfeld Lund, "Doceo + Mentum—A Ground for a New Discipline," paper presented at the Annual Meeting of the Document Academy, Berkeley, CA, August 13–15, 2003, http://thedocumentacademy.org/resources/2003/papers/lund .paper.html; see also Niels Windfeld Lund, "Building a Discipline, Creating a Profession: An Essay on the Childhood of 'Dokvit'," *A Document (Re)turn: Contributions from a Research Field in Transition*, eds. Roswitha Skare et al. (Frankfurt am Main: Peter Lang, 2007), 23; and Niels Windfeld Lund, "Documentation in a Complementary Perspective," *Aware and Responsible: Papers of the Nordic-International Colloquium on Social and Cultural Awareness and Responsibility in Library, Information, and Documentation Studies (SCARLID)*, ed. W. Boyd Rayward (Lanham, MD: Scarecrow Press, 2004), 100.

42. Orson Scott Card, *How to Write Science Fiction and Fantasy* (Cincinnati: Writer's Digest Books, 1990), 28–32.

43. Day, "Role and Purpose," 11. The quotation comes from a comment on the questionnaire sent by Day to Anderson. In the questionnaire itself, Anderson's answer to whether he felt the map should be created after the story is written was "Not At All," the questionnaire's strongest possible negative choice (12).

44. Tolkien to Naomi Mitchison, April 25, 1954, in *The Letters of J. R. R. Tolkien*, ed. Humphrey Carpenter (Boston: Houghton Mifflin, 2000), 177; see also Tolkien to Rayner Unwin, April 11, 1953, 168.

45. A contributing explanation to the unexpected rarity of maps is the popularity of "paranormal romance," which I had underestimated. When the sampling frame was being set up, such works were classified as fantasy. (For more on this, see appendix A.) This hybrid genre is placed halfway between dark fantasy and romance by Mendlesohn and James, featuring romantic involvement between humans and fantasy creatures. They also note how it developed into its own publishing category during the 2000s; see Farah Mendlesohn and Edward James, *A Short History of Fantasy* (London: Middlesex University Press, 2009), 198, 254. For a more thorough discussion on paranormal romance, see also Lee Tobin-McClain, "Paranormal Romance: Secrets of the Female Fantastic," *Journal of the Fantastic in the Arts* 11, no. 2 (2001). While in many respects (predominantly low) fantasy, paranormal romance does not borrow fantasy's predilection for maps, thus biasing the sample toward fewer maps. Removing the thirteen books that, after the study was completed, were found to have been reclassified as "romances" has only a marginal effect, however. The sample would contain 36 percent books with maps, corresponding to between 29 and 43 percent of all fantasy books.

46. Not only are the maps of Robert E. Howard's *Conan the Warrior* (1967; orig. short stories publ. 1935–36); *Conan the Swordsman* (1978), by L. Sprague De Camp, Lin Carter, and Björn Nyberg; and *Conan of Venarium* (2003), by Harry Turtledove,

drawn in three distinct styles, they contain different amounts of information. In addition, the pictorial elements of the two most recent maps (a galley on the *Swordsman* map and sea dragon on the *Venarium* map) bring different associations to the fictional world portrayed.

47. For instance, in his review of Steph Swainston's *The Year of Our War* (2004), Clute refers to "the absence of any maps, in a fantasy novel with lots of names and campaigns and dynastic shifts from one armed house to another" as a "dislocation effect"; see John Clute, *Canary Fever: Reviews* (Harold Wood, UK: Beccon Publications, 2009), 108.

48. Tolkien, *The Hobbit*, 1. For an interesting commentary on the *Hobbit* maps, see Tam, "Here Be Cartographers."

49. P. D. A. Harvey, *Medieval Maps* (London: The British Library, 1991), 19.

50. Based on diagrams in David Woodward, "Medieval *Mappaemundi*," *The History of Cartography*, eds. J. B. Harley and David Woodward, vol. 1 (Chicago: University of Chicago Press, 1987), 298. The same conclusion is drawn by Asa Simon Mittman, *Maps and Monsters in Medieval England* (New York: Routledge, 2006), 28. Of Raisz's fifteen examples of medieval charts from Europe and the Arab world, eight had east at the top, four north, and three south; see Erwin Raisz, "Timecharts of Historical Cartography," *Imago Mundi* 2 (1937): 11.

51. Ann Swinfen, *In Defence of Fantasy: A Study of the Genre in English and American Literature since 1945* (London: Routledge & Kegan Paul, 1984), 77.

52. John Noble Wilford, *The Mapmakers* (New York: Vintage Books, 1982), 10.

53. Norman J. W. Thrower, *Maps & Civilization: Cartography in Culture and Society* (Chicago: University of Chicago Press, 1996), 42. Of course, once the world was accepted to be spherical, the ocean—while surrounding the landmasses—ceased to be a border between known and unknown space. Still, the tradition of drawing the known world within an edge of ocean seemed to persist. According to J. Lennart Berggren and Alexander Jones, Ptolemy's map was uncommon in that most of its edges consist of land; see J. Lennart Berggren et al., *Ptolemy's Geography: An Annotated Translation of the Theoretical Chapters* (Ptolemy's text orig. second century A.D.; Princeton, NJ: Princeton University Press, 2000), 22.

54. John Clute, "Water Margins," in *The Encyclopedia of Fantasy*, 997.

55. Ibid.

56. See Terry Brooks, *Magic Kingdom for Sale/Sold!* (1986; London: Futura, 1987), 93.

57. The map in Gardner's book clearly derives from the map published in Baum's *Tik-Tok of Oz* (1914), but with the cardinal points facing the traditional way (west to the left and east to the right) and with considerably more detail. A box on the map in Gardner acknowledges the debt to the original map. For a brief but illuminating discussion of the Oz maps, see Michael O'Neal Riley, *Oz and Beyond: The Fantasy World of L. Frank Baum* (Lawrence: University Press of Kansas, 1997), 186–89.

58. Terry Pratchett, *The Colour of Magic* (Reading, UK: Corgi, 1985), 11n.

59. I am grateful to Kim Selling, who first brought to my attention the scarcity of southern-hemisphere settings in fantasy.

60. See, for instance, Wood, *Power*, and Black, *Maps and Politics*.

61. In the actual world, the projection used is called Lambert Azimuthal Equal-Area Projection according to Kirkpatrick, who adds that projection details were included on all the maps in the book but that the publisher removed them (Russell Kirkpatrick, email message to author, April 10, 2009).

62. Arthur Robinson et al., *Elements of Cartography*, 5th ed. (New York: John Wiley, 1984), 159; quoted in Wood, *Power*, 97.

63. Wood, *Power*, 101.

64. I use *topography* in a broader sense, to include terrain, vegetation, and hydrographical features.

65. Jones, *Tough Guide*, [x–xi].

66. Ibid., [xi].

67. See ibid., [xi].

68. See Mendlesohn, *Rhetorics*, 1.

69. Thrower, *Maps & Civilization*, 113. Wood cites Thrower and several other scholars on the subject, claiming that despite the "glib assurance" in most of their statements, little is known of the history of mapmaking (Wood, *Power*, 145).

70. The bird's-eye view gives the impression of seeing at an angle to the horizon—Lynam suggests about 70 degrees—as opposed to a view straight ahead (e.g., a profile view), where the impression is of levelness with the horizon, or a plan view (e.g., contours, street plan, hachures), where the observer looks straight down from above. See Edward Lynam, *The Mapmaker's Art: Essays on the History of Maps* (London: Batchworth Press, 1953), 55.

71. Lynam, *Mapmaker's Art*, 39. According to Lynam, map engraving began in Italy around 1474, and "by 1590 the draughtsmen of manuscript maps were imitating [the line engravers'] style, symbols, script and decoration in every detail."

72. Ibid., 38 (referring to a 1335 map); Harvey, *Medieval Maps*, 23, ill. 16 (describing the seventh century Isidore world map). Another typical example is the Cotton world map (see Harvey, *Medieval Maps*, 26).

73. A feature on which, according to Lynam, "all representation of relief right down to 1850 has been founded" (Lynam, *Mapmaker's Art*, 38).

74. Ibid., 41.

75. Ibid.

76. Thrower, *Maps & Civilization*, 113.

77. Ibid., 101, 104–5, 114, 134; Wood, *Power*, 153–54, and Wilford, *Mapmakers*, 127.

78. Eduard Imhof, *Cartographic Relief Presentation* (1965; Redlands: ESRI, 2007), 13. Imhof finds an isolated case of shaded relief in a 1667 map by Hans Conrad Gyger but notes that the map was kept as a military secret and had no effect on contemporary mapmaking (7).

79. See Wood, *Power*, 98–99.

80. Wood, *Power*, ch. 6, esp. 155–78. In a similar vein, Steve Lundin suggests that pre-Enlightenment hill signs are easier to draw and thus more prevalent (comment at the Thirty-first International Conference on the Fantastic in the Arts, 2010).

81. Kim Selling, "'Fantastic Neomedievalism': The Image of the Middle Ages in Popular Fantasy," *Flashes of the Fantastic: Selected Essays from the War of the Worlds*

Centennial, Nineteenth International Conference on the Fantastic in the Arts, ed. David Ketterer (Westport, CT: Praeger, 2004), 212.

82. Selling, "'Fantastic Neomedievalism'," 211; she cites Umberto Eco, *Faith in Fakes* (London: Secker & Warburg, 1986), 63.

83. Zahorski and Boyer, "Secondary Worlds," 61; Eco, *Faith*, 62.

84. Attebery, *Strategies of Fantasy*, 132.

85. Legends are not much older than thematic maps (Wood, *Power*, 79), which have been around since the late seventeenth century (Wilford, *Mapmakers*, 313). Map projections are often associated with Mercator (sixteenth century) even though Ptolemy (second century), possibly building on earlier sources, had already worked with projections; see O. A. W. Dilke, "The Culmination of Greek Cartography in Ptolemy," *The History of Cartography*, eds. J. B. Harley and David Woodward, vol. 1 (Chicago: University of Chicago Press, 1987), 179.

86. See Berggren et al., *Ptolemy's Geography*, 58.

87. Joseph Conrad, *Heart of Darkness* (1902; London: Penguin, 2000), 21–22.

88. Mendlesohn, *Rhetorics*, 4.

89. J. R. R. Tolkien, *The Lord of the Rings* (1954–55; Boston: Houghton Mifflin, 2004).

90. For further information about the various map editions, see the "Note on the Maps" in Tolkien, *The Lord of the Rings* (before the maps at the back of each volume) and the chapter on the maps in Wayne G. Hammond and Christina Scull, *The Lord of the Rings: A Reader's Companion* (London: HarperCollins, 2005), esp. lv–lvi, lxvii.

91. Wood, *Power*, 22 ff. In a later chapter (ch. 5), Wood develops his analysis.

92. References to *The Lord of the Rings* are given parenthetically in the text. The following abbreviations are used: FR—*The Fellowship of the Ring*, TT—*The Two Towers*, RK—*The Return of the King*, Appx—appendices to *The Lord of the Rings*. Book and chapter are given in Roman numerals before the page reference. See Tolkien, *Lord of the Rings* (1993).

93. In many editions misspelled with an "a" instead of an "o": "Bindbale Wood"; see Hammond and Scull, *Reader's Companion*, lvii.

94. Tolkien to H. Cotton Minchin (draft), April 1956, 247.

95. Private correspondence quoted in Hammond and Scull, *Reader's Companion*, lvi.

96. Wayne C. Booth, *The Rhetoric of Fiction* (Chicago: University of Chicago Press, 1983), 71 ff.; Seymour Chatman, *Story and Discourse: Narrative Structure in Fiction and Film* (1978; Ithaca, NY: Cornell Paperbacks, 1980), 147 ff.; and Shlomith Rimmon-Kenan, *Narrative Fiction: Contemporary Poetics* (1983; London: Routledge, 2002), 87 ff.

97. Wood, *Power*, 24.

98. About general reference map themes and map discourse, see Wood, *Power*, 113.

99. Mendlesohn, *Rhetorics*, 2.

100. Tom Shippey, *The Road to Middle-earth: How J. R. R. Tolkien Created a New Mythology* (Boston: Houghton Mifflin, 2003), 101.

101. Shippey, *Road*, 103, and Hammond and Scull, *Reader's Companion*, lvi–lxi. (The names may seem exotic to non-English readers, of course.)

102. See, e.g., J. B. Harley, *The New Nature of Maps: Essays in the History of Cartography* (Baltimore: Johns Hopkins University Press, 2001), 59, and Black, *Maps and Politics*, 136–38.

103. See Alan M. MacEachren, *How Maps Work: Representation, Visualization, and Design* (New York: Guilford Press, 1995), 315–17, and Wood, *Power*, 112, 125–30.

104. Wood, *Power*, 112, 126.

105. Ibid., 112, 127; see generally 125–30.

106. All maps have historical perspectives, see Wood, *Power*, 113; his analysis is broadened in MacEachren, *How Maps Work*, 312–17.

107. See Lynam, *Mapmaker's Art*, 39.

108. Harvey, *Medieval Maps*, 82, ill. 64.

109. David Turnbull and Helen Watson, *Maps Are Territories: Science Is an Atlas: A Portfolio of Exhibits* (Chicago: University of Chicago Press, 1993), 3, 5, and Black, *Maps and Politics*, 11. For a more comprehensive discussion, see Wood, *Power*, ch. 5.

110. Tolkien to Allen & Unwin, October 9, 1953, 171.

111. See, for instance, Harley's discussion on the centering of world maps (*New Nature*, 66) and Black's account of map Eurocentrism (*Maps and Politics*, 37–39).

112. Knowing the *origin* of the names, one finds them less belittling (see Shippey, *Road*, 103, and Hammond and Scull, *Reader's Companion*, lvii–lviii), but the impression remains.

113. Harley, *New Nature*, 67. See also ch. 3 of the same book: "Silences and Secrecy: The Hidden Agenda of Cartography in Early Modern Europe."

114. J. R. R. Tolkien, "Nomenclature of *The Lord of the Rings*," in Hammond and Scull, *Reader's Companion*, 775.

115. Robinson and Petchenik, *Nature of Maps*, 61 ff.

116. Christopher Tolkien discusses this mistake in *The Return of the Shadow*; see J. R. R. Tolkien and Christopher Tolkien, *The Return of the Shadow*, vol. 1 (London: HarperCollins, 2002), 387n10; see also Hammond and Scull, *Reader's Companion*, lx. From the second edition of *The Lord of the Rings*, it is clear from the text that the Yale is an area: "[the road] bent left and went down into the lowlands of the Yale" (FR, I, iii, 75).

117. "Note on the Maps" found at the end of each volume in Tolkien, *Lord of the Rings* (1993). See also Hammond and Scull, *Reader's Companion*, lv.

118. J. R. R. Tolkien, *The Silmarillion* (London: Allen & Unwin, 1977), 22, 54.

119. See the first sentence in note 127.

120. See Tolkien, "On Fairy-stories," 37, and Shippey, *Road*, 101.

121. Shippey, *Road*, 100–101.

122. For their respective roots, see Hammond and Scull, *Reader's Companion*, lxiii, 769–70, 774–75.

123. For further discussion about this ambivalence, see the thought-provoking piece by Verlyn Flieger, "Taking the Part of Trees," and in particular part II in Dickerson and Evans, *Ents*. See also the discussion about Lothlórien in chapter 3 of this book. The meeting between nature and culture will be explored further in chapter 4.

124. Jourde, *Géographies imaginaires*, 126–28.

125. Black, *Maps and Politics*, 101–2.

126. Padrón, "Mapping," 275.

127. Both Elrond and Treebeard mention how there were forests reaching from the Misty Mountains to the Blue Mountains; according to Elrond, the Old Forest is a remnant of that ancient woodland, and Treebeard explains how Fangorn Forest is but the easternmost part of the great forests (FR, II, ii, 258; TT, III, iv, 457). For further discussion on Tom Bombadil and Treebeard as the oldest beings, see David Elton Gay, "Tolkien and the *Kalevala*: Some Thoughts on the Finnish Origins of Tom Bombadil and Treebeard," *Tolkien and the Invention of Myth: A Reader*, ed. Jane Chance (Lexington: University Press of Kentucky, 2004), and Matthew R. Bardowell, "J. R. R. Tolkien's Creative Ethic and Its Finnish Analogues," *Journal of the Fantastic in the Arts* 20, no. 1 (2009).

128. Padrón, "Mapping," 275.

129. More if the appendices are taken into account; they trace not only the remaining members of the Fellowship but also their families. See also chapter 5, note 11.

130. The hero's journey seen from a Campbellian perspective will be discussed further in chapter 3.

131. For Fangorn, see note 127. Lothlórien's relation to time and history is discussed in chapter 3; also in, e.g., Verlyn Flieger, *A Question of Time: J. R. R. Tolkien's Road to Faërie* (Kent, OH: Kent State University Press, 1997), ch. 4; and Stefan Ekman, "Echoes of Pearl in Arda's Landscape," *Tolkien Studies* 6 (2009).

132. Attebery, *Strategies*, 15.

133. The significance of the Fangorn and Lothlórien juxtaposition, and the disappearance of magic foreboded by it, is similarly evident in Peter Jackson's *The Lord of the Rings* movies, the first of which opens with Treebeard's words, but spoken by Galadriel/Cate Blanchett; see Peter Jackson, dir., *The Fellowship of the Ring* (New Line Cinema, 2001).

3. BORDERS AND BOUNDARIES

1. John Clute, "Thresholds," in *The Encyclopedia of Fantasy*, 945.

2. John Clute, "Borderlands," in *The Encyclopedia of Fantasy*, 128.

3. Clute, "Thresholds," 945; John Clute, "Crosshatch," in *The Encyclopedia of Fantasy*, 237.

4. Clute, "Borderlands," 128; Clute, "Crosshatch," 237.

5. Clute, "Thresholds," 945.

6. John Clute, "Land," in *The Encyclopedia of Fantasy*, 558.

7. Roz Kaveney, "Maps," in *The Encyclopedia of Fantasy*, 624; David Langford, "Talents," in *The Encyclopedia of Fantasy*, 919–20.

8. "threshold, n.," 2a, *OED Online*, December 2011 (Oxford University Press).

9. Clute, "Thresholds," 945.

10. See Clute, "Taproot Texts."

11. J. R. R. Tolkien, *Smith of Wootton Major* (1967; London: HarperCollins, 2005), 38, cf. 46.

12. Lord Dunsany, *The King of Elfland's Daughter* (1924; London: Gollancz-Orion, 2001), 2 et passim.

13. Neil Gaiman, introduction to *The King of Elfland's Daughter*, by Lord Dunsany (London: Gollancz-Orion, 2001), xii.

14. "Mundanity, n.," 3, *OED Online*, December 2011 (Oxford University Press).

15. Clute, "Crosshatch," 237.

16. References to Steven Brust, *Taltos. The Book of Taltos* (1988; New York: Ace, 2002), and Steven Brust, *The Paths of the Dead* (New York: Tor, 2002), are given parenthetically in the text.

17. So far, that is. The Vlad Taltos series is scheduled to be nineteen books in total, but as of August 2012 only thirteen had been published.

18. The Khaavren Romances are written as a pastiche (or, as Brust calls it, a "blatant rip-off") of Alexandre Dumas's d'Artagnan Romances. The first novel is thus called *The Phoenix Guards* (1990), the second *Five Hundred Years After* (1994), and the third *The Viscount of Adrilankha*. The last novel is published in three volumes: *The Paths of the Dead* (2002), *The Lord of Castle Black* (2003), and *Sethra Lavode* (2004). See Steven Brust, "Books by Steven Brust," *The Dream Café*, last modified October 25, 2006, http://dreamcafe.com/books.html.

19. See Dante Alighieri, *Inferno*, trans. Robert M. Durling, vol. 1 (1320?; New York: Oxford University Press, 1996), xiv, xvi.

20. "[T]he descent into Avernus is easy [. . .] but to retrace your steps and return to the upper air, that is the task and the toil." Virgil, *Eclogues, Georgics, Aeneid I–VI* (c. 19 B.C.; Cambridge, MA: Harvard University Press, 1999): bk. 6 (my translation).

21. References to Neil Gaiman and Charles Vess, *Stardust: Being a Romance within the Realms of Faerie* (1997–98; New York: DC Comics, 1998), are given parenthetically in the text. Quotations come from the illustrated edition. Page references within square brackets are to the text-only edition: Neil Gaiman, *Stardust* (New York: Avon, 1999). As there are textual differences between the two editions, discrepancies may exist between the quotations given here and the corresponding text in the text-only edition.

22. See Genette, *Paratexts*, 1–2.

23. Attebery, *Strategies of Fantasy*, 131.

24. In 1838: Queen Victoria was on the throne; furthermore "Mr. Charles Dickens was serializing his novel *Oliver Twist*; Mr. Draper had just taken a photograph of the moon" and "Mr. Morse had just announced a way of transmitting messages down metal wires" (7 [5]). The Morse code was presented in 1838. Queen Victoria had ascended the throne in June 1837 and *Oliver Twist* ran until April 1839. Since the Market is on May Day, it must be in 1838. (This does not fit with Draper's photograph of the moon, however, which was taken in 1840 in the actual world.)

25. Among the most notable examples are the tales of Oisín/Ossian, who believes himself to spend three years in the Land of the Young but returns to find that three centuries have passed; and Thomas the Rhymer, who returns after a time in Elfland to find that seven years have gone by. Fantasy examples range from adaptations of folktale themes or entire stories to more imaginative uses. Examples of the former include the fairy hill in which one night corresponds to a century on the outside in Poul Anderson's *Three Hearts and Three Lions*, the Faerie land of the "nether forest"

where time stands still in some regions (in part two of Bertil Mårtensson's series Maktens vägar: *Vägen tillbaka* [The Roads of Power: The Road Back; 1980]), and Ellen Kushner's *Thomas the Rhymer* (1990). More imaginatively, Jeffrey Ford creates a Faerie ("Twilmish") time scale predicated on the duration of the sand castle a Twilmish inhabits ("The Annals of Eelin-Ok" 2004).

26. David Langford, "Time in Faerie," in *The Encyclopedia of Fantasy*, 948.

27. Evelyn Edson, *Mapping Time and Space: How Medieval Mapmakers Viewed Their World*, vol. 1 (London: British Library, 1997), 16. The thirteenth century Hereford world map provides numerous examples of such monsters; see, e.g., Harvey, *Medieval Maps*, especially the detail of Africa (33). For a more thorough discussion, see Mittman, *Maps and Monsters*, ch. 3.

28. Erin C. Blake, "Where Be '*Here Be Dragons*'?" *MapHist*, April 1999, http:// www.maphist.nl/extra/herebedragons.html.

29. Which, it should be noted, is changed to "anyone" in the text-only edition.

30. "Dionysus," in *Encyclopaedia Britannica Online: Academic Edition* (Encyclopaedia Britannica, 2010); Ovid, *Metamorphoses*, trans. Mary M. Innes (c. 8 A.D.; London: Penguin, 1955), 94 [bk. 4].

31. "thyrsus," in *Encyclopaedia Britannica Online: Academic Edition* (Encyclopaedia Britannica, 2010).

32. Together with the man in the silk top hat, Charmed stands behind Dunstan during his first meeting with the fairy girl who is to become Tristran's mother (23), and once she regains her freedom from Madame Semele, he watches from the shadows (203). The hairy little man also watches when Yvaine gives the Power of Stormhold to Tristran (206). Finally, Charmed can be seen in the illustrations on pages 7 and 9 among the people arriving at Wall for the Market without being mentioned in the text. He obviously manages to keep out of sight, however. When Tristran asks around for him at the Market, no one admits to having seen him (204 [316]).

33. John Clute, "Thinning," in *The Encyclopedia of Fantasy*, 942.

34. Clute, "Thinning," 942.

35. Mendlesohn, *Rhetorics*, 3.

36. Vess explains that he had free rein when painting this particular picture, since very little had been written about the book or the characters yet. It is therefore rife with people from history and fiction: the Victorian fairy painter Richard Dadd, Ludwig van Beethoven, Merlin and Nimue, Hayao Miyazaki's anime characters Kiki and Totoro, Prince Valiant, and many others, including Neil Gaiman and Vess himself. He adds that for the appearance of the goblin market sellers, he was inspired by Lawrence Housman's illustrations for Christina Rossetti's poem *Goblin Market* (Charles Vess, email message to author, February 15, 2006).

37. Tolkien, "On Fairy-stories," 37.

38. William Shakespeare, *A Midsummer Night's Dream. The Norton Shakespeare*, eds. Stephen Greenblatt et al. (1600; New York: Norton, 2008), 5.1.7–8. Gaiman and Vess have used this line to connect imagination and Faerie before. In their "A Midsummer Night's Dream," Shakespeare's play is performed in front of Auberon, Titania, and a nightmarish fairy court. The imaginations proclaimed by the text

are revealed as truths by Vess's accompanying illustrations; see Neil Gaiman and Charles Vess, "A Midsummer Night's Dream," in *The Sandman: Dream Country* (New York: DC Comics, 1995), 82.

39. References to Garth Nix, *Sabriel* (New York: HarperCollins, 1995); Garth Nix, *Lirael: Daughter of the Clayr* (New York: HarperCollins, 2001); Garth Nix, *Abhorsen* (New York: Eos-HarperCollins, 2003); and Garth Nix, "Nicholas Sayre and the Creature in the Case," in *Across the Wall: A Tale of the Abhorsen and Other Stories* (New York: Eos-HarperCollins, 2005), are given parenthetically in the text.

40. The name suggests that the country mirrors the Old Kingdom; Fr. *ancien* "old" and *terre* "land, domain." A number of names suggest a Francophone origin, for instance the Ancelstierran mist-covered capital Corvere; Fr. *couvert* "covered, overcast."

41. James Frazer, *The Golden Bough: A Study in Magic and Religion* (1922; Ware, UK: Wordsworth Editions, 1993), 594.

42. Mendlesohn, *Rhetorics*, 1, 3.

43. Joseph Campbell, *The Hero with a Thousand Faces* (1949; London: Fontana-HarperCollins, 1993), 30, 36–38.

44. See Attebery, *Strategies*, 87–88.

45. Campbell, *Hero*, 217. What Campbell refers to as worlds may, in my terminology, equally well be domains.

46. Campbell, *Hero*, 217.

47. Ibid., 77–78.

48. Ibid., 78.

49. Ibid., 217.

50. John Clute, *Scores: Reviews 1993–2003* (Harold Wood, UK: Beccon Publications, 2003), 127.

51. John Clute, "Polder," in *The Encyclopedia of Fantasy*, 772.

52. Ibid., 773.

53. Ibid.

54. References to Tolkien, *The Lord of the Rings*, are given parenthetically in the text. The following abbreviations are used in the references: FR — *The Fellowship of the Ring*, TT — *The Two Towers*, RK — *The Return of the King*, Appx — appendices to *The Lord of the Rings*. Book and chapter are given in Roman numerals before the page reference.

55. Tom Shippey, *J. R. R. Tolkien: Author of the Century* (London: HarperCollins, 2000), 197.

56. See, e.g., Tolkien, "On Fairy-stories," 9–10.

57. Shippey, *Author*, 198.

58. Ibid.

59. Shippey, *Author*, 199. See also Shippey, *Road*, 218.

60. Flieger, "Taking the Part of Trees," 155.

61. Flieger, *Question of Time*, 110; cf. Tolkien to Naomi Mitchison, September 25, 1954, in *The Letters of J. R. R. Tolkien*, ed. Humphrey Carpenter (Boston: Houghton Mifflin, 2000), 197.

62. Clute, "Polder," 772.

63. John Clute, "Time Abyss," in *The Encyclopedia of Fantasy*, 947. According to Clute, "*The Lord of the Rings* [. . .]—once the immense backstory contained in *The Silmarillion* [. . .] and other texts is understood—seems to hover at the very lip of [. . .] a profound T[ime] A[byss]."

64. Tolkien, "On Fairy-stories," 68.

65. The following paragraphs are based on my discussion of Lothlórien's time in Ekman, "Echoes of *Pearl*," 67–68.

66. Flieger, *Question of Time*, 107–8.

67. Paul H. Kocher, *Master of Middle-earth: The Fiction of J. R. R. Tolkien* (Boston: Houghton Mifflin, 1972), 98–99.

68. Flieger, *Question of Time*, ch. 4.

69. J. R. R. Tolkien and Christopher Tolkien, *The Treason of Isengard*, vol. 2 (London: HarperCollins, 2002), 367–69.

70. Flieger, *Question of Time*, 107; cf. Tolkien and Tolkien, *Treason*, 369.

71. Hammond and Scull, *Reader's Companion*, 718.

72. Flieger, *Question of Time*, 100.

73. References to Robert Holdstock, *Mythago Wood* (1984; London: Voyager-HarperCollins, 1995); Robert Holdstock, *Lavondyss* (1988; New York: Avon, 1991); Robert Holdstock, *The Hollowing* (1993; New York: ROC-Penguin, 1995); Robert Holdstock, *Gate of Ivory* (London: Voyager-HarperCollins, 1998) (originally published as *Gate of Ivory, Gate of Horn*); and Robert Holdstock, *Avilion* (2009; London: Gollancz-Orion, 2010), are given parenthetically in the text. The novella "The Bone Forest" (1991), a prequel to the events in *Mythago Wood*, is left out of the discussion as it does not add much to the analysis.

74. Mendlesohn, *Rhetorics*, 156.

75. Marek Oziewicz, "Profusion Sublime and the Fantastic: *Mythago Wood*," in *The Mythic Fantasy of Robert Holdstock: Critical Essays on the Fiction*, eds. Donald E. Morse and Kálmán Matolcsy (Jefferson, NC: McFarland, 2011), 81. He refers to *Mythago Wood* only, but the description is equally true for the other three novels.

76. Clute, *Scores*, 179. Original publication is given as the *Washington Post*, October 1997.

77. Mendlesohn, *Rhetorics*, 154.

78. W. A. Senior, "The Embodiment of Abstraction in the Mythago Novels," in *The Mythic Fantasy of Robert Holdstock*, 14.

79. For a more comprehensive discussion of mythotopes, see Stefan Ekman, "Exploring the Habitats of Myths: The Spatiotemporal Structure of Ryhope Wood," in *The Mythic Fantasy of Robert Holdstock*. The discussion about mythotopes here draws on this text.

80. Clute, *Scores*, 178.

81. Mendlesohn even goes so far as to claim that Steven is not important to the story of the forest, that he is part of an imported narrative rather than a tale native to the forest. Although her argument is rather persuasive, I would suggest that all narratives in the forest are, in some respect, drawn from outsiders, even when they are only part-outsiders, as in the case of Jack and Yssobel in *Avilion* (also see the

episode with the World War I infantryman [*Mythago Wood* 263–77]). See Mendlesohn, *Rhetorics*, 156.

82. Umberto Eco, *Semiotics and the Philosophy of Language (Advances in Semiotics)* (Bloomington: Indiana University Press, 1986), 80.

83. Penelope Reed Doob, *The Idea of the Labyrinth: From Classical Antiquity through the Middle Ages* (Ithaca, NY: Cornell University Press, 1992), 19.

84. Doob, *Idea of the Labyrinth*, 18.

85. Eco, *Semiotics*, 81.

86. Ibid. However, Aarseth questions whether Eco's net is a labyrinth at all; see Espen J. Aarseth, *Cybertext: Perspectives on Ergodic Literature* (Baltimore: Johns Hopkins University Press, 1997), 6.

87. Eco, *Semiotics*, 81.

88. Paul Kincaid, review of *Avilion*, by Robert Holdstock, *SF Site*, 2010, http://www.sfsite.com/01b/al312.htm.

89. Clute, *Scores*, 178.

90. Paul Kincaid, "Of Time and the River: Time in the Fiction of Robert Holdstock," *Vector* 260 (Summer 2009): 9.

91. References to Terry Pratchett, *Pyramids* (1989; London: Corgi, 1990), are given parenthetically in the text.

92. Andrew M. Butler, *Terry Pratchett* (Harpenden, UK: Pocket Essentials, 2001), 33.

93. It should be noted that with the introduction of the History Monks, especially in *Thief of Time* (1994) and *Night Watch* (2002), the nature of time in the Discworld universe developed in quite a different direction from *Pyramids*.

94. Clute, "Polder," 772.

95. David Langford, introduction to *Terry Pratchett: Guilty of Literature*, 2nd ed., eds. Andrew M. Butler et al., (2001; Baltimore: Old Earth Books, 2004), 11.

96. Clute, "Polder," 772.

97. Richard Mathews actually claims that time travel—explicit or implicit—is as important to fantasy as space travel is to science fiction; see Mathews, *Fantasy*, 26.

98. Suvin appears to use this term to refer to high fantasy found near the center of Attebery's fuzzy set, but he muddies the terminological water somewhat by referring to *The Encyclopedia of Fantasy*, where Clute, in fact, sees little use for the term and suggests that it is a marketing euphemism for Sword and Sorcery; see John Clute, "Heroic Fantasy," in *The Encyclopedia of Fantasy*. It is possible that Suvin sees no difference between the (portal or) quest-driven fantasy of Tolkien and the immersive fantasy of, for instance, Michael Moorcock or Fritz Leiber.

99. Darko Suvin, "Considering the Sense of 'Fantasy' or 'Fantastic Fiction': An Effusion," *Extrapolation* 41, no. 3 (2000): 226–27.

100. Swinfen, *In Defence of Fantasy*, 81.

101. Manlove, *Modern Fantasy*, 10. Note that the definition as it stands on p. 1 erroneously uses only "the supernatural." The error is corrected in Colin. N. Manlove, "On the Nature of Fantasy," in *The Aesthetics of Fantasy Literature and Art*, ed. Roger C. Schlobin (1975; Notre Dame, IN: University of Notre Dame Press, 1982), 16.

102. Manlove, *Modern Fantasy*, 3; cf. Manlove, "On the Nature," 19.

103. Manlove, "On the Nature," 29.

104. W. R. Irwin, *The Game of the Impossible: A Rhetoric of Fantasy* (Urbana: University of Illinois Press, 1976), 9. Some writers have introduced "meta-rules" for how the internal rules are allowed to change; see, for instance, Lyndon Hardy's *Master of the Sixth Magic* (1984), a sequel whose plot focuses mainly on how the rules for magic of the previous novel can be changed.

105. Doležel, *Heterocosmica*, 128–29.

106. Ibid., 131.

4. NATURE AND CULTURE

1. For instance, Christopher Manes, "Nature and Silence," *The Ecocriticism Reader: Landmarks in Literary Ecology*, eds. Cheryll Glotfelty and Harold Fromm (1992; Athens: University of Georgia Press, 1996), vx; Lynn White, Jr., "The Historical Roots of Our Ecological Crisis" (1967), *The Ecocriticism Reader*, 14; Lynn White, Jr., "Continuing the Conversation," *Western Man and Environmental Ethics: Attitudes toward Nature and Technology*, ed. Ian G. Barbour (Reading, MA: Addison-Wesley, 1973), 62; Frederick Turner, "Cultivating the American Garden" (1991), *The Ecocriticism Reader*, 41 (referring to Lévi-Strauss); Herbert N. Schneidau, *Sacred Discontent: The Bible and Western Tradition* (Berkeley: University of California Press, 1977), 58, and René Dubos, "A Theology of the Earth" (1969), *Western Man and Environmental Ethics*, 44–45.

2. Attebery, *Fantasy Tradition*, 186.

3. Andrew Brennan, *Thinking about Nature: An Investigation of Nature, Value and Ecology* (Athens: University of Georgia Press, 1988), 88. See also the discussion in Turner, "American Garden," 40–54.

4. Kate Soper, *What Is Nature? Culture, Politics, and the Non-Human* (Oxford: Blackwell, 1998), 1.

5. "nature, n.," esp. 14b, 9c, *OED Online*, December 2011 (Oxford University Press).

6. "nature, n.," 11a, *OED Online*.

7. Soper, *What Is Nature?*, 15. Such a distinction also agrees with what Andersson defines as the basic concept of nature (for a nature-centered environmental ethics), that nature "has not been anthropogenically affected"; see Petra Andersson, *Humanity and Nature: Towards a Consistent Holistic Environmental Ethics* (Gothenburg: Acta Universitatis Gothoburgensis, 2007), 71.

8. Brennan, *Thinking about Nature*, 88. He admits to the circularity of the definition.

9. Keekok Lee, *The Natural and the Artefactual: The Implications of Deep Science and Deep Technology for Environmental Philosophy* (Lanham, MD: Lexington Books, 1999), 82–83.

10. David Kaplan and Robert A. Manners, *Culture Theory* (Englewood Cliffs, NJ: Prentice-Hall, 1972), 3.

11. Alfred Louis Kroeber and Clyde Kluckhohn, *Culture: A Critical Review of Concepts and Definitions* (Cambridge, MA: Peabody Museum, 1952), 149, n4a.

12. Peter Worsley, "Classic Conceptions of Culture," *Culture and Global Change*, eds. Tracey Skelton and Tim Allen (London: Routledge, 1999), 13.

13. Daniel G. Bates, *Cultural Anthropology* (Boston: Allyn & Bacon, 1996), 5.

14. Bill McKibben, *The End of Nature* (London: Viking, 1990), 9–42, 55. Keekok Lee discusses McKibben's position in terms of Lee's seven senses of "nature"; see Lee, *The Natural and the Artefactual*, 86. For an overview of the so-called end-of-nature thesis and its treatment by supporters of a nature-centered environmental ethics, see Andersson, *Humanity and Nature*, 74–79.

15. White, "Historical Roots," 3–4; Turner, "American Garden," 40.

16. Marcus Tullius Cicero, *The Nature of the Gods*, trans. P. G. Walsh (44 B.C.; Oxford: Oxford University Press, 1998), 313 [2.152].

17. See, e.g., Turner, "American Garden," 48. Reflections on this subject derived from hands-on experience can be found in Michael Pollan, *Second Nature: A Gardener's Education* (New York: Grove Press, 1991).

18. Andersson clarifies the distinction between *nature* (which I refer to as *wild nature*) and *wilderness*: the former is "all (biotic) entities and processes that are unaffected by human beings" while the latter is "natural landscapes"; see Andersson, *Humanity and Nature*, 81.

19. Verlyn Flieger similarly defines *nature tamed* as "nature cultivated according to human standards"; see Flieger, "Taking the Part of Trees," 154.

20. For a comprehensive discussion of this conundrum, see Andersson, *Humanity and Nature*, ch. 5.

21. White, "Historical Roots"; White, "Continuing"; Manes, "Nature"; Dubos, "Theology." For an alternative view, see, e.g., Lewis W. Moncrief, "The Cultural Basis of Our Environmental Crisis" (1970), *Western Man and Environmental Ethics*.

22. Gen 1:28 (KJV).

23. Manes, "Nature," 21; Michael T. Ghiselin, "Poetic Biology: A Defense and Manifesto," *New Literary History* 7, no. 3 (1976): 497. Cf. Aristotle, *History of Animals*, 8.1.

24. Tolkien, *The Silmarillion*, 18.

25. Lewis Mumford, *The City in History: Its Origins, Its Transformations, and Its Prospects* (Harmondsworth, UK: Penguin, 1961), 19, 124.

26. John Clute, "Urban Fantasy," in *The Encyclopedia of Fantasy*, 975–76.

27. John Clute, "City," in *The Encyclopedia of Fantasy*, 204.

28. References to Tolkien, *The Lord of the Rings*, are given parenthetically in the text. The following abbreviations are used in the references: FR—*The Fellowship of the Ring*, TT—*The Two Towers*, RK—*The Return of the King*, Appx—appendices to *The Lord of the Rings*. Book and chapter are given in Roman numerals before the page reference.

29. See Gimli's comments on this: FR, II, iv, 307.

30. Tolkien to Rayner Unwin, January 22, 1954, in *The Letters of J. R. R. Tolkien*, ed. Humphrey Carpenter (Boston: Houghton Mifflin, 2000), 173. Interestingly enough, after some hesitation, Tolkien decided that the title of the second volume, *The Two Towers*, could not refer to either of those towers but must "if there is any real reference in it to Vol II refer to *Orthanc* and the *Tower of Cirith Ungol*." Tolkien's

original design for the jacket of this volume, however, shows Orthanc and Minas Morgul (see note in *Letters* 444).

31. Kocher, *Master of Middle-earth*, 125. He refers to TT, IV, v, 663.

32. Presumably, this is the same substance that the Númenoreans used for the Stone of Erech, which has also remained unchanged, smooth and black, over the millennia (RK, V, ii, 771–72).

33. Flieger, "Taking," 152.

34. Ibid., 155.

35. Dickerson and Evans, *Ents*, 66–67.

36. The discussion in this section is based on Charles de Lint's Newford novels and short fiction published until 2006.

37. Charles de Lint, *Moonlight and Vines* (New York: Tor, 1999), blurb; Charles de Lint, "Charles de Lint: Frequently Asked Questions," *SF Site*, http://www.sfsite .com/charlesdelint/faq01.htm. Accessed December 28, 2011.

38. Charles de Lint, *From a Whisper to a Scream* (1992; New York: Orb–Tom Doherty, 2003), 125.

39. Charles de Lint, *The Onion Girl* (2002; London: Gollancz-Orion, 2004), 244.

40. Charles de Lint, *Forests of the Heart* (2000; London: Gollancz-Orion, 2002). Further references to *Forests* are given parenthetically in the text.

41. Charles de Lint, *Widdershins* (New York: Tor, 2006), 77. Further references to *Widdershins* are given parenthetically in the text.

42. The Otherworld (also called *dreamlands*) provides a setting for numerous stories. The following de Lint novels deal with journeys to the Otherworld in one way or another: *The Dreaming Place* (1990), *Trader* (1997), *Onion Girl* (2002), *Forests of the Heart*, *Spirits in the Wires* (2003), *Widdershins*, and, to some extent, *Medicine Road* (2004). The dreamland city of Mabon created by Sophie in her dreams but visitable by others in theirs (in, e.g., "Mr. Truepenny's Book Emporium and Gallery" [1992]) is similar to the Otherworld created by the author Cat Midhir's dreams in de Lint's early novel *Yarrow* (1986).

43. Charles de Lint, "Ghosts of Wind and Shadow," *Dreams Underfoot* (1990; New York: Tor, 1994). Further references to "Ghosts" are given parenthetically in the text.

44. Charles de Lint, "The Stone Drum" (1989), *Dreams Underfoot*, 57–59; see also Charles de Lint, "Winter Was Hard" (1991), *Dreams Underfoot*, 160–61. Further references to "Winter" are given parenthetically in the text.

45. See, e.g., Charles de Lint, *Spirits in the Wires* (New York: Tor, 2003), esp. 413–16. Further references to *Spirits* are given parenthetically in the text.

46. Charles de Lint, *Trader* (1997; New York: Orb–Tom Doherty, 2005), 44; Charles de Lint, "Tallulah" (1991), *Dreams Underfoot*, 444–45; Charles de Lint, "Pal o' Mine," *The Ivory and the Horn* (1993; New York: Tor, 1995), 222. Further references to *Trader* are given parenthetically in the text.

47. Charles de Lint, "But for the Grace Go I" (1991), *Dreams Underfoot*, 326.

48. For instance, Megan Lindholm's *Wizard of the Pigeons* (1986) and Neil Gaiman's *Neverwhere* (1996). For further discussion on invisibility and homelessness in these two works, see Stefan Ekman, "Down, Out and Invisible in London and Seattle," *Foundation: The International Review of Science Fiction* 94 (2005).

49. Charles de Lint, "The Invisibles" (1997), *Moonlight and Vines*, 217.

50. Charles de Lint, "Waifs and Strays" (1993), *The Ivory and the Horn*, 34. Further references to "Waifs" are given parenthetically in the text.

51. Charles de Lint, "The Forest Is Crying" (1994), *The Ivory and the Horn*, 53. Further references to "Forest" are given parenthetically in the text. The quotation is from Gary Snyder, *The Practice of the Wild* (San Francisco: North Point Press, 1990).

52. Max Oelschlaeger, *The Idea of Wilderness: From Prehistory to the Age of Ecology* (New Haven: Yale University Press, 1991), 261.

53. Charles de Lint, *Someplace to Be Flying* (1998; London: Pan, 1999), 85. Further references to *Someplace* are given parenthetically in the text.

54. According to, e.g., "The Buffalo Man" and *Spirits in the Wires*. The earlier stories "The Stone Drum" and "Ghosts of Wind and Shadow," on the other hand, place their house a few blocks to the north, on McKennitt Street. See Charles de Lint, "The Buffalo Man," *Tapping the Dream Tree* (1999; New York: Tor, 2002), 104, and de Lint, *Spirits*, 151; and cf. de Lint, "Stone Drum," 45, and de Lint, "Ghosts," 197. Further references to "Buffalo Man" are given parenthetically in the text.

55. Charles de Lint, "Pixel Pixies" (1999), *Tapping the Dream Tree*, 276.

56. Charles de Lint, *Memory and Dream* (New York: Tor, 1994), 32 et passim. Further references to *Memory* are given parenthetically in the text.

57. Charles de Lint, *The Blue Girl* (2004; New York: Firebird-Penguin, 2006), 251. Further references to *Blue Girl* are given parenthetically in the text.

58. Charles de Lint, "Held Safe by Moonlight and Vines," *Moonlight and Vines*, 117. Further references to "Held Safe" are given parenthetically in the text.

59. Charles de Lint, "In This Soul of a Woman" (1994), *Moonlight and Vines*, 51.

60. Charles de Lint, *The Dreaming Place* (1990; New York: Firebird-Penguin, 2002), 23. Further references to *Dreaming Place* are given parenthetically in the text.

61. Charles de Lint, "That Explains Poland" (1988), *Dreams Underfoot*, 108. Further references to "That Explains" are given parenthetically in the text.

62. Charles de Lint, "The Sacred Fire" (1989), *Dreams Underfoot*, 139.

63. The story of the tree that grows on stories is told mainly in "The Conjure Man" (1992) but is also referred to in "A Tempest in Her Eyes" (1994) and *Onion Girl*.

64. In this respect, Kellygnow is similar to Tamson House, which acts as a genius loci, for instance by magically keeping a severely wounded man alive. See Charles de Lint, *Moonheart* (1990; London: Pan, 1991), esp. 20–22, 24, 256.

65. References to China Miéville, *Perdido Street Station* (2000; New York: Del Rey–Ballantine, 2001); China Miéville, *The Scar* (New York: Del Rey–Ballantine, 2002); China Miéville, *Iron Council* (2004; New York: Del Rey–Ballantine, 2005); and China Miéville, "Jack," *Looking for Jake: Stories* (New York: Del Rey–Ballantine, 2005), are given parenthetically in the text.

66. Joan Gordon, "Reveling in Genre: An Interview with China Miéville," *Science Fiction Studies* 30, no. 3 (2003): 362.

67. Joan Gordon, "Hybridity, Heterotopia, and Mateship in China Miéville's *Perdido Street Station*," *Science Fiction Studies* 30, no. 3 (2003): 456, and Mendlesohn, *Rhetorics*, xx. Even the later Bas-Lag novels have been considered to blur the genre

boundaries; see, for instance, the review of *Iron Council* by Andrew Hedgecock, *Foundation: The International Review of Science Fiction* 94 (2005): 123. Miéville also claims that he writes fiction located at the intersection of science fiction and fantasy; see Gordon, "Reveling in Genre," 359, and China Miéville, "Messing with Fantasy," *Locus* (March 2002): 5. Jeff VanderMeer refers to *Perdido Street Station* as the "flash point" for "the New Weird," fiction in which the setting "may combine elements of both science fiction and fantasy"; see Jeff VanderMeer, "The New Weird: 'It's Alive?'," *The New Weird*, eds. Ann VanderMeer and Jeff VanderMeer (San Francisco: Tachyon Publications, 2008), xi, xvi. For further discussion on genre-blurring and the New Weird, see also Darja Malcolm-Clarke, "Tracking Phantoms," *The New Weird*, 341, and Jukka Halme, "Blurring the Lines," *The New Weird*, 355.

68. Rich Paul Cooper, "Building Worlds: Dialectical Materialism as Method in China Miéville's Bas-Lag," *Extrapolation* 50, no. 2 (2009): 220–21.

69. Christopher Palmer, "Saving the City in China Miéville's Bas-Lag Novels," *Extrapolation* 50, no. 2 (2009): 225–26.

70. Gordon, "Hybridity," 456–63.

71. Yagharek's prologue, epilogue, and interludes are printed in italics but are quoted in roman type here.

72. The city's size is inferred from figures given in *Perdido Street Station* (146).

73. Pratchett repeatedly makes a similar point about the river through Ankh-Morpork, which is, owing to silt and refuse, almost viscous enough to walk on.

74. Mendlesohn, *Rhetorics*, 64. The constructs are so greatly feared that they are eventually wiped out in a conflict called the Construct Wars (*Iron* 87–88).

75. Gordon, "Hybridity," 461.

76. References to Patricia A. McKillip, *Ombria in Shadow* (New York: Ace Books, 2002), are given parenthetically in the text.

77. For a discussion on loyalty in *Ombria in Shadow*, see Christine Mains, "For Love or for Money: The Concept of Loyalty in the Works of Patricia McKillip," *Journal of the Fantastic in the Arts* 16, no. 3 (2006).

78. Christine Mains, "Bridging World and Story: Patricia McKillip's Reluctant Heroes," *Journal of the Fantastic in the Arts* 16, no. 1 (2005): 43.

79. John Clute, "Edifice," *The Encyclopedia of Fantasy*, 309–10.

80. Clute, "Water Margins," 997.

81. Mains, "Bridging," 44.

82. Meeker suggests that we limit our choices by establishing "artificial polarities" such as good/evil, true/false, and pain/pleasure. Nature/culture would make another such set. See Joseph W. Meeker, *The Comedy of Survival: Studies in Literary Ecology* (New York: Charles Scribner's Sons, 1972), 32.

83. Don. D. Elgin sees the transition from hunting and gathering to farming as one of the roots to our ecological crisis. The other two roots are Western religion and the ideas that came out of the French and Industrial Revolutions; see Elgin, *Comedy*, 4–9. It should be noted that, for instance, Breivik and (more recently) Hilbert find that the Old Testament advocates humanity's stewardship—rather than ownership—of the world; see Gunnar Breivik, "Religion, livsform og natur [Religion, way of life, and nature]," *Økologi, økofilosofi* [Ecology, Ecophilosophy], eds. Paul Hofseth

and Arne Vinje (Oslo: Gyldendal, 1975), and Betsy S. Hilbert, "Beyond 'Thou Shalt Not': An Ecocritic Reads Deuteronomy," *Beyond Nature Writing: Expanding the Boundaries of Ecocriticism*, eds. Karla Armbruster and Kathleen R. Wallace (Charlottesville: University Press of Virginia, 2001).

84. The latter position has been forcefully argued, e.g., by Patrick Curry, "Nature Post-nature," *New Formations* 64 (2008): 53–54.

85. In their anthology of critical texts aimed at developing the field of ecocriticism, Armbruster and Wallace go so far as to claim that "understanding nature and culture as interwoven rather than as separate sides of a dualistic construct" is one of ecocriticism's "central conceptual challenges"; see Armbruster and Wallace, *Beyond Nature Writing*, 4.

86. Tolkien, "On Fairy-stories," *The Tolkien Reader*, 57.

87. The evil landscape in Tolkien is discussed in detail in chapter 5.

5. REALMS AND RULERS

1. Moorcock, *Wizardry*, 64.

2. References to Tolkien, *The Lord of the Rings*, are given parenthetically in the text. The following abbreviations are used in the references: FR—*The Fellowship of the Ring*, TT—*The Two Towers*, RK—*The Return of the King*, Appx—appendices to *The Lord of the Rings*. Book and chapter are given in Roman numerals before the page reference.

3. A handful of Dark Ladies can be found in the genre, such as the White Witch in C. S. Lewis's *The Lion, the Witch and the Wardrobe* (1950), but the overwhelming majority of these personifications of evil are male, so I therefore refer to a Dark Lord as *he*.

4. Tolkien, "On Fairy-stories," 68. Clute briefly notes that tragic fantasy exists but is uncommon; see Clute, "Fantasy," 339.

5. The model is presented by Clute in *The Encyclopedia of Fantasy* and described in somewhat more detail in his Guest Scholar Speech at the Twentieth International Conference on the Fantastic in the Arts (Fort Lauderdale, 1999; later published in *Journal of the Fantastic in the Arts*); see Clute, "Fantasy," 338–39, and John Clute, "Grail, Groundhog, Godgame: Or, Doing Fantasy," *Journal of the Fantastic in the Arts* 10, no. 4 (2000). Clute's model is effectively used by Farah Mendlesohn in her fantasy taxonomy; see Mendlesohn, *Rhetorics*, xv et passim. The quotation is from a review of Mendlesohn's book; see Clute, *Canary Fever*, 369, originally published as "Drawn and Quartered" in *Strange Horizons*, June 2008.

6. Attebery, *Fantasy Tradition*, 12–13.

7. Ibid., 13–14. Elsewhere, Attebery observes that *The Lord of the Rings* conforms to Propp's morphology; see Attebery, *Strategies of Fantasy*, 15.

8. V[ladímir] Propp, *Morphology of the Folktale* (1928; Austin: University of Texas Press, 1968), 63–64.

9. Clute, "Fantasy," 338–39.

10. John Clute, "Healing," in *The Encyclopedia of Fantasy*, 458.

11. Don D. Elgin notes that even Aragorn's line will fail, however, and that Sam

and his children are the future of Middle-earth; see Elgin, *Comedy*, 50. Elgin's point suggests a telling comparison between the two characters: it is possible to argue that whereas Aragorn is the monarch who ascends the throne, marries, and heals the land, Sam heals the land, marries, and becomes a successful, democratic representative of his people (he is elected Mayor seven times; see Appx B 1071–72). Rather than the pro-monarchy tract it has often been accused of being, Tolkien's text leaves it to the reader to decide who is the "proper" ruler.

12. Mendlesohn, *Rhetorics*, 3.

13. Jones, *Tough Guide*, 108.

14. The association between Aragorn's ascending the throne and the introduction of nature in Minas Tirith (discussed in chapter 4) is a result of his policy (such as allowing the elves to plant trees in the City) and Gandalf's help in finding the scion of the dead Tree; there is no *direct* link.

15. Ursula Le Guin, *The Farthest Shore. The Earthsea Quartet* (1973; London: Puffin-Penguin, 1993).

16. Michael Ende, *The Neverending Story*, trans. Ralph Manheim (Harmondsworth, UK: Penguin, 1984), 31–32. Original: "Die Kindliche Kaiserin galt zwar— wie ihr Titel ja schon sagt—als die Herrscherin über all die unzähligen Länder des grenzenlosen phantásischen Reiches, aber sie war in Wirklichkeit viel mehr als eine Herrscherin, oder besser gesagt, sie war etwas ganz anderes. [. . .] Sie war nur da, aber sie war auf eine besondere Art da: Sie war der Mittelpunkt allen Lebens in Phantásien." Michael Ende, *Die unendliche Geschichte* (Stuttgart: K. Thienemanns Verlag, 1979), 33–34.

17. Patricia A. McKillip, *The Riddlemaster of Hed* (1976; New York: Del Rey-Ballantine, 1978), 85.

18. Terry Pratchett, *Wyrd Sisters* (1988; London: Corgi, 1989), 127.

19. Ibid., 90–92.

20. Ibid., 92.

21. In the Discworld novels, the legitimate heir often does not ascend the throne. See, e.g., *Pyramids* (discussed in chapter 3), in which Teppic renounces the throne in favor of his (maybe) half-sister; and *Guards! Guards!* (1989) and *Men at Arms* (1993), in which Carrot has all the signs marking him an heir to the throne but these signs are quite emphatically ignored, and he remains an officer of the Ankh-Morpork Watch. Carrot's superior in the Watch is even explicitly against the idea of kings in, e.g., *Feet of Clay* (1996).

22. Brooks, *Magic Kingdom*.

23. Tad Williams, *The War of the Flowers* (New York: Daw Books, 2003).

24. William's Oberon and Titania recall the fairy rulers in William Shakespeare's *A Midsummer Night's Dream*, who are also directly linked to the land. Cf. Titania's description of how their quarrel has caused a large number of ills to befall the land and its people: Shakespeare, *A Midsummer Night's Dream*, 2.1.81–117.

25. References to Tim Powers, *Last Call* (1992; New York: Avon-HarperCollins, 1993), are given parenthetically in the text.

26. Fiona Kelleghan and Tim Powers, "Interview with Tim Powers," *Science Fiction Studies* 25, no. 1 (1998): 7. The second book, *Expiration Date* (1996), focuses

on ghosts and people who ingest them, and the two sets of protagonists are brought together in *Earthquake Weather* (1997), when another bid is made for the kingship. The books are also referred to as the Fault Lines series.

27. Gary K. Wolfe, *Soundings: Reviews, 1992–1996* (Harold Wood, UK: Beccon Publications, 2005), 23. From a review originally published in *Locus* #374, March 1992.

28. For a discussion on Weston's influence on and a Fisher King reading of *The Waste Land*, see Marianne Thormählen, *The Waste Land: A Fragmentary Wholeness* (Lund: Gleerup-LiberLäromedel, 1978), 68–74.

29. T. S. Eliot, *The Waste Land*. *The Waste Land and Other Poems*, ed. Helen Vendler (1922; New York: Signet–New American Library, 1998), l. 189, 191–92. Further references to the poem are given parenthetically in the text.

30. Thormählen points out that the "king my brother's wreck" "could be a modified excerpt from Isis' mournful chants" (71). Since, in *Last Call*'s mythical domain, Osiris and the Fisher King are linked to the same figure, that reading would still agree with the Fisher King reading the novel calls for.

31. Tim Powers, *Earthquake Weather* (New York: Orb–Tom Doherty, 1997), 194.

32. Jessie L. Weston, *From Ritual to Romance* (1920; New York: Anchor-Doubleday, 1957), 118–19.

33. Urban T. Holmes, Jr., and M. Amelia Klenke, *Chrétien, Troyes, and the Grail* (Chapel Hill: University of North Carolina Press, 1959), 103; Thomas Malory, *Le Morte Darthur* (1485; Ware, UK: Wordsworth Editions, 1996), 646 (bk. 17, ch. 5).

34. Arthur Groos, *Romancing the Grail: Genre, Science, and Quest in Wolfram's Parzival* (Ithaca, NY: Cornell University Press, 1995), 145, 205–6. It is worth noting that Groos, citing an article by Brunel, claims that the leg wound of Chrétien's Fisher King is, in fact, a wound to the genitals: "'parmi les hanches ambedeus' [. . .] has a widespread meaning of 'genitalia'" (145n3); see also C. Brunel, "Les Hanches du Roi Pêcheur (Chrétien de Troyes, *Perceval* 3513)," *Romania* 81 (1960).

35. Weston discusses the connection between Tammuz and Adonis and suggests a connection to the Fisher King figure (Weston, *From Ritual*, ch. 4). James Frazer also observes the Tammuz-Adonis link and includes further discussion on, e.g., Attis and Osiris; see Frazer, *The Golden Bough*, esp. chs. 29–42.

36. Weston, *From Ritual*, 114.

37. Barber persuasively argues that there is no "reflex effect" causing the desolation of the Fisher King figure's realm—in the earliest Grail stories, the wasteland is simply the result of the ruler's inability to lead his men into battle; see Richard Barber, *The Holy Grail: The History of a Legend* (London: Penguin, 2005), 205. "[Weston] emphasizes the Waste Land, which [. . .] is a minor theme in all but the very late romances," Barber claims, "and even in these romances it becomes important only because the writer was anxious to tie up the loose ends left by his predecessors" (Barber, *Holy Grail*, 249).

38. Dáithí Ó hÓgáin, *The Sacred Isle: Belief and Religion in Pre-Christian Ireland* (Woodbridge: Boydell Press / Wilton: Collins Press, 1999), 170.

39. In "Cath Maige Tuired" (The Battle of Maige Tuired), James MacKillop claims that this and similar Irish and Welsh tales are believed to be antecedents to the

maimed Fisher King by some Arthurian commentators; see James MacKillop, *Dictionary of Celtic Mythology* (Oxford: Oxford University Press, 1998), 253.

40. MacKillop, *Dictionary of Celtic Mythology*, 253.

41. References to Lisa Goldstein, *Tourists* (1989; New York: Orb–Tom Doherty, 1994), are given parenthetically in the text.

42. Wolfe, *Soundings*, 209. From a review of Goldstein's short-story collection *Travellers in Magic*, originally published in *Locus* #406, November 1994.

43. "palimpsest, n. and adj.," 2a–b, *OED Online*, December 2011 (Oxford University Press).

44. See, e.g., Bob Brier and Hoyt Hobbs, *Daily Life of the Ancient Egyptians* (Westport, CT: Greenwood Press, 1999), 24–26; Charles W. Hedrick, *History and Silence: Purge and Rehabilitation of Memory in Late Antiquity* (Austin: University of Texas Press, 2000), 109; and "palimpsest," *Encyclopaedia Britannica Online: Academic Edition* (Encyclopaedia Britannica, 2010).

45. Hedrick, *History and Silence*, 93.

46. Five categories of palimpsests relevant to the field of archaeology are discussed by Geoff Bailey, "Time Perspectives, Palimpsests and the Archaeology of Time," *Journal of Anthropological Archaeology* 26 (2007): 203–10. An architectural palimpsest is described as "the partial erasing and constant overworking of sites and buildings over time. This can involve building over, within, above or alongside the previous or existing structure" in Tom Porter, *Archispeak: An Illustrated Guide to Architectural Terms* (London: Spon Press–Taylor & Francis, 2004), 135; see also Robert Cowan, *The Dictionary of Urbanism* (Tisbury, UK: Streetwise Press, 2005), 279.

47. A brief but well-reasoned overview of the subject, which may serve as a starting point for such an exploration, is provided by Roz Kaveney, "Dark Lord," in *The Encyclopedia of Fantasy*, 250.

48. Examples of the former include the evil god Torak in David (and Leigh) Eddings's Belgariad sequence (1982–84); the wrathful and destructive Rakoth Maugrim in Guy Gavriel Kay's Fionavar Tapestry (1985–86); and the power-hungry Morgoth in Tolkien's *The Silmarillion* (1977). Examples of the latter include Voldemort in J. K. Rowling's Harry Potter series (1997–2007); Darken Rahl in Terry Goodkind's *Wizard's First Rule* (1995); and the Warlock Lord in Terry Brooks's Shannara books (1977–present).

49. Including the White Witch/Jadis in *The Lion, the Witch and the Wardrobe* and *The Magician's Nephew* (1955), who is mortal but from a different world and with powers far beyond those of normal people; Arawn in the Prydain series by Lloyd Alexander (1964–68), who is a supernatural character but not divine; and the Storm King in Tad Williams's Memory, Sorrow, and Thorn series (1988–93), who is an undead lord of the immortal Sithi.

50. And therefore easily parodied. Examples include Diana Wynne Jones's *The Dark Lord of Derkholm* (1998), in which "Dark Lord" is just a role thrust upon a wizard to provide a suitable opponent for tourists from another world, and Mary Gentle's *Grunts* (1992), in which the Dark Lord returns in a female body and announces that rather than conquer the world by military means, she will win by elec-

tion. In "Another End of the Empire" (2009), Tim Pratt portrays a Dark Lord who decides to educate the children prophesied to overthrow him and finds himself adopting them and reforming his realm in the process.

51. Mendlesohn, *Rhetorics*, 50.

52. Texts that predate the emergence of generic fantasy, but that include the fantastic, and are of heightened significance to the genre. See Clute, "Taproot Texts," 921–22.

53. Michael Alexander, ed., *Beowulf* (London: Penguin, 1995), l. 1357; cf. *Beowulf: A Verse Translation*, trans. Michael Alexander (Harmondsworth, UK: Penguin, 1973).

54. John Milton, *Paradise Lost*, in *Paradise Lost: An Authoritative Text, Backgrounds and Sources, Criticism*, 2nd ed., ed. Scott Elledge (1674; New York: Norton, 1993), 50 (bk. 2, lines 624–26).

55. Robert Browning, "Childe Roland to the Dark Tower Came," *Robert Browning's Poetry: Authoritative Texts, Criticism*, ed. James F. Loucks (1855; New York: W. W. Norton, 1979), st. 10:2–3. Further references to this poem are given parenthetically in the text.

56. Tom Shippey, introduction to *The Wood beyond the World*, by William Morris (Oxford: Oxford University Press, 1980), ix; see also Shippey, *Road*, 184. In the latter work, Shippey also mentions that "Childe Rowland" is a story in Joseph Jacobs's *English Fairy Tales* from 1890 (346). This story takes Rowland to Elfland, however, rather than to any evil landscape. Edgar's line comes at the end of *King Lear* 3.4.

57. Astrid Lindgren, *Mio, My Son*, trans. Marianne Turner (1954, English trans. 1956; London: Puffin-Penguin, 1988), 88, 103. It is interesting to notice the many similarities—even on a fairly detailed level—between Lindgren's book and *The Lord of the Rings*, especially since the original Swedish edition of *Mio, My Son* was published in the same year as *The Fellowship of the Ring*: a small boy and his steadfast friend, the gardener's son, venture to the Dark Land to defeat a Dark Lord in his dark tower. For aid, they receive magical bread that sustains them, cloaks that hide them, and a special blade; and they avoid the black soldiers by entering the Dark Land through mountain tunnels.

58. Milton, *Paradise Lost*, 10 (bk. 1, l. 63).

59. Homer, *The Odyssey*, trans. A. T. Murray, vol. 1 (Cambridge, MA: Harvard University Press, 1995), bk. 10; Virgil, *Eclogues, Georgics, Aeneid I–VI*, bk. 6.

60. Glen Cook, *The Black Company* (New York: Tor, 1984), 240. The two following books of the series also introduce a male Dark Lord.

61. Dickerson and Evans, *Ents*, 190.

62. For a more thorough discussion on authorities in portal–quest fantasies, see Mendlesohn, *Rhetorics*, 12–16 et passim.

63. Tolkien, *The Hobbit*, 183 [ch. 11].

64. Tolkien, *The Silmarillion*, 151 [ch. 18].

65. J. R. R. Tolkien and Christopher Tolkien, *The Shaping of Middle-earth*, vol. 4 (London: HarperCollins, 2002), 11, 26–27, 58–59.

66. Randel Helms, *Tolkien's World* (Boston: Houghton Mifflin, 1974), 98.

67. This is also the position of Dickerson and Evans, *Ents*, 186.

68. John Garth, "'As under a Green Sea': Visions of War in the Dead Marshes," *Tolkien 2005: 50 Years of The Lord of the Rings*, ed. Sarah Wells, vol. 1 (Birmingham: The Tolkien Society, 2005), I:18–19. He mainly treats the Dead Marshes and Dagorlad in connection with Tolkien's experiences at the Somme, however, referring to an interview from 1968. The same interview (Keith Brace, "In the Footsteps of the Hobbits," *Birmingham Post*, May 25, 1968) is cited in Hammond and Scull, *Reader's Companion*, 455, in connection to Dagorlad.

69. J. R. R. Tolkien and Christopher Tolkien, *The War of the Ring*, vol. 3 (London: HarperCollins, 2002), 105.

70. Dickerson and Evans call it "one of the lengthiest and most gruesome passages describing environmental degradation in modern literature" (186). They also argue persuasively that both Isengard and the Shire under Saruman offer more potent images because they strike closer to home for the reader (Dickerson and Evans, *Ents*, 193, 204).

71. Swinfen, *In Defence of Fantasy*, 85.

72. For further discussion on the felling of trees in *The Lord of the Rings*, see Flieger, "Taking the Part of Trees," as well as Dickerson and Evans, *Ents*, 195–96, 211–13.

73. Helms, *Tolkien's World*, 79; see also 81.

74. Dickerson and Evans, *Ents*, 190; cf. RK, VI, ii, 897; iii, 916.

75. For a similar discussion, see Dickerson and Evans, *Ents*, 191.

76. References to Stephen R. Donaldson, *The Power That Preserves* (1977; New York: Del Rey–Ballantine, 1980), are given parenthetically in the text.

77. W. A. Senior, *Stephen R. Donaldson's Chronicles of Thomas Covenant: Variations on the Fantasy Tradition* (Kent, OH: Kent State University Press, 1995), 87–88.

78. Senior, *Stephen R. Donaldson's Chronicles*, ch. 3. For his discussion of the rings, see esp. 85–97. A similar comparison can be found in the discussion on evil in Donaldson's Chronicles in Christine Barkley, *Stephen R. Donaldson and the Modern Epic Vision: A Critical Study of the "Chronicles of Thomas Covenant" Novels* (Jefferson, NC: McFarland, 2009), ch. 5.

79. Senior, *Stephen R. Donaldson's Chronicles*, 79–80.

80. Stephen R. Donaldson, *Lord Foul's Bane* (1977; Glasgow: Fontana-Collins, 1978), 38–41.

81. Barkley, *Stephen R. Donaldson*, 148–49.

82. Senior, *Stephen R. Donaldson's Chronicles*, 67.

83. Ibid., 79.

84. References to Robert Jordan, *The Eye of the World* (New York: Tor–Tom Doherty, 1990), are given parenthetically in the text.

85. Dante, *Inferno*, xiii.

86. Ibid., xiii, ll. 31 ff.

87. Other parallels to nuclear weapons in Jordan's Wheel of Time series are discussed in the blog *The Thirteenth Depository* (Linda [pseud.], "The Age of Legends," *The Thirteenth Depository: A Wheel of Time Blog*, March 26, 2002, http://13depository.blogspot.com/2009/02/age-of-legends.html).

88. At least Gandalf implies that Sauron is behind the storm (FR, II, iii, 281), a point also noted in Senior, *Stephen R. Donaldson's Chronicles*, 88.

89. Tolkien's anti-industrialism is brought out even more plainly in Peter Jackson's movies, where the servants of Sauron are portrayed as engineers. A typical example would be when Jackson's ents flood Isengard by tearing down Saruman's dam rather than (as in Tolkien's text) damming the river themselves—destroying technology that harnesses nature rather than building such a harness themselves.

90. Pratchett, *Wyrd Sisters*, 127.

91. Mendlesohn, *Rhetorics*, 3.

92. Peter Barry, *Beginning Theory: An Introduction to Literary and Cultural Theory* (Manchester: Manchester University Press, 2002), 260.

APPENDIX A: METHOD FOR THE MAP SURVEY

1. In the construction of this study, I am much indebted to the careful description of methodology provided by Helena Francke, *(Re)creations of Scholarly Journals: Document and Information Architecture in Open Access Journals* (Borås, Sweden: Valfrid, 2008), ch. 5.

2. Attebery, *Strategies*, 12–14. See also chapter 1.

3. International Federation of Library Associations and Institutions: Study Group on the Functional Requirements for Bibliographic Records, *Functional Requirements for Bibliographic Records* (Munich: K. G. Saur, 1998), http://www.ifla.org/files/cataloguing/frbr/frbr.pdf.

4. Baker, "What We Found," 239.

5. For the nonrepresentativeness of convenience samples, see Chava Frankfort-Nachmias and David Nachmias, *Research Methods in the Social Sciences* (New York: St. Martin's Press, 1996), 184.

6. November 7, 2007. SF-Bokhandeln has stores in Sweden's three largest cities as well as a web store at http://www.sfbok.se.

7. See Clute, "Taproot Texts," 921–22.

8. G. H. Jowett, "The Relationship between the Binomial and F Distributions," *The Statistician* 13, no. 1 (1963), and Mikael Elenius, "Några metoder att bestämma konfidensintervall för en binomialproportion: en litteratur-och simuleringsstudie [Some methods to determine confidence intervals for a binomial proportion: A literature review and simulation study]" (C-essay [bachelor's thesis], University of Gothenburg, 2004), 7; cf. Francke, *(Re)creations*, 186–87.

Bibliography

Aarseth, Espen J. *Cybertext: Perspectives on Ergodic Literature*. Baltimore: Johns Hopkins University Press, 1997.

Alexander, Michael, ed. *Beowulf*. London: Penguin, 1995.

Andersson, Petra. *Humanity and Nature: Towards a Consistent Holistic Environmental Ethics*. Acta Philosophica Gothoburgensia 20. Gothenburg: Acta Universitatis Gothoburgensis, 2007.

Armbruster, Karla, and Kathleen R. Wallace, eds. *Beyond Nature Writing: Expanding the Boundaries of Ecocriticism*. Charlottesville: University Press of Virginia, 2001.

Attebery, Brian. *The Fantasy Tradition in American Literature: From Irving to Le Guin*. Bloomington: Indiana University Press, 1980.

———. *Strategies of Fantasy*. Bloomington: Indiana University Press, 1992.

Bachelard, Gaston. *The Poetics of Space*. 1958. Translated by Maria Jolas. Boston: Beacon Press, 1994.

Bailey, Geoff. "Time Perspectives, Palimpsests and the Archaeology of Time." *Journal of Anthropological Archaeology* 26 (2007): 198–223.

Baker, Deirdre F. "What We Found on Our Journey through Fantasy Land." *Children's Literature in Education* 37 (2006): 237–51.

Balfe, Myles. "Incredible Geographies? Orientalism and Genre Fantasy." *Social and Cultural Geography* 5, no. 1 (2004): 75–90.

Barber, Richard. *The Holy Grail: The History of a Legend*. London: Penguin, 2005.

Bardowell, Matthew R. "J. R. R. Tolkien's Creative Ethic and Its Finnish Analogues." *Journal of the Fantastic in the Arts* 20, no. 1 (2009): 91–108.

Barkley, Christine. *Stephen R. Donaldson and the Modern Epic Vision: A Critical Study of the "Chronicles of Thomas Covenant" Novels*. Critical Explorations in Science Fiction and Fantasy 17. Jefferson, NC: McFarland, 2009.

Barry, Peter. *Beginning Theory: An Introduction to Literary and Cultural Theory*. 2nd ed. Manchester: Manchester University Press, 2002.

Bates, Daniel G. *Cultural Anthropology*. Boston: Allyn & Bacon, 1996.

Beowulf: A Verse Translation. Translated by Michael Alexander. Harmondsworth, UK: Penguin, 1973.

Berggren, J. Lennart, Alexander Jones, and Ptolemy. *Ptolemy's Geography: An Annotated Translation of the Theoretical Chapters*. Ptolemy's text originally from second century A.D. Princeton, NJ: Princeton University Press, 2000.

Black, Jeremy. *Maps and Politics*. Chicago: University of Chicago Press, 1997.

Blake, Erin C. "Where Be '*Here Be Dragons*'?" *MapHist*. April 1999. www.maphist .nl/extra/herebedragons.html.

Booth, Wayne C. *The Rhetoric of Fiction*. 2nd ed. Chicago: University of Chicago Press, 1983.

Bradley, Raymond, and Norman Swartz. *Possible Worlds: An Introduction to Logic and Its Philosophy*. Oxford: Blackwell, 1979.

Branch, Michael P., and Sean O'Grady, eds. *Defining Ecocritical Theory and Practice*. The Association for the Study of Literature and the Environment, 1994. www.asle.org/site/resources/ecocritical-library/intro/defining/.

Branham, Robert J. "Principles of Imaginary Milieu: Argument and Idea in Fantasy Fiction." *Extrapolation* 21, no. 4 (1980): 328–37.

Breivik, Gunnar. "Religion, livsform og natur [Religion, way of life, and nature]." In *Økologi, økofilosofi* [Ecology, ecophilosophy], edited by Paul Hofseth and Arne Vinje, 82–90. Oslo: Gyldendal, 1975.

Brennan, Andrew. *Thinking about Nature: An Investigation of Nature, Value and Ecology*. Athens: University of Georgia Press, 1988.

Brier, Bob, and Hoyt Hobbs. *Daily Life of the Ancient Egyptians*. Westport, CT: Greenwood Press, 1999.

Brooks, Terry. *Magic Kingdom for Sale/Sold!* 1986. London: Futura, 1987.

Browning, Robert. "Childe Roland to the Dark Tower Came." 1855. In *Robert Browning's Poetry: Authoritative Texts, Criticism*, edited by James F. Loucks, 134–39. New York: W. W. Norton, 1979.

Brunel, C. "Les Hanches du Roi Pêcheur (Chrétien de Troyes, *Perceval* 3513)." *Romania* 81 (1960): 37–43.

Brust, Steven. "Books by Steven Brust." *The Dream Café*. Last modified October 25, 2006. http://dreamcafe.com/books.html.

———. *The Paths of the Dead*. New York: Tor, 2002.

———. *Taltos*. 1988. In *The Book of Taltos*, 3–174. New York: Ace, 2002.

Butler, Andrew M. *Terry Pratchett*. Harpenden, UK: Pocket Essentials, 2001.

Campbell, Joseph. *The Hero with a Thousand Faces*. 1949. London: Fontana-HarperCollins, 1993.

Canavan, A.-P. "Calling a Sword a Sword." *The New York Review of Science Fiction* (May 2012): 1, 6–8.

Card, Orson Scott. *How to Write Science Fiction and Fantasy*. Genre writing series. Cincinnati: Writer's Digest Books, 1990.

Chatman, Seymour. *Story and Discourse: Narrative Structure in Fiction and Film*. 1978. Ithaca, NY: Cornell Paperbacks, 1980.

Cicero, Marcus Tullius. *The Nature of the Gods*. 44 B.C. Translated by P. G. Walsh. Oxford: Oxford University Press, 1998.

Clute, John. "Borderlands." In Clute and Grant, *The Encyclopedia of Fantasy*, 127–28.

———. *Canary Fever: Reviews*. Harold Wood, UK: Beccon Publications, 2009.

———. "City." In Clute and Grant, *The Encyclopedia of Fantasy*, 204–5.

———. "Crosshatch." In Clute and Grant, *The Encyclopedia of Fantasy*, 237.

———. "Edifice." In Clute and Grant, *The Encyclopedia of Fantasy*, 309–10.

———. "Fantasy." In Clute and Grant, *The Encyclopedia of Fantasy*, 337–39.

———. "Grail, Groundhog, Godgame: Or, Doing Fantasy." *Journal of the Fantastic in the Arts* 10, no. 4 (2000): 330–37.

———. "Healing." In Clute and Grant, *The Encyclopedia of Fantasy*, 458.

———. "Heroic Fantasy." In Clute and Grant, *The Encyclopedia of Fantasy*, 464.

———. "Land." In Clute and Grant, *The Encyclopedia of Fantasy*, 558.

———. "Notes on the Geography of Bad Art in Fantasy." In *Pardon This Intrusion: Fantastika in the World Storm*, 111–22. Harold Wood, UK: Beccon Publications, 2011.

———. "Polder." In Clute and Grant, *The Encyclopedia of Fantasy*, 772–73.

———. *Scores: Reviews 1993–2003*. Harold Wood, UK: Beccon Publications, 2003.

———. "Taproot Texts." In Clute and Grant, *The Encyclopedia of Fantasy*, 921–22.

———. "Thinning." In Clute and Grant, *The Encyclopedia of Fantasy*, 942–43.

———. "Thresholds." In Clute and Grant, *The Encyclopedia of Fantasy*, 945.

———. "Time Abyss." In Clute and Grant, *The Encyclopedia of Fantasy*, 946–47.

———. "Urban Fantasy." In Clute and Grant, *The Encyclopedia of Fantasy*, 975–76.

———. "Water Margins." In Clute and Grant, *The Encyclopedia of Fantasy*, 997.

Clute, John, and John Grant, eds. *The Encyclopedia of Fantasy*. New York: St. Martin's Griffin, 1999.

Coleridge, Samuel Taylor. *Biographia Literaria*. The Collected Works of Samuel Taylor Coleridge. 1815. Vol. 7:2. London: Routledge & Kegan Paul, 1983.

Conrad, Joseph. *Heart of Darkness*. 1902. London: Penguin, 2000.

Cook, Glen. *The Black Company*. New York: Tor, 1984.

Cooper, Rich Paul. "Building Worlds: Dialectical Materialism as Method in China Miéville's Bas-Lag." *Extrapolation* 50, no. 2 (2009): 212–23.

Cowan, Robert. *The Dictionary of Urbanism*. Tisbury, UK: Streetwise Press, 2005.

Curry, Patrick. "Nature Post-nature." *New Formations* 64 (2008): 51–64.

Dante Alighieri. *Inferno*. The Divine Comedy of Dante Alighieri, vol. 1. 1320? Translated by Robert M. Durling. New York: Oxford University Press, 1996.

Day, Frank W. "The Role and Purpose of the Map in Science Fiction and Fantasy Literature." M.A. thesis, Bowling Green State University, 1979.

de Lint, Charles. *The Blue Girl*. 2004. New York: Firebird-Penguin, 2006.

———. "The Buffalo Man." 1999. In *Tapping the Dream Tree*, 103–32. New York: Tor, 2002.

———. "But for the Grace Go I." 1991. In *Dreams Underfoot*, 321–38. New York: Tor, 1994.

———. "Charles de Lint: Frequently Asked Questions." *SF Site*. Accessed December 28, 2011. www.sfsite.com/charlesdelint/faq01.htm.

———. *The Dreaming Place*. 1990. New York: Firebird-Penguin, 2002.

———. "The Forest Is Crying." 1994. In *The Ivory and the Horn*, 53–76. New York: Tor, 1995.

———. *Forests of the Heart*. 2000. London: Gollancz-Orion, 2002.

———. *From a Whisper to a Scream*. 1992. New York: Orb–Tom Doherty, 2003.

———. "Ghosts of Wind and Shadow." 1990. In *Dreams Underfoot*, 187–220. New York: Tor, 1994.

———. "Held Safe by Moonlight and Vines." 1996. In *Moonlight and Vines*, 116–31. New York: Tor, 1999.

———. "In This Soul of a Woman." 1994. In *Moonlight and Vines*, 41–55. New York: Tor, 1999.

———. "The Invisibles." 1997. In *Moonlight and Vines*, 202–20. New York: Tor, 1999.

———. *Memory and Dream*. New York: Tor, 1994.

———. *Moonheart*. 1990. London: Pan, 1991.

———. *Moonlight and Vines*. New York: Tor, 1999.

———. *The Onion Girl*. 2002. London: Gollancz-Orion, 2004.

———. "Pal o' Mine." 1993. In *The Ivory and the Horn*, 221–34. New York: Tor, 1995.

———. "Pixel Pixies." 1999. In *Tapping the Dream Tree*, 259–89. New York: Tor, 2002.

———. "The Sacred Fire." 1989. In *Dreams Underfoot*, 138–51. New York: Tor, 1994.

———. *Someplace to Be Flying*. 1998. London: Pan, 1999.

———. *Spirits in the Wires*. New York: Tor, 2003.

———. "The Stone Drum." 1989. In *Dreams Underfoot*, 31–60. New York: Tor, 1994.

———. "Tallulah." 1991. In *Dreams Underfoot*, 440–59. New York: Tor, 1994.

———. "That Explains Poland." 1988. In *Dreams Underfoot*, 100–17. New York: Tor, 1994.

———. *Trader*. 1997. New York: Orb–Tom Doherty, 2005.

———. "Waifs and Strays." 1993. In *The Ivory and the Horn*, 15–45. New York: Tor, 1995.

———. *Widdershins*. New York: Tor, 2006.

———. "Winter Was Hard." 1991. In *Dreams Underfoot*, 152–70. New York: Tor, 1994.

Dickerson, Matthew, and Jonathan Evans. *Ents, Elves, and Eriador*. Lexington: University Press of Kentucky, 2006.

Dilke, O. A. W. "The Culmination of Greek Cartography in Ptolemy." In *The History of Cartography*, edited by J. B. Harley and David Woodward. Vol. 1, 177–200. Chicago: University of Chicago Press, 1987.

"Dionysus." In *Encyclopaedia Britannica Online: Academic Edition*. Encyclopaedia Britannica, 2010.

Doležel, Lubomír. *Heterocosmica: Fiction and Possible Worlds*. Baltimore: Johns Hopkins University Press, 1998.

Donaldson, Stephen R. *Lord Foul's Bane*. 1977. Glasgow: Fontana-Collins, 1978.

———. *The Power That Preserves*. 1977. New York: Del Rey–Ballantine, 1980.

Doob, Penelope Reed. *The Idea of the Labyrinth: From Classical Antiquity through the Middle Ages*. Ithaca, NY: Cornell University Press, 1992.

Duane, Diane. "Cartography for Other Worlds: A Short Look at a Neglected Subject." *SFWA Bulletin* 11, no. 5 (1976): 10–14.

Dubos, René. "A Theology of the Earth." 1969. In *Western Man and Environmental Ethics: Attitudes toward Nature and Technology*, edited by Ian G. Barbour, 43–54. Reading, MA: Addison-Wesley, 1973.

Dunsany, Lord [Edward John Morton Drax Plunkett]. *The King of Elfland's Daughter*. Fantasy Masterworks. 1924. London: Gollancz-Orion, 2001.

Eco, Umberto. *Faith in Fakes*. London: Secker & Warburg, 1986.

———. *Semiotics and the Philosophy of Language (Advances in Semiotics)*. Bloomington: Indiana University Press, 1986.

Edson, Evelyn. *Mapping Time and Space: How Medieval Mapmakers Viewed Their World*. Vol. 1. The British Library Studies in Map History. London: British Library, 1997.

Ekman, Stefan. "Down, Out and Invisible in London and Seattle." *Foundation: The International Review of Science Fiction* 94 (2005): 64–74.

———. "Echoes of *Pearl* in Arda's Landscape." *Tolkien Studies* 6 (2009): 59–70.

———. "Exploring the Habitats of Myths: The Spatiotemporal Structure of Ryhope Wood." In Morse and Matolcsy, *The Mythic Fantasy of Robert Holdstock*, 46–65.

Elenius, Mikael. "Några metoder att bestämma konfidensintervall för en binomialproportion: en litteratur-och simuleringsstudie [Some methods to determine confidence intervals for a binomial proportion: A literature review and simulation study]." C-essay (bachelor's thesis), University of Gothenburg, 2004.

Elgin, Don D. *The Comedy of the Fantastic: Ecological Perspectives on the Fantasy Novel*. Contributions to the Study of Science Fiction and Fantasy 15. Westport, CT: Greenwood Press, 1985.

Eliot, T. S. *The Waste Land*. 1922. In *The Waste Land and Other Poems*, edited by Helen Vendler, 32–59. New York: Signet–New American Library, 1998.

Ende, Michael. *Die unendliche Geschichte*. Stuttgart: K. Thienemanns Verlag, 1979.

———. *The Neverending Story*. 1979. Translated by Ralph Manheim. Harmondsworth, UK: Penguin, 1984.

Falconer, Lee N. *A Gazet[t]eer of the Hyborian World of Conan, Including Also the World of Kull, and an Ethnogeographical Dictionary of Principal Peoples of the Era, with Reference to the Starmont Map of the Hyborian World*. West Linn, OR: Starmont House, 1977.

Flieger, Verlyn. *A Question of Time: J. R. R. Tolkien's Road to Faërie*. Kent, OH: Kent State University Press, 1997.

———. "Taking the Part of Trees: Eco-Conflict in Middle-earth." In *J. R. R. Tolkien and His Literary Resonances: Views of Middle-earth*, edited by George Clark and Daniel Timmons, 147–58. Contributions to the Study of Science Fiction and Fantasy 89. Westport, CT: Greenwood Press, 2000.

Fonstad, Karen Wynn. "Writing 'TO' the Map." *Tolkien Studies* 3 (2006): 133–36.

Francke, Helena. *(Re)creations of Scholarly Journals: Document and Information Architecture in Open Access Journals*. Borås, Sweden: Valfrid, 2008.

Frankfort-Nachmias, Chava, and David Nachmias. *Research Methods in the Social Sciences*. 5th ed. New York: St. Martin's Press, 1996.

Frazer, James. *The Golden Bough: A Study in Magic and Religion*. 1922. Ware, UK: Wordsworth Editions, 1993.

Gaiman, Neil. Introduction to *The King of Elfland's Daughter*, by Lord Dunsany, xi–xiii. London: Gollancz-Orion, 2001.

———. *Stardust*. New York: Avon, 1999.

Gaiman, Neil, and Charles Vess. "A Midsummer Night's Dream." In *The Sandman: Dream Country*, 62–86. New York: DC Comics, 1995.

———. *Stardust: Being a Romance within the Realms of Faerie.* 1997–98. New York: DC Comics, 1998.

Garth, John. "'As under a Green Sea': Visions of War in the Dead Marshes." In *Tolkien 2005: 50 Years of The Lord of the Rings*, edited by Sarah Wells. Vol. 1, 9–21. Birmingham: The Tolkien Society, 2005.

Gay, David Elton. "Tolkien and the *Kalevala*: Some Thoughts on the Finnish Origins of Tom Bombadil and Treebeard." In *Tolkien and the Invention of Myth: A Reader*, edited by Jane Chance, 295–304. Lexington: University Press of Kentucky, 2004.

Genette, Gérard. *Paratexts: Thresholds of Interpretation.* Translated by Jane E. Lewin. Literature, Culture, Theory 20. Cambridge: Cambridge University Press, 1997.

Ghiselin, Michael T. "Poetic Biology: A Defense and Manifesto." *New Literary History* 7, no. 3 (1976): 493–504.

Glotfelty, Cheryll. "Introduction: Literary Studies in an Age of Environmental Crisis." In Glotfelty and Fromm, *The Ecocriticism Reader*, xv–xxxvii.

Glotfelty, Cheryll, and Harold Fromm, eds. *The Ecocriticism Reader: Landmarks in Literary Ecology.* Athens: University of Georgia Press, 1996.

Goldstein, Lisa. *Tourists.* 1989. New York: Orb–Tom Doherty, 1994.

Gordon, Joan. "Hybridity, Heterotopia, and Mateship in China Miéville's *Perdido Street Station*." *Science Fiction Studies* 30, no. 3 (2003): 456–76.

———. "Reveling in Genre: An Interview with China Miéville." *Science Fiction Studies* 30, no. 3 (2003): 355–73.

Groos, Arthur. *Romancing the Grail: Genre, Science, and Quest in Wolfram's Parzival.* Ithaca, NY: Cornell University Press, 1995.

Halme, Jukka. "Blurring the Lines." In VanderMeer and VanderMeer, *The New Weird*, 355–58.

Hammond, Wayne G., and Christina Scull. *The Lord of the Rings: A Reader's Companion.* London: HarperCollins, 2005.

Harley, J. B. *The New Nature of Maps: Essays in the History of Cartography.* Baltimore: Johns Hopkins University Press, 2001.

Harvey, P. D. A. *Medieval Maps.* London: The British Library, 1991.

Hedgecock, Andrew. Review of *Iron Council*, by China Miéville. *Foundation: The International Review of Science Fiction* 94 (2005): 122–24.

Hedrick, Charles W. *History and Silence: Purge and Rehabilitation of Memory in Late Antiquity.* Austin: University of Texas Press, 2000.

Helms, Randel. *Tolkien's World.* Boston: Houghton Mifflin, 1974.

Hilbert, Betsy S. "Beyond 'Thou Shalt Not': An Ecocritic Reads Deuteronomy." In *Beyond Nature Writing: Expanding the Boundaries of Ecocriticism*, edited by Karla Armbruster and Kathleen R. Wallace, 29–40. Charlottesville: University Press of Virginia, 2001.

Holdstock, Robert. *Avilion.* 2009. London: Gollancz-Orion, 2010.

———. *Gate of Ivory.* London: Voyager-HarperCollins, 1998.

———. *The Hollowing.* 1993. New York: ROC-Penguin, 1995.

———. *Lavondyss.* 1988. New York: Avon, 1991.

———. *Mythago Wood.* 1984. London: Voyager-HarperCollins, 1995.

Holmberg, John-Henri. *Fantasy: Fantasylitteraturens historia, motiv och författare* [The history, motifs, and authors of fantasy literature]. [Viken, Sweden]: Replik, 1995.

Holmes, Urban T., Jr., and M. Amelia Klenke. *Chrétien, Troyes, and the Grail.* Chapel Hill: University of North Carolina Press, 1959.

Homer. *The Odyssey.* Translated by A. T. Murray. Vol. 1. Cambridge, MA: Harvard University Press, 1995.

Hume, Kathryn. *Fantasy and Mimesis: Responses to Reality in Western Literature.* New York: Methuen, 1984.

Hunt, Peter. "Landscapes and Journeys, Metaphors and Maps: The Distinctive Feature of English Fantasy." *Children's Literature Association Quarterly* 12, no. 1 (1987): 11–14.

Imhof, Eduard. *Cartographic Relief Presentation.* 1965. Redlands, CA: ESRI, 2007.

Ingram, Elizabeth M. "Maps as Readers' Aids: Maps and Plans in Geneva Bibles." *Imago Mundi* 45 (1993): 29–44.

International Cartographic Association. "ICA Mission." Last modified March 18, 2012. www.icaci.org/mission/.

International Federation of Library Associations and Institutions: Study Group on the Functional Requirements for Bibliographic Records. *Functional Requirements for Bibliographic Records.* Munich: K. G. Saur, 1998. www.ifla .org/files/cataloguing/frbr/frbr.pdf.

Irwin, W. R. *The Game of the Impossible: A Rhetoric of Fantasy.* Urbana: University of Illinois Press, 1976.

Jackson, Peter, dir. *The Fellowship of the Ring.* New Line Cinema, 2001. Film.

James, Edward, and Farah Mendlesohn, eds. *The Cambridge Companion to Fantasy Literature.* Cambridge: Cambridge University Press, 2012.

Jones, Diana Wynne. *The Tough Guide to Fantasyland.* 1996. Rev. and updated ed. New York: Firebird-Penguin, 2006.

Jordan, Robert [James Oliver Rigney, Jr.]. *The Eye of the World.* New York: Tor–Tom Doherty, 1990.

Jourde, Pierre. *Géographies imaginaires de quelques inventeurs de mondes au XXe siècle: Gracq, Borges, Michaux, Tolkien* [Imaginary geographies by some twentieth century inventors of worlds: Gracq, Borges, Michaux, Tolkien]. Paris: José Corti, 1991.

Jowett, G. H. "The Relationship between the Binomial and F Distributions." *The Statistician* 13, no. 1 (1963): 55–57.

Kaplan, David, and Robert A. Manners. *Culture Theory.* Englewood Cliffs, NJ: Prentice-Hall, 1972.

Kaveney, Roz. "Dark Lord." In Clute and Grant, *The Encyclopedia of Fantasy,* 250.

———. "Maps." In Clute and Grant, *The Encyclopedia of Fantasy,* 624.

Kelleghan, Fiona, and Tim Powers. "Interview with Tim Powers." *Science Fiction Studies* 25, no. 1 (1998): 7–28.

Kincaid, Paul. "Of Time and the River: Time in the Fiction of Robert Holdstock." *Vector* 260 (Summer 2009): 5–9.

———. Review of *Avilion*, by Robert Holdstock. *SF Site*, 2010. www.sfsite.com /01b/al312.htm.

Kocher, Paul H. *Master of Middle-earth: The Fiction of J. R. R. Tolkien*. Boston: Houghton Mifflin, 1972.

Kroeber, Alfred Louis, and Clyde Kluckhohn. *Culture: A Critical Review of Concepts and Definitions*. Papers of the Peabody Museum of Archaeology and Ethnology, 47:1. Cambridge, MA: Peabody Museum, 1952.

Lakoff, George. *Women, Fire, and Dangerous Things: What Categories Reveal about the Mind*. Chicago: University of Chicago Press, 1987.

Lakoff, George, and Mark Johnson. *Metaphors We Live By*. Chicago: University of Chicago Press, 1980.

Langford, David. Introduction to *Terry Pratchett: Guilty of Literature*. 2nd ed., edited by Andrew M. Butler, Edward James, and Farah Mendlesohn, 3–13. Baltimore: Old Earth Books, 2004.

———. "Talents." In Clute and Grant, *The Encyclopedia of Fantasy*, 919–20.

———. "Time in Faerie." In Clute and Grant, *The Encyclopedia of Fantasy*, 948.

Lee, Keekok. *The Natural and the Artefactual: The Implications of Deep Science and Deep Technology for Environmental Philosophy*. Lanham, MD: Lexington Books, 1999.

Le Guin, Ursula K. *The Farthest Shore*. 1973. In *The Earthsea Quartet*, 301–478. London: Puffin-Penguin, 1993.

———. "Changing Kingdoms: A Talk for the Fourteenth International Conference on the Fantastic in the Arts, March 17–21, 1993." In *Trajectories of the Fantastic: Selected Essays from the Fourteenth International Conference on the Fantastic in the Arts*, edited by Michael A. Morrison, 3–12. Contributions to the Study of Science Fiction and Fantasy 70. Westport, CT: Greenwood Press, 1997.

Lewis, David. "Truth in Fiction." 1978. In *Philosophy of Literature: Contemporary and Classic Readings: An Anthology*, edited by Eileen John and Dominic McIver Lopes, 119–27. Oxford: Blackwell, 2004.

Linda [pseud.]. "The Age of Legends." *The Thirteenth Depository: A Wheel of Time Blog*. 26 March 2002. http://13depository.blogspot.com/2009/02/age-of-legends.html.

Lindgren, Astrid. *Mio, My Son*. 1954. Translated by Marianne Turner. London: Puffin-Penguin, 1988.

Lund, Niels Windfeld. "Building a Discipline, Creating a Profession: An Essay on the Childhood of 'Dokvit'." In *A Document (Re)turn: Contributions from a Research Field in Transition*, edited by Roswitha Skare, Niels Windfeld Lund, and Andreas Vårheim, 11–26. Frankfurt am Main: Peter Lang, 2007.

———. "Doceo + Mentum—A Ground for a New Discipline." Paper presented at the Annual Meeting of the Document Academy, Berkeley, CA, August 13–15, 2003. http://thedocumentacademy.org/resources/2003/papers/lund.paper .html.

———. "Documentation in a Complementary Perspective." In *Aware and*

Responsible: Papers of the Nordic-International Colloquium on Social
and Cultural Awareness and Responsibility in Library, Information, and
Documentation Studies (SCARLID), edited by W. Boyd Rayward, 93–102.
Lanham, MD: Scarecrow Press, 2004.

Lynam, Edward. *The Mapmaker's Art: Essays on the History of Maps*. London:
Batchworth Press, 1953.

MacEachren, Alan M. *How Maps Work: Representation, Visualization, and*
Design. New York: Guilford Press, 1995.

MacKillop, James. *Dictionary of Celtic Mythology*. Oxford: Oxford University
Press, 1998.

Mains, Christine. "Bridging World and Story: Patricia McKillip's Reluctant
Heroes." *Journal of the Fantastic in the Arts* 16, no. 1 (2005): 37–48.

———. "For Love or for Money: The Concept of Loyalty in the Works of Patricia
McKillip." *Journal of the Fantastic in the Arts* 16, no. 3 (2006): 217–32.

Malcolm-Clarke, Darja. "Tracking Phantoms." In VanderMeer and VanderMeer,
The New Weird, 337–43.

Malory, Thomas. *Le Morte Darthur*. 1485. Ware, UK: Wordsworth Editions, 1996.

Manes, Christopher. "Nature and Silence." 1992. In Glotfelty and Fromm, *The*
Ecocriticism Reader, 15–29.

Manlove, Colin N. "The Elusiveness of Fantasy." In *The Shape of the Fantastic:*
Selected Essays from the Seventh International Conference on the Fantastic
in the Arts, edited by Olena H. Saciuk, 53–65. Contributions to the Study of
Science Fiction and Fantasy 39. New York: Greenwood Press, 1990.

———. *Modern Fantasy: Five Studies*. Cambridge: Cambridge University Press,
1975.

———. "On the Nature of Fantasy." 1975. In *The Aesthetics of Fantasy Literature*
and Art, edited by Roger C. Schlobin, 16–35. Notre Dame, IN: University of
Notre Dame Press, 1982.

Mathews, Richard. *Fantasy: The Liberation of Imagination*. New York: Routledge,
2002.

McKibben, Bill. *The End of Nature*. London: Viking, 1990.

McKillip, Patricia A. *Ombria in Shadow*. New York: Ace Books, 2002.

———. *The Riddlemaster of Hed*. 1976. New York: Del Rey–Ballantine, 1978.

Meeker, Joseph W. *The Comedy of Survival: Studies in Literary Ecology*. New
York: Charles Scribner's Sons, 1972.

Mendlesohn, Farah. "*Conjunctions 39* and Liminal Fantasy." *Journal of the*
Fantastic in the Arts 15, no. 3 (2005): 228–39.

———. *Rhetorics of Fantasy*. Middletown, CT: Wesleyan University Press, 2008.

———. "Toward a Taxonomy of Fantasy." *Journal of the Fantastic in the Arts* 13,
no. 2 (2002): 169–83.

Mendlesohn, Farah, and Edward James. *A Short History of Fantasy*. London:
Middlesex University Press, 2009.

Miéville, China. *Iron Council*. 2004. New York: Del Rey–Ballantine, 2005.

———. "Jack." In *Looking for Jake: Stories*, 199–212. New York: Del Rey–
Ballantine, 2005.

———. "Messing with Fantasy." *Locus* (March 2002): 4–5, 75–76.

———. *Perdido Street Station*. 2000. New York: Del Rey–Ballantine, 2001.

———. *The Scar*. New York: Del Rey–Ballantine, 2002.

Mighall, Robert. *A Geography of Victorian Gothic Fiction: Mapping History's Nightmares*. Oxford: Oxford University Press, 1999.

Miller, J. Hillis. *Topographies*. Stanford, CA: Stanford University Press, 1995.

Milton, John. *Paradise Lost*. 1674. In *Paradise Lost: An Authoritative Text, Backgrounds and Sources, Criticism*. 2nd ed., edited by Scott Elledge, 7–301. New York: Norton, 1993.

Mittman, Asa Simon. *Maps and Monsters in Medieval England*. Studies in Medieval History and Culture. New York: Routledge, 2006.

Moncrief, Lewis W. "The Cultural Basis of Our Environmental Crisis." 1970. In *Western Man and Environmental Ethics: Attitudes toward Nature and Technology*, edited by Ian G. Barbour, 31–42. Reading, MA: Addison-Wesley, 1973.

Moorcock, Michael. *Wizardry and Wild Romance*. London: Victor Gollancz, 1987.

Moretti, Franco. *Atlas of the European Novel, 1800–1900*. London: Verso, 1998.

Morse, Donald E., and Kálmán Matolcsy, eds. *The Mythic Fantasy of Robert Holdstock: Critical Essays on the Fiction*. Critical Explorations in Science Fiction and Fantasy 26. Jefferson, NC: McFarland, 2011.

Mumford, Lewis. *The City in History: Its Origins, Its Transformations, and Its Prospects*. Harmondsworth, UK: Penguin, 1961.

Nix, Garth. *Abhorsen*. New York: Eos-HarperCollins, 2003.

———. *Lirael: Daughter of the Clayr*. New York: HarperCollins, 2001.

———. "Nicholas Sayre and the Creature in the Case." In *Across the Wall: A Tale of the Abhorsen and Other Stories*. New York: Eos-HarperCollins, 2005.

———. *Sabriel*. New York: HarperCollins, 1995.

Oelschlaeger, Max. *The Idea of Wilderness: From Prehistory to the Age of Ecology*. New Haven: Yale University Press, 1991.

Ó hÓgáin, Dáithí. *The Sacred Isle: Belief and Religion in Pre-Christian Ireland*. Woodbridge, UK: Boydell Press / Wilton: Collins Press, 1999.

Ovid [Publius Ovidius Naso]. *Metamorphoses*. c. 8 A.D. Translated by Mary M. Innes. London: Penguin, 1955.

Oziewicz, Marek. *One Earth, One People: The Mythopoeic Fantasy Series of Ursula K. Le Guin, Lloyd Alexander, Madeleine L'Engle and Orson Scott Card*. Critical Explorations in Science Fiction and Fantasy 6. Jefferson, NC: McFarland, 2008.

———. "Profusion Sublime and the Fantastic: *Mythago Wood*." In Morse and Matolcsy, *The Mythic Fantasy of Robert Holdstock*, 81–95.

Padrón, Ricardo. "Mapping Imaginary Worlds." In *Maps: Finding Our Place in the World*, edited by James R. Akerman and Robert W. Karrow, Jr., 255–87. Chicago: University of Chicago Press, 2007.

Palmer, Christopher. "Saving the City in China Miéville's Bas-Lag Novels." *Extrapolation* 50, no. 2 (2009): 224–38.

Pollan, Michael. *Second Nature: A Gardener's Education.* New York: Grove Press, 1991.

Porter, Tom. *Archispeak: An Illustrated Guide to Architectural Terms.* London: Spon Press–Taylor & Francis, 2004.

Post, J. B. *An Atlas of Fantasy.* 1973. 2nd ed. New York: Ballantine, 1979.

Powers, Tim. *Earthquake Weather.* New York: Orb–Tom Doherty, 1997.

———. *Last Call.* 1992. New York: Avon-HarperCollins, 1993.

Pratchett, Terry. *The Colour of Magic.* Reading, UK: Corgi, 1985.

———. *Pyramids.* 1989. London: Corgi, 1990.

———. *Wyrd Sisters.* 1988. London: Corgi, 1989.

Propp, V[ladímir]. *Morphology of the Folktale.* 1928. Austin: University of Texas Press, 1968.

Rabkin, Eric S. *The Fantastic in Literature.* Princeton, NJ: Princeton University Press, 1976.

Raisz, Erwin. "Timecharts of Historical Cartography." *Imago Mundi* 2 (1937): 9–16.

Ranson, Clare. "Cartography in Children's Literature." In *Sustaining the Vision: Selected Papers from the Annual Conference of the International Association of School Librarianship,* 164–66. Worcester, UK: International Association of School Librarianship, 1996.

Riley, Michael O'Neal. *Oz and Beyond: The Fantasy World of L. Frank Baum.* Lawrence: University Press of Kansas, 1997.

Rimmon-Kenan, Shlomith. *Narrative Fiction: Contemporary Poetics.* 1983. 2nd ed. London: Routledge, 2002.

Robinson, Arthur H., and Barbara Bartz Petchenik. *The Nature of Maps: Essays toward Understanding Maps and Mapping.* Chicago: University of Chicago Press, 1976.

Rosebury, Brian. *Tolkien: A Cultural Phenomenon.* 2nd ed. Basingstoke, UK: Palgrave Macmillan, 2003.

Ryan, Marie-Laure. *Possible Worlds, Artificial Intelligence, and Narrative Theory.* Bloomington: Indiana University Press, 1991.

Schlobin, Roger C. "'Rituals' Footprints Ankle-Deep in Stone': The Irrelevancy of Setting in the Fantastic." *Journal of the Fantastic in the Arts* 11, no. 2 (2000): 154–63.

Schneidau, Herbert N. *Sacred Discontent: The Bible and Western Tradition.* Berkeley: University of California Press, 1977.

Selling, Kim. "'Fantastic Neomedievalism': The Image of the Middle Ages in Popular Fantasy." In *Flashes of the Fantastic: Selected Essays from the War of the Worlds Centennial, Nineteenth International Conference on the Fantastic in the Arts,* edited by David Ketterer, 211–18. Contributions to the Study of Science Fiction and Fantasy 107. Westport, CT: Praeger, 2004.

Senior, W. A. "The Embodiment of Abstraction in the Mythago Novels." In Morse and Matolcsy, *The Mythic Fantasy of Robert Holdstock,* 13–25.

———. *Stephen R. Donaldson's Chronicles of Thomas Covenant: Variations on the Fantasy Tradition.* Kent, OH: Kent State University Press, 1995.

Shakespeare, William. *A Midsummer Night's Dream.* 1600. In *The Norton Shakespeare*, edited by Stephen Greenblatt, Walter Cohen, Jean E. Howard, and Katharine Eisaman Maus, 849–96. New York: Norton, 2008.

Shippey, Tom. Introduction to *The Oxford Book of Fantasy Stories*, edited by Tom Shippey, ix–xxii. Oxford: Oxford University Press, 1994.

———. Introduction to *The Wood beyond the World*, by William Morris, v–xix. Oxford: Oxford University Press, 1980.

———. *J. R. R. Tolkien: Author of the Century.* London: HarperCollins, 2000.

———. *The Road to Middle-earth: How J. R. R. Tolkien Created a New Mythology.* Boston: Houghton Mifflin, 2003.

Slovic, Scott. "Ecocriticism: Containing Multitudes, Practising Doctrine." In *The Green Studies Reader: From Romanticism to Ecocriticism*, edited by Laurence Coupe, 160–62. London: Routledge, 2000.

Snyder, Gary. *The Practice of the Wild.* San Francisco: North Point Press, 1990.

Soper, Kate. *What Is Nature? Culture, Politics, and the Non-Human.* Oxford: Blackwell, 1998.

Stableford, Brian. "The Discovery of Secondary Worlds: Notes on the Aesthetics & Methodology of Heterocosmic Creativity." *The New York Review of Science Fiction* (August 2004): 1, 6–19.

Suvin, Darko. "Considering the Sense of 'Fantasy' or 'Fantastic Fiction': An Effusion." *Extrapolation* 41, no. 3 (2000): 209–47.

Swinfen, Ann. *In Defence of Fantasy: A Study of the Genre in English and American Literature since 1945.* London: Routledge & Kegan Paul, 1984.

Tam, Nicholas. "Here Be Cartographers: Reading the Fantasy Map." *Nick's Café Canadien* (blog). April 18, 2011. www.nicholastam.ca/2011/04/18/here-be-cartographers-reading-the-fantasy-map/.

Thormählen, Marianne. *The Waste Land: A Fragmentary Wholeness.* Lund Studies in English 52. Lund: Gleerup-LiberLäromedel, 1978.

Thrower, Norman J. W. *Maps & Civilization: Cartography in Culture and Society.* Chicago: University of Chicago Press, 1996.

Tobin-McClain, Lee. "Paranormal Romance: Secrets of the Female Fantastic." *Journal of the Fantastic in the Arts* 11, no. 2 (2001): 294–306.

Todorov, Tzvetan. *The Fantastic: A Structural Approach to a Literary Genre.* Ithaca, NY: Cornell University Press, 1975.

Tolkien, J. R. R. *The Hobbit, or, There and Back Again.* 1937. Boston: Houghton Mifflin, 1997.

———. *The Letters of J. R. R. Tolkien*, edited by Humphrey Carpenter. Boston: Houghton Mifflin, 2000.

———. *The Lord of the Rings.* 1954–55. Boston: Houghton Mifflin, 1993.

———. *The Lord of the Rings.* 1954–55. Fiftieth Anniversary ed. Boston: Houghton Mifflin, 2004.

———. "Nomenclature of *The Lord of the Rings*." In Hammond and Scull, *The Lord of the Rings: A Reader's Companion*, 750–82.

———. "On Fairy-stories." 1947; original lecture 1938. In *The Tolkien Reader*, 3–84. New York: Ballantine, 1966.

———. *The Silmarillion*. London: Allen & Unwin, 1977.

———. *Smith of Wootton Major*. 1967, edited by Verlyn Flieger. London: HarperCollins, 2005.

Tolkien, J. R. R., and Christopher Tolkien. *The Return of the Shadow*. The History of *The Lord of the Rings* 1. London: HarperCollins, 2002.

———. *The Shaping of Middle-earth*. The History of Middle-earth 4. London: HarperCollins, 2002.

———. *The Treason of Isengard*. The History of *The Lord of the Rings* 2. London: HarperCollins, 2002.

———. *The War of the Ring*. The History of *The Lord of the Rings* 3. London: HarperCollins, 2002.

Traill, Nancy H. *Possible Worlds of the Fantastic: The Rise of the Paranormal in Fiction*. Toronto: University of Toronto Press, 1996.

Turnbull, David, and Helen Watson. *Maps Are Territories: Science Is an Atlas: A Portfolio of Exhibits*. Chicago: University of Chicago Press, 1993.

Turner, Frederick. "Cultivating the American Garden." 1991. In Glotfelty and Fromm, *The Ecocriticism Reader*, 40–51.

VanderMeer, Ann, and Jeff VanderMeer, eds. *The New Weird*. San Francisco: Tachyon Publications, 2008.

VanderMeer, Jeff. "The New Weird: 'It's Alive?'" In VanderMeer and VanderMeer, *The New Weird*, ix–xviii.

Virgil. *Eclogues, Georgics, Aeneid I–VI*. c. 19 B.C. Cambridge, MA: Harvard University Press, 1999.

Walker, R. C. "The Cartography of Fantasy." *Mythlore* 7, no. 4 (1981): 37–38.

Westfahl, Gary. "Fantastic." In Clute and Grant, *The Encyclopedia of Fantasy*, 335.

Weston, Jessie L. *From Ritual to Romance*. 1920. New York: Anchor-Doubleday, 1957.

White, Lynn, Jr. "Continuing the Conversation." In *Western Man and Environmental Ethics: Attitudes toward Nature and Technology*, edited by Ian G. Barbour, 55–64. Reading, MA: Addison-Wesley, 1973.

———. "The Historical Roots of Our Ecological Crisis." 1967. In Glotfelty and Fromm, *The Ecocriticism Reader*, 3–14.

Wilford, John Noble. *The Mapmakers*. New York: Vintage Books, 1982.

Williams, Tad. *The War of the Flowers*. New York: Daw Books, 2003.

Wolfe, Gary K. *Critical Terms for Science Fiction and Fantasy: A Glossary and Guide to Scholarship*. New York: Greenwood Press, 1986.

———. "Evaporating Genres." In *Evaporating Genres: Essays on Fantastic Literature*, 18–53. Middletown, CT: Wesleyan University Press, 2011.

———. *Soundings: Reviews 1992–1996*. Harold Wood, UK: Beccon Publications, 2005.

Wood, Denis. *The Power of Maps*. London: Routledge, 1993.

———. *Rethinking the Power of Maps*. New York: Guilford Press, 2010.

Woodward, David. "Medieval *Mappaemundi*." In *The History of Cartography*, edited by J. B. Harley and David Woodward. Vol. 1, 286–370. Chicago: University of Chicago Press, 1987.

Worsley, Peter. "Classic Conceptions of Culture." In *Culture and Global Change*, edited by Tracey Skelton and Tim Allen, 13–21. London: Routledge, 1999.

Zahorski, Kenneth J., and Robert H. Boyer. "The Secondary Worlds of High Fantasy." In *The Aesthetics of Fantasy Literature and Art*, edited by Roger C. Schlobin, 56–81. Notre Dame, IN: University of Notre Dame Press, 1982.

Index

. . . .

Eliot, T. S., *The Waste Land*, 185–86

Elmore, Larry and Robert, *Runes of Autumn*, 41–42

empty map space. *See* blank spaces

Ende, Michael, *The Neverending Story*, 92, 181–83, 215

eucatastrophe, 107, 179. *See also* happy ending

Evans, Jonathan, 141, 198, 202, 261n70

evil lands. *See* landscapes of evil

Faerie, 6, 11, 71–72, 85, 219, 246–47n25, 247n38; in *Stardust* (Gaiman and Vess), 12, 82–92, 98–100, 128; Lothlórien, related to, 101–2, 105, 109; in Newford (de Lint), 141, 143–44, 147–148, 151; in *War of the Flowers* (Williams), 183. *See also* mundanity, descriptions of

fantastic, definition of, 4–5, 234n20

fantasy, definitions of, 4–7, 126–27. *See also* high fantasy, low fantasy

Farthest Shore, The (Le Guin), 180–81

Feist, Raymond E.: *A Darkness at Sethanon*, 70; *The King's Buccaneer*, 28; *Magician*, 17, 38

Fforde, Jasper, *Something Rotten*, 70

Fisher King figure, 13, 178, 183–91, 219, 258n30, 258nn34–35, 258n37, 258–59n39

Fletcher, Charlie, *Stoneheart*, 23

Flieger, Verlyn, 106–7, 138, 140

folktales, 6, 71, 85, 90, 179, 246n25

Ford, Jeffrey, "The Annals of Eelin-Ok," 247n25

Frazer, James, 95, 185–86

fuzzy set, fantasy as, 4, 6–9, 219, 221, 236n28, 250n98

Gaiman, Neil, 23, 71, 222, 236n33, 247n38; *Stardust*, 12, 72, 82–93, 95, 98, 247n36

Gardner, Martin, *Visitors from Oz*, 27, 241n57

Garner, Alan: *Elidor*, 178; *The Weirdstone of Brisingamen*, 23

Garth, John, 200

Gate of Ivory (also *Gate of Ivory, Gate of Horn*; Holdstock). *See* Holdstock, Robert

Genette, Gérard, 20–21. *See also* paratexts

Gentle, Mary, *Grunts*, 259n50

Glotfelty, Cheryll, 3

Goldstein, Lisa, 13, 178, 190–94, 214, 236n33

Goodkind, Terry, 259n48

Gordon, Joan, 155, 160

Granström, Erik, *Svavelvinter*, 236n34

Groos, Arthur, 258n34

hachures, 40, 42, 242n70. *See also* hill signs

Hambly, Barbara, *The Magicians of Night*, 195–97

Hammond, Wayne G., 108

happy endings, 64, 179, 182. *See also* eucatastrophe

Hardy, Lyndon, *Master of the Sixth Magic*, 251n104

Harley, J. B., 51–52

Harvey, P. D. A., 25, 50

healing, 103, 138; and rulers, 139–40, 179–80, 182, 187, 190, 256–57n11

Hedrick, Charles W., Jr., 191

hells, 72, 91, 196–97; in Dante, 14, 18, 20, 74, 196–97, 212; in Milton, 196–97, 209, 212

Helms, Randel, 199, 201

"Here be dragons" (expression), 39, 85–86

Hickman, Tracy, Dragonlance Chronicles, 236n34

high fantasy, 2, 42, 250n98; definition of, 10; maps in: 14–15, 22–23, 65, 223; as pseudomedieval, 41, 66. *See also* portal-quest fantasy; immersive fantasy; secondary worlds

Hilbert, Betsy S., 255n83

hill signs, 39–42, 49–50, 66, 242n80.
See also contours; hachures; oblique
view; profile view
Hobbit, The (Tolkien), 17, 62, 199;
subtitle describes plot, 47, 63, 99;
Thror's map, 21, 24–26, 31, 42. *See
also* Tolkien, J. R. R.; Tolkien maps
Holdstock, Robert: Merlin Codex, 70,
116, 236n33; Mythago Wood Cycle,
12, 101, 109–117, 122, 249n81
Hollowing, The (Holdstock). *See* Hold-
stock, Robert
Homer, *The Odyssey*, 70, 127, 197
Howard, Robert E., Conan stories,
10, 240n46. *See also* Conan the
Barbarian
Hume, Kathryn, 4, 234n20
Hunt, Peter, 16–17

Imhof, Eduard, 242n78
immersive fantasy, 8, 115, 135, 212,
250n98; description of, 7
Inferno (Dante). *See* Dante Alighieri
International Federation of Library
Associations and Institutions (IFLA),
221
introduction, formulaic, 10, 84
intrusive fantasy, 8, 110–11, 135; de-
scription, 7
Iron Council (Miéville). *See* Miéville,
China
Irvine, Ian, *Geomancer*, 30, 33–34
Irwin, W. R., 6, 235n24

"Jack" (Miéville). *See* Miéville, China
Jackson, Peter, 245n133, 262n89
James, Edward, 240n45
Johnson, Mark, 236n28
Jones, Alexander, 241n53
Jones, Diana Wynne, 127, 259n50; *The
Tough Guide to Fantasyland*, 15, 17,
35–37, 180, 188
Jordan, Robert, 13, 16, 178, 195, 199,
208–12, 214
Jourde, Pierre, 17, 60, 239n22

Jowett, G. H., 223
Jung, Carl, 143, 184

Kavenay, Roz, 14, 69, 99–100, 238n4
Kay, Guy Gavriel, Fionavar Tapestry,
259n48
Kincaid, Paul, 115–16
King Lear (Shakespeare), 196
Kirkpatrick, Russell, *The Right Hand of
God*, 30–32, 40–41, 242n61
Kluckhohn, Clyde, 130
Kocher, Paul H., 107, 136
Kroeber, Alfred L., 130
Kushner, Ellern, *Thomas the Rhymer*,
247n25

labyrinths, 113–17, 171
Lakoff, George, 236n28
land of the dead, 11, 70, 196–97, 217,
219; Dragaeran (Brust), 12, 56,
72–82, 98, 127; returning from,
78–79, 93
landforms. *See* hill signs
landscape, definition of, 11
landscapes of evil, 13, 178, 194–213,
218–19, 260n57; in Donaldson, 13,
178, 204–8, 209–13; in Jordan, 13,
178, 208–13; in Tolkien, 13, 60, 63,
176, 178, 195–98, 199–205, 207–13
Langford, David, 69, 85, 122
Larke, Glenda, *Gilfeather*, 28–29
Last Call. See Powers, Tim
Lavondyss. See Holdstock, Robert
Lee, Keekok, 130–31, 165
legends. *See* maps
Le Guin, Ursula K., Earthsea, 16, 18,
28–29, 180–81
Leiber, Fritz, "The Price of Pain-Ease,"
70
Lewis, C. S., 233n2, 238n4; *The Last
Battle*, 177; *The Lion, the Witch and
the Wardrobe*, 198, 256n3, 259n49;
The Magician's Nephew, 133, 259n49
liminal fantasy, 219, 236n38; descrip-
tion of, 7–8

Midsummer Night's Dream, A (Shakespeare), 71, 92, 247n38, 257n24
Miéville, China, 8, 254–55n67; Armada, 162–65; Iron Council, 164–65; New Crobuzon, 12, 135, 144, 154–67, 173–76, 218, 220
Mighall, Robert, 4
Miller, J. Hillis, 4
Milton, John, *Paradise Lost*, 196–97, 209, 212
Mirrlees, Hope, *Lud-in-the-Mist*, 72, 221
Miyazaki, Hayao, *Spirited Away*, 177
monomyth. *See* Campbell, Joseph
Moorcock, Michael, 177
More, Thomas, *Utopia*, 14, 17–18
Moretti, Franco, 4
mundanity, descriptions of, 71–72, 184. *See also* Faerie; Gaiman, Neil; Powers, Tim; Vess, Charles
Mythago Wood. See Holdstock, Robert
mythotopes, 113–17

Narnia. *See* Lewis, C. S.
nature: cultural representations of, 136, 138, 141, 163–65, 167–68, 172–73; definitions of, 130–33; feral, 132, 136, 143, 146, 148, 152–53, 158–60, 163, 165–66, 171. *See also* culture; Darwinism; *scala naturae*; second nature
neomedieval. *See* pseudomedieval
Newford stories. *See* de Lint, Charles
New Weird, the, 255n67
"Nicholas Sayre and the Creature in the Case." *See* Nix, Garth
Niven, Larry, *The Burning City*, 33, 35
Nix, Garth, 12, 72, 92–98, 220, 248n40
nuclear weapons, 97, 211–12

oblique view, 39–40, 42, 49–50, 66, 242n70. *See also* hill signs
Ombria in Shadow. See McKillip, Patricia A.
"On Fairy-stories" (Tolkien), 5–7, 9, 91,
102, 179, 235n24, 235n26; recovery, 6, 175. *See also* Cauldron of Story; Tolkien, J. R. R.
Oziewicz, Marek, 111

Padrón, Ricardo, 18–19, 60–62, 238n4
palimpsests, 13, 158, 165–66, 178, 190–94, 214, 259n46
Palmer, Christopher, 155
paranormal romance, 240n45
paratexts, 20–22, 31–32, 39, 45, 54–55, 59, 66–67, 82; definition of, 20
Paths of the Dead, The. See Brust, Steven
Perdido Street Station. See Miéville, China
Perilous Realm, the. *See* Faerie
periphery. *See* center and periphery
Petchenik, Barbara Bartz, 19–20, 53
plan view, 21, 30, 50, 242n70
polders, 12, 69, 77, 99, 126–28, 217, 219; definition of, 100; Djelibeybi (Pratchett), 101, 117–26; Lothlórien (Tolkien), 101–9, 125–26, 128; Ryhope Wood (Holdstock), 101, 109–17, 125–26; and time, 85, 100, 104, 106–9, 116–20, 124–26, 217
portal-quest fantasy, 36, 39, 96, 115, 135, 218, 250n98; description, 7; landscapes of evil in, 195–96, 198, 212; ruler/realm connection in, 178, 180; starting point of, 46, 91
Porter, Tom, 259n46
possible-worlds semantics, 10
Post, J. B., *An Atlas of Fantasy*, 15
Pournelle, Jerry, *The Burning City*, 33, 35
Powers, Tim, 13, 178, 183–90, 191, 219, 258n30; *On Stranger Tides*, 91
Power That Preserves, The. See Donaldson, Stephen. R.
Pratchett, Terry, 29, 221–22, 257n21; *Eric*, 134; *Pyramids*, 12, 101, 117–25, 257n21; *Small Gods*, 91; the Watch, 257n21; *Wyrd Sisters*, 181–82, 213

72, 75, 77, 98–99, 126–28, 169, 172–73 (*see also* borders; boundaries)

Thror's map. See *Hobbit, The*; Tolkien maps

Thrower, J. W., 39

time: between worlds or domains, 10, 74, 93, 143, 217; in Faerie, 84–85, 246–47n25; and geography, 12, 125–26; maps, encoded in, 48–49, 60–62; and polders, 100–101, 104–9, 109–110, 114–26; time abysses, 106, 116, 125, 249n63

Tobin-McClain, Lee, 240n45

Todorov, Tzvetan, 234n20

Tolkien, Christopher, 45, 55

Tolkien, J. R. R., 70, 71–72, 140, 199; anti-industrial sentiments, 200–201, 206, 261n70, 262n89; epigones, 15, 96, 236n35. See also *Hobbit, The*; *Lord of the Rings, The*; "On Fairy-stories"; *Silmarillion, The*; Tolkien maps

Tolkien maps, 12, 14, 38, 44, 238n4; creation of, 25, 45, 47, 50; history encoded in, 48–49, 60–62; names on, 47, 52, 59, 65–67; "A Part of the Shire," 23–24, 44–55, 66; previous studies of, 16–18; roads on, 46–47, 59, 61 (*see also* roads); "The West of Middle-earth," 23–24, 39, 55–67; as world creation, 14–15, 21–22. See also *Hobbit, The*; *Lord of the Rings, The*; Tolkien, J. R. R.

T-O maps, 25–26, 41

topofocal, 2–4, 11, 216, 218–20

topographical map elements, 36–37, 46–47, 49–50, 56–57

Tough Guide to Fantasyland, The (Jones), 15, 17, 36–37, 180, 188

Tourists. See Goldstein, Lisa

Traill, Nancy H., 10–11

Turner, Frederick, 131

VanderMeer, Jeff, 255n67

Vess, Charles, 247–48n38; *Stardust*, 12, 72, 82–92, 93, 95, 98, 247n36

Virgil, *Aeneid*, 70, 78, 197

Walker, R. C., 16, 238n4

Wallace, Kathleen R., 256n85

water margins, 26–28, 30, 37, 47, 173

Weis, Margaret, Dragonlance Chronicles, 236n34

Welch, Michelle M., *Chasing Fire*, 27–28

Westfahl, Gary, 233–34n20

Weston, Jessie L., 185–88, 258n37

White, Lynn, Jr., 131

white spaces. *See* blank spaces

Wilford, John Noble, 26

Williams, Tad, *Caliban's Hour*, 236n33; Memory, Sorrow, and Thorn, 259n49; *War of the Flowers*, 71, 183

Windling, Terry, Borderlands, 72

Wizard of Earthsea, A (Le Guin), 16, 18, 28–29

Wolfe, Gary K., 4, 9, 184–185, 190

Wolfe, Gene: The Book of the New Sun series, 10; the *Soldier* series, 222

Wolfram von Eschenbach, *Parzival*, 188

Wood, Denis, 20, 32–33, 41, 44, 46, 48

world, definition of, 9. *See also* actual world; dyadic worlds

worlds. *See* dyadic worlds; primary worlds; secondary worlds

Worsley, Peter, 131

Wyndham, John, "Confidence Trick," 91–92

Wyrd Sisters (Pratchett), 181–82, 213

Zahorsky, Kenneth J., 2, 10, 41

Zelazny, Roger, *Jack of Shadows*, 72

ABOUT THE AUTHOR

Stefan Ekman is a freelance lecturer on fantasy,

role-playing games, and manga, and serves as the head of

the Fantasy Literature Division at the International Conference

on the Fantastic in the Arts. He teaches in the creative

writing program at Lund University in Sweden.